RESISTANT PRACTICES

in **COMMUNITIES** of **SOUND**

RESISTANT PRACTICES in COMMUNITIES of SOUND

Edited by **DEANNA FONG** and **COLE MASH**

MCGILL-QUEEN'S UNIVERSITY PRESS
Montreal & Kingston · London · Chicago

© McGill-Queen's University Press 2024

ISBN 978-0-2280-2121-6 (cloth)
ISBN 978-0-2280-2122-3 (paper)
ISBN 978-0-2280-2174-2 (ePDF)
ISBN 978-0-2280-2175-9 (ePUB)

Legal deposit third quarter 2024
Bibliothèque nationale du Québec

Printed in Canada on acid-free paper that is 100% ancient forest free
(100% post-consumer recycled), processed chlorine free

This book has been published with the help of a grant from the Canadian Federation for the Humanities and Social Sciences, through the Awards to Scholarly Publications Program, using funds provided by the Social Sciences and Humanities Research Council of Canada.

We acknowledge the support of the Canada Council for the Arts.
Nous remercions le Conseil des arts du Canada de son soutien.

McGill-Queen's University Press in Montreal is on land which long served as a site of meeting and exchange amongst Indigenous Peoples, including the Haudenosaunee and Anishinabeg nations. In Kingston it is situated on the territory of the Haudenosaunee and Anishinaabek. We acknowledge and thank the diverse Indigenous Peoples whose footsteps have marked these territories on which peoples of the world now gather.

Library and Archives Canada Cataloguing in Publication

Title: Resistant practices in communities of sound / edited by Deanna Fong and Cole Mash.
Names: Fong, Deanna, editor. | Mash, Cole, editor.
Description: Includes bibliographical references and index.
Identifiers: Canadiana (print) 20240297164 | Canadiana (ebook) 20240297318 | ISBN 9780228021223 (paper) | ISBN 9780228021216 (cloth) | ISBN 9780228021759 (ePUB) | ISBN 9780228021742 (ePDF)
Subjects: LCSH: Sound art—Political aspects—Canada. | LCSH: Sound art—Social aspects—Canada. | LCSH: Communication in art—Canada. | LCSH: Art and literature—Canada. | LCSH: Authors, Canadian—Interviews. | LCSH: Artists—Canada—Interviews.
Classification: LCC NX650.S68 R47 2024 | DDC 709.04/074—dc23

For Maxine, Cedar, and Heath

CONTENTS

Figures and Scores xi

Introduction: Resistant Practices in Communities of Sound 3
Deanna Fong and Cole Mash

On Transcription:
A Prelude (in Conversation with Deanna Fong) 26
Deanna Radford

1 "We make something out of what records we can find":
An Interview with Wayde Compton 50
Deanna Fong

2 Race, Multiplicity, and Dis/Located Voices:
Wayde Compton's Turntablist Poetics 62
Eric Schmaltz

3 "The fact of my mouth": An Interview with Jordan Scott 77
Deanna Fong

4 Listening as Access: Toward Relational Listening for
Nonnormative Speech and Communication 89
Faith Ryan

5 "That in-between space":
An Interview with Oana Avasilichioaei 105
Deanna Fong

CONTENTS

6 New Forms of Digital, Temporal, and Auditory Poiesis 118
prOphecy sun and Reese Muntean

7 "It doesn't mean anything except talking":
An Interview with Tracie Morris 136
Cole Mash and Deanna Fong

8 "It's resistance but it's also embrace":
Tracie Morris's Collaborative Ear, An Open Letter 155
Nicole Brittingham Furlonge

9 "What is being resisted is our 'yes'": An Interview
with Tawhida Tanya Evanson, El Jones, and Erin Scott 163
Cole Mash

10 The Whatever-icity of Spoken Word:
Community, Identity, Performativity 196
Corey Frost

11 "A taking in, a holding with":
An Interview with Jordan Abel 213
Deanna Fong

12 Can We Think of Sound (or Voice) without Sight (or the Gaze)?
Lacanian Theory and the Horror of Community 233
Clint Burnham

13 Transcript of *Lesbian Liberation Across Media:
A Sonic Screening* Podcast, Introduction 246
Felicity Tayler

CONTENTS

14 Listening to LGBTQ2+ Communities at the Lesbian Liberation Across Media Watch Party 273
Mathieu Aubin

15 "It was an extension of the moment": Five Poets in Conversation on Analog Audio Recording and Creative Practice 286
Karis Shearer and Erín Moure

16 Curatorial Agency at Véhicule Art Inc.: "Openness was a guiding spirit to VÉHICULE" 324
Klara du Plessis

17 "Songs are so much more than songs": An Interview with Dylan Robinson 339
Clint Burnham

18 "Misaudition" 353
Kate Siklosi

Contributors 359
Index 365

FIGURES AND SCORES

Figures

- **0.1** Structural mapping of chapters in *Resistant Practices in Communities of Sound* 12
- **6.1** *A Small Piece of Sky*, photo 119
- **6.2** *A Small Piece of Sky*, performance photo 120
- **6.3** *A Small Piece of Sky*, performance photo 120
- **6.4** *A Small Piece of Sky*, performance photo 120
- **6.5** *A Small Piece of Sky*, performance photo 121
- **6.6** *A Small Piece of Sky*, performance photo 121
- **6.7** *A Small Piece of Sky*, performance photo 121
- **6.8** *A Small Piece of Sky*, performance photo 124
- **6.9** *Choreography Walk* map, sketch 125
- **6.10** *Choreography Walk* map, sketch 125
- **6.11** *A Small Piece of Sky*, performance photo 126
- **6.12** *A Small Piece of Sky*, performance photo 126
- **6.13** *A Small Piece of Sky*, process photo 132
- **18.1** "Misaudition 1" 354
- **18.2** "Misaudition 2" 355
- **18.3** "Misaudition 3" 356
- **18.4** "Misaudition 4" 357

Scores

6.1 *Rules and Intentions, Performance Score*   127
6.2 *Performance Score 1*   130
6.3 *Performance Score 2*   130

RESISTANT PRACTICES

in COMMUNITIES of SOUND

INTRODUCTION

Resistant Practices in Communities of Sound

Deanna Fong and Cole Mash

A recording of the "Politics and Poetics of Mediated Sound" opens with a buzz of ambient conversation during the event. A few voices stand out in their specific tone and timbre, but the words they speak are unintelligible – at least to our straining ears, domed in headphones / stuffed with earbuds. There are coughs and peals of laughter. Around the five-minute mark, the conversational pulse slows: something is happening, or is about to happen. The Vancouver crowd reacts accordingly and voices soften to a murmur. A voice once obscured by conversational static suddenly becomes clear and audible: "Do you have a glass of water?"

At the forty-nine-minute mark, British Columbia–based poet Jordan Scott and sound artist Jason Starnes take the stage. After the audience's applause dwindles, Scott's voice cuts through the vacuum of silence: "skin-like / deer's sylph arbour / secret legs / scintilla me / hush too / debarkful forest / I am moving / teeth / soft / ache in yes / panting ..."[1] His voice lifts these lines from his book *Night & Ox* into the air, projecting them as sound to the audience – both the audience in the room, present that evening, and to us more than three years after the original performance.

What we can't conjure in writing is the way that, as a stutterer, Scott's voice grapples with this text. We could transcribe the places that the stutter "ambushes" the voice (to use Scott's evocative description) – where syllables are caught and refuse to "land"[2] – but this would not evoke the timbre, affect, and labour required to bring these syllables into sound. We could slide into metaphor and say: we hear the voice's *muscularity* as it grapples with language. However, the thought of doing so brings us back to the lines that open Scott's 2008 book of poetry, *blert*: "It is part of my existence to be the parasite of metaphors, so easily am I carried away by the first simile that comes along. Having been carried away, I have to find my difficult way back, and slowly return, to the fact of my mouth."[3] *The fact of the mouth* (and, metonymically, the voice) is that it is an obstinate and unyielding referent that resists description in language. In trying to capture Scott's performance in writing, we are reminded of the paucity of language for describing sound: our limited vocabularies for describing sonic qualities other than amplitude and pitch, the scattershot of metaphor.

It should be emphasized that the difficulty of describing sound is not particular to Scott's performance of the poetics of dysfluency. Rather, Scott's performance foregrounds that this difficulty attends all sounds that make the transition into print, whether through transcription or graphical/musical notation. However, in sound's resistance to being codified in signs, a generative space emerges through acts of attentive, intentional listening – especially when these acts are founded on a willingness to embrace the difficulty, impasse, and uncertainty that sound and its reception demand. As American scholar Nicole Brittingham Furlonge writes in her book *Race Sounds*, the "gap or expressive abyss" between orality and print in fact "invite[s]...readers to listen as they read."[4] It engenders a textual interaction that is multimodal and multisensory. Or, as Canadian poet and sound artist Oana Avasilichioaei puts it in her interview in this collection, "I'm more interested in that passage – that in-between space – rather than the end points."[5] This is as true for the passage from sound to text as it is between languages, which Avasilichioaei gestures to as a translator. Crucially, this in-between space – its own "possible world," to quote Salomé Voegelin – is co-constructed between speaker and auditor, between author and reader.[6] It is one in which difference becomes an operative rather than inhibiting condition, as we strive to find tools in our respective vocabularies, lexicons, an sensory experiences that allow us to meaningfully connect with those just out of reach of our sensoria.

To Resist

Stemming from this place of creative impasse, *Resistant Practices in Communities of Sound* collects scholarly chapters, interviews, and creative works, pairing print- and oral-based genres to interrogate the ways that sonic practices (speaking, vocalizing, hearing, listening, recording, etc.) can act as forms of aesthetic and political resistance. As a collection, the works in this volume probe the specificity of sound as a communicative medium in art and literature, asking what its affordances enable within a particular social and historical milieu: contemporary Canadian cultural production (literature, film criticism, and fine art). It ponders the places that sound might infiltrate when visual markers are redacted or obscured. It contemplates the technologies, practices, and techniques that sound artists and literary performers mobilize in the service of unsettling the status quo. Perhaps most importantly, it endeavours to articulate an ethics of enunciating and listening to sound that is grounded in the nuances of individual subjectivities and, by proxy, differences in vocal and aural practices. In naming *resistance* as the focus of this collection, we gesture not only toward the cultural dominance of visual and printed materials in arts and literary practices but also regimes of social and political hegemony that are upheld through normative sonic frameworks.

Toward the former point – the dominance of the visual regime – this book meditates on the ways that visuality and writing retain their primacy in literary, artistic, and academic spheres in Canada. Indeed, many of the interviews with creative practitioners in this book describe the struggles that attend lifting poetry off the page into voiced, sounded, or otherwise time-based media. As Nisga'a poet Jordan Abel says of the sampler-produced poetic performances of his book *Injun*, he has often had to contend with questions of legitimacy in the vein of, "Is this even poetry?"[7] – questions that react to the digital mediation of the text both as a sonic object and the product of computational collation and indexing.

Likewise, critical work in this collection, such as prOphecy sun and Reese Muntean's essay describing their 2015 Vancouver-based multimedia performance *A Small Piece of Sky*, orients itself toward the possibilities of multisensory engagement with the world that extends beyond the visual, guiding us toward an ethics of artistic attunement that hinges upon the interaction between our senses – especially hearing and touch – and external stimuli.

Underpinning the collection's discussion of sensory bias is a conversational thread not only with communications and media theorists concerned with the differentiation and determination of the senses – R. Murray Schafer, Marshall McLuhan, Walter Ong, and Eric Havelock, among others – but also successive scholarship that rebuts a naturalized (and thus neutralized) reading of the senses as self-evident and ahistorical. Jonathan Sterne's critique of "the audiovisual litany" – a set of assumptions about the faculties of vision and hearing – becomes an important keystone for notions of *relationality* that attend every communicative act.[8] As Faith Ryan's essay in this collection reminds us, communication is a two-way street: the listener is as much an agent in making meaning as the speaker in the ways that they interpret speech.

An interrogation of sound's relationality opens up onto the latter formulation of resistance: sound as a site of political and social opposition, refusal, and transformation. Here, we are in dialogue with a community of recent sound studies texts that centre questions of equity and justice in their approaches to sound. Brandon LaBelle's *Acoustic Justice* insists that an important part of sonic justice work remains, at a basic level, diversifying the soundscape and creating the conditions to amplify voices that are unaccustomed to occupying public acoustic space. In his words, "To 'open the mic' is already to transform the dynamics of representational politics, upsetting the balance of power by giving way to new forms of social movement and articulation."[9] Justice not only demands a recalibration of the acoustic public sphere but also asks us to reconsider our default listening practices and imagine how we might listen differently. Stó:lō scholar Dylan Robinson's book *Hungry Listening* is cited often in this collection as a paradigmatic study of extractive or appropriative listening practices – what Robinson refers to as the hunger of settler-colonial forms of audition – as well as the dismantling of those practices by way of sustained, self-reflexive meditation on the positions we listen from (and what we listen *for*).

Nina Sun Eidsheim's *The Race of Sound* is also a keystone in this collection in its foregrounding of "the acousmatic question" – *Who is this?* – that attends every act of listening to a human voice.[10] In marking the acousmatic question as politically and culturally salient, Eidsheim refutes the long-standing equation of the voice and the subject – especially one whose personhood is stable, identifiable, and certain – and moves toward a relational model that is informed by the listener's material situation and life experience. We believe that art and literature offer space to elaborate and expand these theories of sound's resistant qualities, owing to the reader/listener's active role in a work's reception and interpretation, and also the ways that language – particularly poetic language – embraces uncertainty, multiplicity, and contradiction in its modes of making meaning.

Thus, we hear resistance in the creative works of Canadian performers Wayde Compton and Jason de Couto, whose collaborative turntablist performances unsettle a naturalized relationship between the voice and the body, the poet and the text. We hear resistance in scholar Mathieu Aubin's call to create space for dialogue across Canadian queer communities, using time-based, auditory media to overcome the barriers of geographical distance and generational difference. We attempt to formally enact resistance in our resonant – and sometimes dissonant – pairings of spoken and written words, acknowledging that their comparison and/or reconciliation is at times impossible. In this book, impossibility is productive: a gap leading not to inaction, silence, and disconnection but rather to the necessary and intentional work of listening and dialogue, and mutually created links of possibility despite the distance between.

Embedded within a colonial state, Canadian literary studies has historically reproduced the power imbalances between white settler Canadians and the Indigenous Peoples this country has sought to displace and exploit. Canadian poet and scholar Smaro Kamboreli writes of Canadian literature: "As a literature with a colonial descent, it has always been inscribed by the anxiety and insecurity typifying the ambivalent desire of settler cultures: to differentiate themselves from their imperial origins by establishing a literary idiom representative of the local even while craving recognition from the metropole under the rubric of its presumed universal literary values."[11] In other words, a Canadian literary context carries a colonial legacy (and the literary values inherent to that legacy) even as it tries to carve out its own unique identity. It transmits, even while attempting to distance itself from, the legacy of British literature and the values it upholds. To quote El Jones from this collection, in the Western tradition, "a good poem rewards frequent engagement."[12] For Jones, who situates her work within the Black oral tradition, work that is ephemeral, improvised, or oral runs counter to ideas of "a particular kind of very Europeanized, intellectual exercise" because it privileges the oral/aural elements of poetry over traditional elements of craft. As she puts it: "I just did it because it sounded good and it was what I wanted to do in this moment."[13] Canadian literature then, broadly, still holds onto colonial markers of literary value that reward intellectual, print-based forms of writing rather than oral, improvisational, or experimental forms of writing – a value system that is rooted in colonialism and white supremacy.

This is not to say that Canadian literature has not been /is not a space open to experimentation or sonic approaches. For CanLit, the identity of the past half-century is one that has been greatly influenced by the sonic experimentation of American avant-garde and the rise of new media formats like reel-to-reel recording, led by experimental writers and sound artists such as bpNichol, bill bissett, Jackson Mac Low, and Maxine Gadd, to name only a few. More recently, Indigenous writers like Jordan Abel and Tanya Tagaq have foregrounded sonic approaches in their work, as well as Black Canadian writers like Montreal-based Kaie Kellough and Tawhida Tanya Evanson, whose practices are deeply entrenched in oral, sonic, and musical approaches to making through language. Yet, even though we are seeing more Black, Indigenous, and writers of colour than ever before being published and amplified in Canada – and more work that breaks aforementioned page-bound colonial markers of craft handed down by the Crown – ultimately, when we think about this formal radicality alongside the still-unanswered calls of the Truth and Reconciliation Commission or the failure of the Canadian government to respect Indigenous culture and sovereignty, there is still a large power gap between the needs and values of the nation-state of Canada, and therefore the institution of Canadian literature, and the oral cultures and literatures that it feigns to uphold and value. In this way, in interviews with Jordan Abel, Tawhida Tanya Evanson, and El Jones, *Resistant Practices in Communities of Sound* showcases the incongruent multiplicity of sonic literary resistance in Canada as both a formal creative act (often performed uncritically by white settlers) and as an act of cultural vitality by creators and thinkers from Black and Indigenous communities.

Engaging the difference of such irreconcilable gaps, this collection argues that the oppositional potential of sonic practice cannot be realized without contending with the complexities of auditory and textual representation, and that sound in its fullness requires a plurality of directions and approaches. As such, the collection's pairings of the creative and the critical, the oral and the written, as well as the mediated and the live not only enrich one another through discourse but also mirror the complex iterations of academic and creative communities of sound that exist in Canada, and the cultural sphere more generally, today.

To Practise

This book is the product of much listening, dialogue, and experimentation. In assembling the collection, we grappled with how to present such tonally diverse and wide-ranging material in a way that strikes the reader as harmonious and purposeful. Some of the essays in this collection originated from the 2019 SpokenWeb Symposium, which was hosted at Simon Fraser University in Vancouver, British Columbia. Centring on the theme of "resonance," the two-day conference offered manifold perspectives on performed poetry, sound art, recording technologies, and collective sounds, and culminated in the event featuring Scott and Starnes's performance (somewhat inadequately) described above. The theme of "resistance" in its various forms emerged from the papers that we collected, and we solicited more work that we felt reverberated our understanding of this concept. However, we believed that to fully engage with sound's resistance as it had come to signify in our fledgling book, we also needed to introduce an element that concretely enacted and performed it. With Mash's background in spoken word and slam poetry – a long-time co-organizer of the Inspired Word Café in Kelowna, British Columbia – and Fong's in oral history interviewing, we were drawn to the interview as a critical form: one that diversified the "vocal" range of the page by presenting different voices, and that left room for recursions of speech, experimental position-taking, and debate.

We feel that this collection offers a unique methodological approach to both sound and Canadian cultural studies in its curation of critical writing alongside orally sourced works – primarily interviews with creative sound practitioners but also transcriptions of round-table proceedings and a podcast episode. In switching between expressive forms – writing and speech represented in writing – it asks its audience members to (re)attune themselves as listeners as well as readers and conscripts a variety of audile techniques to hear them in the mind's ear. It invites us to think about the rhetorical differences in communicative forms occurring between people, face to face, and those occurring between a writer and their reading public. However, the division between direct interpersonal speech (i.e., a conversation) and the more abstract notion of public discourse becomes muddied, especially in a Canadian context of pandemic-era communication, when dialogues are often happening asynchronously and interlocutors can enter the conversation after the fact. Many works in the collection self-consciously play with the temporality of digitally remediated sounds as they circulate in the context of the pandemic. For example, Mathieu Aubin and Felicity Tayler's *Lesbian Liberation Across Media: A Sonic Screening* podcast stacks layers of remediation as participants watch digitized films over Zoom and the ensuing dialogue is collaged into a podcast, which is then reproduced textually in this volume. Tayler's introduction to the transcript asks where intimacy and community reside in each of these transformations, what each iteration brings to the community represented in this ever-evolving gathering, and ethical considerations attend each shift in medium.

The interaction between speech and writing in the form of transcription is an object of self-reflexive practice throughout the book. It is our conviction that the political and ethical dimensions of sound cannot be separated from its materiality in the real world, and so we felt it was important to stylistically retain the markers of its origins in orality: dates, timestamps, speaker tags, sound cues, etc. However, while we sought to preserve the "flavour" of orality in these works, the transcripts are by no means verbatim. Our decision to bring the text closer to the flow of written language is based on a number of factors. One, a sympathetic edit attempts to *mirror audition* by representing what the ear (or, specifically, *our* ears) actually hear in a conversation, rather than what is explicitly said. That is, it's easy to follow an oral conversation with its aborted sentences and trail-offs, non-verbal filler words and non-linear syntax, because the mind fills in the gaps to make it comprehensible and whole. This is less so the case with verbatim transcripts, which attempt to impose language intended for aural reception onto the completely disparate activity of page-reading – an act which, personally speaking, has disastrous consequences for readerly patience and comprehension.

Additionally, we had no qualms about letting authors edit their spoken words after the fact (ourselves included), so as to enrich and enlarge what was said in speech. Any specific iteration of a conversation represents only a fraction of what might be said on the topic; the same questions with the same interviewee might yield a completely different response on another day, depending on the weather. Interviewees were given the opportunity to review and revise their transcripts several times before publication to ensure that what appears on the page actually represents what they wanted to convey. Thus, the overarching goal in reproducing the interviews in print was not to uphold some kind of idealist fidelity to the speech act (which, in actuality, is impossible), but to think through speech as a critical *genre*: its formal qualities and rhetorical gestures, its rhythms and patterns. We are indebted to Montreal-based poet and scholar Deanna Radford's thoughtful transcription work and preface that opens this collection for shaping our thoughts on the representation of speech in writing.

In addition to pairing spoken and written language, the collection also brings conversations about creative practice into contact with critical works on and around cultural production. This structure bridges the too-often separate worlds of creative and critical sonic praxis, producing generative dialogue in which work from one field speaks to and

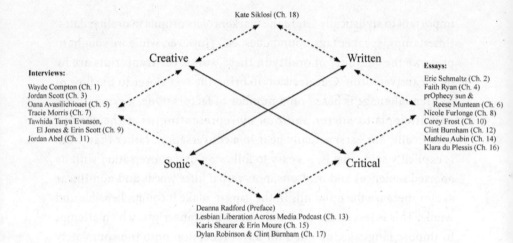

FIGURE 0.1 • Structural mapping of chapters in *Resistant Practices in Communities of Sound*

enriches work from the other, whether through resonance, inquiry, or counterpoint. The collection examines, on the one hand, *critical methods* of engaging with sound – particularly bodies of literary and artistic work in their specific materiality as read, recited, performed, mediated, archived, and remixed objects. On the other hand, it engages with *creative practices* that mobilize sound as a political aesthetic, taking on questions of identity, racialization, ability, mobility, and surveillance. Chapters showcase diverse approaches to the equally complex formations of sound and community: the former an interaction of physiology, cognition, and environment, and the latter a relational network of individuals, institutions, and physical/social spaces.

Figure 0.1 maps the collection's contents along two central axes: (1) Sonic – Written and (2) Creative – Critical. The first axis indicates a work's origin in either sound or writing: sonic works are pieces that were transcribed from spoken recordings, and written works those that were composed on the page. The second axis designates whether a work is primarily oriented toward creative practice (literature, performance, visual art) or critical interpretation (hermeneutics, history, theory). This second axis is more porous than the first, in that creative and critical practices shape one another in significant ways; however, for the purposes of the collection, it was useful to mark *the positions from which the authors speak*, whether primarily as artists reflecting on their craft or as cultural critics speaking to (and from) a particular argumentative standpoint.

The left-hand quadrant of the square lists the works in the collection that are both sonic and creative: interviews with poets and performers who use innovative sonic techniques in the presentation of their work. The lower quadrant represents works that are sonic and critical: transcripts of events emerging from communities with particular relationships to sound and practice. The right-hand quadrant is works that are both written and critical: essay chapters by scholars from diverse disciplines, including literary study, the visual arts, performance studies, oral history, and education. Finally, the upper quadrant represents work that is both written and creative, pointing to Kate Siklosi's visual poems that close the book, which were composed as a direct response to Clint Burnham's interview with Dylan Robinson. While there is only one piece in this quadrant, its ultimate position in the collection and centrality to the collection's research questions and methods make it a crucial component of the book. This mapping is intended as a non-hierarchical representation of the collection's central methodological and thematic threads.

To Commune

Sonic communities and sounded cultural production have historically been constituted of, and championed by, the marginalized and the underserved. Modern modes of spoken word, sound poetry, or poetry in performance more generally owe far more to Black and Indigenous orature and oral culture than they do to the Western oral tradition or the English literary canon, despite the fact that avant-garde sound poetry has frequently advanced itself through the appropriation and erasure of other cultures. In a Canadian context, this appropriation and erasure within artistic communities is paralleled by the ongoing appropriation, erasure, and genocide enacted upon Indigenous peoples through, among other practices, a systematic destruction of oral language and culture.

One of the primary goals of the Canadian residential school system was assimilation of Indigenous children through replacing their traditional oral culture and knowledge with a print-based, Western education. Thus, the tyranny of the visual that this book resists refers to not merely an aesthetic domination but a cultural one: the suppression and appropriation of oral forms and cultures, which has been a fulcrum of colonialism. Though the irony of a print manuscript is not lost on us, in focusing this book on sound and orality, we felt it was important to amplify the voices of equity-deserving writers and creative practitioners – not only to honour these writers' ties to communities of oral tradition and sonic cultural innovation but also to uphold the voices and communities who have historically done, and continue to do, an unequal share of the labour of speaking truth to power today.

As such, one of our goals from the outset was to present a diverse range of insights and experiences from BIPOC+ authors and artists, women and femmes, members of the queer community, disabled people, and multiple generations, who bring their personal experiences to bear on the phenomenological and social experience of sound. This mandate guided our choices to interview contemporary sound practitioners with diverse backgrounds and lean into the places where their subjective positionality intersects their work. As interviewers, we too endeavoured to not shy away from our own layered subjective positioning (as early-career academics, as poets, as parents, etc.) and to approach the conversation with curiosity, openness, and a willingness to be unsettled in our thinking. As philosopher Gemma Corradi Fiumara writes in *The Other Side of Language*, genuine, attentive listening requires "a relationship to thinking anchored in humility and faithfulness," an approach that resolutely rejects "grasping, mastering, [and] using."[14]

Listening, as much as speaking, requires vulnerability (if we're to do it well), and the contributors in this collection acted not only as authors of language but also its *auditors*. Contributors read each other's work in progress and incorporated the thoughts and ideas of others into their prose; the content of one interview served as a talk-point in another and sound practitioners frequently commented upon the impact of others' work in their own practice. As a record of listening acts, this book celebrates a number of shared discoveries: the parallels, say, between Wayde Compton's notion of pheneticization – that is, "[r]acially perceiving someone based on a subjective examination of his or her outward appearance"[15] – and Faith Ryan's discussion of "the ableist ear" which "hear[s] vocal difference and account[s] for it with the indexes 'disabled,' 'unintelligent,' and/or 'unhealthy,' rather than considering how their positionality and skill in listening impacts the outcome of the communication."[16] In both of these cases, the observer/listener's role in making meaning by way of their "diagnosis" of an other is effaced, and the qualities being interpreted – as being "raced" or "disabled"– are attributed to the person being heard or observed as though they were natural or self-evident qualities. Slam practitioners/spoken word artists El Jones, Tawhida Tanya Evanson, and Tracie Morris find affinities in their parallel observations that resistance cannot simply involve refusal, but also on a fundamental level must embrace the "yes" of solidarity, allyship, and building alternative forms of community. "[A]dvocacy is 90 percent listening" as Jones reminds us.[17]

Ultimately, this book embraces *difference* as the foundation of its intended solidarity work. By this we mean that it not only seeks to be representationally diverse, but it also grapples with differences of perspective without seeking to homogenize or reconcile them. We believe that sustained attention to the sonic world necessitates difference *as methodology*. Difference is an inherent part of the speech and listening acts that form the basis of communication, the ways that they succeed or fail to connect. Difference also expresses itself in minute fluctuations in attention, perception, and interpretation that constitute an individual's listening practice. Ultimately, this collection's aim is to foreground sound's difference-making capabilities as a source of strength and political vigour. As Dylan Robinson writes in *Hungry Listening*: "Listening and sounding responsively (responsibly) are coterminous processes. If we're doing both well, we are constantly being pulled off center and then recentering to a new position, which entails being open to exploring new ideas. The problems occur when we think we can prehear the outcome; and I think that applies as much to listening in the audience as it does to composition or performance."[18] This openness to disparity humbly asks for a kind of textual mindfulness: not anticipating through meditation on the past or the future, but a genuine focus on that which lies in front of us.

We hope the audience for this book, then, is not just readers interested in aesthetic or formal criticism on the creative and critical sounded work being produced in the world today but also those interested in the ways that sonic practices are deeply political practices, shaping and reshaping the standard socio-cultural narratives we see and hear. We hope the audience for this book is as wide-ranging as the poets and critics within it. We hope that despite a Canadian focus within the book, that its message crosses borders and ideological boundaries. We hope our readers can see (hear) themselves herein in a way not previously experienced in other books in Canadian cultural studies. We hope that *Resistant Practices in Communities of Sound* will guide readers to hear – and be moved by – different experiences, voices, and pasts in order to carry them forward into the hum of possible futures.

Chapter Overview

On Transcription: A Prelude by Deanna Radford
(in conversation with Deanna Fong)

The collection opens with a meditation on transcription as a poetic, affective, and embodied practice that introduces one of the central themes of the collection: the interface between speech and text. Deanna Radford, a poet, organizer, and performer, transcribed the majority of the interviews in the collection during the fall of 2020. The preface weaves in a transcribed conversation with editor Deanna Fong, exploring the features of transcription that are obscured when we think of it as neutral, transparent, or merely "technical" labour. Radford's written remarks, in both essay and poetry form, thread into the conversation as additional frequencies of critical thought. Radford pays close attention to the physicality of transcription and the gestures of care that mark a *fidelity* to the speech event: its speakers, their words, and the extralexical gestures that give language its meaning. Opening the collection with this prelude re-centres the important intellectual and creative labour of transcription that often goes uncredited in academic production. It also introduces the driving questions at the heart of this book by consciously navigating the interaction between spoken and written language and proposing an ethos of care in our approach to sonic cultural material.

Chapters 1 and 2, Compton / Schmaltz

The first pairing in the collection places Fong's interview with British Columbia poet and novelist Wayde Compton alongside Canadian poet-critic Eric Schmaltz's chapter "Race, Multiplicity, and Dis/Located Voices: Wayde Compton's Turntablist Poetics." Fong's conversation with Compton discusses his work with the avant-garde turntablist collective the Contact Zone Crew, focusing on the recording and performance technologies that they use to mobilize their unique poetic and political practice. Compton and Fong consider the ways in which the materiality of sound technologies have changed over time; how historical forms of media are tied to traditions of Black music and orature; and how turntablism resists reductive ideas of authorship and ownership through the acts of remixing and recirculation. Schmaltz's essay offers insight into Compton's poetic work, both on the page and in performance. He analyzes Compton's interventions into composer R. Murray Schafer's essentializing noise/music paradigm, as well as the aesthetics and ethics of sonic sampling. Schmaltz suggests, through a series of short, interrelated textual "cuts" that Compton's turntablist poetics and multimodal artistic practice resist the intertwining forces of nationalism, capitalism, racism, and literary exceptionalism. Together, these pieces argue that collaborative, multimedia practice can generate new possibilities for art to resist dominant modes (or technologies) of production, while probing the relationship between subjects, language, and media that serve as the material support for creative works.

Chapters 3 and 4, Scott / Ryan

The following chapters pair Fong's interview with Vancouver Island poet Jordan Scott and Faith Ryan's essay "Listening as Access: Toward Relational Listening for Nonnormative Speech and Communication." Fong's discussion with Scott explores listening to nonnormative speech from his perspective. Scott's work is based around his relationship to language as a stutterer. He describes the labour of nonnormative speaking and the physical toll of trying to force his body to feign fluency. Ryan's paper argues for listening as a "form of access." Fong engages Scott's work alongside that of multimedia artist Alice Wong, reading through scholarship on disability studies, sound studies, and critical race theory to consider how communication is an essentially intersubjective activity. Listening relationally means "generating access" for disabled or nonnormative speakers, which can only occur when able-bodied listeners "[assume] meaningfulness" on the part of the speaker.[19] That is, the listener accepts responsibility and care in the act of listening and rejects preconceived notions of fluency and beauty in order to honour relations between particular bodies with their own unique speech patterns. There are strong echoes between Scott and Ryan's ideas on listening and access: they both speak to the labour of hearing and vocalizing, and how accessibility can be fostered through conscious engagement with self-reflexive listening practices.

Chapters 5 and 6, Avasilichioaei / sun and Muntean

Focusing on questions of geographical and social space – and artistic representations thereof – the book's third pairing brings together Fong's interview with poet and multimedia artist Oana Avasilichioaei and the chapter "New Forms of Digital, Temporal, and Auditory Poiesis," co-written by Vancouver-based artists and educators prOphecy sun and Reese Muntean. Fong's conversation with Avasilichioaei discusses her newest work, a chamber opera titled *Cells of Wind*, for which she wrote the libretto. Avasilichioaei comments upon collaborative methods of composition and improvisation, as well as the ways that translation, remediation, and polyvocality become methods of creating work that is, within itself, multiple and relational. The interview finds resonance in sun and Muntean's chapter, which elaborates on the theoretical, technological, and aesthetic resonances of their 2015 site-specific interdisciplinary performance, *A Small Piece of Sky*. Choreographing human, non-human, and environmental actors according to a chance-based script, the piece invited deliberate, sustained engagement with the normally suppressed sonic elements of the participants' surroundings. In reflecting on the complex and often asymmetrical relations between human beings and the material world *through sound*, this piece espouses a post-human ethics, recognizing the agency of non-human actors and of sound itself. The two pieces find affinity through their interest in multimedia art production: both pieces discuss visual and textual reference points from the creative work that they document. Both are interested in the permeable boundaries between public and private spaces that express themselves sonically through movement, proximity, mediation, amplification, noise, and signal.

Chapters 7 and 8, Morris / Furlonge

Fong and Mash's interview with Brooklyn-based avant-garde sound poet Tracie Morris finds direct response in American scholar and educator Nicole Brittingham Furlonge's chapter "'It's resistance but it's also embrace': Tracie Morris's Collaborative Ear, an Open Letter." The interview opens with a meditation on Morris's extensive career as a collaborator – with contemporaries in literature, music, dance, and the visual arts, but also as a reader, auditor, interpolator, and perennial "hand-holder" of texts. Morris draws upon her own experience as a slam and avant-garde sound poet to dig into the tacit assumptions underpinning value-judgments such as "popular," "literary," "canonical," and "amateur," resisting aesthetic absolutism in favour of nuanced, personally and culturally inflected definitions of value. Furlonge's chapter directly responds to Morris's interview, tuning in to what it means to be in a collaborative relationship with another artist. Furlonge argues that Morris's poetry demonstrates a profound interest in intersubjective listening as a ground for her own sonic compositions and improvisations. Morris's ways of listening – what Furlonge terms her "collaborative ear" – lean into the uncertainty and possibility in the space of collaborators' different perceptions. In the form of an open letter, this piece listens to Morris's listening. It champions the "collaborative ear" as a dynamic, ethical, and inclusive auditory practice that resists absolutism and embraces what it could mean for the poet – and for us as educators, scholars, and critics – to be listeners to and for each other in a fractured, polarized world.

Chapters 9 and 10, Evanson, Jones, and Scott / Frost

Mash's interview with Montreal-based spoken word poet Tawhida Tanya Evanson, Halifax's former poet laureate and activist El Jones, and Kelowna poet-organizer Erin Scott pairs with Corey Frost's chapter "The Whatevericity of Spoken Word: Community, Identity, Performativity." The interview with these three veteran sound performers is wide-reaching in scope. It covers broad terrain, including spoken word as a community formation; its place within the literary canon and popular culture; its historical roots; the role of sound in composition and performance; and the socio-cultural and racial politics within not only Canadian spoken word and slam communities but also so-called CanLit as a whole. The interview thinks through the performativity of spoken word and slam, and that performativity's roots in historically Black traditions, such as the West African griot among other historically oral traditions. As a complement, Frost's essay thinks through the relation of slam and spoken word to formulations of "the popular," and the racial politics in those communities. He suggests that there is an inclusion/exclusion loop often inherent to community formation: the circumscription of community boundaries is simultaneously an act of inclusion of those who meet the criteria for citizenship and an exclusion of those who don't. Together, this pairing suggests the ways that slam poetry resists cultural and aesthetic elitism through an artistic ethos of openness and through championing modes of poetry that have seen less critical and pedagogical attention than their print counterparts.

INTRODUCTION

Chapters 11 and 12, Abel / Burnham

A tense yet productive dialogue about sound, performance, racialization, and white privilege emerges from Fong's interview with Nisga'a sound poet Jordan Abel alongside Vancouver-based poet and critic Clint Burnham's chapter "Can We Think of Sound (or Voice) without Sight (or Gaze)? Lacanian Theory and the Horror of Community." In his interview with Fong, Abel discusses his perspective as a Nisga'a poet performing in public spaces that are created largely for, and by, white settler audiences. He describes the myriad subtle ways that these spaces produce a fetishized notion of Indigeneity, discrediting and disciplining subjective experiences that do not conform to those expectations. Abel explains how his own use of mediated performance resists those expectations, mobilizing the difficulty of sonic poetry to perforate the settler-colonial structures of academic and literary spheres. The latter half of the interview turns to Abel's recent book NISHGA (2021), which marks cues of auditory liveness as a poetic strategy, examining the possibility of literature acting as a form of witness to intergenerational trauma and lateral violence. Burnham's chapter draws on Lacanian theories of voice and gaze as lacking, partial objects to discuss two recent horror films: John Krasinski's *A Quiet Place*, and Suzanne Bier's *Bird Box*, both released in 2018. Taking these two cultural objects as case studies, this chapter counters the pervasive idea that listening is an unalloyed social good – that listening, on its own, can create more equitable material conditions for marginalized peoples. Rather, Burnham points out that, in the context of the Truth and Reconciliation Commission on Canadian residential schools, listening is often the activity of the powerful and serves as a substitute for meaningful reparative action. Burnham's reading of the two films exposes the faulty logic of aligning listening with benevolence and voicing with power, inviting us to consider ways that we might listen differently – first and foremost, relinquishing the practice of listening as a form of mastery. While these two texts are quite distant in terms of the cultural fields they examine, perhaps better than any other pairing they enact this book's methodology of listening through and across difference, sharing a compelling common interest in settler-colonial modes of perception and the resurgent practices of witness that can act as decolonizing forms of resistance.

Chapters 13 and 14, Aubin and Tayler / Aubin

A transcription of the podcast *Lesbian Liberation Across Media: A Sonic Screening* (with an introduction by Ottawa-based scholar, curator, and librarian Felicity Tayler) pairs with Franco-Ontarian co-creator Mathieu Aubin's critical reflection on the sonic object and the event that occasioned its making. This unique pairing invites an author to directly reflect upon one of their own sonic works. We "hear" the stories of Canada's Lesbian Liberation Movement through a transcription of the episode, which weaves together ambient sound and conversation from a Zoom-era watch party for three lesbian liberation films produced in the 1970s and '80s. Aubin's accompanying essay, in which he positions himself as a producer of this event, explores the "activist potential of the watch party as a queer community-building practice that relies on audio-visual (AV) materials and oral histories."[20] The transcription reproduces the podcast's audio collage, which weaves together archival clips, participant commentary, and an original musical score. It explores the community-building potential of media-focused gatherings – a method that not only lends itself to dispersed global populations but also those separated by the COVID-19 pandemic. Aubin insists that watch parties such as Lesbian Liberation Across Media have the potential to create intergenerational, dialogical space for queer people to reflect together on their communities and the multiplicity within them. They also offer an opportunity to re-animate the past in the present – an important methodological feature of oral history – creating continuity between generations of activists.

Chapters 15 and 16, Shearer and Moure / du Plessis

"'It was an extension of the moment': Five Poets in Conversation on Analog Audio Recording and Creative Practice" offers a transcript of a 2013 University of British Columbia Okanagan round table on sound recording and poetic production, framed by an introduction from co-facilitators Canadianist Karis Shearer and Montreal-based poet Erín Moure. This piece is in dialogue with Montreal-based poet-scholar Klara du Plessis's chapter "Curatorial Agency at Véhicule Art Inc.: 'Openness was a guiding spirit to Véhicule.'" Both texts consider historical literary communities for whom sound recording and self-documentation were constitutive practices. The 1960s Vancouver-based *TISH* poetry community – represented on the panel by George Bowering, Frank Davey, Daphne Marlatt, Sharon Thesen, and Fred Wah – archived their own literary lives via reel-to-reel, and later, cassette tapes and digital recordings. The round table discusses the embodied nature of listening to poetry and the crucial community-building function of recording and circulating recorded audio materials to a prolific community of writers. Du Plessis's chapter discusses the work of the Montreal-based Véhicule Art Inc., a collective of artists and writers who, in early formations, held literary readings and open mics that invited reading and performance practices that pushed the boundaries of aesthetic value and taste. The chapter proposes the term "curatorial agency" to describe the various activities that organizers of literary events undertake in cultivating the auditory space of a public reading. She demonstrates how Véhicule Art Inc.'s weekly bilingual poetry reading events were defined by an ethos of openness and aesthetic experimentation, favouring the new (and, indeed, sometimes shocking and offensive) over the politically oppositional *and* the literary status quo. The result is a profoundly ambivalent and conflictual space: on the one hand, this curatorial openness created grounds for burgeoning queer, feminist, political consciousness; on the other, its deliberate structurelessness opened the door for works that rehearsed the racist, sexist, and homophobic rhetoric of the era. What connects these two works is a nuanced discussion of communities and the sound technologies that they employ as a double-edged possibility of resistance and re-inscription of normative power.

Chapters 17 and 18, Robinson and Burnham / Siklosi

The book's final pairing departs from previous content by bringing together an oral critical interview with a visual creative piece commissioned as a response. Clint Burnham's conversation with Stó:lō sound scholar Dylan Robinson touches upon the intersubjective sound practices that reverberate between human, environmental, and spiritual agents. Burnham and Robinson wend through discussions of the relationality of silence – that silence can be audible and, indeed, articulate in some circumstances, depending on the listener – as well as the importance of engaging one's own critical listening positionality, that is, the social and cultural influences that shape our perceptions and which orient our hearing toward and away from different sounds. Invited as an interpreter/interpolator of Burnham and Robinson's interview, Toronto-based concrete poet Kate Siklosi's "Misaudition" is a suite of visual poems that respond to the themes, images, and topics presented in the text. Siklosi's work interfaces the forensic materiality of the natural world (leaves, bark, seeds, and shells) with the formal materiality of language through techniques of collage, weaving, and stitching. Siklosi's work figuratively engages with Robinson's notions of intersubjective sound practices, resisting the idea that verbal agency is an exclusively human faculty and instead distributing the meaning of speech acts between a network of environmental actors. We feel it is important to close the collection with this pairing in order to solidify the book's two overarching aims: one, to foreground sonic works that enact decolonial forms of resistance and, two, to highlight works that act on our sensoria as well as our intellect, inscribing political resistance on affective and aesthetic levels.

NOTES

1 Jordan Scott, *Night & Ox* (Toronto: Coach House Books, 2016), 66.
2 Jordan Scott, "'The fact of my mouth': An Interview with Jordan Scott" by Deanna Fong, in this volume, 80.
3 Jordan Scott, *blert* (Toronto: Coach House Books, 2008), 7.
4 Nicole Brittingham Furlonge, *Race Sounds: The Art of Listening in African American Literature* (Iowa City: Iowa University Press, 2018), 4.
5 Oana Avasilichioaei, "'That in-between space': An Interview with Oana Avasilichioaei" by Deanna Fong, in this volume, 108.
6 Salomé Voegelin, *Sonic Possible Worlds: Hearing the Continuum of Sound* (New York: Bloomsbury, 2014).
7 Jordan Abel, "'A taking in, a holding with': An Interview with Jordan Abel," by Deanna Fong, in this volume, 219.

INTRODUCTION

8 Jonathan Sterne, *The Audible Past: Cultural Origins of Sound Reproduction* (Durham: Duke University Press, 2003), 15.
9 Brandon LaBelle, *Acoustic Justice: Listening, Performativity, and the Work of Reorientation* (New York: Bloomsbury Academic, 2021), 2.
10 Nina Sun Eidsheim, *The Race of Sound: Listening, Timbre, and Vocality in African American Music* (Durham: Duke University Press, 2018), 3.
11 Smaro Kamboureli and Christl Verduyn, eds, *Critical Collaborations: Indigeneity, Diaspora, and Ecology in Canadian Literary Studies* (Waterloo: Wilfrid Laurier University Press, 2013), 1.
12 El Jones, "'What is being resisted is our "yes"': An interview with Tawhida Tanya Evanson, El Jones, and Erin Scott" by Cole Mash, in this volume, 179.
13 Ibid., 180.
14 Gemma Corradi Fiumara, *The Other Side of Language: A Philosophy of Listening* (London: Routledge, 1990), 14.
15 Wayde Compton, *After Caanan: Essays on Race, Writing, and Region* (Vancouver: Arsenal Pulp Press, 2010), 25.
16 Faith Ryan, "Listening as Access: Toward Relational Listening for Nonnormative Speech and Communication," in this volume, 94.
17 Jones, "'What is being resisted,'" 170.
18 Dylan Robinson, *Hungry Listening: Resonant Theory for Indigenous Sound Studies* (Minneapolis: University of Minnesota Press, 2020), 250.
19 Ryan, "Listening as Access," 98.
20 Mathieu Aubin, "Listening to LGBTQ2+ Communities at the Lesbian Liberation Across Media Watch Party," in this volume, 274.

On Transcription

A Prelude (in Conversation with Deanna Fong)

Deanna Radford

The formal act of transcription is a channelling of spoken information into written form; it renders words that are spoken legible upon the page. The transcriber's starting point and means of livelihood is a field of sound reception – the corporeal, phenomenal self. As transcriber, my relationship with the field of sound involves close listening to words spoken, to voiced and voiceless utterances, and to the spaces in between them. I am not passively muted while I work. I listen with ears in sync with eyes, mind, breath, heartbeat, balance, and hands. I do not communicate verbally while transcribing but I am often not expressionless. The array of sounds I emit while fingers tap on the keyboard for intense stretches of time depend on what I hear – laughter at wordplay and jokes; suspense with the inhalation and holding of breath; physical release with a sigh; empathy in a short hum from my throat; confusion with an overt misapprehension

ON TRANSCRIPTION: A PRELUDE

of syllables; I click my tongue. In-/exhale. I release the headphones from my ears and the room tone where I am sitting washes over me. My sense of proprioception recalibrates. I take a pause and stretch my neck, forearms, and shoulder blades. Start over and repeat. Echo. Have I been here before? What can I learn from my sensate motions at this very moment? In retrospect?

I find a way through the sensate motions, through disorientation in a field of sound that I am part of.

I began the work of speech-to-text transcriber for the interviews collected in *Resistant Practices in Communities of Sound* as an MA student in creative writing and research assistant for Jason Camlot at Concordia University in Montreal. While I transcribed each conversation, Deanna Fong and Cole Mash's subject matter resonated with me: the questions they asked of each poet and their responses, and the quality of voice and engagement captured in sound. These features spoke to my own personal interests in poetry, sound, listening, and poetics. Completing the transcripts and thinking alongside the ideas put forward in each conversation accentuated the value in listening from a place of curiosity and embodiment. My contribution derives from my responsiveness and receptivity and not from words that I spoke. There is a particular kind of quiet that's required of the transcriber, and it served me as both home base and guide in the process. I was excited to contribute to the project. Which is why, when Fong invited me to contribute to the collection, I was moved and surprised. Throughout my experience as a transcriber for students, television, as a music writer, and in other academic settings, I never imagined that I would get to contribute in this way. The invitation was generous and collegial. In extending it, Fong overturned a traditional dynamic between those who are identified as "the client" and "the service provider" in the common parlance of transcription work.

Conceptualist poet Kenneth Goldsmith refers to transcription as a *subjective* process in the context of his uncreative writing framework – and it is.[1] Taking uncreative writing's blueprint for a novel approach toward creative writing practices, the invitation to contribute my thoughts as a transcriber for this project broadens the scope of subjectivity within the authorial process. It prompts a pragmatic reconsideration of terms such as "listening," "authorship," "authority," and "transcription" that become activated within an ecosystem of care. For instance, it is rare for a transcriber to engage at length with a person they have transcribed on the record. It is fortuitous that Fong and I share a given name: Deanna. It is a personal twist that has enabled us to converse from two sides of the same coin.

After I transcribed the interviews, Deanna and I met at Hinnawi Bros Bagel & Café near Concordia University (a neighbourhood standard) to discuss in further depth. The text that follows is composed of three elements: (1) my transcription of that conversation; (2) poems, which convey the affective experience and challenges of transcription; and (3) essay reflections intended to put even further pressure on transcription's fraught relationship to speech and sound. Many theorists and thinkers of sound, art, and language have guided my reflections, in addition to post-interview written exchanges with Deanna by email and shared documents.

Deanna Fong: ... It's so weird. I think you can hear it particularly in my interview with Jordan [Scott] where we're talking and talking, and then we hit record, and then all of a sudden he starts stuttering again. The interview was actually the first thing I had done since I got back from maternity leave, and we both got *so* nervous! We were having such a nice conversation beforehand. Hitting record totally changes the tenor of everything that happens.

ON TRANSCRIPTION: A PRELUDE

Deanna Radford: It does! The gesture of hitting the record function can be imbued with so much in the moment. Like it's a gust that brings a change in temperature. The pause in conversation and turning of attention to the gesture can remind us of the conversation's purpose and also pulls one out of the actual conversation. I know I have felt self-conscious as both interviewee and interviewer in that moment. I find it a struggle to recall what was said *before* that gesture and to rearticulate my thoughts coherently. There can be discomfort from hearing one's own voice on a recording if playback figures into such moments, especially if one isn't used to hearing it.

DF: Which is an act of mercy that you're doing the transcription! [Laughter] Because I truly hate transcribing my own voice – just hearing how many of my sentences I just trail off or restart!

DR: I relate to that!

A microphone that amplifies the human voice is parallel to a microscope in that it transmits a blow-up of the speaking subject. What results is a version of personal aural embodiment that we might have less familiarity with, in comparison to retinal reproductions of ourselves or our likeness in photo or video. Douglas Kahn writes about the microphone as a microscope in how it relates to early sound thinking. I think that the latter half of what follows is a nice proxy for what the listening engagement of the transcriber can be like: "Telephony was a new day for sound, not just for talking. The reality and idea of phonography contributed to the surge of sound thinking and auditory imagination during the same period (the latter half of the 1870s), but the way people talked about telephony was different. The telephone was celebrated for its unprecedented sensitivity in rendering incredibly small amounts of energy audible, just as its associated technology, *the microphone, zoomed into a new universe of sounds, real and imagined, like a microscope with ears peering all the way down to the molecular level.*"[2]

Close listening is a constituent of the transcription process. How Kahn depicts the vantage point of listening on behalf of a microphone, as during transcription, is emblematic. If one accepts Kahn's depiction, which conveys both a sense of scientific rigour and of wonder, then one would be able to reimagine the potential for transcription as a creative form wherein the sound of the human voice is a material object in its own right. The zoom-in or microscopic effect of the microphone enables the transcriber to consider the interview from a vantage point that the recorded subject or conversants don't have: as an external observer of the interview process, for the embodied attunement of close listening, and from a mental perspective at a distance. Returning to the example with Jordan Scott, a break in a conversation emerged when Fong pressed the record button. There could be discomfort experienced by conversants in a moment like that. As Fong took care in the moment to resume the conversation, care too must be taken in treating that moment within the transcript. Can that moment of onboarding toward an officially recorded conversation – that might be somewhat tumultuous – also be regarded after the fact in the transcript like a candid photo worthy of memento? Can transcripts take root in the auditory imagination instead of treating the sound as an eventual offcut? What can we learn from that moment of quiet, if it remains uncensored and present, within the transcribed document as a historical record or literary document?

DF: I had this thought on the topic of conceptual poetry that we were talking about on the way here. I was thinking about Kenneth Goldsmith's introduction to *Day*. Is that on your radar, that book?

DR: No, it's not. Though I spent time with Goldsmith's essays in *Uncreative Writing* when it came out in 2011. A couple of years later, I attended the *Postscript: Writing After Conceptual Art* exhibit at the Power Plant in Toronto, which included his work. I was excited to see the work of artists and writers who explored the material possibilities of language up close. Tell me about *Day*!

ON TRANSCRIPTION: A PRELUDE

DF: To be fair, it's not meant to be read, either. Or at least Goldsmith says it's not. He basically took one day of the *New York Times* and transcribed it into book format. I was thinking of the introduction he has for that book and his discussion of the transcription process is so much about mastery. He's like, "I'm an OCR wizard! I'm a transcription GURU!"[3] [Laughter] It's so much about that.

I was thinking about how different your approach is to it. In your writing, you talk about loyalty or fidelity to the voice, and there's a real openness or receptiveness to letting the text move you. I was thinking about those two different approaches. I think it has a lot to do with this feeling of your own embodiment in relation to the text. Because his body's nowhere to be seen around that. It's all things the machine does, you know?

DR: Yes! From one perspective, transcription can take a significant amount of time, attention, and physical endurance to complete a given project or job. I appreciate the advantage of using OCR (optical character recognition) to convert images of text into text that's legible to machines. "OCR Master" is funny and perhaps even self-effacing. Personally, I question that missing body, though, almost subconsciously. In response to the context surrounding *Day* that you describe, and in general, I want to welcome and name the people who have traditionally done transcription and transcription-adjacent work since the arrival of the typewriter. I want to invite them into the interview space, to take hold of the proverbial microphone, and to share their experiences of "copying text," as it were. I have had these people in my thoughts since I seriously began writing poetry – the messengers. My mother worked as a secretary; my paternal grandfather was a radio-telegrapher in World War II. I identify as a messenger.

> The phone operator, the typist, and the secretary wear a scent, or traces of a scent, called *messenger*: a trusted intermediary mandated to document and deliver information from one source to another. As in

a relay system, a messenger is not an author for they do not write. Rather, they listen, witness, note, trace, enter, store, and then reproduce the words and expressions of others in order to transmit. Each of these positions within the category I call *messenger* are distinct (I prefer to label them as germinal contributors to the foundations of digital technology) and are not to be understood as the distillations of the messenger function listed here. Instead, I propose the discussion of an image stereotype designated by twentieth-century popular culture; one that is lodged in my psyche as a white, able-bodied, cis-gendered woman, and late Generation X-er.

If young, she is quiet and servile but shrewd. If old or old*er*, she is a matronly and savvy gatekeeper to the boss (presented in the image of a handsome, powerful, middle-aged, white, able-bodied, cis-gendered businessman). This messenger I speak of is an example of labour in binary code, of feminized labour; soft and crucial, but not overly technical, never challenging, and usually white.

≡

The supposed ideal image of a messenger I have conjured isn't as potent as it may once have been. But feminized labour as a social construct does exist and does not operate in isolation. It is made of layers developed over time, which continue to exist and reinforce sexist and racist structures not disconnected from the interests of Western colonialism and hegemony. In her book on women in electronic music and sound cultures, Tara Rodgers writes, "Broadcast radio developed in conjunction with military investment around World War I, and subsequent amplification and recording technologies emerged directly from wartime expenditures or were funded for their potential military applications."[4] This historical information is relevant to a discussion of transcription's form and limits to better understand its material footprint and lineage. That is, we still often approach listening without considering an ethical approach or, "the relationship between listener and the listened-to" as Dylan Robinson writes in *Hungry Listening*.[5]

Reflecting on audio recording tools, the audio recording function on my smartphone for example, what is the relationship between me once I discard the phone and the individual who refurbishes it or harvests it for rare minerals? What is the sound that my disused smartphone makes when intermingled in a pile of other disused smartphones as e-waste in a warm climate under the sun? Who is the listener and who is the listened-to in these instances? How do I develop a listening technique to explore these questions? What biases prevent me from trying to pursue these questions? Broadly, the historical material circumstances that informed the creation of broadcast radio and amplification and recording technologies are relevant to these questions, and to the discussions that are centred in this collection. Their discussions do important work by asking *who and what matters* in the listening practices among sound poets, artists, scholars, and transcribers who engage with sound.

═══

To the interview space, I dream of inviting the people who assemble the keyboards, laptops, microphones, and digital audio recorders; the people who cull valuable rare earth materials from those tools once done for, rejected, and shipped to be recycled in distant countries. I want to bring these people together from across time and into a shared space – to listen to their stories in recognition of their labour, smarts, grit, speed, accuracy, and listening ability. To this list of skills and aptitudes I would add the ability to take quiet risks and to put one's own body on the line for the work of the messenger.

The location of the interview space would be a land site where deep earth materials that comprise tools for recording and documentation come from in order to initiate a broader collective listening experience that includes earth, non-human living things, and the elements.

DR: There was this beautiful moment in one of your questions where you asked, how can we leave the body out of transcription when we talk about it? And that when you step away from the work, you're a bit dizzy and your soul is crushed and still; it's discombobulating somehow. What is that? It's not a desirable place to be, but I think it's ephemeral and can possibly operate as a creative well to draw from, in some aspects. Because you do become tied to the work, to the conversation, as a transcriber. Maybe you feel a part of it. But also you've put in intense labour to materialize the conversation.

DF: Yeah. The only thing I can liken it to is I've gotten really into weightlifting – like doing really heavy squats and presses. The moment where you re-rack it, and then all of a sudden it feels like your body is about to float away because you've just put down this super heavy thing. I feel like that's the physical equivalent of the mental work of transcription. That when you step away from it, it was so intense that somehow you're just almost out-of-body.

ON TRANSCRIPTION: A PRELUDE

I wanted to ask you about that. If you had to describe what transcription feels like ... Is there a standard thing that it feels like? Or is it a bunch of different things?

DR: I love that question. What I was thinking about, part of the reason why we don't really talk about it in scholarship, or the academy, or research, is maybe, well, it's often viewed as support work. I think of the body as an infrastructure supporting, in service to, transcribing a conversation, and with any infrastructure, we really only notice it generally when it starts to break down. [Laughter] And I think that's where the questions about perfection and imperfection can come in. The body becomes elided in service to the work. All of this then draws attention to the working conditions, or your tools, or that complex name for what you experienced –

DF: Ulnar tunnel syndrome.

DR: – Ulnar tunnel syndrome. Or tennis elbow! I've written poetry about my bodily response to manual labour and what I appreciate about your question about this is that you're raising it as valuable work and I'm often angry and sad about manual labour and power imbalances of work.

But I think there's also more to say about it. It's really important to acknowledge this work because it cuts across different kinds of support work. If I were to take a Marxist analysis of the labour, of the tools, of the boss, the pay ... Even if you could be paid really well to do transcription, would you really want to do it if you got carpal tunnel syndrome? [Laugher] It's valuable to think through as an exercise. Maybe if it's something that we want to read and it's about documenting conversations and art and ideas.

Transcription also is connected to providing service to people with various disabilities. In my work at the Concordia Access Centre for people who had mobility issues or who are blind, for example, for me doing that work heightened my awareness of the failure of all of the infrastructure around us to support people who have such challenges. And as you say, the geopolitical nature of the work for people who live in Southeast Asia doing transcription work.

DF: Yeah. Definitely. Here we open up the question of what goes into the production of creative work, which we generally think of as immaterial or merely cognitive. It never, ever is. But I think one of the important things, at least in my mind and why I wanted to ask you to write about your experience for the collection, is that I think this work is often imagined as just technical. This is built into the labour structure of everyday transcription where people often get paid by the word. It's like this micro-transactional thing where it's like, "Every time I transcribe one word, I get one cent." Or whatever it is. When we boil it down to the material product like that, it's saying that the rest of the things that are involved in that labour don't matter. Like ulnar tunnel syndrome. Or just feeling so emotionally drained after you've connected with a recording and have been present for it for two hours and you just want to lie on the couch afterward and do nothing for another two hours while it settles in! [Laughter]

And yet there are all these creative decisions that you make into putting into this, figuring out how you're going to represent this conversation with care. None of that is represented in what we see and also what we think we're paying for in the traditional model of transcription. So I think when you factor in all those different kinds of labour that go into it, we should be paying transcribers a lot more!

To transcribe is to listen and capture, listen, mis-hear, miss, shear, rewind, try again. It is to press play, change playback speed, increase volume, capture, listen, refine. Breathe. Stop. Stand up and stretch. Start over.

To transcribe is to adjust the posture and headphones for comfort and to push through to the next ten-minute mark while there remains forty minutes of recording to listen through.

ON TRANSCRIPTION: A PRELUDE

Transcription brings a rhythm I feel compelled by, even when my body heat increases from sitting in front of a monitor for long stretches, when the tension in my lower neck becomes loud, even when I feel frustrated for not being able to decipher something that was expressed after having to rewind and replay more times than I'd prefer to mention.

Typing for transcription may appear easy to do. Those who master a skill make its performance look effortless. A completed transcript may mirror a conversation that took place in real time and appear luminous on the page or screen. Does successful transcription demand mastery? Can artful mastery of a skill imply that the body is no longer needed for its performance?

DF: Is there intention behind some of these more subconscious gestures, these verbal tics in speech? Do we keep them in because they mean? Or is it better to skip over them? What's your intuitive sense about that?

DR: I do think subconscious gestures can have meaning. I try to determine if or how a gesture adds or detracts from what is being said when I encounter them. Context plays a part: it will be less important to include within the transcript of a weekly university lecture than, say, from a conversation for anthropological research purposes. My intuitive approach is to consider them. A more intentional subconscious gesture can function as a rhetorical device or imply emphasis on a certain, more embodied level, for example.

It's possible that what a speaker says will guide me in whether or not to include a subconscious gesture with some tacit indication that I pick up on. Deciding to do so or not can be a quandary, but whatever the case, I want to represent the speakers on the page with care and respect.

Those subconscious gestures are part of a living sound space generated by the conversational exchange or talk. That sound space also includes the technology that facilitates conversation recording and the environment where the recording took place. Including subconscious gestures within a transcript can inform the liveness and character of the transcript.

The topic of intention reminds me of a comment you shared with me from Carole Itter that I find beautiful. It was about the tonality of a transcript while editing the oral historical book *Opening Doors* with Daphne Marlatt. She remarked that they added no parenthetical cues (i.e., [laughs],) but pretty much any time there was an exclamation point, you could be sure that they were all laughing![6] It's an example of where craft and artfulness can enter into the transcription process, where a subjective treatment of a conversational element also clearly reflects what was verbalized.

Listening for the intention of a speaker can be fascinating. What I noticed in your and Cole's conversation with Tracie Morris, for example, is that she moved through registers in speaking about Shakespeare and interdisciplinary artistic collaboration with terminology, slang, and jokes. [DF: "About *Schitt's Creek!*"] The poet's music! The effects of speech might not necessarily appear as intentional when spoken by others, but of course what is *communicated* instead can be. To take a long drag from a cigarette as punctuation. The transcriber can listen to the language of the speaking body, as well.

DF: One of my verbal tics is "you know?" or "right?" This constant effort to confirm that what I'm saying is landing. But I think those things fade away to the mind's ear in a very different way than the deliberateness with which Tracie plays with language even in conversation, as lightly as skipping across rocks.

DR: Yes!

DF: Yeah. I think those default dynamics of conversation are things that are really hard to unlearn. They just take so much conscious effort to try and find different pathways. Even this thing I was telling you about this morning, about this guy following me and my daughter as I walked her to daycare, and the fact that my husband said, "Well, why didn't you just tell him to fuck off?" And I was like, "Because, I couldn't!" I have so many years of socialization assessing risk and danger in those scenarios, trying to decide whether an offensive approach or a more subtle defensive approach is going to be less risky to me – and now to me and my child. You know? Completely lost on him, this idea of risk. I spoke my piece with my tone and my body. I think in interviews, too, all those things are at play. The question of: (a) how to navigate those in the interview, and, (b) how those choices must inform how you hear the speech on the other end, as a transcriber. How you represent those kinds of things, those tensions, can be so meaningful. Certain non-verbal things. Like a really lengthy pause or a sigh. How do you grapple with things like that?

DR: Addressing tensions or conflict when they arise can be a challenge to witness *in medias res* and to grapple with how to capture it on record. I know that I would easily experience tension within a conversation I'm transcribing as if it were my own because of how closely I receive the reverberations of voice in my body, and how I feel so very interconnected with the conversation I'm working on.

How can my subjectivity and bias not be implicated in capturing such a moment? The transcriber can be privy to significant moments such as these and other more intimate expressions. The transcriber can occupy a strange position. This is a good example of the transcriber as witness and what Dylan Robinson refers to as *witness attentiveness.*[7] What does one do with the information? What is the transcriber's responsibility in relation to the transcript?

The transcript I produce does not end with me. What would other transcribers as labourers say about their work and their position within the project? In relationship to the primary content/speaker at hand? Their bodily experience in relation to that work and tools? The tools, the tech, and my body, in general and in function, aren't neutral.

To grapple with risk and tension and to learn how to navigate them as a transcriber bears practical similarities to the journalistic conventions of fairness and neutrality. Transcripts are a record of what the transcriber heard from the conversants' exchange. From this we can gather that what was recorded in an exchange must be factual. Editorializing on the page by the transcriber doesn't align with the primary function of the transcript. As a literary form, transcripts often tend to appear as a final product in Q&A interviews and the reader is to understand that the interview is based on truth. Transcription as a project bears creative similarities to cinéma-verité (the transcriber observes and is like a fly on the wall).

ON TRANSCRIPTION: A PRELUDE

DR: Earlier this week when I was working on the transcript with you and Jordan [Abel], I had done the bulk of transcription in two separate chunks then listened through to insert timecodes and check for accuracy. I know that during that process of quickly reviewing the transcript, the quality of my listening the first time around was so close, and I could feel his energy and your energy in exchange as friends. It sounded as if he was always smiling when he spoke! [Laughter]

DF: Which I'm sure he was, actually! He's got this like, "Yeah!" And there's a little tiny smile every time. [Laughs]

DR: Yeah! That friendship-energy was really nice to listen to and that wasn't self-conscious. I observed that as two friends in exchange. My first listen I was struck with how dear the energy was. When I was doing the quick review, I knew I had distance from that and didn't feel the vastness of the conversation the first time around. I could gloss over the sound of a smile at the end of a sentence more quickly.

DF: Yeah. Which is incredible, too. Because it's maybe the one sort of activity in life where you enable all kinds of distances and durations of listening to the same thing, and each one activates something slightly different, right? I think, honestly, anybody who has done a lot of transcription has a sense of the immense variety of forms that listening can take.

DR: For the work that you transcribed for your PhD, how did you receive the act of listening?

DF: I feel like my own approach and my own listening in general is perhaps not as multimodal as you describe. For me, I find listening is always vertical and deep. This is the thing. I have albums that I've been listening to for twenty years from bands that I love. Let's say they have released five other albums since and I'm like, "Okay! I'll move onto those other albums once

I have figured this one out." But then I just never figure it out and really obsessively drill down into it. I'm like, "Oh, wow, that tiny little hi-hat after that note! *Yes!*" I feel like it's to my detriment, especially in transcription, which is something that requires a certain efficiency that I'm so fucking bad at it! [Laughter] I will obsess over the particular phrasing of a sentence and make sure I got all of the words in order. I find I'm not good at it, in that sense. But that said, it's a way for me to have intimacy with a conversation. Because of the particular way that my memory works, I'll often walk away from a really great conversation and only retain like three things. "Wow! That was really profound!" But then all these other things will escape me. But if you work on it as a transcriber, half of it you can quote verbatim! I found that facet of it really interesting.

DR: I do think about babies and listening and the connection of the child's ear to the mother's chest and voice and a similar scenario with transcription – that throughline between two people in conversation and listening as transcriber. Well, yeah, it's typing at a computer but that's slow time.

It's that combination of things. I feel that depth of connection when I listen to music or to voice for transcription. This is part of my process.

DF: Yeah. Because I think that's not the case for everyone. I remember my mom saying, "If something is just auditory, I don't retain anything." Which is funny because she's a speech therapist.

DR: Right! People retain things from different sensory perspectives.

In *Hungry Listening,* Dylan Robinson lays out a framework for ethical listening practices that involve "a reflection on sonic encounters between particular perceptual logics, and between particular bodies, within a larger conceptual framework of critical listening positionality."[8] The term "hungry listening" "emerges from the historical encounter between xmélmexw (Stó:lō people) and the largest influx of settlers to the territory during the gold rush,"⁹ and the work shares further cultural, social, and linguistic context for the conceptual development of *hunger* as the dominant characteristic of settler-colonial perception. The framework is critical and rich. With each reading, Robinson's work reverberated with aspects of the ongoing conversation between us Deannas – our shared subject. For example, hungry listening "prioritises the capture and certainty of information over the affective feel, timbre, touch, and texture of sound"[10] and fixates on "possession" and "extraction."[11]

These ideas touch on what could be a tender nerve. The task of transcription can be characterized as *necessarily* relying upon the capture and certainty of information. And yet, the uncustomary invitation to contribute to an academic project in a substantial way complicates the idea of transcription as being strictly about capture and certainty. It suggests a particular relationship to emerge from a work dynamic (i.e., "the client" and "the service provider") that can be collaborative, mutual, flexible, and imaginative (i.e., relational) instead of top-down, prescriptive, inclement, and isolated (i.e., possessive over ideas or things, or extractionist for cultural, academic, or monetary gain). These salient qualities don't override the physicality, time, and endurance transcription work demands, but in view of critical listening positionality and transcription that involves "sonic encounters between particular perceptual logics, and between particular bodies,"[12] they bring to mind that transcription can stem from a partnership between the transcriber and the transcribed. In recognizing that the noun "transcription" can part ways from a fixation on capture, extraction, and possession, it may be equally generative to recognize that the nouns "transcriber" and "transcribed" are also not absolute personifications. Rather, they are each a layering of positionalities. The lesson that *words matter* rings true here as ever.

To have engaged in this project of *reciprocal* or *mutual transcription* – as Fong has suggested labelling the approach to transcription described herein – puts forward a potential model for future forms of transcription in the field of literary writing and collaboration in the literary arts.

DF: Do you feel that you, personally, in terms of your own senses, have a sort of auditory attunement naturally?

DR: Yes. It comes from a number of familial, friend, and community sources: growing up around a lot of music at home and learning how to play music; being a big music fan from an early age; becoming very connected to radio programming in campus/community radio; and becoming a presenter of sound art, punk bands, and new music in my twenties and thirties. All a big part of my identity.

To talk about personal auditory attunement, I need to return to the body and what I have come to understand about myself as an adult with ADHD and my corresponding sensory profile, which has a lot of over-responsivity built into it: to smells, certain fabrics, lighting, and of course, sound. I know that if I become very tired or stressed, overresponsivity to these things can be uncomfortable or distressing. That sensitivity can also be wonderful for the magnitude at which I can observe them on a good day. It has things to teach me. I'm learning to seek out ways of being and making spaces for myself, and how I relate to others that works with my experience of these things rather than trying to smooth over my surroundings. The ways in which I can be overresponsive to my environment also inform the quality of listening I have during the transcription process, whether in a live or pre-recorded setting.

Though what I'm describing is seemingly about material effect upon my embodied self, the materials and I don't exist alone. It is also about where I'm situated while I carry out the work, how the audio is being transmitted to me, and what I can perceive of the transmission. Perhaps my skin and my senses function ephemerally – as the microphone and microscope that Douglas Kahn describes.

DF: Is that where the impetus comes for poetry, too? Is that related?

DR: Yes. Totally. My trajectory to poetry is from music. They are intertwined as forms. And maybe since sound is what both forms take to launch from the two-dimensional surface of the page, acknowledging that not all

ON TRANSCRIPTION: A PRELUDE

poetry or music begins on the page, this is nonetheless where I love to find myself situated and to work from in my own practice.

DF: Yeah. Fittingly, Édith Piaf is just fluttering into the conversation, which is a really lovely moment of coincidence. It is an oral form and something that's interested in the particularities of the voice, and really getting at something that's behind or beyond language through language. Which I think speaks very much to all the other qualities of language and speaking that we've just discussed.

On the particularities of voice, Tricia Rose writes in her discussion of rap music:

> Rhythm and polyrhythmic layering is to African and African-derived musics what harmony and the harmonic triad is to Western classical music ... The voice is also an important expressive instrument. A wide range of vocal sounds intimately connected to tonal speech patterns, "strong differences between the various registers of the voice, even emphasizing the breaks between them," are deliberately cultivated in African and African-influenced musics. Treatment, or "versioning," is highly valued. Consequently, the instrument is not simply an object or vehicle for displaying one's talents, it is a "colleague in the creation."[13]

With Rose's description of the human voice in relation to African and African-derived music and the breaks between voicings, I'm interested in thinking about the transcription process. What can a momentary rupture in a recorded conversation – a "break between" voices, to borrow Deanna's question – mean? What is alive in that moment of speech? Or on a recording of that moment of speech? Can a break between voices become a "colleague in the creation" and impact the outcome of the transcript? These questions rely in part on the quality of audio recording and on the attunement of the transcriber's ear. These questions also remind us that the job of the transcriber is to help bring voices forward to the reader.

DF: But I wanted to ask you, too, circling back, you were talking about being in service to a conversation and I think one of the threads that we picked up on in our writing exchange was this idea of transcription as an act of care. I wanted to first ask you: do you have a personal connection to any of the interviewees?

DR: Only Oana. I'm not close friends with her but absolutely connected to her through working on the Atwater Poetry Project and we've hung out as friends. It was very exciting to hear your conversation with her and to listen to both of you working through your ideas in the conversation. Otherwise, my connection to everyone that I transcribed is as a fan. [Laughter]

DF: Yeah, mostly me too, actually. [Laughs] I was thinking in terms of care work, how does that care express itself? What are the gestures of that care? How do you demonstrate care for a conversation?

DR: I immediately think about when I was transcribing for students with disabilities. As long as you could type seventy words a minute they'd hire you. During the lectures I would type everything that would be said. That's partly my fixation on detail and hyperfocus. It's a challenge and maybe I have a martyr-like interest in making sure I get everything. I started to notice in comparison to some other people, a colleague, we both worked for the same student. She said the student preferred to work with the both of us because we were the most thorough with the transcripts and other transcribers in the position wouldn't work as if they were on fire doing this kind of work. It's the kind of labour where you get what you pay for in that context.

How do I take care? I'm not sure. I feel that I've been fortunate to work on conversations and material that I care about. I feel responsible.

ON TRANSCRIPTION: A PRELUDE

DF: I think of some of the things that you've signalled to me in our email exchanges around the transcripts. Like the parentheticals of Jordan's daughter, Phoenix, that were inserted into the conversation; "They can be removed if you so prefer" – which I do not![14] But I don't think it's everybody who would notice that and think of it as important. That in itself, and your sensitivity to the context of the conversation, have been really apparent throughout in those kinds of exchanges.

DR: That's so lovely. Thank you. It's such a pleasure. Also, it's very much that having Phoenix in the conversation *is* a part of the conversation. I think it's about the approach from *Hungry Listening* and what are the expectations and why should we follow a certain sterility in transcription? I know it's an academic text but ...

DF: We'll see what the reviewers say! I'm going to be heartbroken if they want to take that out. Although let's put this part of the conversation in so they know how deliberate it is.

But that gesture in itself – I'm thinking about the ways in which this work connects to all these different avenues. It's a way of reinserting Jordan's labour as a caregiver and as a father into that conversation. It's a way of situating the context in which we have our conversations, which are sometimes divided, and sometimes produced under difficult circumstances. All this stuff. Which I think really is at the heart of the collection, too. I think that in itself is a completely resistant practice. [Laughs]

DR: Making these things visible.

DF: Through listening! [Laughter]

DR: Yeah!

The words and expressions I observe as a transcriber, corporeally situated within a field of sound, are not mine to take liberties with. I'm loyal to this idea. Committed, even. The job isn't to enter substitutes or translations of words spoken for brevity or convenience. Otherwise, the resulting documentation would be a set of notes instead of a transcript. There is a sense of urgency in my experience of transcription, which derives from the physical demands of the work and the endurance connected with it (e.g., having to sit for long periods in a fixed seated position, process a large volume of words spoken); from time pressures (e.g., the need to complete the work with a short turnaround time); and in relation to the needs of the client or benefactor of the work (e.g., capturing spoken utterances and expressions with nuance). This sense of urgency is perhaps a mode of responsiveness to the job environment and a way of listening. It is an energy force that enables me to persist through the material. Despite this sense of urgency, transcribing a conversation from audio recordings is a slow and iterative process. Two hours of conversation takes me roughly six hours to complete to my satisfaction before sending to the authors of the conversation for approval. In spite of the machine-like typing speed transcription calls for, it isn't a machine-like process. Transcription is easy to do. Transcription is not easy to do.

ON TRANSCRIPTION: A PRELUDE

NOTES

1 Kenneth Goldsmith, *Uncreative Writing: Managing Language in the Digital Age* (New York: Columbia University Press), 11.
2 Douglas Kahn, *Earth Sound Earth Signal: Energies and Earth Magnitude in the Arts* (Berkeley: University of California Press, 2013), 2–3 (emphasis added).
3 The actual quotation is from Goldsmith's essay "Being Boring" that appears on *PennSound*, which reads: "I've needed to acquire a whole new skill set: I've become a master typist, an exacting cut-and-paster, and an OCR demon. There's nothing I love more than transcription; I find few things more satisfying than collation." See https://writing.upenn.edu/library/Goldsmith-Kenny_Being-Boring.html.
4 Tara Rodgers, *Pink Noises: Women on Electronic Music and Sound* (Durham: Duke University Press, 2010), 6.
5 Dylan Robinson, *Hungry Listening: Resonant Theory for Indigenous Sound Studies* (Minneapolis: University of Minnesota Press, 2020), 58.
6 Daphne Marlatt and Carole Itter, "Re-Opening Doors into Vancouver's Strathcona Neighbourhood: A Conversation With Daphne Marlatt And Carole Itter," an interview with Mathieu Aubin and Deanna Fong presented as part of the Festival metropolis bleu / Blue Metropolis Festival, 5 May 2021, www.facebook.com/watch/?v=467210441277897.
7 Robinson, *Hungry Listening*, 52.
8 Ibid., 2.
9 Ibid.
10 Ibid., 38.
11 Ibid., 10.
12 Ibid., 2.
13 Tricia Rose, *Black Noise: Rap Music and Black Culture in Contemporary America* (Hanover: Wesleyan University Press, 1994), 86.
14 Referring to an email from Deanna Radford to Deanna Fong, 16 June 2021.

1

"We make something out of what records we can find"

An Interview with Wayde Compton

Deanna Fong, recorded over Zoom
TRANSCRIBED BY DEANNA RADFORD

Deanna Fong: In *After Canaan*, you open with the quotation from Heraclitus, which reads, "Everything flows and nothing abides; everything gives way and nothing stays fixed."[1] Seeing as 2020 is actually the tenth anniversary of the publication of that book, I thought I would open by asking you what, if anything, has given way or become unfixed in your thinking since then?

Wayde Compton: Quite a lot in terms of this essay, I think. Because, speaking of subjective time, the surprise – everybody goes through it – but the surprise for me of the last twenty years is how, when you get to be forty-eight, it really does feel like 2001 was a few years ago! So, the technological changes from the time that I first conceived of doing that turntable project to now are huge and sweeping but in my mind, they're not. They happened really quickly. They didn't happen quickly but it feels like they happened quickly.

The conditions have changed a lot. Turntablism survives but it's increasingly feeling like a deliberately antiquated thing to do. It feels like learning how to play the lute or something like that. I guess it's cooler than the lute. It still has space in popular culture, but it's just further and further away from being a common technology. I even remember going to a show where somebody was DJing and they had a guest come up on stage and put something on the platter. I remember looking at this young person using the turntable as though it were a musical instrument and I thought that was funny, because we grew up with them as furniture. Every home had one and it was just a piece of furniture that anybody could use. I realized in that moment that it's passed into being *primarily* a musical instrument now, really. Or, a specialized technology and that's kind of interesting.

So I think that that essay is written at the very, very tail end of the turntable as the normative means of schizophonophilia.[2] Now that's all so gone. The fragmentation of media and YouTube. All the various ways that we get sound now are very different. The multiplying of platforms and all of that is so different.

DF: In rereading "Turntable Poetry, Mixed-Race, and Schizophonophilia" from that collection – I first read it in 2014, which also seems like no time ago but it's now six years ago – I remember feeling sort of frustrated-slash-intrigued by the précis of the performance. I couldn't hear it because it involves so many simultaneous elements in performance. To be honest, some of them were not super well-known tracks, either. So I had a hard time tracking down everything. But this time in 2020, I reread it and just made a Spotify playlist! [Laughter]

WC: See, that's different. That's exactly what I'm talking about. I was thinking about this today when thinking about doing this interview, and I thought about turntables as stricture. Jason and I were very deliberately very aware of thinking of that as a stricture because at that time we had access to all sorts of other ways of playing music. Sometimes we sampled stuff from podcasts, or this and that. But whenever we did it, it was with some guilt, because we were kind of like, "The project is turntable-based." That's what it has to be. So every once in a while, we would throw in a sample from some other source and feel a bit like we were cheating. Because the idea was: we make something out of what records we can find. That's where crate-digging is part of the creative process. It's like that found-art side of it.

It all fed back into the performances because when we did a performance in Kamloops – Ashok Mathur brought us up there for a performance – we were like, "Oh, this is great! Because we get to go to small-town Salvation Armies and stuff like that, thrift stores so we can look for records here." And sure enough, we found the weirdest records that we incorporated into that performance. We found a record – it might have been an acetate of a hockey game. Somebody had recorded some peewee hockey game and put it onto an acetate. You'd only get that in small-town Canada, really. That was part of the process: where we went, and what records we could find, and how those records somehow got to us.

DF: Discovery. And being serious about having the physical objects themselves there to manipulate. That makes me think of two different things: one is that in the essay you make an analogy between the deep global denaturing of hip hop and Afro-peripheral experience, in that the mainstream idea of Black experience and of hip hop are both coming to you through this increasingly globalized media – I guess at the time radio, internet radio, TV, that sort of thing. But now that those media have become not only denaturized but also don't have a physical form anymore, how does that shift for you? How does it make that analogy different – or does it?

WC: It's so interesting. I remember making this observation a long time ago. It had occurred to me in the aughts that it's weird that we're still at hip hop – that Black culture is *still* using hip hop at all. That's not been the pattern of how African American music has worked. There have been innovations in it in smaller cycles than this. This is why my dad always put it to me that Black music lasted as long as it took for white people to find it. And then Black people will change it up. That was the thing. This is a bit simplistic and there's been a lot of interesting work done on this, of appropriation and reappropriation and – who does the essay about the Black Bottom? There was a dance that was African American in origin and then it was appropriated – I guess this was maybe by the '20s – by white folks who imitated the dance poorly and it became a craze and then Black people saw that dance and did their own version of it, not realizing it was a corruption of the original one.

DF: Yeah, it seems like we're in a very longue durée, late-capitalist moment where we just keep encountering the same sort of impasses again and again. There's not the change happening that we would hope for, which is frustrating. I'm tired of living in this moment over and over!

WC: I am too! In global terms, I think it's not much different than it was then, when I made some of those observations about the global place of hip hop, that it's a kind of variant of American imperialism at this point. But, that's how it arrives in places, but then sometimes Indigenous or minority populations in different countries receive it and then they recognize something of that resistance in it and so they can kind of reconstitute it for their own resistance. So we see that happening in places where hip hop *comes in* like American imperialism but it can be like this, "Oh, but, there's a useful political corollary there with what's happening here." So that's interesting. But even that feels like it's less and less so as time goes on. I'm also getting old. Maybe I'm just ready for something else!

DF: When was the last time that you performed that work, the series of performances that incorporate "The Reinventing Wheel"?

WC: I don't actually know. It's one of those things where I think the last time we performed it we didn't know it was the last time we were going to perform it. We both had kids within a few years of each other. It was before my daughter was born. So probably twelve years ago, maybe. Could it be that long ago? Part of the problem was that it just took us so long to practise. Because we didn't do it frequently enough, that was one problem. We would do a different set every time and because we didn't do it frequently enough. It made sense to do something different each time because we had to learn it all over again anyway. But we would practise for two days, three days sometimes, to do a fifteen-minute performance. That got really irritating as our time got much more crunched. Then I think we just drifted off and stopped doing it.

DF: Would you be interested in returning to it or do you feel like that project has run its course?

WC: No. It's run its course. I think I actually gave my turntables away. Jason teaches high school. He's a high school music teacher and so I donated them to his class so kids can learn on them. That seemed like the right thing to do. Jason still has all that equipment and stuff and he'd probably do it. I feel like I did a thing and it made its point. It was never that much fun! [Laughs] It was never that much fun for me! [Laughter] It was always so stressful because I was not a turntablist. And Jason was. Maybe he had a bit of fun but I think he was stressed out too because it wasn't really – it was just this weird thing that had its own sensibility and so it always just felt like we were just barely making this thing work.

DF: The essay, which kind of stands as the record of it, is still super relevant and really fascinating in how it articulates its particular form of resistance. It's a media-specific form of resistance through art. One of the things that I always think about is how you once stated that one of the goals was to make the poem an art object outside the body, which is to resist this sort of tendency to naturalize and specularize Black speech and a specific type of commodified Black performance. So, I was wondering if you had any thoughts on that and how the relationship of the body changes by putting your voice out there on something else in this very deliberate gesture.

WC: That didn't quite happen the way I originally thought it might. I thought it would be used as a source more. It *was* a bit, which was great. It was fascinating. There was a guy named DJ Kentaro (Kentaro Ide) who sampled it, so it had mutated and become something else. It was neat because he was dealing with race in a different way, too. That was very cool. I think I had originally thought of pressing the vocal track and having it out there but that never happened so it wasn't really available as a source material for anybody. In terms of it being this disembodied thing that would go out and have another life, it didn't really work that way. We did it ourselves. And that was all right. We had other ideas. It could have gone in different directions because at a certain point I was looking into buying a lathe.

This is what I mean by the technology being so different. If you want to cut your own acetates, it's so expensive. It's just prohibitively expensive because to buy a lathe, to actually do it and to have the skill to do it properly – you couldn't do it. I think at the time there was maybe one person in Vancouver doing it, who had a lathe and was doing acetates for people.

Maybe if we had stayed in it and done that, it would have been a different thing. We could have kept pressing stuff and releasing things. But it just didn't really head in that direction.

DF: It's interesting that it used to be this cheap, portable medium to make the music accessible to everybody and now it's become this extremely elite, expensive, nostalgic kind of venture. Really just in a matter of a couple decades. That's interesting in itself.

WC: I will say, when I first saw Jordan Abel perform the way that he does, I thought, "*That's* the next thing." That's how I would do it now if I were doing it now. He's still mixing things live. But he's relying on smaller, more mobile digital technology. It's less about the stricture of the object, but it's still performative. It actually made me feel really good seeing it. That, "Okay, there's still a way to do this and somebody's doing this." It felt really great to see.

DF: Absolutely. Another way of externalizing the performance so that it's not coming from the body. I don't know if you've ever thought about this – I feel like maybe we've talked about this a long time ago. It's not in line with that kind of athletic, masculine *Ursonate*-type sound poetry. It's not about pushing the voice to its limit or inhabiting it in a certain authentic space or what we might imagine as that fantasy about bodily authenticity. It's very resolutely being like, "My voice and my body are not commensurate." It's maybe creating a little fissure between your symbolic body as an author and your physical body as a human being.

WC: Absolutely. Because for me that's there in spoken word and it's there in the MC side of hip hop culture, that embodiment of it. And that's fine. People can do that and it's got its place, but it's not a coincidence that the DJ has kind of dropped out of hip hop culture that we were talking about, the development or endurance of hip hop and the longer it goes, the less the DJ is relevant. If you go back to the '80s, the DJ is everything! If you go back to the beginning, the DJ *creates* it. And the DJ gets eclipsed by the MC to the point now where that's everything. To me, that makes perfect sense because that's always been the most marketable aspect of the culture and it's the most tropic element in terms of Black culture as popular spectacle and consumer product, really: the Black body as entertainer. I don't say that to disparage anybody who's doing that but it's not what I wanted to do, and I think it does change the way you think about the voice when it's externalized that way and you can operate upon it.

In doing my performances, I always felt like it's almost like there were two audiences. We're the audience and the audience is the audience. And then my voice is there on this technology and we're all listening to it on stage, we're manipulating it, too – but we're decentred in a way. I've always really, really liked that. I thought that was the best part of it.

DF: That's interesting. As a collaborative project, how did that come about? How did you find Jason?

WC: I think I met Jason at the University of British Columbia [UBC] and it was a class. I feel like it was because some instructor brought me out to read in a class that he was in. Then we started talking after, and then we stayed in touch. I was already thinking at that point about doing stuff with DJs and then I met him and realized he *was* one. He was very smart and we just clicked as people and I just felt like we had so much in common and he just had very interesting thoughts about mixed race. He was a big Fred Wah fan. We just hit it off. It felt like one of those things that I wouldn't have been able to do if I didn't have the right person to do it with and it just evolved. We were just hanging out and I was asking him stuff about DJing and telling him about this idea. We tried things out and just jumped in and started really going for it.

I had the idea and I wanted to do it before I met him, but I don't think I would have been able to do it. I might have done a really half-assed thing that I would have done a few times but I don't think it would have been as well-developed unless I had met somebody who had the skills that he had to bring to it. It was also that he could understand the theory behind it. That was really important, too, because I couldn't have done it just with some DJ who just had fast hands or whatever. Because so much of it was counter to what DJs normally do. So he had to be pretty open-minded to have long stretches of weird sounds and stuff that the music drops away and there's some voice going on for a while. It doesn't sound like music most of the time or part of the time. That took somebody who was ready to do something that was experimental and could enjoy that.

I just remember long hours in his basement with the turntables out and all these records and trying things out and playing with different ideas.

DF: That's an amazing thought. That's the substrate of the fifteen minutes of what actually gets performed. All of the infinite variations and permutations that went into mixing that into exactly the form that it becomes in performance. Of course, the archivist in me is like, "Damn! I wish you recorded it."

WC: That's my biggest regret about the whole project: my lack of understanding about the importance of recording things. [Laughs] What we were doing was performance art without understanding we were doing performance art. It was *later* that I realized that, "Oh, performance artists all document their shit!" That's what it's actually about. They *think about* the way they're going to document it as they're doing it. We were just doing the thing and late in the project going, "Wow! We should probably document this. Oh, no! We got a performance coming up," and scramble it together and be like, "Oh, yeah! We should have documented that!" [Laughs]

So we just didn't have it together to do that. Now it bothers me. At the time I didn't really care, I guess. But now it bugs me. I don't feel like there's a good video recording. There is one – Warren Dean Fulton showed me one once. He videotaped a performance – that might have been one I did alone at Simon Fraser University, actually. Early on. There's one that Kevin McNeilly did at UBC. There were a couple, here and there, and some sound. Jason started to actually do sound recordings. So there are some sound recordings that he has of later performances. It's all scattered everywhere.

DF: So you performed the work at universities, and also in art galleries, and clubs, and a bunch of different venues. I was wondering who, other than yourselves in discovery, you considered to be the work's audience. Who did you perceive as the receiving community of that work?

WC: I didn't think about it very much at the beginning. Although partway through, I realized at a certain point that it was poetry. I started to speak of it as a poetry reading. Or a performance of poetry. Mainly because we did a couple of music venue events that did not feel right. We did one at Under the Volcano, I think it was, where I realized people have to know they're in a poetry reading so they'll consume it that way. Otherwise, there's a beat going for a while and then the beat will just stop and if there's people dancing, they'll be like, "What? Why did that stop?" [Laughter] It doesn't make sense.

The only place that that didn't happen, where it worked fine, was actually in Montreal. We did a performance at a cabaret type thing in Montreal. People were dancing during the beats and then when it dropped away, people just seemed to flip over into that mode. I think that's the cabaret culture of Montreal. It's like, "Oh, you're going to go to a thing and there's going to be five different genres that will happen and they're going to be very different from each other and so people will be like, 'Oh! It's changing now. So now, we'll stand and listen. Then the music will come back and we'll dance.'" That was really great. We have to do this as poetry in places where people are expecting to hear poetry.

The thing that I misunderstood about that, too, is that in the early days of the project I thought it would be easier than it was in terms of performing because I didn't realize that everywhere we went we had to build the sound system. We didn't have a PA. Because if we were doing a classroom, or the Kootenay School of Writing or wherever, they would not have anything there. So we'd have to bring in the speakers and everything. So it was arduous. We'd have to come in super early, build everything, sound check it. Whereas, I guess I was thinking in terms of actual DJs who fly from city to city with a bag of records! 'Cause they know every club will have the same model of turntables there. They can bring their mixer and they can bring their records and they're ready to go. Whereas we had to bring an entire PA, the turntables themselves, the mixer, everything. That was really, really annoying. We'd have to build this whole system. Play the thing. Fifteen minutes! Break it all down again. It was just such a nightmare.

DF: Yeah. But it also says a lot about the state of contemporary poetry, that it's still so rooted in the single author standing in front of a microphone or not a microphone. Although I think that's maybe changing a little bit. What's exciting for me is that for this collection I'm also interviewing Jordan Scott, Jordan Abel, Oana Avasilichioaei, and there are a lot of people who are doing really, really innovative sound practice around poetry that's absolutely integral to the reading of it. So maybe reintroducing sound as an important component – but not in the elocutionary sense – as a semantic component itself.

WC: That's actually interesting because also, in the middle of it, I remember thinking – where this occurred to me was when we did that gig in Kamloops with Ashok because he had the brilliant idea – he had a bunch of artists and writers and people come up for Thompson Rivers University and he had rented a house – or was it his house? There was a house and we were all staying in the house together for however many days, five days or something.

That was the best, because Jason and I were able to set up the turntables and do a performance every night. But they were already set up so we could have an idea and do it or do something that evolved over a few performances. I remember after that thinking, "This would be the way to do it." If it was a permanent gig or a long-term gig at a place like a residency or something where people could come to you rather than us going into these spaces that aren't made for it. I don't know what that looks like or what that is but that would have made it very different if there had been a way to do that long-term.

DF: It changes the scale a lot. Something like that requires a certain sort of intimacy that you presume that you'll probably have a returning audience who's going to be there for the journey. I remember Roy Kiyooka saying that he considers his public to be about twelve people! I think for him, it ultimately made him produce better poetry because it was like his public were people he could be intimate and honest with, and really integrate his everyday life into his artistic practice. So I don't know if that would have been like a similar vibe with something like that.

WC: Oh, yeah. Absolutely! That makes complete sense to me. The way we did it, there was *no way* it could have reached a mass audience. We deliberately hobbled it in a way that that couldn't happen! [Laughter] Because I did want it to be a performance.

In the very, very early, early, earliest stages of the project, before I met Jason, I was just thinking about what I was doing. My original intention was to compose the poem, "The Reinventing Wheel," without writing anything down. I was going to compose it entirely orally and then record it and then work from that. So I wanted there to be absolutely no text and in the process of doing it I discovered that was beyond me. I wasn't able to do that. And then I wrote it and then I started thinking differently about the interplay of the textual version and the oral version as being different parts of the same thing.

But I was thinking of it in that way – of ephemera – of wanting it to be ephemeral. It was never about a product and more about a performance, and just having a small, intimate number of people having seen it. So maybe it's good that we didn't document it, in a way – because maybe it lived in the people who happened to be there and they saw it and they could talk about it.

DF: Which also resonates with the other writing in *After Canaan*, right? Which is this sort of interrogation of fixation, especially symbolic fixation, acts of reading, the threat and the harm that these acts of reading in "pheneticization" and that sort of thing are prone to. In a way it's maybe a fitting aesthetic gesture that goes along with that argument.

WC: Yeah. I guess the thing is, like I said, it just trailed off. So I never really feel like I had a chance to kind of go, "Now what will I do now that I know we're not going to do it anymore?" We didn't have that phase of it. We didn't have a third act, I guess! [Laughs]

DF: Well, perhaps this interview will prompt a resuscitation of it ... or maybe this is the third act!

AN INTERVIEW with WAYDE COMPTON

NOTES

1 Quoted in Wayde Compton, *After Caanan: Essays on Race, Writing, and Region* (Vancouver: Arsenal Pulp Press, 2010), 8.
2 Compton defines "schizophonophilia" as "the love of audio interplay, the pleasure of critical disruptions to natural audition, the counter-hegemonic affirmation that can be achieved through acoustic intervention." Compton, *After Caanan*, 199.

2

Race, Multiplicity, and Dis/Located Voices
Wayde Compton's Turntablist Poetics

Eric Schmaltz

British Columbia–based poet Wayde Compton's intermedia poetics disrupt assumptions about sound, soundscapes, and vocalization. Compton's aesthetic deployment of the rupture and fragmentation of sound, especially electroacoustically mediated sound, lead to significant reconsiderations and revisions of what it means to listen to and contribute to soundscapes – both as sonic environments and fields of study. Compton's notion of "turntablist poetics" identifies a poetry that is informed by the DJ's techniques of the scratch, cut, and delay to move from track to track and sound to sound, which is mobilized in his multimedia literary works, such as his live audio collaborations with Jason de Couto as the Contact Zone Crew and the combination book and compact disc, *Performance Bond* (2004). Compton's poetry is grounded in literary experimentation with consideration given to how vocalization, media, and identity have historically come to bear on understandings of the soundscape. Motivated by Compton's poetics, this chapter presents a series of interrelated "cuts" that attend to aspects of his intermedial practice.[1] These cuts intervene into currents of critical thought regarding the configuration of three sonic planes – the literary, nationalist, and capitalist – as they relate to Compton's poetry.

Cut One: Expanding the Soundscape

Drawn to Canadian composer R. Murray Schafer's theories of the soundscape, Compton briefly examines these in his essay "Turntable Poetry, Mixed-Race, and Schizophonophilia" (2010). Schafer's benchmark study of acoustic ecology, *The Soundscape: Our Sonic Environment and the Tuning of the World* (1977), listens to the histories of progress and modernity, and the impacts those forces have on soundscapes across the world. The two underlying theses of his book are as follows: "When the rhythms of the soundscape become confused or erratic, society sinks to a slovenly and imperiled condition" and, further, that "the soundscape is no accidental by-product of society; rather it is a deliberate construction by its creators, a composition as much distinguished for its beauty as for its ugliness."[2] Stated differently, Schafer laments the impacts that modern technologies have had on the composition of soundscapes. For Schafer, electronic and motorized devices with sound-producing capabilities ranging from radios to lawnmowers create sounds that overpower quieter soundscapes. Quieter soundscapes – those not populated by modern technological sounds – symbolize an ordered and stable society. On the other side of this binary, a proliferation of industrial and electronic sounds represent a deteriorating society. He attempts to substantiate these arguments by listening to the technological apparatuses of modernity – from trans-Canada steam engines to audio amplifiers and beyond – with attention to their consequent alteration of sonic life.

Schafer's conception of acoustic ecology is underwritten by anxiety stimulated by the effects of technological development on hearing. However, Schafer's arguments, as sound critic Marie Thompson has noted, are reductively comprised of binary oppositions such as music and noise, or natural and unnatural, and he assumes that there is a primordial or pure soundscape that acoustic environmentalists should defend. Thompson investigates Schafer's anxiety by attending to what she calls his "aesthetic moralism," which refers to the value that Schafer ascribes to some sounds over others. Some sounds are "good" and others are "bad."[3] "Noise" is used indiscriminately to refer to both noise pollution and unwanted sound. Thompson explains that in Schafer's thinking, "Noise is heard as the product of urbanization and capitalism – it is aligned with the city and industry. Silence and quietness, by contrast, are imbued with a spiritual, naturalism – they characterize the acoustic territories of the church and countryside." Thompson continues, "silence is equated with tranquility; tranquility is equated with the natural; and the natural is equated with the good."[4]

Schafer's position represents a nostalgia for a "before-time" that harks back to pre-modernizing processes, and risks leaning on the fallacy of historical inversion. Schafer provides a variety of cases to support his theses, most of which (if not all) rely on the assumption that, as suggested by Thompson's summary of Schafer's position, *all* noise is unwanted. His arguments lead him to consider the implementation of noise abatement laws as remedies for noisy soundscapes. However, such assumptions and proposals, as Thompson points out, are acts of silencing. By dictating which sounds are "good" and "bad," Schafer thus indicates which sounds are permitted and which are not. Schafer's conception of acoustic ecology (and the role of the acoustic ecologist) leads to the exclusion of sound and sound makers from acoustic space.

Schafer's theory of the soundscape assumes that sounds have ideal environments. Thus, if extended to the realm of vocalization, his argument suggests that vocal emittance is best grounded in silence, without the risk of interruption and unaided by electroacoustic technologies. This is fantasy; the spoken voice must always navigate the conditions of the site where it is emitted. There is no idealized flow of speech or song, and vital musical traditions have emerged in the twentieth century that are predicated on the interaction of body, sound, and electroacoustic technologies (such as the turntable, vinyl record, tape player, etc.). Electroacoustic technologies lead to "schizophonia," which is Schafer's ableist term for the split between the original sound source via electronic devices. These devices contribute to a synthetic soundscape, which Schafer laments. His depreciation problematically identifies recording artists and makers of synthetic music and sounds to exceed his moralist vision. By disparaging music and sound work at this intersection, Schafer's position consequently labels certain practitioners as "bad" since it is not merely electroacoustic devices that contribute to soundscapes but human beings who choose to use sound technologies. Artists who embrace electroacoustic technologies effectively undermine Schafer's depreciation of schizophonia to recognize the intrinsic value of technologically inclined culture and cultural producers. Compton is one of those artists.

Cut Two: Performing Schizophonically

Compton's turntablist poetic embraces the concept of schizophonia. He calls this embrace "schizophonophilia," which is, as he describes it, "the love of audio interplay, the pleasure of critical disruptions to natural audition, the counter-hegemonic affirmation that can be achieved through acoustic intervention."[5] Schizophonophilia draws attention to Schafer's reactionary position when he expresses anxiety about audio recording technologies for the ways they dislocate sounds, like the voice, from their source. By categorizing schizophonia as a significant contributing factor to the "imperiled condition"[6] of society, Schafer haphazardly categorizes whole traditions of Black musical arts – rap, hip hop, and techno, for example – as a threat to auditory life. For Compton, the concept of schizophonophilia departs from Schafer's conception of electroacoustic technologies. Instead, it opens the creative field to expansive traditions from a diverse range of practitioners and resists exclusionary practices while facilitating contact between sonic communities and traditions through mixing and sampling.

In their poetic experiments with electroacoustic technologies, Compton and his collaborator Jason de Couto – known together as the Contact Zone Crew – advance a version of schizophonophilia which is grounded in the DJ's techniques of sampling and mixing. They work with sounds from instrumental hip hop, jazz, Black spirituals, podcasts, audio autobiographies, and custom-made acetate dubplates with recordings of Compton's voice.[7] As Compton points out in his interview with Deanna Fong (included in this collection), few recordings of their mixes actually exist. In performance, they use up to six analog turntables, a digital turntable, and a sampler to sound out a diverse range of recorded sounds and voices that are culled from their crate of vinyl records and acetate dubplates. The Contact Zone Crew welcomes the rupture of the voice and revels in the dislocation of sound. Their performances challenge the limits of the body as the origin point of vocalization and ask: What sounds are recognized in the act of poetic meaning-making? What voices are permitted in this soundscape?

Part of the group's impetus is in their name – "contact zone" – a phrase drawn from "Arts of the Contact Zone" (1999) by Mary Louise Pratt. She uses this term "to refer to social spaces where cultures meet, clash, and grapple with each other."[8] Creating zones of contact is the work of the Contact Zone Crew, wherein they investigate fragmentation and cultural clashes as subjects that resonate with Compton's identity as a mixed-race person[9] while also foregrounding this project's mixture of sounds – the creation of a *contact zone* of sonic materials. Thus, the Contact Zone Crew sees the layering of voices, sounds, and textures with one another to create auditory experiences that resist any kind of projection of the voice as that which flows "naturally" from the mouth while also analogizing Compton's mixed-race experience. Contra Schafer's lament that "[v]ocal sound ... is no longer tied to a hole in the head,"[10] the Contact Zone Crew invites and integrates a multiplicity of voices into the mesh of their creations. Their sampling, mixing, and modulations offer alternative possibilities for vocalization in poetry and create an expansive zone for the meeting and alteration of rhythms, sounds, voices, and identities.

There are few publicly available recordings of the Contact Zone Crew's live performances. However, their thirty-minute appearance at the 2008 Signal+Noise Media Art Festival in Vancouver is excerpted on video streaming site Vimeo and demonstrates how their collaboration creates expansive zones for the intermixture of sound, voice, and interruption. In this nearly seven-minute excerpt, I can hear at least three voices emitted from their sound system: the first voice is Brian Dunning lecturing on the topic of pareidolia; the second is the voice of *Roots: The Saga of an American Family* (1976) author Alex Haley, which is a sample taken from his two-hour audio autobiography, *Alex Haley Tells the Story of His Search for Roots* (1977); and the final voice belongs to Compton, which was recorded on an acetate dubplate. Interspersed between, and accompanying these voices, are samples from instrumental tracks and de Couto's scratching and backspinning.

RACE, MULTIPLICITY, and DIS/LOCATED VOICES

The first voice comes from the Crew's sample of Dunning that explains pareidolia – the perception of patterns, shapes, images, or sounds in random or accidental arrangements. The sample from Dunning's podcast begins with a short phrase that has been electroacoustically manipulated to isolate the sine waves of the recording, thus making it difficult to discern what is said. This distorted voice is followed by Dunning's audible, didactic voice; he says, "Almost does sound like speech, doesn't it? But it's not quite clear what it's saying. Well, suppose someone tells you that it says [the sample is played again without modification], 'It was a sunny day and the children are going to the park.'"[11] The statement, now audible, is played twice, followed by the first electroacoustically distorted sample. "This time," Dunning says, "it is almost impossible not to hear the words you've been preconditioned to hear."[12] As Dunning explains the powers of pareidolia – powers of pattern recognition that allow us to recognize and interpret language and sound – the Contact Zone Crew moves into a sample of percussion-forward instrumental music.

Dunning's explanation of pareidolia effectively establishes preliminary tenets that can be drawn from the Contact Zone Crew's work. It foregrounds the power of expectation and pattern recognition when encountering acts of creative communication, pheneticization,[13] and the poetry reading as a soundscape. Audiences often come to the poetry reading with expectations for how words and sounds function and signify and how the voice, mouth, and body – especially the racialized body – are used and positioned in these spaces. That which falls outside of an audience's powers of recognition falls outside, or disrupts, what we have previously conceived as belonging and meaningful in that acoustic space.

As a poetry performance group, The Contact Zone Crew confound expectations of what is recognizable in the reading and enlarge our understanding of what constitutes a soundscape. They undermine what is too often assumed to come "naturally" to an audience. Their performance at the 2008 Signal+Noise Festival, for example, is not focused on a single author reading from the page into a microphone. Instead, there are two artists behind their sound system, speaking no words with their mouths. Drawing from traditions of Black musical arts and turntablism, they select, mix, and scratch vinyl and acetate. They speak through their selections and the modifications they make to those sounds. The performances comprise the typical sonic flows of language that come from Compton's recorded voice, but it is emitted from the sound system while the duo also integrate musical rhythms and beats, sampled from music such as DJ Krush's laid-back trip-hop track, "Ha-Doh." Such juxtapositions and layers reconfigure the sonic composition of the typical poetry reading into a dynamic collagist space.

With the Contact Zone Crew, the entanglement of sound and audience is no longer based solely on the receptive transmission of the spoken word. The "reading" now forcefully underscores the body. First, the absence of the typical positioning and movement of the poet's body makes Compton's and de Couto's bodies more visible. They move, dig, scratch, and spin before the audience. This draws attention to their bodies and the audience's assumptions about the poet's body and its role in the room. As an event "still so rooted," as Fong points out in her interview with Compton, "in the single author standing in front of a microphone," the introduction of Black cultural forms such as turntablism actively breaks with the expectations of the forum.[14] The reading is not typically a space for extensive technological involvement, as Compton points out when he discusses the significant labour he and de Couto undertook when setting up and tearing down for their sets.

Second, their performances invoke rhythms for dance and movement, which draws the audience's body into the sonic fold.[15] Finally, the cuts between voices and sounds draw attention to the voice as a vulnerable sonic material. They emphasize this, for example, when de Couto picks up Haley's speaking voice on the turntable and begins to repetitively scratch it back and forth, warping Haley's words into a purely rhythmic material. The Contact Zone Crew expand the reading into a polyvocal and polysonic space, composed by the meeting of disparate sounds, sampled instrumentals, and ruptured voices that are pushed through electroacoustic amplification to bring the body forcefully into the foreground.

Cut Three: Polyvocality and Multiculturalism

Dislocation through schizophonic emittance is not merely a ramification of Compton's choice to channel poetry through technologies of sonic extension and amplification. In her essay, "Ghosts in the Phonograph: Tracking Black Canadian Postbody Poetics" (2018), critic Emma Cleary describes Compton's schizophonic poetry as an experiment in "posthumanism"[16] since audio recording technologies permit the voice an itinerant path from its bodily source. Cleary suggests that "sound technologies serve as a kind of material postbody that transmits across and acoustically challenges spatial, temporal, and body boundaries."[17] Though the poem is typically projected from the mouth at the poetry reading, Compton's experiments with turntablism dislocate the poem from his body. This sense of dislocation is integral to the politics of his poetry.

While Compton's schizophonic experiments may reflect a posthuman and "postbody" impulse as Cleary suggests, I draw the thinking of critic Alexander Weheliye into this entanglement, who argues that technologically focused Black cultural practices rearticulate human concerns thereby resisting assumptions that "information has lost its body."[18] Instead, he claims that "black cultural practices do not have the illusion of disembodiment, they stage the body of information and technology as opposed to the lack thereof."[19] I am alternatively suggesting, then, that Compton's posthumanist poetic effectively gestures toward humanist concerns. Compton's turntablist poetic advances nuanced perspectives on issues of race and identity, especially for persons who are systemically marginalized. Compton's embrace of "schizophonia" not only acknowledges the itinerant quality of the voice that travels from the body but also the travellers – their bodies and identities – who carry their voice. It recognizes the chorus of diasporic voices that have travelled to Canada to comprise the Canadian soundscape.

In her analysis of Compton's *49th Parallel Psalm* (1999), poet and critic Kate Siklosi finds that "place is constructed from the interaction of human rhythms into a territory."[20] The construction of place through interaction and human rhythm – along with a variety of sonic phenomena – is also relevant to Compton's interrogations of race, identity, and place in poems such as "Performance Bond." This poem revises poet Dennis Lee's canonical essay, "Cadence, Country, Silence: Writing in Colonial Space" (1974), which addresses how, for Lee, sounds develop a sense of personal and Canadian national identity. Lee claims that he struggled with the absence of a distinctly Canadian language in the face of colonial pressures and influence. Lee's language, he felt, was not his own; so, he finds a solution in listening to what he describes as *cadence*: "What I hear is initially without content; but when the poem does come, the content must accord with the cadence I have been overhearing or I cannot make it."[21] Interestingly, Lee's process of finding poetic language resonates with the concept of pareidolia discussed above – that is, the process of finding patterns in seeming randomness as a result of our own expectations and preconditioning. The act of listening to the "cadence" of Canada gives Lee a clear sense of who and what comprises the self and nation.

Compton's poetry indicates that the relationship between sound, identity, and belonging is more complex than Lee's influential essay on literary nationalism suggests. Canada – just as it is a country made of many cultural identities – is comprised of many soundscapes. Harbour sounds on the east coast are significantly out of tune with sounds of the fields in the prairies. What sounds, then, comprise the Canadian soundscape that Lee listens to? Who and what is left out of his listening? Lee seems to be making a case for a mythological cadence that emanates from the landscape without considering that what makes up his idea of Canada is cultivated and constructed by not only what he hears but also what he chooses and is able to listen to. Lee's discussion of cadence and listening is a striking example of what xwélméxw (Stó:lō) critic Dylan Robinson refers to as the "tin ear" of settler-colonialism. The "tin ear" describes a problem related to listening, wherein settlers refuse to hear sounds in ways that may exceed or require a reorientation of their understanding of them.[22] This problem is paralleled in Schafer's privileging of "natural" sounds in the soundscape, which fails to account for the importance of listening to and understanding industrial and urban soundscapes.

Though Lee's essay responds to the pressures of Canada's colonial ties to Britain and the additional cultural influence of the United States, his efforts to advance a Canadian national literary identity are limited. We now know that the efforts to promote a Canadian identity in the 1960s and 1970s were limited mainly to promoting a white Canadian identity of European descent.[23] And further, efforts to diversify Canada's national identity with cultural policies such as the Multiculturalism Act in the 1980s did not adequately acknowledge diversity nor undo systemic conditions of racism.[24] As critic Richard Cavell recognizes, "the multiculturalist approach was characterized by claims of authenticity that merely reverted to the principle of the nation-state, and the fall-back position was the same one that subtended [Northrop] Frye's work – White, British, and liberal."[25]

A similar point is more forcefully advanced by Yellowknives Dene scholar Glen Sean Coulthard, who writes, "Instead of ushering in an era of peaceful coexistence grounded on the ideal of reciprocity or mutual recognition, the politics of recognition in its contemporary liberal form promises to reproduce the very configurations of colonialist, racist, patriarchal state power that Indigenous peoples' demands for recognition have historically sought to transcend."[26] Even at the time of this writing, popular Canadian sentiment is largely ignorant of these arguments, falsely maintaining that Canada is a multicultural space of equal opportunity. This pervasive issue makes Compton's poetry ever more powerful.

In "Performance Bond," Compton creates a fragmented and polyvocal space on the page to engage issues related to multiculturalism, travel, race, and belonging. The poem contains not only his words but also the words of politician Rosemary Brown, poet and activist Jamie Reid, anonymous dancers, artist George Clutesi, and writer Miguel de Unamuno. The page poem, like his audio poetry, embraces a rupture of the individual poetic voice to open the field of the poem to broader considerations of identity. The "poly" of the poem's polyvocality gestures toward the "multi" of multiculturalism, a central issue in the poem:

multiculturalism can't arrive
by forgetting, but by remembering
every hectare taken, every anti-Asian defamation
because those who don't remember
repeat.[27]

Compton focuses on issues of multiculturalism, specifically in British Columbia; however, the poem's lessons exceed any provincial context. Transposing techniques of mixing from the realm of DJ into that of the page poem, Compton culls the province's title, dissects it, and rewrites it to reflect the racial and cultural identities that comprise the diverse population of the province:

Chinese Columbia
Haida Columbia
Punjabi Columbia
African Columbia
Vietnamese Columbia
Squamish Columbia
Jewish Columbia
Salish Columbia
and
British Columbia.[28]

On the one hand, this sequence suggests that the identity of a collective (and an individual) is hardly stable: "If only being yourself was a simple trick,"[29] writes Compton. Furthermore, this act of sampling and rewriting undermines the prevalence and normalization of Canada's historical colonial ties, and thereby its ongoing legacies of white supremacy, as they are encoded by the adjective "British." Instead, in Compton's rewriting (and in my humanist reading of it), the province's multiculturalism is recognized as Compton expands the language of identity to acknowledge the Indigenous, Asian, Indian, and African cultures that form the population and thereby populate the Canadian soundscape (which does not acknowledge its non-human elements). The aforementioned Dunning sample on pareidolia and powers of recognition is relevant here. In this brief section of "Performance Bond," Compton rewrites the pattern of racist colonial legacies as they are encoded within the province's name by altering the pattern itself. By changing these patterns, Compton's poem recognizes the power of altering linguistic codes as part of the process of opening the field of belonging to truly welcome other identities and voices.

Cut Four: Collaborative Logics

In *The Soundscape*, Schafer calls for collective resistance against capitalist technologies for the way they infiltrate and alter the soundscape. Today, the entanglement of technology, capital, and sound is likely more complex than Schafer understood it in 1977, which simply cannot be reduced to "good" or "bad." Many vital forms of cultural works are indebted to the mechanisms of sonic technologies that enabled groups and individuals new forms of expression. So, while Schafer may advocate for the removal of industrial and electric sounds from our collective soundscapes, electric – and now digital – sounds are deeply embedded into our sonic realities. What requires further consideration here is the intersection of capital, copyright, and sound as clearly articulated in debates about copyright – the legal ownership of particular sounds and music.

Compton's schizophonophilic practice tends toward the short-circuiting of capitalist logic but without denouncing electroacoustic technologies. In fact, Compton acknowledges the complex relationship between his turntablist poetic and copyright. When reflecting on releasing a version of "The Reinventing Wheel" on compact disc, Compton acknowledges that his performances with de Couto "involve extensive use of copyrighted material by other artists" thus, he chose "only samples from the public domain."[30] Compton and de Couto abide by the DJ's practices, mixing pre-recorded works in a live setting. This practice accrues a certain amount of symbolic cultural capital without claiming ownership over these sounds. And, as seen in the excerpt from the 2008 Signal+Noise festival, they display the record sleeves to identify the source of the samples they use, indicative of an ethics of ownership that honours the labour of the original artist. In doing so, their practice enriches the cultural context of the sounds, voices, and labour of other musicians, artists, and poets.

In the backdrop of Compton's work with de Couto are the literary debates regarding what Stephen Voyce refers to as "open source poetics," which describes "a decentralized and non-proprietary model of shared cultural codes, networks of dissemination, and collaborative authorship" in the twenty-first century.[31] To some extent, the work of the Contact Zone Crew could be located within this milieu of poetic expression.

However, Compton's work circumvents this matrix by carefully treating copyrighted sounds since he, as indicated above, chooses not to violate ownership laws by reproducing the sounds of others as his own. "The Reinventing Wheel," for example, does not include the sounds of DJ Krush, Urbaniak, Alex Haley, or the others whom he samples in the live setting. Appropriative literary strategies should not be wholly depreciated, but we have recently seen the impact of such "open source poetics" when those tactics risk the exploitation of persons and groups.[32] In these instances, "open source" works do not embody the "collaborative logic"[33] that Voyce describes.

In contrast, Compton's work deflects the exploitative possibilities of these strategies and respects the copyright of other creators. The artists they sample – like Haley – do not seem like appropriate targets for challenging notions of property and ownership when compared to the targets of appropriative projects like Rachel Zolf's *Janey's Arcadia* (2014), Jordan Abel's *Injun* (2016), or M. NourbeSe Philip's *Zong!* (2008), whose works disparately unsettle racist and colonial legacies. Rather, in Compton's sound work, I find a similarly profound model that seeks to navigate the complexities of sound and ownership with a collaborative logic grounded in care and compassion.

Final Cut: Spinning Back

The textual and sonic cuts of Compton's turntablist poetics, in turn, cut into perceptions of literary, nationalist, and capitalist sonic planes. In his sampling and mixing of materials, Compton intervenes into and reconfigures moralist exclusivist assumptions about sounds and soundscapes that marginalize persons, histories, and forms of expression. Rather, Compton's collaborative, creative risk-taking activities are imbued by a generous spirit that welcome voices, practices, and modes of being into a contact zone and resists a logic of ownership and singularity. This is a model of collaborative and resistant logic urgently needed in this world.

NOTES

1 I use the term "cut" here in reference to the form of this essay. In its most basic sense, "cutting" refers to a technique that DJs use while cross-fading to "cut" sounds in and out of a mix. In a similar fashion, I think of my movements between these sections as a kind of textual "cut" since each of these sections quickly brings into focus a specific idea or concept before moving to the next.
2 R. Murray Schafer, *The Soundscape: Our Sonic Environment and the Tuning of the World* (Rochester, VT: Destiny Books, 1993), 237.
3 Marie Thompson, *Beyond Unwanted Sound: Noise, Affect, and Aesthetic Moralism* (New York: Bloomsbury Academic, 2017), 88.
4 Ibid., 92.
5 Wayde Compton, *After Canaan: Essays on Race, Writing, and Region* (Vancouver: Arsenal Pulp Press, 2010), 199.
6 Schafer, *The Soundscape*, 237.
7 In "Turntable Poetry, Mixed-Race, and Schizophonophilia," Compton provides a précis that outlines a performance the duo did at the 2008 Scream in High Park Literary Festival in Toronto. Compton provides details about the samples they use, identifying specific cue points as well as blending and scratching techniques. This précis informs my listening and my understanding of the general arc of their work and, specifically, the recorded 2008 performance in Vancouver discussed below.
8 Mary Louise Pratt, "Arts of the Contact Zone," in *Profession* (1991): 34.
9 Compton, *After Canaan*, 189.
10 Schafer, *The Soundscape*, 90.
11 The Contact Zone Crew, *Wayde Compton, Jason de Couto – The Contact Zone Crew*, uploaded by Signal+Noise Media Art Festival, 23 July 2009, video, 6:55, https://vimeo.com/5736532.
12 Ibid.
13 Compton coined this term in his 2010 book of essays *After Canaan* (Arsenal Pulp). He defines pheneticization as "the classification of a person's race or ethinicity based only on eyeball examination, rather than the cladisitic inquiry that would require knowing the person's actual family background" (24).
14 Wayde Compton, "'We make something out of what records we can find': An Interview with Wayde Compton" by Deanna Fong, in this volume, 59.
15 Watch Compton's 2013 performance and Q&A with Nick Storring at the University of Waterloo's Critical Media Lab, for his remarks on how audiences have occasionally responded to the Contact Zone Crew with dance and movement. See "Wayde Compton & Nick Storring at the Critical Media Lab," YouTube, uploaded by UWaterlooEnglish, video, 47:03, 7 March 2013, www.youtube.com/watch?v=4MuUirGB2Oo.

16 Emma Cleary, "Ghosts in the Phonograph: Tracking Black Canadian Postbody Poetics," in *Canadian Literature*, no. 236 (2018): n.p., Gale Literature Resource Center, accessed 13 July 2023.
17 Ibid.
18 Alexander Weheliye, "'Feenin': Posthuman Voices in Contemporary Black Popular Music," *Social Text* 71, 20, no. 2 (Summer 2002): 39.
19 Ibid.
20 Kate Siklosi, "'Caught in the Few Feet Between': (Re)negotiations of Place in the Architextural Lacunae of Dionne Brand's *Thirsty* and Wayde Compton's *49th Parallel Psalm*," in *MaComère* 14, no. 1 (2013): 153.
21 Dennis Lee, "Cadence, Country Silence: Writing in Colonial Space," in *boundary2* 3, no. 1 (1974): 152.
22 Dylan Robinson, *Hungry Listening: Resonant Theory for Indigenous Sound Studies* (Minneapolis: University of Minnesota Press, 2020), 44.
23 In the literary context, we see these efforts reflected in the homogeneous body of writings included as part of McClelland & Stewart's New Canadian Library series (edited by Malcolm Ross), which ushered in the formation of a Canadian literary tradition by reissuing such works as Susanna Moodie's *Roughing It in the Bush*, John Richardson's *Wacousta*, and many others.
24 "Canadian Multiculturalism Act," Justice Laws Website, 1988, last edited 1 April 2014, https://laws-lois.justice.gc.ca/eng/acts/c-18.7/page-1.html.
25 Richard Cavell, "World Famous Across Canada, or Transnational Localities," in *Trans.Can.Lit.*, eds. Smaro Kamboureli and Roy Miki (Waterloo: Wilfrid Laurier University Press, 2007), 87.
26 Glen Sean Coulthard, *Red Skin, White Masks: Rejecting the Colonial Politics of Recognition* (Minneapolis: University of Minnesota Press, 2014), 3.
27 Wayde Compton, *Performance Bond* (Vancouver: Arsenal Pulp Press, 2004), 42.
28 Ibid., 44.
29 Ibid., 47.
30 Compton, *After Canaan*, 189.
31 Stephen Voyce, "Toward an Open Source Poetics: Appropriation, Collaboration, and the Commons" in *Criticism* 53, no. 3 (Summer 2011): 407.
32 See Mongrel Coalition Against Gringpo, "MCAG Presents the Best Conceptual Poem of the Year: Interrupting the Maintenance of White Supremacy," *Internet Archive: Wayback Machine*, snapshot of *Gringpo.com* from 05 April 2015, https://web.archive.org/web/201504 05002803/http://gringpo.com/; or Jillian Steinhauer, "Kenneth Goldsmith Remixes Michael Brown Autopsy Report as Poetry," *Hyperallergic*, 16 March 2015, https://hyperallergic.com/190954/kenneth-goldsmith-remixes-michael-brown-autopsy-report-as-poetry/.
33 Voyce, "Toward an Open Source Poetics," 425.

3

"The fact of my mouth"

An Interview with Jordan Scott

Deanna Fong, recorded over Zoom
TRANSCRIBED BY DEANNA RADFORD

Deanna Fong: I was just listening to the recording of the performance that you did at the SpokenWeb Symposium at Simon Fraser University [SFU] and figured that actually that might be a really nice way to get into things. Seeing as most of the readership probably wasn't at the performance, I wonder if you could give a brief summary of what you did there.

Jordan Scott: Yeah, sure. I've always been interested in experimenting with delayed auditory feedback which is a proven therapeutic method to ease or even erase someone's stutter. The way it does that is it produces an echo inside of the stutterer's ear so you're essentially hearing yourself on a delay. That delay produces a kind of fluency. I tried it when I was a child and then again when I started at university, mostly due to anxiety of having to speak and present. Jason [Starnes] and I had talked about that when we had collaborated on other work together and we thought that it would be interesting to try that one day. So, we thought that that particular reading would be a good time to actually try that. A couple weeks before the performance we recorded a section of my book, *Night & Ox*. I read without the delay and then I read with the delay to give the audience a sense of what the delayed auditory feedback would do to the poem and my voice and the stutter.

DF: One of the things that struck me in your description of the reading was you were talking about the labour of speech, which is not something that I've ever really thought about and I don't think most people think about – that it *is* a form of labour. I, myself, am terrified of public speaking. I hate it so much. There's always this immense emotional labour that goes into bringing one's self to speak in public and then the big affect-dump after it happens. I wanted to ask you more about that idea of speech as labour, and what that labour means to you.

JS: Speech for me always has and continues to be a very physical and painful experience. Physically and emotionally. This example puts a fine point on it: most recently, I've been having to go to the dentist a lot because my teeth are wearing down because of the way that I feign fluency. I do a lot of clenching. Over the years I've worn my teeth away. That's been recent, where all the dentists I've seen have raised the alarm for that.

I never thought about that before. I never thought that the stutter would have those kinds of physical impacts. When they told me about that and told me how long I would have had to be doing something like that to get my teeth to where they are, it just reminded me of this really long haul of always having to negotiate public and private spaces at the same time I'm negotiating the physicality of speech. At the same time, I'm negotiating how I'm perceived and how I sound. Then at the same time, in a very odd way, understanding that when it comes to aesthetics and my life as a poet, that's almost what is expected. I think that was so intriguing to me, with the performance that you asked me to give where I read fluently for the first time ever and thinking about that long-term. I'm wondering if maybe that's just what I'll do because sometimes the performative aspect of reading poetry where I'm not allowing myself to try to be fluent is very physically taxing. It's more so. And, as you said, there's that affect-dump at the end. That's very complex for me.

DF: I remember Helen Potrebenko saying that it took her two weeks to work herself up to a reading and two weeks to recover afterward! I wanted to ask you about that. It leads me back to the idea that the line is always being led in poetry back to the fact of one's mouth. I was thinking, also one of the things you said in that performance is that, upon trying delayed auditory feedback, all of a sudden sensing this verbal fluency for the first time felt inauthentic somehow.

JS: Jason and I were in his studio in his backyard the first time we did it. We both just looked at each other after and started laughing. It was this really strange kind of childhood laughter. We were laughing at how different I sounded and he was also laughing at me because it was such a glorious feeling. I was just like, "Let's do it again! Let's read the whole book like this!" Because it was so fast. *So* fast. I read so fast and so easy and I think that's where a lot of the discomfort came from. Because it didn't sound like me at all. It very much removed me from my poetics as well. It was very odd to read that particular poem in that way. But on the other hand, I think there was a certain pleasure in that speed that I took a lot from. It's really hard to describe. It just felt like I could finally concentrate on the line breaks and I could finally concentrate on not being self-conscious or removing the fact of my mouth from the equation.

DF: And sliding into metaphor, as it were?[1]

JS: Yeah, exactly.

DF: But, if I think about *blert* and the way that your poetics are articulated there, there's a sort of interrogation of the very structure of what we think of as linguistic fluency. I suppose in performing the work in this unusual voice – this voice that feels not quite your own, as if it's your absented voice that's coming back at you that produces the effect – do you feel like that somehow runs against the grain of the book's content itself?

JS: I think so. In a sense it relinquishes any type of resistance to that, the line I've used before, "the regime of fluency." It surrenders to that, in a sense. For me, it was surrendering to a more therapeutic way of speaking like when I used to see a speech pathologist back in the day. I assume they have different ways of dealing with this now but, back in the day, it was like, "Okay, how do we get you to speak without stuttering." Right? I do feel that it was definitely against the grain as you say, of *blert*. Almost going in the complete opposite direction.

DF: Yeah. However, with the way that the line breaks are in *Night & Ox* – with those very short lines – it's a long poem that doesn't have quite the same sort of normative syntax as *blert*. It's a long poem that to me really relies on the line as a form of breath, which you talk about in the afterword. The form necessitated by this small, breathing being that you're holding in your arms. But I wanted to ask you if there's a different kind of authenticity in being able to relay that and carry those line breaks forward with a certain velocity? It may not be an authentic bodily experience but maybe it's a somewhat different embodied physicality that belongs to that particular book.

JS: I think that's a great way of saying it. I think that in *blert*, the normative syntax was almost like a "fuck you," in a way. Because syntax is in a way meaningless to me in a performative sense. It doesn't matter. Commas, periods, don't really matter. So I wanted to embed that in there and then have the performative aspect of me reading those pieces do something to the sentence. But the line breaks in *Night & Ox* in terms of authenticity – this is what's so fascinating to me about the stutter *still* – is how it's so improvisational or it's so based and structured on ambush, right? There's no way to exactly tell which parts of those lines or syllables I'm going to land on or not land on. So every time I read that poem, it's different. So then it becomes really interesting how to compose something like that when you realize that every time you read it, it's not going to be an authentic representation of your voice.

DF: It's interesting because Jordan Abel read that evening, too. In his performance there's this layer of mediation that chops up the poem and distends it. It's the only way of actually authentically representing the text because, he said, "If I just read it, it's not the poem on the page." In a way too, the way that he performs his piece also relies on these chance interventions but it's digitally manipulated.

AN INTERVIEW with JORDAN SCOTT

JS: Yes, that's right. And every time I hear Jordan's work, even if it's the same piece, you're right: it's always different, in that sense. Because, as you said, it just depends on the way that he is manipulating his poem on any given evening. In terms of the stutter – which some of his work is that, in a sense, that kind of manipulation of language to distend it, or break it apart, or to produce fragments and whatnot – that to me seems is edging towards an authenticity in the way that dysfluency actually functions in somebody's mouth.

DF: I wanted to think about the idea of resistance in *blert*: that it's resisting the idea of a normative fluency, drawing on these different lexicons from the Zurich Dadaists – Tristan Tzara who frames the afterword to Lewis Carroll's "Jabberwocky." I guess it is in a way resisting the idea that there's a possible linguistic fluency, but then also thinking about your project, *Lanterns at Guantánamo*, which I think is a pointed critique of state systems of power and ways that they redact people's humanity. I was wondering how, or if, linguistic resistance and, say, something like political resistance, connect for you.

JS: I think the best example I can give of how they connect, for me at least, is through interrogation and through the structure and consequences of that particular procedure. Just because in that particular way of talking and coercing, there are so many linguistic and political consequences wrapped up in that moment that two people share together in a really unequal power dynamic. That's where that begins, for me. [Pause] I think that's where that happens for me, is in that particular space. That's most definitely how I measure the collision between the linguistic and the political and to get at – not only what happens in those moments – but what's at stake for the mouth and how people speak and the consequences of dysfluency within a larger power structure. I felt like, for me, I could contribute somehow to that.

DF: Because it's so intimately involved in these acts of reading other people's speech, reading other people's bodies – these gestures that are so tied up with power, right?

JS: Yeah. Then the idea that these power structures hold that is also a cultural idea, too. That when somebody is dysfluent, they are somehow lying or not telling the truth. That these kinds of ruptures in speech mean that somebody is dishonest. Obviously, those moments of interrogation, those kinds of ruptures in speech become ways to manipulate someone or to incarcerate them or to harm them.

DF: Following on that, I thought I would ask you where your interest in the sonic aspect of performance comes from.

JS: For me, I've always been really aware of, obviously, my own body and the way that I speak and the way that I sound. There's something that's really interesting and intriguing to me with the way that the stutter in particular finds a home to a certain degree in poetry and poetics. That's really interesting to me. There's a certain level of comfort there, to understand that the way that I speak can find some solidarity in poetics. In terms of level of syllable, which the sound poets have been practising, as well. So, I think that's where sound always comes in for me on that level. Also, I discovered this a couple of years ago, that I do like to compose in a kind of musicality because I do find it easier to speak in that way. For a while it was an unconscious way of preparing myself for the inevitability of performing something. I knew if I produced some kind of rhythm or paid attention to the sound, that the performative aspect would somehow be smoother.

DF: Speaking of the affinities with other sound poets, my ears perked up at the Tzara quote at the end of *blert* – "Thought is made in the mouth"[2] – because of the way the language in the book travels through all of these different argots that are often not very familiar to most readers – remind me to never play Scrabble against you, okay? But it does almost have a similar effect of defamiliarization that the Dadaists were searching for, in a way. There are some words in there that are unfamiliar and there are some that are used, but in a totally unfamiliar sense. There are some that are not totally words. They at least have a sort of linguistic sense but they're not exactly *the sign*. I'm thinking about the Dadaist project of trying to find this Ur-language that's before speech. Say, where thought and speech are coincident, without having to deal with that nasty business of the signifier in-between. In service of that project, Tzara and Hugo Ball co-opted Oceanic, African, and Indigenous languages, and placed them in this position of "before-speech." I know your work might have a similar effect, in terms of defamiliarizing language, but it's not at all interested in trying to find something "before sense," right?

JS: Yes. Most definitely. I think that that's what always really inspired me about Lewis Carroll, who also had a stutter. I'm using these nonce words. It's definitely in *blert*, that defamiliarization, but also intimacy at the same time was what I was trying to do, at least: a kind of cycling through the dictionary as a means of both labour but also survival. Also, the contradictory absolute joy in the sounds and weirdness of words, but also the terror of trying to approach them and navigate through them.

DF: What I love about it is it never says, "This other kind of language is out there." Intimacy is exactly the word and is, for me, what separates it from that kind of Dadaist sound poem project. It's not exteriorizing it in a way and projecting onto someone, or something, else. It's very intimately felt.

JS: Yes, most definitely. That kind of materiality of it.

DF: So, you've worked in collaboration with Jason Starnes and lots of other people. I was wondering if you could say a little bit about what collaboration has meant for your work or maybe even sociality more broadly. How has that affected your production?

JS: Collaboration for me has made such a difference in my poetics and my practice and my life. I would not have been able to do all of those things without collaborating with all those people. It's almost my favourite thing to do when it comes to poetry. Especially when I collaborate with people such as Jason, who have real expertise, and joy, and love for something that I don't know anything about. That's always for me where the excitement is. To give your work over to someone else with no restrictions or expectations and then just see where that process takes you. I think that it's definitely also the way that I feel like I can quietly contribute to a community. I feel like over the years I maybe haven't – I'm not so much for going out a lot and doing that kind of thing that sometimes poetry requires or wants of you.

DF: To see and be seen.

JS: Yeah, right. I think that I find collaboration to be much quieter and I like to get to know people that way. To build friendships through this kind of mutual work on these weird and wonderful things together. In the case of Steve [Collis] and I with *Decomp*, or in the case with Jason Starnes, or even that documentary that I did a long time ago, all those people were able to take my work to places that I could never do and that kind of extension of poetics into those fields has been very, very formative for me because it changes my thinking beyond the page. Then when I return to the page, I'm thinking beyond the page as well. It's been really fascinating.

DF: It's great, too – it makes the labour that goes into those projects very visible in a way that a book doesn't. Collaboration credits that labour, which we don't always hear in single-author book production.

JS: Yes, exactly.

DF: So. I have this question that I've been wanting to ask you basically since I wrote on *Lanterns at Guantánamo*, which was under a different name at the time.[3]

JS: Yeah, *Clearance Process*.

DF: I've been thinking through the acousmatic sound you use in that piece. Sound that has been absented from its source. As always, it conjures the body, but it conjures the body through absence. I remember you saying in the speech that you gave for your Poet-in-Residence talk at SFU that in listening to the sound of the air conditioners, which is a constant thrum throughout that piece, that one is listening to a certain kind of torture without the body being present. At the time I was writing about it, I was reading Sara Ahmed's *The Cultural Politics of Emotion*. She brings up this question that she doesn't totally answer, which is: what do we do with the fact that we can't feel somebody else's pain? What is the ethical way to feel alongside somebody whose pain you can't actually access? I think that's the deep ethical question at the heart of *Lanterns at Guantánamo*. I throw that out there as a big meatball.

JS: I was certainly always conscious of not going to that place to try in any way to attempt to represent someone else's pain. That's something that's very important to me poetically as well as ethically, too. But I think what became clear is, in the recording, I felt like there was an opportunity to attempt a kind of navigation of all the structures around them that are designed to cause pain. The media tour was one of them. Trying to navigate this very bureaucratic form of erasure that was pretending to be a very transparent look into this prison and to the detainees. I think that the recording of the absences and the redactions are, in a sense, a way to maybe come close to a form of violence I wouldn't experience because of my body and its privilege. I wouldn't experience that kind of trauma. But those redactions and those silences within themselves definitely function that way.

Spending so much time with those documents and spending so much time on the tour, behind every redaction, there's something there. Oftentimes that's a name or that's a form of abuse. So I think that there was this idea that this kind of tour as a form of state redaction that I could record that somehow and maybe allow those silences and absences to speak for themselves. But, what I still haven't answered – there's a lot of things I haven't answered – but, one of them that's very interesting to me is that on almost all those recordings you can hear my body, my footsteps, or the rustle in my shirt or my breathing.

That for me is a whole other set of ethical questions that I think what I've written on it maybe gestures towards some kind of an answer but I definitely haven't got there at all. But, just to say that recording those silences was not a neutral act. I still had to decide where I was going to put my body to record those sounds and as I've said repeatedly, where I could place my body was also restricted to the point of sometimes being touched and moved into certain spots where I couldn't record.

DF: That's interesting. I had never thought of that. In an effort to avoid the obvious question of positionality that would be there if you were going and writing poems about it – where your position as author would be very obvious and kind of suspect – even I, for a second, skimmed over the positionality of your body in the recording. I think we tend to do that a lot in thinking that it's this neutral, objective medium that just records everything indiscriminately – because it's not the case.

JS: Completely. I remember before I went, the poet angela rawlings – I'd never done sound recordings before and it was her idea – she just said record everything. That was her advice, to try to make it as random as possible. Try not to pay attention to where you are walking or whatever. But for me, once I got there, I realized that that was an impossibility. The decisions that I made – the ones that I was *allowed* to make, where I was like, "I should record within this cell" or "I should record right up against this fence at night" or "I should record the air conditioner or the sound of the ocean right outside of the prison walls" – all those are decisions. I didn't know how to do it without it. I wasn't sure how to do it without it. Even when I tried just to leave.

I remember ryan [fitzpatrick] asked the question after the talk about the manipulation of the recordings, how that actually happened. He's right. I keep going back to how they're not neutral recordings whatsoever. They were all decisions of where to place myself. What makes it even more complicated is the kind of access that I was allowed as not being a journalist, as being a poet, as being a Canadian, as being a man, as being white, all these things – that kind of access was also really present there, too. It was like, "Oh, he can go there because he's harmless, but you can't. You have to stay here with us. But he can go off into that field over there." All those things for me are still very present in the way that I still think about that project.

DF: It's a good one to not come to a resolution on.

JS: The other thing that I think sometimes is that even though it's ethically problematic, and I still think it is, there is some type of importance in that kind of archived sound because some of those places now, especially Camp X-Ray, they don't let people in at all and they're just razing it. They're taking everything down. They don't let people go into that field anymore.

So I think that there's something to that. I don't know how to articulate it but there's something to the soundscape of a place that however it was recorded bears some kind of witness to what that space is trying to redact or trying to keep from the public because this tour, which is called a media tour, part of its core structure is to make sure that all of the media that comes out is all the same. So all the pictures have to be the same. All the videos have to be the same. All of the stills have to be the same. Everything is. So you produce a witnessing that the state condones and controls and redacts again and then puts out into the world as this kind of release valve. But I think there's something to that ambient sound that's more porous, that escapes those levels of redaction.

DF: As a function of the medium itself. I imagine they didn't listen through all of your recordings.

JS: No, they did not. Not at all.

DF: Not in the same way they scrutinized every single picture that you took to ensure that everything was up to snuff.

JS: That's right. And the journalists who did video, they spent hours and hours with them. Hours with them going over every reel, every frame. Everything.

DF: I think that there is definitely something: the fact that the absence strikes us as so prominent. The redaction is made transparent and not just what is inside the frame of it. We get a sense of the act of framing itself.

JS: Yes, exactly. Yes.

NOTES

1 Referring to the lines that open the Preface to Scott's book of poems, *blert:* "It is part of my existence to be the parasite of metaphors, so easily am I carried away by the first simile that comes along. Having been carried away, I have to find my difficult way back, and slowly return, to the fact of my mouth." Jordan Scott, *blert* (Toronto: Coach House Books, 2008), 7.
2 Tristan Tzara, quoted in Jordan Scott, *blert*, 64.
3 See Deanna Fong, "Jordan Scott: Clearance Process," *Tripwire* 12 (2016): 263–5.

4

Listening as Access
Toward Relational Listening for Nonnormative Speech and Communication

Faith Ryan

The *Disability Visibility Podcast* [DVP], started in 2017 by media-maker Alice Wong, said goodbye to fans of the show with a celebratory one-hundredth episode in April 2021. The DVP's near four-year run is a historic event in media creation because of the show's commitment to providing space for disabled people to share their stories, its focus on access, intersectionality and culture, and its use of sound to further disability politics and build crip futures.[1] Among the podcast's innovative uses of sound, it centres and amplifies the voices of disabled speakers. Wong, who hosts the podcast, uses a BiPAP machine: a mask and tube that cover her nose attached to a machine that supports her breathing. The BiPAP gives Wong's voice a unique texture and rhythm. Wong's voice, along with those of many of her guests, sonically signals the podcast's defiance of the politics of voice that keep disabled speakers absent from aural media.

In disability and media scholar Bill Kirkpatrick's 2013 article on the exclusion of disabled speakers from radio, he notes that podcasting is a space where disabled speakers can gain greater representation. Four years before the DVP's first episode, Kirkpatrick wrote that it would be "an extraordinary moment if a cottage-produced podcast [brought] greater vocal non-normativity with any regularity to more than the smallest of audiences."[2] When the DVP concluded, I joined in with fellow listeners stating my thanks to Wong for the years of listening and community. The "extraordinary moment" Kirkpatrick imagined, in which disabled speakers were featured on a podcast with an immense listenership, had come and gone.

Many would say that the exclusion of disabled voices from radio is a result of audiences' desire for "smooth" and "easy" listening. Under colonial capitalism, "desirable" voices are effortlessly digested and understood.[3] Amidst this cultural definition of "good" sound and voice, the realities of the labour and pain of speech for some communicators does not make for easy consumption. Jordan Scott, a poet and performer who writes about his experience as someone who stutters, describes speaking as a "painful experience. Physically and emotionally."[4] To achieve fluency Scott clenches his teeth, wearing them down over time and causing pain. Any sign of the physicality, labour, and pain of communication render diverse vocalizations, sounds, and gestures unconsumable to the ableist ear,[5] which grants value based on a communication's similarity to the norm. In opposition to the ableist ear's desire for speed, certainty, and ease, the DVP fosters a community of listeners who enjoy sounds and voices that meander, destabilize, and labour. Averse to the common-sense appeal of the "smooth" and "beautiful," listeners of the DVP desire sound and voice beyond these constructed boundaries.

As a listener of the DVP, I long to hear Lateef McLeod's crip-cool introduction, "this is the *Disability Visibility Podcast* with your host Alice Wong," voiced through his AAC (augmentative and alternative communication device) as the Krip-Hop beats of Wheelchair Sports Camp drum behind. I repeat the intro and wiggle my fingers seaweed-like while I listen, my excitement growing as Wong's pausing, dysrhythmic voice says, "Hello, all you glorious creatures, welcome to the *Disability Visibility Podcast*."[6] Is there anything better for a crip (and in my case, a baby crip just starting the process of coming out) than to be greeted as a "cyborg," an "earthling," or a "glorious creature" by a visionary self-proclaimed cyborg whose vocal magnificence conveys a crip politics, a rejection of compulsory normativity, a claim to beauty for those society deems "bad" or "ugly"?

My desire for the sounds of crip aesthetics is echoed in Wong's manifesto for crip voices on the radio, in which she writes:

On radio, I want to hear people who ...
lisp
stutter
gurgle
stammer
wheeze
repeat themselves
pause when needing to breathe
make noises when they talk
salivate and drool
communicate, enunciate, and pronounce differently
use different speech patterns and rhythms
use ventilators or other assistive technology
use sign language interpreters or other people that facilitate speech
use computer-generated speech[7]

The sheer number of listeners of the DVP, and my own experience of longing for crip sounds, has led me to question why some experience vocal alterity as "disturbing, an impingement from which they need relief,"[8] while many in the disability community and beyond hear these sounds as authentic and stylistic. I contend that the exclusion of disabled communicators from media is less a result of disabled speech and more a matter of audiences' *disabling listening*. Disabling listening is a function of the ableist ear that rejects speech and communication which deviates from normalcy. The communication is disabled by the ear that is unwilling and/or unable to comprehend and appreciate messages communicated across modality, through texture, tone, affect, and context, or through nonnormative speech.

In this chapter, in order to develop – or rather, *find* – a method for listening equitably to disabled communicators, I begin by discussing how the ableist ear acts as a barrier to communication, effectively disabling communication through bias and habit. Next, I present communications as interdependent – arising from the relationship between speaker and listener – and emphasize the listener's role in communication. Finally, through introducing Mia Mingus's concept of "access intimacy," I argue that *listening is a form of access*. By focusing on the negotiation of access that happens while listening, we can promote practices of listening otherwise, in the cultivation of an archive, in classrooms where aesthetics are named, or in everyday encounters where listening means the speaker's access to medical care, housing, relationships, and safety.

The medical model sees disability as the deviation or disease of a body or mind. But decades of disability activism have revealed that disabilities are not simply medical realities, they are "misfittings" between the individual and the "material-discursive world."[9] Disabilities are created in the relationship between an individual who has an impairment, the environment they are in, the resources (un)available to them, and the attitudes of those in the environment. If we recognize the relational nature of all disabilities, including those related to speech and communication, we can attend to all aspects of a communication, particularly the part played by the listener. Attending to the cultural ways we listen to nonnormative speech and communication provides an opportunity to not only recognize how a speaker's access to communication is precluded by attitudes of ableism but also to heed the knowledge and wisdom of those who have already developed methods for listening otherwise.

The Listener as a Barrier to (Co)mmunication

In an interview for *The Vocal Fries Podcast*, Alice Wong comments on the politics of sonic aesthetics and presents the listener as a barrier to understanding disabled speech: "In our goal for 'good' sound we leave out a lot of kinds of sounds that are organic to so many of us. And that's one of my ulterior, hidden agendas in my podcast, it's my attempt to actually try to get people to be uncomfortable. To force the listeners to actually think, 'Oh, I gotta put a bit more work into listening and into understanding.'"[10] Wong's suggestion that audiences "put a bit more work into listening" reveals that listening to, and understanding, different voices and communication styles is a *learned skill requiring practice*; a skill disabled people in community practice daily. Still, outside of disability communities the skill of listening patiently, on crip time,[11] and toward recognizing style and technique, is not taught or valued. Instead, listeners learn to diagnose and reject sonic or communicative differences. Disgust and impatience intervene in the chain of communication and seek a separation between the speaker and listener: "I can't understand *them* because *they're* disabled."

Sara Ahmed writes about the affect of disgust in *The Cultural Politics of Emotion* as a "sensuous proximity" that causes the subject to "[recoil] from the object; it pulls away with an intense movement that registers in the pit of the stomach."[12] The relation between, in this case, communicator and listener is felt as "too close" as particular histories of social and cultural practice, which construct the "bad voice," abide in the moment of contact. The close collaboration required for communication produces a proximity between communicator and listener, which "threaten[s] the ontology of 'being apart' from others,"[13] especially others to whom disgust "sticks."[14] Ahmed shows that whether disgust sticks to an object is a matter of "a certain history, rather than being a necessary consequence of the nature of things."[15] Divergent bodyminds are not inherently disgusting but are impacted by histories that reproduce sticky associations between difference, pain, or struggle, and ugliness or contamination. The listener's process of diagnosing and recoiling from the communicator operates from within a medical approach to disability,[16] which (along with forgotten histories of emotion) conceals the role of the listener in disabling the voice.

Similar to the function of what Stó:lō scholar Dylan Robinson calls the settler "tin ear," a pattern of listening that limits comprehension of the affect and texture of sound,[17] the ableist ear restricts what kinds of communications and sounds listeners are willing or able to perceive, appreciate, and understand. Namely, the ableist ear is attuned to "normal speech": a cultural ideal that grants authority to voices that "sound" white, middle-class, gender-conforming, and abled. In the twentieth century, performing "normal" speech was considered a sign of rationality and moral character.[18] Alternately, "bad" voices (including foreign accents, gender-nonconforming pitch and inflection, and/or speech disability) were thought to pose a corrupting danger to the population if allowed to circulate.[19] Today, the concept of "normal" speech continues to use ableism to render all linguistic differences a sign of disability –

an indication of intellectual or mental divergence. The ableist ear is thereby deeply entwined with settler-colonialism, since white supremacy and binary gender need ableism in order to continue to pathologize and criminalize those of working-class or impoverished queer, trans, Black, Indigenous, and people of colour populations. The ableist ear affectively rejects differences in modality, vernacular, pronunciation, time, texture, timbre, fluency or articulation, and diagnoses deviations from normalcy. Listening with an ableist ear is a culturally taught method of perceiving and valuing that reflects ableism's function as an everyday diagnostic that distributes and restricts power across populations.

In our limited categories for sound, the indexes of "disabled" and "unhealthy" are often applied instinctively by the listener. The Accessible Canada Act defines disability according to the social model, as "any impairment, including a physical, mental, intellectual, cognitive, learning, communication or sensory impairment ... that, *in interaction with a barrier* [emphasis added], hinders a person's full and equal participation in society."[20] A speech or communication disability arises when impairment meets the ableist ear. Listeners hear vocal difference and account for it with the indexes "disabled," "unintelligent," and/or "unhealthy," rather than considering how their positionality and skill in listening impacts the outcome of the communication. Listeners may overlook that communication is mutual labour and that disability is created in the relation.

Often, appeals to health are used in discourse around disability, race, and gender to conceal the role of society in disabling individuals and groups. Wong discusses a time that a stranger sent her a message on Twitter saying, "I'm a nurse and I'm very concerned about your voice. And, by the way, if I just heard your voice, I would think you were in respiratory distress!"[21] This expression of concern obscures racist and ableist discrimination behind a seemingly apolitical matter: "I'm just worried about your health!" Naturalizing the ideology of ability, the concept of health distracts from the political dimensions of the listener's concern: the uncomfortable emotions the listener experiences hearing a disabled Asian American woman, whose voice simply being recorded and garnering listenership threatens current distributions of power along the intersections of ability, race, and gender. The unnamed Twitter user shields the political dimensions of their rejection of Wong's audio work by emphasizing Wong's impairment.

The medical paradigm of disability aligns with (outdated) theories of the voice as independent (created only by the speaker) to conceal a cultural crisis of listening. Theories and myths of the independent voice obscure the reality that nonnormative voices are disabled – made less effective in communicating a message – by ableist ways of listening, not simply by a quality of the speaker's bodymind. If we put pressure on the idea of independence in theories of voice, it becomes less singular where the voice is "failing," and more evidently a matter of the listener's willingness to be in relation with the speaker.

The Voice as Interdependent

The myth of vocal essence has long imagined the voice as an independent entity and an essential expression of an individual's humanity, the quality of the sound conveying aspects of the speaker's character.[22] This myth impels emotions of fear and disgust that operate in the moment of listening since nonnormative speech and communication culturally signal a lack of humanity, intelligence, and rationality.[23] A nonnormative voice, or method of communication (echolalia, AAC, etc.), evokes the spectre of mental disability, which Remi Yergeau states "signals a kind of rhetorical involuntariness" since "rhetorical actions are rendered less as symbolic actions and more as biological motions."[24] The assumed "involuntarity" of messages communicated by neurodivergent people and those with mental health disabilities forecloses the social necessity of listening.[25] Nonnormative speech and communication are often interpreted as a sign that the message lacks meaning, even when the content of the communication expresses evidence otherwise. Theories of the voice as independent and essential render disabled speech lacking without accounting for the ways that ableist ears create barriers to understanding.

Voice scholar Nina Eidsheim's articulation of voice as collective, cultural, and *in the listener* challenges the assumed independence of the voice.[26] The voice (spoken or otherwise) is not independent but rather generated through interaction. She says: "No matter how we present vocally it's really the person who listens to us, who hears us, that is going to define what that voice is. So, we can make any number of sounds, but it is always somehow in the receiver that that sound is going to be defined and named and known, and sometimes there is no connection or correlation between the two."[27] To clarify, Eidsheim is not suggesting that there is one voice that emerges. She is submitting that everyone, including the speaker, hears the voice differently. Not only are voices produced collectively and culturally, but also the listener assigns meaning to the voice from within their positionality and cultural context. Eidsheim shows that the listener's interpretation of the voice – their answer to the acousmatic question – reflects the "culture's impression of who the vocalizer is."[28]

While Eidsheim's work in *The Race of Sound* utilizes an analysis of timbre, I extend her focus on the listener to emphasize how *listening through a culture of ableism disables voices and messages*. Eidsheim states that "regardless of the actual vocal signal emitted, listeners will produce their own assessment of what they did hear. We actually assign value when we pose and respond to the acousmatic question."[29] Measurable observations such as "this voice stutters," "this voice is interrupted by breaths," and "this voice is high-pitched" are given as supporting evidence for the cultural conclusion "this is a bad voice."

Following Eidsheim's rejection of the voice as independent, or arising from a single source, I suggest that we think about voices as *interdependent*. Voices are made through a relationship between many different variables including: the vocal cords, air, vibration, the listener, the culture(s) the speaker and listener are part of, vocal training and therapies, technologies, and the material conditions of the speaker and the listener's bodies. The many variables that interact within the vocal event reflect communications' interdependence: a concept and method from disability culture that Kelly Fritsch and Aimi Hamraie define as "the weaving of relational circuits between bodies, environments, and tools to create non-innocent, frictional access."[30] The voice arises out of a particular entanglement of environmental, physiological, and cultural elements and forms in the relationship between the vocalizer and the listener.[31] The two are interdependently entwined.

In turning toward the listener's role in creating the communication, I do not wish to discount the significance of the speaker's performance. The communicator possesses agency in their performance and utilizes rhetorical techniques[32] in the moment of expression. Nonetheless, no matter the performative decisions made by the communicator, it matters how the listener decides to interpret the sounds. Eidsheim points out that the listener has a choice to "either reinforce or refuse to engage naturalized notions and values,"[33] since in the interpretive moment of listening "the technology of narrative comes into play."[34] The listener chooses the meaning of the voice through their negotiation of affect, positionality, and relation. Understanding the listener's role in the interpretation of voice or communication reveals that listening is a way of generating or precluding access.

Listening Toward Access in Relation

In making the claim that listening is a form of access, I am not referring to access that can be legislated or enacted at arm's length. I am not talking about compelled access that treats accommodations as optional forms of benevolence: in such instances, disabled people are left to carry the weight of shame and gratitude for inclusion in unsafe spaces. I am invoking author and co-creator of the Disability Justice framework,[35] Mia Mingus's concept of *access intimacy* to imagine listening in a way that generates access as "an act of love" that results from recognizing and honouring relation.[36] Access intimacy reorients access away from ableist rehabilitation models and toward the needs and desires of disabled people, welcoming the transformation that takes place when individuals' needs for safety, respect, resources, and more – all the expansive holdings of access – are understood as essential for all lives. This concept highlights that many forms of access are created relationally, built between people in moment-to-moment interactions and fostered by attitudes and affinities. Inclusion fails when only physical access is accounted for and the attitudinal barriers to access remain undisturbed. It is not enough to make it appear like access is happening; access intimacy is a matter of what is felt.

Mingus writes: "Access intimacy is that elusive, hard to describe feeling when someone else 'gets' your access needs. The kind of eerie comfort that your disabled self feels with someone on a purely access level. Sometimes it can happen with complete strangers, disabled or not, or sometimes it can be built over years. It could also be the way your body relaxes and opens up with someone when all your access needs are being met."[37] The concept's focus on intimacy highlights that access is collaborative labour – a thing two or more people make together. In this way, access intimacy is a matter of desire and attraction: a desire to know, and be known for, all the parts of one's identity, or to relate on the level of access and disrupt the structures of power that attempt to isolate oppressed people. Within this framework, access is not commodifiable or enforceable but it is deep, personal, and affective.

The vocal event is overflowing with moments where access intimacy can be built or found. In the moment of listening, access intimacy means learning to decipher the speaker's unique techniques of reaching out and connecting. Generating access might entail the listener learning a communicator's rhetorics and addressing personal biases and ableism, or it might require learning another language entirely. In either case, generating access is only possible when the listener assumes meaningfulness. Mingus states that in her life, access intimacy "has looked like able-bodied people listening to [her] and believing [her]."[38] Regardless of particular disability (mental, physical, speech, learning, etc.), listening to a disabled person in an ableist world entails *believing* disabled people. Moreover, listening to nonnormative communications, sound, or speech requires *valuing* sonic difference as aesthetically and politically meaningful.

Sounds and voices that do not conform to the "smooth," the "beautiful," or the "timely" are crucial within disability culture and activism because they create what Fritsch and Hamraie call "generative frictions."[39] They push against the interlocking operations of white supremacy, capitalism, and ableism and expose the tensions between the myths of the normative, independent subject and the lived experience of disabled people. Voices that possess qualities of friction are disruptive, bringing normative aesthetics into crisis and calling on a history of, to quote

Fritsch and Hamraie, "access-making as disabled peoples' acts of noncompliance and protest."[40] The sounds of disruption and untimeliness are timbres and rhythms crips welcome in listening.

If colonial capitalism is about speeding up time, standardization, and streamlining, crip voices interfere in these operations with aesthetics and listening practices that value dis-order and slowness. Political geographer, radio maker, and sound artist Anja Kanngieser puts it this way: "As disabled people what we know is how to wait, we know how to sit, we know how to watch, we know how to listen, we know how to take our time. We know the value of time."[41] Kanngieser connects the diverse relationship that disabled people have to time to crip ways of listening. They state that colonial capitalism "didn't like the fact that we took longer, that we saw time differently."[42] Listening in a way that values different pacing and timbral qualities is not so much a new way of listening as it is an old part of a disabled episteme. It is part of being disabled, and living with, loving, and desiring other disabled people: partners, lovers, friends, and family.

Disability culture acknowledges and celebrates the radical poetics of nonnormative speech and communication. These are transformative aesthetics that free us from captivation by the echoes of the desirable and the beautiful. Mingus writes about "moving beyond a politic of desirability to loving the ugly. Respecting Ugly for how it has shaped us and been exiled. Seeing its power and magic, seeing the reasons it has been feared. Seeing it for what it is: some of our greatest strength."[43] Mingus's call to turn away from normative definitions of "aesthetic" and toward those exiled under colonial capitalism highlights the resistance of turning toward rejected sounds, "toward the ugly," the dysfluent, the shaky, the drooling, the silent, the echoing: toward the "undesirable" sounds humans make. These are the sounds of lives full of experience and knowledges long ignored.

By tuning in to the audio work of Alice Wong, the music and poetry of Leroy Moore and Keith Jones of Krip-Hop Nation, and the spoken word poetry of Jordan Scott and Lateef McLeod, individuals can learn about sound and listening from those who have always already listened otherwise. Listening toward generating access is a learned skill that happens by recognizing one's always-shifting positionality, confronting affects and learned ableism, and desiring intimacy and relationships with disabled people. Performing this kind of listening requires the rejection of mastery and knowing, categorization and diagnosis. Instead, access listening happens in the recognition of relation and the choice to respect and cocreate. It is an open answer to the acousmatic question – "who is this?" – with the only adequate response: "maybe if I listen they will tell me."

NOTES

1 "Crip" is an abbreviation of the derogatory word "crippled" that was recovered by the disability community in the first wave of the disability rights movement. Scholar Alison Kafer describes "crip" as an identity, an affiliation, a politics, and a method. See Alison Kafer, *Health Rebels: A Crip Manifesto for Social Justice*. YouTube, uploaded by uwocp, video, 6 April 2017, www.youtube.com/watch?v=YqcOUD1pBKw&list=PLjhniCMyj1VeLhbrQf1dESaPuP1xrD7-O&index=6&ab_channel=uwocp. One can claim crip identity, be in relation to crips, develop and assert a crip politics, or one can crip as a verb; "to crip" is to actively resist social mandates of normalcy (16:45). The word holds an uncomfortable affect; it is meant to disturb and "jolt people out of their everyday understandings of bodies and minds, of normalcy and deviance." See Alison Kafer, *Feminist, Queer, Crip* (Bloomington: Indiana University Press, 2013), 15. To "build crip futures" denotes the work that disabled people and activists do to imagine and create the conditions for disabled people to survive and thrive in the future.
2 Bill Kirkpatrick, "Voices Made for Print: Crip Voices on the Radio," in *Radio's New Wave: Global Sound in the Digital Era*, ed. Jason Loviglio and Michele Hilmes (New York: Routledge, 2013), 120.
3 Dylan Robinson's *Hungry Listening: Resonant Theory for Indigenous Sound Studies* (Minneapolis: University of Minnesota Press, 2020) discusses the settler colonial "tin ear" – a pattern of normative listening that "prioritizes the capture and certainty of information over the affective feel, timbre, touch, and texture of sound" (38). Robinson describes settlers as "hungry listeners" whose "subjectivity emerges out of a state of consumption" (47). He utilizes the metaphor of consumption – of sound, knowledge, culture, bodies, and resources – to link the settler desire to own and possess (settler hunger) with settler ways of listening that seek to extract meaning and certainty, and exclude "'action, speech, or thought'" that is not deemed valuable (Panagia quoted in Robinson, 40). I utilize the same metaphor of consumption to draw connections between the settler "tin ear" that is unable to "hear Indigenous song as a form of legal evidence in land claims" (40) and the ableist ear, which is unable and/or

unwilling to listen to voices and communication styles that resist standardization and easy consumption. The settler "tin ear" intersects with the anti-relational ear that enforces colonial capitalist mandates of normalcy and what a "good" body, mind, communication, and voice are. Both settler and ableist ways of listening, in their drive for content and efficiency, miss the meanings conveyed through affect and context.

4   Jordan Scott, "'The fact of my mouth': An Interview with Jordan Scott" by Deanna Fong, in this volume, 78.
5   The "ableist ear" is a prevailing habit of listening in which disabled speech and communication is not heard as worthy of attention or understanding. I model the concept of the ableist ear after Dylan Robinson's notion of the "tin ear" of hungry listening. The ableist ear accounts for the immediacy with which listeners dismiss the authority of disabled communicators and fail to recognize meanings and sensations communicated through modalities other than speech, or through dysfluent speech. The ableist ear does not refer to actual physiological differences in hearing but to the learned psychological and cultural ways of valuing certain sounds and communication modalities that are not "normal." This habit of listening arises from a culture of ableism that is essential to, and inextricable from, colonization and capitalism. Talila "TL" Lewis defines "ableism" as "a system that places value on people's bodies and minds based on societally constructed ideas of normality, intelligence, excellence, desirability, and productivity. These constructed ideas are deeply rooted in anti-Blackness, eugenics, misogyny, colonialism, imperialism and capitalism." See Talila A. Lewis, "Working Definition of Ableism," *Talila A. Lewis*, 1 January 2021, www.talilalewis.com/blog. Lewis describes how the system of ableism – that unevenly distributes worth and value to human lives – is used to pathologize and criminalize predominantly working-class, disabled, queer, trans, Black, Indigenous, and people of colour.
6   Alice Wong, "Ep. 100 Podcasting," *Disability Visibility Podcast* (The Disability Visibility Project, 2021), 00:22.
7   Alice Wong, "Diversifying Radio with Disabled Voices," in *Transom*, 2016, https://transom.org/2016/alice-wong/.
8   Caitlin Marshall, "Crippled Speech," *Postmodern Culture* 24, no. 3 (2014): n.p., www.pomoculture.org/2017/09/09/crippled-speech/.
9   Rosemarie Garland-Thomson quoted in Kelly Fritsch and Aimi Hamraie, "Crip Technoscience Manifesto," *Catalyst: Feminism, Theory, Technoscience* 5, no. 1 (2019): 7, https://catalystjournal.org/index.php/catalyst/article/view/29607. See also Fritsch and Hamraie, 10.
10 Alice Wong, "The (In)visibility of Disability," *The Vocal Fries: The Podcast About Linguistic Discrimination*, hosted by Carrie Gillon and Megan Figueroa, 7 October 2019, 21:42, https://radiopublic.com/the-vocal-fries-GOoXdO/s1!84f7b.

11 "Crip time" refers to the different approaches to time and pacing that disabled people inhabit. Alison Kafer writes that "rather than bend disabled bodies and minds to meet the clock, crip time bends the clock to meet disabled bodies and minds." See Kafer, *Feminist, Queer, Crip*, 27. Many say that listening to disabled speakers and communicators requires patience (it does!). But patience assumes an allegiance to normative, capitalist time; the listener chooses to be patient though they are always aware of the time "lost" waiting for voices and communications that take longer. Listening on crip time happens when the listener holds an understanding of time wherein "slow" does not have a negative connotation but may be valued as politically and rhetorically effective, or simply vital in order for knowledge to be shared.
12 Sara Ahmed, *The Cultural Politics of Emotion* (Edinburgh: Edinburgh University Press, 2004), 85.
13 Ibid., 86–7.
14 Ibid., 90.
15 Ibid., 87.
16 Jordan Scott discusses what he terms the "'regime of fluency'" which applies medical and therapeutic interventions to linguistic and vocal differences to produce normative communicators. See Scott, "'The fact of my mouth,'" in this volume, 79. Under the "regime of fluency," despite discomfort or pain arising from therapy and intervention, the individual must strive for standardization and normalcy, rather than listeners widening their conceptions of what "good" communication can be. This medical approach to speech and communication disability sees diverse communicators as a problem to be fixed, rather than recognizing how listening practices contribute to – and create – disability.
17 Robinson, *Hungry Listening*, 38.
18 See James Deaville, "The Moaning of (Un-)Life: Animacy, Muteness and Eugenics in Cinematic and Televisual Representation," *Journal of Interdisciplinary Voice Studies* 4, no. 2 (2019): 226; Charis St Pierre and Joshua St Pierre, "Governing the Voice: A Critical History of Speech-Language Pathology," *Foucault Studies*, no. 24 (2018): 166; and Nina Sun Eidsheim and Jessica Holmes, "'A Song for You': The Role of Voice in the Reification and De-naturalization of Ablebodiedness," *Journal of Interdisciplinary Voice Studies* 4, no. 2 (2019): 132.
19 St Pierre and St Pierre, "Governing the Voice," 157.
20 "Accessible Canada Act," Government of Canada, Justice Laws Website, 2019, https://laws-lois.justice.gc.ca/eng/acts/A-0.6/page-1.html.
21 Wong, "The (In)visibility of Disability," 36:20.
22 See Johnathan Sterne, "Ballad of the Dork-o-Phone: Towards a Crip Vocal Technoscience," *Journal of Interdisciplinary Voice Studies* 4, no. 2 (2019): 180; and Nina Sun Eidsheim, "Sound Studies Podcast: Nina Sun Eidsheim, 'The Race of Sound: Listening, Timbre and Vocality in African American Music,'" *New Books in Sound Studies*, Radio.com, 11:50, 19 February 2020, www.radio.com/

podcasts/new-books-in-sound-studies-21532/nina-sun-eidsheim-the-race-of-sound-listening-timbre-and-vocality-in-african-american-music-duke-up-2019-128555841.

23 See Deaville, "The Moaning of (Un-)Life," 226; and St Pierre and St Pierre, "Governing the Voice," 166.
24 Remi Yergeau, *Authoring Autism: On Rhetoric and Neurological Queerness* (Durham: Duke University Press, 2018), 10.
25 Ibid.
26 Nina Sun Eidsheim, *Race of Sound: Listening, Timbre and Vocality in African American Music* (Durham: Duke University Press, 2018), 9.
27 Eidsheim, "Sound Studies Podcast," 9:56.
28 Eidsheim, *Race of Sound*, 13.
29 Ibid.
30 Fritsch and Hamraie, "Crip Technoscience Manifesto," 12.
31 I focus on voice here because this section draws heavily from Eidsheim's work, but this conclusion applies across communication styles. A gesture, vocalization, or expression made by a communicator will be defined by the interpreter. Communication methods beyond speech often rely even more on the interdependence of communication; forming a relationship is a central component of understanding and relating.
32 See Jay Dolmage, *Disability Rhetoric* (Syracuse: Syracuse University Press, 2014); and Yergeau, *Authoring Autism* for more on disability rhetorics.
33 Eidsheim, *Race of Sound*, 25.
34 Ibid., 26.
35 Writer and organizer Leah Lakshmi Piepzna-Samarasinha informs us that "'Disability justice' is a term coined by the Black, brown, queer, and trans members of the original Disability Justice Collective, founded in 2005 by Patty Berne, Mia Mingus, Leroy Moore, Eli Clare, and Sebastian Margaret. Disabled queer and trans Black, Asian and white activists and artists, they dreamed up a movement building framework that would center the lives, needs, and organizing strategies of disabled queer and trans and/or Black and brown people marginalized from mainstream disability rights organizing's white-dominated, single-issue focus" (15). The framework foregrounds intersectionality and collective liberation. For more on this framework and movement, see Leah Lakshmi Piepzna-Samarasinha, *Care Work: Dreaming Disability Justice* (Vancouver: Arsenal Pulp Press, 2018); Mia Mingus, *Leaving Evidence* (blog); and Sins Invalid, "10 Principles of Disability Justice," 17 September 2015, www.sinsinvalid.org/blog/10-principles-of-disability-justice; and/or Sins Invalid, *Skin, Tooth, and Bone: The Basis of Movement is Our People* (Berkeley: Dancers' Group, 2016).
36 Alice Wong, "Ep. 82 Americans with Disabilities Act," *Disability Visibility Podcast*, The Disability Visibility Project, 2020, 23:05.

37 Mia Mingus, "Access Intimacy, Interdependence and Disability Justice," Leaving Evidence (website), 12 April 2017, n.p., https://leavingevidence.wordpress.com/2017/04/12/access-intimacy-interdependence-and-disability-justice/.
38 Mia Mingus, "Access Intimacy: The Missing Link," Leaving Evidence (website), 5 May 2011, n.p., https://leavingevidence.wordpress.com/2011/05/05/access-intimacy-the-missing-link/.
39 Fritsch and Hamraie, "Crip Technoscience Manifesto," 2.
40 Ibid., 10.
41 Anja Kanngieser, "The Last Disable Oracle," *Assembly for the Future*, 6 August 2020, 29:14, www.thethingswedidnext.org/assembly-for-the-future/.
42 Ibid., 29:17.
43 Mia Mingus, "Moving Toward the Ugly: A Politic Beyond Desirability," Leaving Evidence (website), 22 August 2011, n.p., https://leavingevidence.wordpress.com/2011/08/22/moving-toward-the-ugly-a-politic-beyond-desirability/.

5

"That in-between space"
An Interview with Oana Avasilichioaei

Deanna Fong
TRANSCRIBED BY DEANNA RADFORD AND DEANNA FONG

Deanna Fong: It's been a minute since we last spoke.

Oana Avasilichioaei: Yes, it has.

DF: Some things have happened between then and now.

OA: Yeah.

DF: So, to begin, would you mind telling me a little bit about what you're working on at the moment?

OA: I just returned from one week in Toronto, where we workshopped a one-hour, multimedia chamber opera, for which I wrote the libretto. Titled *Cells of Wind* and written mostly in English with some French and Romanian, it was commissioned and is being developed by FAWN Chamber Creative, a small company in Toronto, and the composer is Victoria-based Anna Höstman. She's amazing. She wrote a 90 per cent graphic score, so it's very compelling and demanding on the singers and instrumentalists because they have to make decisions and come up with certain sounds, textures, and ways of making music. The opera's premise is about surviving solitary confinement through the resilience of the mind and power of the imagination. It's inspired by the ordeal of Lena Constante, a Romanian artist who was a political prisoner and kept in solitary confinement for eight years, which is a mind-boggling amount of time. She survived it by developing a routine of writing in her mind several plays, thousands of verses of poetry, short stories, and novellas – mentally editing and perfecting the work over time.

Though inspired by Constante's experience, *Cells of Wind* is written out of and set in a contemporary Canadian context. Both the libretto and the score are very fragmented – there are many wisps of sound and splinters of presence/absence. Often phrases or even words are split between several singers. There is dialogue, but it's very fractured. It's about surviving an extreme place of deprivation, a space that's meant to break a person, deny their personhood. So how does one hang on to a sense of themselves? Not an easy topic to work with. All the people involved are amazing, bringing their individual artistry to a collaborative endeavour and going through their own processes of how to tackle such a challenging subject matter.

DF: It sounds incredible. Especially because it has such a fulsome cast of collaborators, which is interesting in that it's representing the idea of solitary confinement – perhaps almost counterintuitively – through a whole host of people.

OA: Yes, in writing the libretto, it was important for me to have a closer focus on one individual, while also showing that this is one among many living through such detrimental experiences. During the week of the workshop, FAWN also organized a panel discussion with two experts in this area from the University of Toronto, Dr Kelly Hannah-Moffat and Dr Paula Maurutto. Canada, by the way, does not officially use the term "solitary confinement" but rather other euphemisms such "administrative segregation," "quiet time," or "therapeutic observation."

DF: No.

OA: Yes. Dr Hannah-Moffat talked about the current conditions in Canada – because solitary confinement is still actively used today – and it was amazing to me how similar the situation is to the one in 1950s Romania that initially inspired the opera. There's basically no difference. It's sad and frightening.

DF: It seems like the rehearsal space was an intense period of collaboration and collective attunement because you were working through different compositional, practical, and technical aspects of the project. I wanted to ask you what it's been like working across different media in this context, for one, and then different disciplines: writing, music, visual art – you mentioned there is a video component as well. What is this process like, and how do you get in tune with all of the different people who you're working with on this project?

OA: I've learned a lot. It's been a really eye-opening experience for me. I wrote most of the libretto before Anna started writing the music, though I was in conversation with her from very early on, so there was a sense of common endeavour from the start. Once she started composing the music, I also made adjustments based on what she was doing. Yet I was always writing something that was only going to be a very small part of a much larger whole, without yet knowing what that whole would be. It had to be something that had openings or gaps in which the other components – the music, staging, lighting, costumes, etc. – could fit and grow, yet also provide enough direction or basis for those elements. I've never worked on anything quite like this before. When I work on my own performances, for example, I'm creating them in their totality – the sound, which objects I choose to interpret, which texts I write, or how they will behave in the space or in my voice. With the opera, on the other hand, I feel that only now, after this week of hearing how it could sound, how it could exist in people's bodies, and what space is being created, that I am beginning to have an experience of the whole. And no doubt, we are going to make more changes and adjustments based on this experience.

DF: This reminds me of my interview with Tracie Morris in this collection, who's done a lot of collaborative cross-disciplinary work as well, that she was working with a choreographer and that that relationship was about tuning into somebody else's particular expressive vocabulary. Thinking, for example, "I'm a poet. I use words." But as a choreographer perhaps your vocabulary is the gesture. Or the musical fugue for a composer.[1] Did you find you had to engage a different part of your "listening brain" as a poet to get into those different vocabularies?

OA: Certainly. It's so intriguing. I've learned so much about musical, vocal, visual vocabularies through this process, but also about the types of communication, interpretation, transference, translation that is possible (and sometimes not possible) between these different vocabularies.

DF: So, following on this idea of translation, you've done quite a lot of translation work in poetry, and it sounds like this current work is a form of translation as well. Are there similarities or differences in how those two kinds of translations take place for you?

OA: You mean, do I take certain ideas from translation and use them in composition?

DF: Yeah. Broadly, I guess. [Laughs]

OA: Absolutely. One aspect that comes to mind right away is that I think of translation as a passage between two or more things, two or more languages. But I'm more interested in that passage – that in-between space – rather than the end points. I work a lot with these in-between spaces in my own work – the space that can exist between denotative sense and noise or non-sense, for example. I've also worked with applying the syntax, grammar rules, or turns of phrase of another language to English so that they estrange the English in certain ways. For instance, by using French grammar as the underpinnings of an English phrase, I can create a different type of phrase. I've also worked with translingual texts that have more than one language in them simultaneously. I'm interested in the friction, tension, and potential opening that happens when one places fragments of different languages side by side and gives them equal weight. Translation also necessarily implies a dialogue with an other or others and thus a multiplicity or diversity of voices and perspectives. Multiplicity, diversity, and simultaneity are ideas I work a lot with in my compositions.

DF: I love what you said about it not being the end destination of representing one language in the other, but the strangeness of the passage between. I often think about things like – as an anglophone speaker of French – what does the mistake of using the wrong gendered article for a noun sound like to a French speaker's ear? I can't know that; there's no equivalent in English. Or, my family speaks Cantonese, for example, so what does the mistake of using the wrong intonation for a word sound like? You could almost break your brain trying to find equivalents of what that mispronunciation would sound like in English. So, I think that's an interesting project, trying to keep some of that strangeness and impasse between languages.

OA: Definitely.

DF: With that in mind, I was wondering if there's something about working in language, or poetry in particular, that lends itself to this idea of impasse or resistance, that has something to do precisely with its inexactitude or liminality.

OA: I think that poetry can be a space that intensely investigates how language works or breaks down – how it means or resists simplicity, how it forms thought and, through that, invents ways of thinking. It can be a place that produces new and diverse forms – aesthetic, epistemological, linguistic. In situations of domination, oppression, or autocratic modes of being, language and modes of thinking are pared down, minimized, simplified, reduced to a singularity. There is one way of thinking, one way of saying something. In contrast, poetry can be a space that resists this oneness because it's constantly trying to invent other modes of thinking and working with language.

The other thing I would say is that poetry seems to demand more of readers and listeners and through this, offers them more agency. Poetry demands the reader's participation and involvement in constructing meaning, not just absorbing meaning, and is therefore more active. It's hard to be passive when looking at a page of poetry because you have to actively figure out how you make your own meaning out of the text on the page, how you move through that text. This requirement of participation, this immersion, is a form of resistance because it denies passivity and demands individual and diverse contribution.

DF: Also, there is language in poetry that makes us hold multiple and sometimes contradictory things together in our minds at the same time. I'm thinking of your book *Eight Track* and having to hold the different meanings of the word "track" together – an audio track, surveillance in the verb "tracking," and the traces left by an animal as tracks, footprints. We must think of all those things simultaneously every time we see that word.

OA: Exactly. Poetry has the potential to assemble contrasting or opposing signs, which can be threatening, benevolent, harmless, or unruly, and by putting them together creates its own codification, while at the same time offering a few clues to the reader/listener of how to go through this landscape of language and undertake their own decoding of it. Poetry can provide an environment where things that come from diverse points of view are made to exist in the same space-time.

DF: Or "cell," for that matter! [Laughs]

OA: Or cell. Exactly.

DF: In that vein, I wanted to ask you about your recent sound performance piece, "Operator," [https://soundcloud.com/oanalab/operator] which puts two poems from *Eight Track*, "The Drone Operator" and "Drone Operators," in contact. In the performance, we get the simultaneity of the two sides together. Can we think of the two poems as having a similar sort of twinned or simultaneous dynamic?

OA: Yes, definitely. There is much reverberation or doubling throughout *Eight Track* and beyond it – not just across pieces, but also across form or genre. In all the research and interview reading I did on military drone operators, two approaches to the job seemed to emerge. The soldiers either found the disembodied position of doing harm at a great distance ethically and psychologically untenable and it burned them out, or they approached the situation as a video game made extra "cool" by the fact that it's real.

Though I don't usually like to work with dichotomies [laughs], this dual approach led me to various kinds of doublings, including two different voicings of this dynamic: one being my writing and the other, my curating or editing of found material. The poem "Drone Operators" is distilled from a transcript of a drone strike, which is hundreds of pages long, while my piece is only six. Besides singling out certain moments, I was also fascinated by the transcript's initial editing as it had many instances that were redacted, deleted, marked classified, or made "incoherent" by static. The transcript had much material interference, so I made the interference into a voice that can "say" something about certain moments.

DF: Where I think the reading mind tends to skip over the cues of redaction as a stage direction, the audio really draws attention to the fact that what we receive as the transcript is heavily redacted and layered with uncertainty.

OA: Yes. And behind the redaction is decision-making and intentionality. Drone operators don't make the decision to strike; they only make the decision to follow command, which for a soldier is a priori. So, it seemed to me that these bits of interferences and cues of redacted moments are actually where the decision-making is happening.

DF: In its absence, it speaks volumes.

OA: Exactly.

DF: Which the performance really highlights in a very powerful way. Furthermore, in relation "The Drone Operator," we have "the subject" who is the subject of the poem. At times we read the subject as a subject – because this particular subject has a body, stretches, moves, feels tedium, all these sorts of physical things. But on the other hand, the subject, as you describe, is a conduit for executing a command. And so, there's a real tension in this poem, and I think elsewhere in the book also, between subjects as singular, specific, embodied and this kind of universal subject of the state. How do you feel these two subjects interact in this poem? Or in the work more generally?

OA: I think maybe they always coexist. I feel like any individual subject is often more than one subject simultaneously: an embodied subject, a subject of the state, a commanded subject, a subject with agency, without agency. Some of these positions may be stronger than others at any one time, but they coexist and necessarily interact with one another. At times they may be at odds, at times in sync, at times in a kind of reverberation. Yet it's not their adversarial or complementary stance that makes them productive but the subject's awareness of what these positions may be at any one time and how they may be affecting and producing that particular moment. The idea of agency – and the lack thereof – is a key aspect the book. Especially what makes agency possible. Because it's very easy not to have agency. There are many factors in our everyday lives, in the world through which we live, that take agency away from bodies, from all of us. And so I'm constantly questioning: Where to find agency? How to find agency? How to recognize agency? Because it's actually even difficult to see it at times.

DF: So, to follow up on that question, because you work across media in so many of your works, we've talked about what poetic language allows us to do with a certain aptitude – what it does well – but I wondered where language fails, and where other media might be more capable vehicles. I don't want to suggest that it's because of a failing of language that we turn to these other modes of representation – there are different facets of understanding that different media bring to the fore. But what do other media bring out of a topic that you might be investigating?

OA: One aspect that functions very differently between something that exists as static text on the page and something that exists in live or recorded sound is time. The experience of time is significantly different in performance than in the printed page. For example, when listening to a piece of sound, in any one moment you can grasp the moment but not the previous moments or the ones to come; you have to remember or hold the previous moments in your body, in your mind, and maybe even simultaneously imagine or anticipate the ones to come. Any one moment is made up of intense nowness or presence and also total absence. Furthermore, depending on how the performance or sound piece slows something down or speeds something up, creates quieter or louder moments, it affects the quality of how you experience time as a listener or viewer: it can feel fast or slow or endless.

When looking at a piece of text, however, even though you might read the text linearly, you also have the possibility to look at it in its totality (within limits of course), to take it all in at once, to backtrack and reread something or to skip ahead. So all this is interesting to me: exploring how we feel time depending on the media. Other aspects that are harder to represent in writing, yet are very much part of language, are tonality, accent, and volume. I could take the same line and say it five different ways and it slightly changes the meaning. For example, "*What* are you talking about?" and "What are *you* talking about?" are slightly different.

DF: Imagine how we're going to transcribe this interview! [Laughs]

OA: Exactly. But all these are worth exploring, and I'm trying to experiment with and discover ways of rendering tonality or volume, for instance, on the inscribed page. It's been done typographically, of course, indicating loudness through larger, bold type and quieter moments through grey type, for example, but that's pretty basic. I'm trying to think beyond that.

DF: Yeah, it doesn't give us much. I always think about the closed captioning sound cues like, [whispering softly] or [intense music playing]. They're always so interpretive and imprecise. I guess it gives some indication – or maybe gives some interpretation that another auditor wouldn't have read into it.

The other thing that the first part of your answer made me think of is Fanny Howe's essay on "Bewilderment" where she says, "There is literally no way to express two actions occurring simultaneously in language,"[2] and that being a huge problem with the temporality of it, is that you're locked into this sequentiality.

OA: Whereas you can do that in other media, you can certainly express two or more diverse actions simultaneously, and this is something I like to work with a lot. Time-based media also "perform" language differently and therefore encourage varied types of embodiments. It's interesting how in theatre, for example, no one looks at the text of a play and thinks, "That's THE play." [Laughter] That's just one version of the play, and many interpretations or performances of the play are possible. No one thinks there is only one way of interpreting that textual material. Yet it's curious how in other genres, like poetry, we've decided that there's only one way. You have to give this sympathetic, clear reading of the text!

DF: You give a nice frame about the origin of its composition.

OA: And then you enunciate it! And then you go to the next one. That's the way to do it. Why is that? [Laughter] That's one way to do it, and I'm not saying that it's an invalid way, but only that it's one way.

DF: And it shouldn't be the default way, necessarily. Because I think poetry demands this multitudinous kind of reading.

OA: Yes. My reading experience of a page is very layered: not just what the lines say, but how they are assembled; how they look on the page; what the space is enacting; what has come on the previous pages; how the words accumulate across the pages – they all come into play. The silent reading experience of a poem is multilayered, so it seems that one is flattening and singularizing this experience by doing a basic enunciation of it.

DF: There's one question I want to make sure that I ask you because it's very important to me. It's regarding your note on "Trackscapes," the aerial photographs of the Nasca Lines in Peru that appear in *Eight Track*. There you write, "In adding my voice/eye to those who have worked from this desert book" – that is, the Nasca Lines – "my intent is not to tell or document, for their story is not mine to tell."

This brings me to a question that came up in my interview with Jordan Scott, when we discussed his project *Lanterns at Guantánamo*, where he was allowed to tour the Guantánamo detention facility as a poet – not as a journalist, as a poet – and produce work out of that encounter.

One of the things his work thematized is how that space is so heavily redacted, much like the drone strike transcript. My question is: how do we feel alongside someone else's body, someone else's pain when that pain is not ours? Or especially if that person's body is removed from us or absent so as is the case with the detainees at Guantánamo, as is the case with the Nasca, as is the case perhaps with the asylum seeker in your radio drama, "On Origins," too. What is an ethical way to exist alongside?

OA: I think one of the starting points is being aware of one's own position vis-à-vis the others' bodies, pain, or history, and how one's own perspective might actually be shaping that pain, body, or history. I think of it as listening and being present with that listening. Present with the other in whatever capacity is possible, present with their agency or struggles around it, not just your own. Obviously, different kinds of presences are possible across time or spaces. In terms of the Nasca Lines, which were made roughly between 100 BCE and 700 CE, not only am I at an enormous time remove from their makers, but they exist as a palimpsest with multiple histories since they were made by different peoples over centuries. So, there is an attempt not to speak for but alongside them. Maybe not even speak, but bear presence with. Even though one's understanding of any situation, any moment, will always remain partial regardless of one's proximity or distance to it, this doesn't mean that one shouldn't try to seek out as many perspectives or voices (both form the inside and outside) on the situation in order to deepen one's understanding of it; it's a process, not an endgame.

DF: Did photography seem like a more apt medium to capture your presence alongside?

OA: Yes. Many meanings of "track" are negative, yet I see these markings as a positive kind of track-making, so I really wanted to attend to them in some way from fairly early on in the project. Initially I thought it would take the shape of writing, and I did much research and reading on the subject, yet I kept finding that they are not something I can speak. All I could do is bring my eye – the abstract framing of my "I" – on these landshapes.

DF: I'll finish with one final question. I know you've worked collaboratively with lots of folks in Montreal and elsewhere, so I wanted to know who you consider your community for your practice and how that community shapes your work.

OA: My community changes over time and is very amorphous and not localized to a specific place, working language, or art form. I also consider part of "my community" people I interact with directly, such as Moina Pam Dick et al., Erín Moure, Chantal Neveu, Vida Simon, Kaie Kellough, Mark Goldstein, Carla Harryman, Betsy Warland, Margaret Christakos, Andrew Forster, and others, and those whose ideas and ways of being or thinking I access through books, artworks, performances, such as Caroline Bergvall, John Cage, Wolfgang Tillmans, Agnes Martin, Jacques Derrida, Christof Migone, Iannis Xenakis, Helen Mirra, and many more. It's completely necessary to my thinking and work to have these minds in my practice because I learn from them; I'm challenged by them; I'm inspired by them. I can't remain complacent because of them. I think it's important to be challenged in our views and thinking. Of course, we surround ourselves with somewhat like-minded people and that's good. But it's also important to have dissenting views. I might think a certain way about a certain thing, but sometimes I might reach that thinking too quickly. So, it's important to have others who challenge me: "Do I think that? Why do I think that?" Also, people working in other art forms have always been super important to me, not necessarily because I desire to work in that form, but because by seeing how they're working in their painting or photography practice and approaching the materials, I learn about how I might approach materials in sound or word.

AN INTERVIEW with OANA AVASILICHIOAEI

NOTES

1 Tracie Morris, "'It doesn't mean anything except talking': An Interview with Tracie Morris" by Cole Mash and Deanna Fong, in this volume, 137.
2 Fanny Howe, "Bewilderment," Virginia G. Piper Center for Creative Writing, 1998, www.asu.edu/pipercwcenter/how2journal/archive/online_archive/v1_1_1999/fhbewild.html.

6

New Forms of Digital, Temporal, and Auditory Poiesis

prOphecy sun and Reese Muntean

Introduction

Many contemporary artists have investigated the resonance and/or the stillness of sound by creating new forms of technological, corporeal, cultural, and methodological engagements and aesthetic encounters. Over the last century, our world has become louder, and sound has become more important in our experiences. We are more aware of noise polluting our environments. Jim Drobnick deems this phenomenon as the sonic turn, whereby sound is established as a cultural marker or perceptual driver of contemporary reality.[1] We mention this to highlight how such a turn has opened up avenues for artists, designers, scientists, scholars, and theorists to explore auditory stimuli with telecommunication systems; in particular, how digital and spatial tools can extend our hearing, gaze, and perception beyond.[2]

Soundwalks are one example of this exploration, having developed out of the necessity to understand and grapple with levels of sound that fill our everyday life.[3] In the 1970s, composer R. Murray Schafer founded the World Soundscape Project to study the relationship between people and their environments. In this project, Schafer and colleagues Barry Truax, Hildegard Westerkamp, Bruce Davis, and Peter Huse worked together to develop and deepen an ecological understanding of, and perspectives on, the impact of sound. The legacy of this work is diverse and still

NEW FORMS of DIGITAL, TEMPORAL, and AUDITORY POIESIS

FIGURE 6.1 • prOphecy sun and Mireille Rosner, *A Small Piece of Sky*, 2015 (Courtesy of Reese Muntean)

practised fervently today. For example, Vancouver New Music, a non-profit organization, hosts regular creative programs that explore new ways of engagement with urban and rural environments through sound. Collaborative makers Janet Cardiff and Georges Bures Miller's immersive piece *The Murder of Crows* (2007) combines sound composition with sculptural elements, ephemera, objects, and installation. In an interview with Deanna Fong, artist Oana Avasilichioaei similarly articulates the impacts that sound, images, and technology have on her practice and how working through, across, and in-between disciplines allows for her to see and hear differently.[4]

Soundwalks, part of research-creation's expansion of scholarly/artistic practice and output, refer to self-guided or guided walks or series of listening exercises that focus on our relationship to the environment.[5] They are complex focus points where multiple aural ecologies intermix. Exposing our ears to sound in such a listening excursion can impact how we behave and how we understand our interactions with the physical

FIGURES 6.2–6.7 • prOphecy sun and Mireille Rosner, *A Small Piece of Sky*, 2015 (Performance photos courtesy of Reese Muntean)

environment and other species.⁶ We leave physical and auditory traces every time we move or walk. These traces not only affect those around us in ways that are sometimes unavoidable but also in ways we could mitigate if we consciously recognize the impacts our spatio-temporal practices have on others and if we are more thoughtful in our encounters.⁷ Soundwalks are an opportunity to tune into these impacts of our presence on the landscape and adjust our behaviours in ways that consider and decentre the human, aligning the practice with posthumanist notions concerned with multispecies entanglements and ecosystems of relations, rather than foregrounding human activity.⁸

This chapter builds on these ideas and presents a mediated soundwalk as an extension of earlier artworks such as *Remarkable Concussions* (2011) and *Send and Receive* (2015), which explore immersive ways of working with sound, movement, inflatables, and site-specificity. In *A Small Piece of Sky* (2015), we present a durational, site-specific, interdisciplinary piece that was created for Dance in Vancouver's *Choreography Walk*. The walk featured seven distinct performances that were created in response to the everyday sounds and rhythmic movements of the city. The project goals were to create a series of performative interventions and re-shufflings, which would elicit environmental and sensory engagement beyond the limbs, and to experience the world from multiple vantage points.⁹ The following pages illustrate the complex ways that we explored sound through creative making, choreographic scores, performance documentation. They present new vantage points that open up possibilities that do not privilege bodies, materials, or other elements over another. This symbiotic exchange between us and communal relations provided a deeper engagement and level of listening poiesis.

We understand poiesis in the scholarly tradition in relation to the sensory aesthetics of contemporary artmaking with conceptual and empirical implications.¹⁰ We articulate poiesis as more expansive and equate it to sensorial possibilities, entangled in the process and production of immersive sound and performative art practices.¹¹ This includes an openness to wonder and wander in the landscape, and to listen, feel, and experience inter-material engagements, beyond, through, and with technology and our bodies. We argue that poiesis is a state of balance, wherein the borders of human imagination are expanded in such a way that connects past, present, and future experiences through bodily interactions and sonic elements, which in turn creates transformative encounters with technology, space, and environment.

The Artwork: *A Small Piece of Sky*

Traditionally, soundwalks are an auditory experience. *A Small Piece of Sky* (2015) is a contemporary interpretation of a soundwalk because it focuses on listening to the environment and accentuating the physical, visual, and embodied experiences of the practice; here the sensory engagements are expanded to include ears, eyes, and body. Situated on the traditional, ancestral and unceded territory of the Sḵwx̱wú7mesh (Squamish), and Səl̓ílwətaʔ/Selilwitulh (Tsleil-Waututh), and xʷməθkʷəy̓əm (Musqueam) Nations, *A Small Piece of Sky* (2015) is an interdisciplinary project created by artists prOphecy sun and Mireille Rosner. The piece weaves together multilayered choreography, live performance, larger-than-life inflatable forms, and environmental soundscape composition. The piece was curated by dancer Justine Chambers for Dance in Vancouver's *Choreography Walk* in 2015. The performance took place on 19 and 21 November 2015 and was led by prOphecy sun, Mireille Rosner, and dancers Darcy McMurray and Rob Leveroos.

Over two days, the piece was performed in two-hour segments alongside Creekside Park next to Science World, as well as the SkyTrain station and other challenging architectural structures. Chambers led audiences in a silent walk along Vancouver's streets, through alleyways, basketball courts, next to buildings and other social sites. The participants in the soundwalk were encouraged to listen, watch, and be present as they moved for two and a half hours, without stopping, through the landscape. When Chambers commissioned these works, she requested responses to specific locations. We were drawn to the location near Science World because of the way bodies and technologies merged at this intersection of space and time in this particular urban context. In our proposal to Chambers, we outlined how our project would "design the performance

FIGURE 6.8 • pr0phecy sun and Mireille Rosner, *A Small Piece of Sky*, 2015 (Performance photo courtesy of Reese Muntean)

to direct and play with the audience's sensorial experience so as to invite their gaze, ear, and travel flow."[12]

These guiding principles were the seed to our investigations at Creekside Park. Physically, Creekside Park is situated on the east side of False Creek (see figs 6.9 and 6.10). Science World, a science and technology centre built for Expo '86, is housed in a large geodesic dome and sits at the south end of the park. The Georgia Viaduct is visible just to the north of the park. The overpass, which displaced the Black community of Hogan's Alley during its construction in the early 1970s, shuttles vehicle traffic from Vancouver's downtown. The busy Quebec Street runs along the east side of the park, with the rapid transit SkyTrain station and the Pacific Central Station bus and rail depot just beyond. All the while, the elevated rail of the SkyTrain crosses overhead. These physical locations shape the movements of everyday life in the city, with commuters

NEW FORMS of DIGITAL, TEMPORAL, and AUDITORY POIESIS

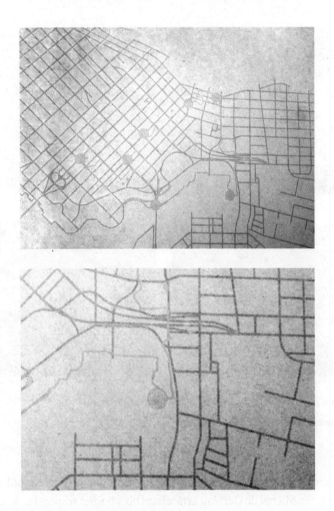

FIGURES 6.9 AND 6.10 • *Choreography Walk* map
(Sketches courtesy of Deanna Peters and Erick Villagomez)

migrating to work, school, and other leisure activities, and the historical context of the location speaks to larger forced migrations of Black and Indigenous communities. Science World, too, is a visible reminder of the impact of technology on the environment and in daily activity.

The seven performances in *Choreography Walk* (2015) offered walking participants an opportunity to reconsider their movements and

FIGURES 6.11 AND 6.12 • prOphecy sun and Mireille Rosner, *A Small Piece of Sky*, 2015 (Performance photos courtesy of Reese Muntean)

experiences through these locations (see figs 6.9 and 6.10). Scholar and philosopher Michel de Certeau articulates how bodies respond to locations in meditative ways, and how they have the power to reshape, reform, and create new patterns in space.[13] Hildegard Westerkamp similarly outlines this further through seminal notions on the intermixing of aural ecologies and recognizing the unsettling impact of walks through urban landscapes.[14]

In *A Small Piece of Sky* (2015), we continuously renegotiated and constructed our relationships with the space, while listening and blending our bodies to the terrain. For example, the rattle of the SkyTrain periodically passing overhead would punctuate the passing of time, or as the light changed at the intersection of Quebec Street and Terminal

Avenue, the repeating chorus of revving engines, tires on pavement, and feet walking footsteps across the crosswalk would begin again. Further, other ambient textural tones from the crinkling of the orbs' plastic moving in the grass or being lifted, and sounds such as airplanes soaring, geese calling, crows cawing, birds chirping, dogs barking in the park, children screaming on the playground, passersby in conversation, and other rhythmic sonic impressions would crescendo and decrescendo, and deepen our engagement with the cityscape. In this way, we suggest that temporal spaces present moments of discovery and produce new knowledge in our bodies, while changing our relationship to the environments that we move through. Thus, soundwalks combine the knowing and the feeling gained from moving through space with sound as it is experienced and expressed through the body.

Score 6.1

A Small Piece of Sky, 2015, *Performance Score, Rules and Intentions* (Courtesy of prOphecy sun and Mireille Rosner)

All the orbs are our collective responsibility
We keep them in bounds and reasonably free from harm
We facilitate their material properties and in this way lend them
    as much freedom of expression as possible
Our actions bring out their expression: their fullest range of sound
    and movement, aside from harmful expressions
If harm comes, we deal with it as openly and practically as possible
We listen with our whole body, the orbs rest
We follow and keep pace, the orbs roll in the wind
We use our whole body to redirect
We roll the orbs in order to travel them somewhere
We toss and throw, they shiver and mobilize, morphing shape

> SCORE 6.1, CONTINUED
>
> We stack them together to give ourselves a new perspective
> We consider the bird's-eye view whenever possible
> We never adopt a single orb
> We never force or drag
> The wind is our partner
> The wind animates
> The wind is not in our control
> The wind causes behaviours in the orbs
> We map the wind's influence on our playing field

When we walk through a landscape, we discover power dynamics in our relationships with the Earth that change our interactions with our surroundings.[15]

Digital devices also played an important role in making and documenting the artwork. We used a variety of tools, apparatuses, and handheld devices to amplify and emote our experiences and capture aspects of the sensorial exchanges. Increasingly used as extensions of ourselves, technologies capture daily rhythms and store memories of these events. This rise of technological apparatuses and devices has provided artists with tools that extend and teleport their reach beyond the body.[16]

We used smartphone cameras, digital photography, walkie-talkies, video and sound apps as tools to capture the durational process of making the work. Creekside Park provided challenging architecture and physical challenges for the performance and thus walkie-talkies were used as devices to communicate across distance. This tool was especially important in conveying the beginning, middle, and end of the performance as multiple performers were moving through various configurations and activities. During the rehearsals, we used three smartphones and tripods as a way to document the sound of the location, the visual progression of our movement, and the variation of weather and other environmental factors. This approach enabled us to understand our imprint on the location, capturing an array of anthropophagic (human), geophonic (non-biological, e.g., wind), and biophonic (natural) sounds with smartphones, which were then amplified in post-production.

Building on the goals of the *Choreography Walk* overall, *A Small Piece of Sky* (2015) incorporated choreographic scores as a way to align our movement and response patterns and generate a sensorial exchange, engaging in a dance between bodies, frequencies, and environment. Like video or photo documentation, which can elicit a visceral response, performance scores can enable a collective rhythm with a work and can be used as a tactic or strategy for performers to jell and connect with one another. Arguably, ephemera and creative propositions such as notes and sketches allow for a deeper engagement with the material conveyed, and sharing research processes has the potential to generate new artistic and scholarly output.[17]

This project included a combination of *Rules and Intentions* and two scores: *Performance Score 1* and *Performance Score 2* (see scores 6.1–6.3), which outline the intentions and guiding principles on how to carry out sequences of throwing, pushing, gliding, and co-constructing improvised shapes and how to listen and give space for sounds to emerge alongside and with the inflatable orbs (see fig. 6.13). For example, "all the orbs are our collective responsibility" and "our actions bring out their expression: their fullest range of sound and movement" (*Rules and Intentions* 2015). The scores were generated from our rehearsal experiences, and they created an adaptable framework for the performance itself.

Now, in this academic writing, the scores serve as an example of the concrete ways this work engaged with our bodies, the audience, responding to the environmental sounds, and urban surroundings through the soundwalk (see figs 6.1–6.12). Rather than improvising the entire performance or making it up on the spot, we created the scores to connect ourselves to the rhythmic sounds and architectural elements and to align our movement with the ebbs and flows of the location. These scores, although unseen by members of the audience, also helped shape the performance and the collaborations between artists, objects,

prOphecy sun AND REESE MUNTEAN

Score 6.2

A Small Piece of Sky, 2015, Performance Score 1
(Courtesy of prOphecy sun and Mireille Rosner)

Collective herding – keep them together as a group, and in bounds
Collective tossing – working together to form a rhythm
Collective rest – find rest, either supporting orb in stillness (using whole body), or moving away from still orb, and contemplating it
Collective building – find way to stack orbs, keeping one on top of another

- step back and witness when possible, but don't step out of bounds
- use whole body to redirect, don't grab, and be specific about intervening in orb's trajectory

Score 6.3

A Small Piece of Sky, 2015, Performance Score 2
(Courtesy of prOphecy sun and Mireille Rosner)

As a collective, keep the orbs in bounds and reasonably free from harm
Allow the orbs to be moved by the wind and intervene only when necessary
Notice how the wind creates a map of orb activity
When the wind has compelled most of them to push against the edge of the field, herd the orbs toward the designated centre (offset by the wind)
Roll the orbs, using whatever body parts are most efficient, to travel them

NEW FORMS of DIGITAL, TEMPORAL, and AUDITORY POIESIS

SCORE 6.3, CONTINUED

Never adopt a single orb
Change places whenever possible, cross paths, share responsibility
Work efficiently with your energy
When the orbs are at rest, watch and wait
Notice the patterns you create - high/low, near/far - with the others and the orbs
Be aware with all your senses, keeping your cool
Whenever you can, put a safe distance between yourself and the orbs
When the wind conditions are right, stack the orbs
Humans can buttress the construction if necessary
Notice when you are visible to the others, and when you are not
Consider the bird's-eye view whenever possible
Do not grab their corners or toss them
Repair any tears immediately with packing tape - work with another person if necessary

- designate gestures for herding, resting, stacking
- designate the offset centre
- designate beginning and end

sounds, and the landscape. Their importance is further highlighted through photographic documentation, which highlights the interwoven exchanges and textual feel of the compositions (see figs 6.1–6.13). For example, the images depict the wind lifting orbs out of our hands, the alignment of bodies moving in co-construction flows, and the formations of stacked orbs, which were ever-changing and adjusting in response to the environmental elements (figs 6.11 and 6.12). Other sounds appeared through chanceful encounters with other bodies walking along the park and came out of moving with the shapes in the landscape.

FIGURE 6.13 • prOphecy sun and Mireille Rosner, *A Small Piece of Sky*, 2015 (Process photo courtesy of Reese Muntean)

The artistic notes and scores presented here are important forms of evidence about the entanglement of the landscape alongside experiences walking and sensing with, and through, the body. They serve as reminders of the priority of understanding and attending to our interactions with the environment – the physical, emotional, and auditory aspects of these interactions – and recognizing the traces we leave behind. We argue that the scores are artifacts of the experiential walk and physical artifacts of the experience. In particular, the scores make an important contribution to understanding the impact of soundwalks in contemporary practice to the arts and humanities.[18] For example, these documents further offer a lens to understand the artistic process and temporal nature of performance. In collecting and revisiting the documentation, we can continue to reflect on our impacts, interactions, and approaches to collective making and site-specificity. Collectively, the scores and documentation demonstrate how attending to various elements like sound, movement, images, and bodily relationships can shift the vantage points – from a place of listening to an active place of emergent transformative encounters with the environment. Further, this layering and multimodal approach mobilize and enliven sensory engagement beyond the body. For instance, the sounds, visuals, movement score, and location do not privilege one element over another, and they become a series of unconscious and conscious choreographies of breath, sound, and movement, which are activated, invigorated, and mingled in bodily expressions that meld personal and public spheres.

Conclusion

Soundwalks have the power to entice, encourage, lift, and shift our understanding of a location. Rather than embodying one measurable form, sensation, sound, or rhythm, we set constraints and parameters with the performance scores that enabled listening with, through, and in between the noise. For instance, a succession of interdependent immaterial/material instances such as the wind, crows and people, movement and sounds traversing. Each element, while unique and present, coalesced in undeniable and unrepeatable ways, reminding us of the importance of being present and open to orchestrated life currents and flows. The scores mobilized a deeper attachment with and through the ecologies at Creekside Park. The exercises, while intentional, were communicated from a poietic perspective, which takes up a multiplicity of unfoldings. Poiesis, thus considered, is a contemporaneous, continually expansive process, full of balanced, kinesthetic engagements, alongside environmental elements, and sonic tonalities, which are shaped by invisible sensorial dimensionalities – between the body, landscape, and other feeling, expressive forms.

Soundwalks also introduce new ways of creative engagement and opportunities to gain insight that can expand notions of subjectivity, especially within our current complex and technologically mediated environments. Compared to other contemporary soundwalks which typically focus on the auditory resonance of the voice and historical narratives of a location, *A Small Piece of Sky* explores how the body mediates, privileges, or accepts sensorial frequencies through and in between social and geographical space. As the piece was developed, our bodies became collaborative tools to extend our experiences beyond technological systems of digital capture. The performance dynamically emerged in felt time, like a temporal collage, in response to, and with, the location and many unseen encounters – where presence and place resonated in a continuous loop of negotiation and mediated communal relationships. Poietic approaches, thus articulated, are transcorporeal, multisensory, entangled, emergent, enacted, and exchanged in mobilizing processes of listening, feeling, and experiencing within and across landscapes.

NOTES

1 See Jim Drobnick, ed., *Aural Cultures* (Toronto: YYZ Books, 2004); and Caleb Kelly, ed., *Sound: Documents of Contemporary Art* (Cambridge, MA: MIT Press, 2011).
2 See Roy Ascott, *Telematic Embrace: Visionary Theories of Art, Technology, and Consciousness* (Berkeley: University of California Press, 2007).
3 See R. Murray Schafer, *The Soundscape: Our Sonic Environment and the Tuning of the World* (New York: Simon & Schuster, 1993); and Hildegard Westerkamp, "Soundwalking," *Sound Heritage* 3, no. 4 (1974).
4 Oana Avasilichioaei, "'That in-between space': An Interview with Oana Avasilichioaei" by Deanna Fong, in this volume, 108.
5 See Stephanie Springgay and Sarah E. Truman, "On the Need for Methods Beyond Proceduralism: Speculative Middles, (In)Tensions, and Response-Ability in Research," *Qualitative Inquiry* 24, no. 3 (2018): 203–14.
6 See Hildegard Westerkamp, "The Practice of Listening in Unsettled Times," keynote address in proceedings of *Invisible Places 2017: Sound Urbanism and Sense of Place*, São Miguel Island, Azores, Portugal, 7–9 April 2017, 29–45; and Westerkamp, "Soundwalking," 1974.
7 Frauke Behrendt, "Cycling the Smart and Sustainable City: Analyzing EC Policy Documents on the Internet of Things, Mobility and Transport, and Smart Cities," in *Sustainability* 11.3 (2019): 763.
8 See Francesca Ferrando, "Posthumanism, Transhumanism, Antihumanism, Metahumanism, and New Materialisms," *Existenz* 8, no. 2 (2013): 26–32.
9 See Justine. A. Chambers, "Choreography Walk @ Dance In Vancouver," Justine A. Chambers (website), 1 November 2015, https://justineachambers.com/2015/11/01/choreography-walk/.

10 See Derek H. Whitehead, "Poiesis and Art-Making: A Way of Letting-be," *Contemporary Aesthetics* 1, no. 1 (2003), 5.
11 See Seán Street, *The Memory of Sound: Preserving the Sonic Past* (New York: Routledge, 2014).
12 Chambers, "Choreography Walk," n.p.
13 See Michel de Certeau, *The Practice of Everyday Life*, trans. Steven Rendall (Berkeley: University of California Press, 1984).
14 Westerkamp, "The Practice of Listening in Unsettled Times," 2017.
15 Alessandro Sbordoni and Antonio Rostagno, eds, "Free Improvisation: History and Perspectives," in *Free Improvisation* (Lucca: Libreria Musicale Italiana, 2018), 101.
16 See William John Thomas Mitchell and Mark B.N. Hansen, eds, *Critical Terms for Media Studies* (Chicago: University of Chicago Press, 2010).
17 See Springgay and Truman, "On the Need for Methods Beyond Proceduralism"; and prOphecy Sun, Kristin Carlson, Kate Hennessy, "Research-Creation as a Generative Approach to Sound Design," in *Doing Research in Sound Design*, ed. Michael Filimowicz (New York: Routledge Press, 2021).
18 Sun, Carlson, and Hennessy, "Research-Creation."

7

"It doesn't mean anything except talking"
An Interview with Tracie Morris

Cole Mash and Deanna Fong, recorded over Zoom
TRANSCRIBED BY DEANNA RADFORD

Deanna Fong: Since we're in this time of extended isolation from other people, I was thinking that a nice way to get into the conversation would be to begin by talking about collaboration. I know that you've collaborated with lots of different folks over your career – other writers, musicians, and artists. Seeing as collaboration is such a substantial part of your process, what would you say is the mark of a good collaborative relationship? Or, maybe differently put, what's the *ethics* of collaboration for you?

Tracie Morris: It's funny you mention that today. A couple of days ago I found out that dancer and choreographer Ralph Lemon, one of my former collaborators whom I worked very closely with on a project called *Geography*, was named a MacArthur Genius Fellow. That was one collaboration that defined my relationship with other artists outside of music, because I had been working with music before I worked with Ralph. What I learned from that experience is that in a collaboration you bring your perspective to the work and assume that your perspective will be different. I don't just mean "I like or don't like a thing," I mean that I learned that Ralph *sees in movement*. He understands how things happen in the world in terms of stillness and movement, and I understand the world with words. I translate images into words. I translate words into images. I have a conceptual framework that is predicated on language while his is predicated on movement.

So, when we worked together on the *Geography* project – I was a burgeoning baby experimental poet even then, and Ralph was a well-known choreographer at that point – one of the things we had to come together with was how to understand what the first part of the *Geography* project was. I think that there is an ethic to *understand* as opposed to trying to get somebody to your point of view. It is to know that your perception of the world is different. How do you come together to make something new based on these different perceptions? For Ralph and I it was easy because he was the director, so what he said went! [Laughs] But it was instructive when we were talking about narrative arcs for the *Geography* project.

For example, he placed the dances in certain ways because of the way that he was considering the momentum of movement, while I was thinking about it as a narrative, like literally this movement means *this*, and that word is a beginning of the idea. So that was kind of interesting. I think one of my greatest compliments that I've gotten as a collaborator with musicians is, "Oh, you're a musician." I get this from members of my band, or people that I sit in with and or I get permission to work with. They're like, "Oh, yeah, yeah. You're a musician." But in my world view, they're poets! I'm like, "Yeah, yeah! You're playing poetry." So, I know that I have my particular biases, too. I think understanding the ethics of collaboration is assuming that your collaborator knows what they're doing, that they're going to teach you something, and you're going to hopefully teach them something, and then something new will come out of that. So that it doesn't seem like they're the backup – which I find a highly problematic dynamic and I'll say a little bit more about that before you go onto the next question.

For collaboration, understanding that you're coming from a particular point of view and that you're making something new is helpful. It also helps in finding where you intersect. For me, when I think about a collaborator, I'm considering, "What do we have in common, conceptually?" I don't do dance. I like *to* dance, but I don't *do* dance. I like visual art but I don't paint. (I've begun to make short films, but I still come to films as experimental poems. I make them by myself, but I consider it a collaboration with my subjects and the film topics.) So it's like, what's the concept that makes us have something in common? We both think about line, we both think about space, we both think about breath, the page, or the two-dimensional space. So what can we bring into that in our own ways? That's one of the other things I try to think about: not how we're different conceptually but also how we're conceptually paired and it seems very high up and very distant from like, "We gotta make a theatre piece," or something. To me it's the foundation. There's a conceptual foundation and then we can both come to it in our perspectival ways.

DF: So the labour part of col*labor*ation is not just making the thing, but approaching the other person's way of viewing?

TM: Yeah. Absolutely. Then seeing how you diverge from your point of view and what you have in common.

Cole Mash: That seems to be your approach to J.L. Austin in *Who Do With Words*, as well. You disagreed with things he was saying when you first encountered his work in a graduate course, but then you learned to find that common ground.

TM: Well, I was very resistant to it. The person who taught that graduate course by the way, was Fred Moten, who also received a MacArthur Genius Award this year. They did very well. It's people I like – Fred! Ralph! [Laughter] Jacquie Woodson, N.K. Jemisin, I was like, "Okay!" And Louise Glück just won the Nobel Prize for Literature, poetry. Yeah, I find this so interesting because a lot of these folks whom I have the pleasure of knowing – I don't know Louise personally very well – but they were kind of on the outside. Or they were appreciated by certain sorts of groups. The ambitious projects, for instance, that Ralph put together were funded by major funders, but it wasn't at the Kennedy Center or anything mainstream. It was at, like, the BAM [Brooklyn Academy of Music] or the Walker Art Center or something. I just think it's very interesting to see certain people come in from the cold, as it were. I mean, be successful and be surviving, but in a mainstream way. I think it's extremely interesting.

But anyway, Austin was someone who I was intrigued by and refused to be friends with because I knew from the first page, as I said in my book, that he was talking bad about my friends. I could just feel at the first page I was gonna be mad. I was like [sucks teeth], "He's gonna say something about poetry!" [Laughs] I thought that the first couple of sentences. Then by the time I got down to the first page, I said, "See! I *knew* he was gonna say something bad about poetry."

DF: This makes me think of a question about generosity versus risk and harm. Fred Moten gave this amazing reading in Vancouver in 2015, or somewhere around there. A couple years ago now. One of the things that he said that has really stuck with me is that one of his worst writing habits is that he has the impulse to critique things sometimes, and it never gets better for him until he finds some sort of rapprochement with the thing that he thought that he hated. But he qualified that by saying, "That can also be dangerous sometimes." That is, coming into proximity with things that you have resistance toward or that might not be so good for you. As Cole was pointing out, in *Who Do With Words*, there's a great deal of generous extension to texts that have ideological or problematic authors, who you nonetheless find a way to get into their orbit or maybe read them in a perlocutionary way – not for what they intended but for what *you* receive from them, as their auditor.[1] The question in all of this is: how do you balance that sense of love and generosity with this possibility of risk or harm?

TM: That's interesting. From the generosity side, I'd have to say, for me, now that you're asking the question, I think it has a lot to do with how I approach the text – how I come to it. With Edgar Allan Poe, I came to it with a great deal of love and affection, probably because of Vincent Price, but also because before I saw Vincent Price's films that were interpretations of Poe, I was reading it and I just felt moved by the language. I read Poe at a very young age and it was quite foundational. Austin, too – I came to him as Fred's student, so I trusted the context in which I approached him but, in a very grad-student way, I still was: *harrumph*. But I figured there was some reason for me to bother. There was a reason for me to get to know this person, at least to learn something. The only reason I took that class was because Fred was teaching it. I knew nothing about Austin. Nothing. So that had something to do with it. It was the generosity that I think is imbued in the language and that comes through the writer's work, despite their other problems, or in Austin's case, what I found problematic.

Danger is an interesting way to think about it. I wonder what that would mean. I think that I grew up in a kind of tough environment and it helped me to have a thicker skin about certain things, and so I don't know if Poe would have hurt my feelings. When I found out that Poe was a pro-slavery person – which means that he was a bigot – I had such a strong opinion about Poe's relevance to my life, and his core meaning for me as a creative person, that I could not and chose not to dissociate myself with his importance. So then what do you do? I was like, "Well, I've got to balance that." I have to say, "Yeah, he was a racist and he was important to me and those things are both true." I just leave it at that. I mentioned in the book several other moments of problematic interaction, especially Shakespeare's *Taming of the Shrew*. It's not only a horribly sexist play, it teaches you how to torture people. It's terrible! But ... There's no "but" to that. That's just, period. I also get a great deal out of what he does with language because that's how I perceive the world, and he's a big part of that. I think it just depends. Sometimes it's how they form you. Others it's how you form *them*.

There are other people who I don't feel that way about. I'll give an example. Well, maybe I shouldn't give an example! [Laughs] I will just say, there are a couple of filmmakers that I have found highly problematic. One filmmaker that I find problematic, like I said, I came to their work and their work had a strong influence on me. Particularly a connection with language and performative utterance that was extremely important and helpful to me. So when I think about that person, I don't support that person's work going forward but I can't dismiss it either, and I'm actually very appreciative of their art in one particular case.

In another case, I never got invested in that person's work and so I don't have a relationship with it, and because of my politics I will not get into the person's work. [Laughs] They just ruin any possible relationship that I would have with their work. So, I think it depends on how you come to it. But I didn't feel any fear about it. I didn't worry about getting my feelings hurt.

I think your question speaks to the notion of disappointment. How disappointment can be a very profound feeling and experience. That's one of the reasons why I made a point to put this commentary in the book because I think being able to make that distinction, on your own terms, whatever your terms are, is extremely important. It's extremely important to be able to do that. I think if you're a marginalized person in any kind of way in society, it's even *more* important. Because I think sometimes people depend on a certain type of absolutism to keep you out of the room, you know? With Shakespeare, I think that's very much the case. I think that's really an issue with him. That's one of the reasons I like to talk about him so much, because there's this sense that only certain people are supposed to be in the room. That not only goes against the idea that Shakespeare influenced language, period, but that exclusion was his intention. It was the opposite. The kind of elitism that he negotiated as a living artist meant that he was talking to several communities at once. But people try to say that he's only talking to one group and if you want to be in *that* one, then it's up to you to demonstrate your relationship to Shakespeare. I'm like, "No, he was talking to everybody." That's my relationship! [Laughter]

CM: I've been thinking lately about audience and elitism, specifically in relation to community art, or local and amateur-art scenes. Community-based forms of contemporary poetry and performance do have the potential to resist the hegemony of capitalist or institutional art economies, creating vibrant communities that rely on, and are constituted by, shared artistic praxis and exchange rather than intellectual or monetary capital. This is arguably most evident in amateur spaces like the open mic, but perhaps to a lesser extent in social media, Instagram poets, etcetera, as well. I hoped you could speak a little bit to the potential for so-called "amateur art" to act as a space for resistance against artistic elitism or hegemony.

TM: Well, I think if we're going to explore amateur art, we have to ask: what is professional art? The reason that there is so-called "amateur art" is because people close the door on what's considered legitimate. There are a lot of ways in which people resist that, because we all have the impulse to create. I think that's an innate and wonderful thing. So, people are not going to be undermined by the fact that people don't consider them legitimate or "real" to stop making art. Then what happens is people deny that it's real, and then they write about it to legitimize themselves as being on the pulse, and then those people eventually move into those spheres and then it becomes legitimate. That's kind of like the generic way that it works. An example is before you right now.

So I think it really depends. What I try to do is balance it from both points of view, you know? I encourage people who are not in my sort of professionalized, legitimized position that what they're doing is real. I talk about it in terms that are, or might be elite, or not. But I also critique the idea of what's elite that keeps people out. So, I think it's a balancing act. I think it's a complex thing. In my position, for example, the slam scene. I guess it would be considered outsider art. One of my great influences as a performer in that scene for years was hip hop, which was considered a marginalized form of Black art that was community based. I grew up hearing that and seeing people perform it when I was little in real time, when it wasn't recorded, which happened a little bit later in the '70s. [Laughs]

I knew something was going on there because, as a language nerd, I was a reader. I knew that what was going on with words was interesting. It was in my poetry, I was advocating that this should be legitimate. Well, now it's a trillion-dollar industry, so no one needs me to legitimize it, or anybody really. But it was an earth-shattering sort of turn to see it go from the margins to the middle. To the centre. I think hip hop influenced the slam scene, but I also think it affected poetry and I see that as a teacher. People may or may not be writing hip hop, but they are with the sort of mechanics of hip hop, the poetic poiesis of hip hop. It certainly influenced how they're approaching poetry and poetics. There's no question about it that there's been a shift across the board, across cultures, geographies, languages, everything. It's been a sea change of how we listen to language as well as how we use it.

So, what does it mean to be an outsider in the context of something like that? What did it mean for the Beat poets to be outsiders? Even though a lot of them went to Columbia, you know? [Laughs] To me this is really classic. People find themselves in the mainstream, they go off, and then the mainstream eventually catches up. I'm not making a value judgment on it, I'm just saying that's what it is. You see that with slams, and you see that with hip hop, and you see that with rock and roll, and you see it with folk music. You name it. Roma culture. You think about the Gypsy-fortune-teller stereotype, right? But now in the self-help section you see like fifty decks of Tarot cards that you can purchase, you know? [Laughs] Next to Eckhart Tolle and Oprah Winfrey. It's just completely changed. I'm using a non-poetic example to present this idea – something that was considered really, really marginal years and years ago but is now extremely mainstream. Marijuana legalization, which was unfathomable thirty years ago. Gay marriage. There are a million things. But now it's like, "So?" And everything I'm talking about has artistic ripples for it. Shows like *Pose*, *Schitt's Creek* – you just name it. It's a million different things. It's interesting, though, to think how "mainstream culture" adjusts to this truth yet still manages to find ways to marginalize …

CM: In some ways, I'm always thinking about amateur art as constructed in opposition to capitalist or institutional economies – so, art that's not making money or art that's "not successful," quote un-quote, by neoliberal markers of success. Do you know the book *Dark Matter* by Gregory Sholette? There, he refers to amateur art as part of what he theorizes as "dark matter." For Sholette, there's a small group of artists at the top who work professionally in the art world, then there are all the people who buy canvases at dollar stores and attend open mics and fill notebooks at home and never share their work. He refers to the latter group as "dark matter," and notes that these people – the amateurs, teachers, and one-timers – prop up the artistic economy. So some amateur art stays amateur. It doesn't follow that same cycle of moving from the margins to the centre, maybe because it resists commodification or something like that. What do you think of that?

TM: I don't know if that's the case though, because I think *somebody* makes money off it. It just might not be the people who create it. But somebody makes the money. I don't know how much money Jean-Michel Basquiat made, but I know that his estate is making a lot of money. I'm sure he made some money, but the real money that his estate made was/

is posthumously. I think about that a lot as an example because I think visual arts culture and the traditions around it that go back to feudal times and the relationship to the patron actually very much affects the entire artistic community, the way that we perceive art's value. It's something that we have to be vigilant about.

One of the interesting things about poetry is that people might consider you a professional artist because you won accolades and sometimes that results in a bit of money. But it's not like you're gonna make money as a poet. There's a certain freedom in that. You can get a teaching job or something but you're not gonna become a wealthy poet, necessarily. I think poets that are wealthier do other things adjacent to or outside of poetry to become wealthier maybe. They might apply a particular poetic sensibility to other things like plays – you know, like Shakespeare. Like plays, or narrative writing, or other kinds of books. But it's not like the average person who's a workaday poet is like, "I'm a full-time poet! That's my profession!" You might be able to make a living if you're really good at it, but you're not going to become wealthy. It gives poets and poetry a different kind of sheen or prestige, I think, in the minds of average people – much less the cognoscenti. When somebody says something they like is "poetic," what do they mean by that? They usually mean it's exalted, it's beautiful, and you're doing it for the love of doing it and not because it's commodified.

DF: So where does slam poetry fit in this cultural economy that we're tentatively feeling out here? It's not exactly mainstream, but I know there's still a resistance in the academy to talking about it as an object of study in the same way as other exalted "high art" kind of stuff.

TM: It's interesting because a lot of times in academia, slams are used to get students into poetry. I've been to a billion of these things at this point! [Laughs] You're going to be a writer-in-residence or you're going to be a visiting poet and somebody will say, "Oh, the students are doing a poetry slam, you wanna come?" And it's like, "I've been to hundreds of those and I've got to get ready for a performance, so I'm not gonna come to the poetry slam." But why I mention it is because it's consistently used as a vehicle. It's like a gateway poetry environment for folks who get students into it. I think that the complication is slam poetry has two things happening. One is the performance of poetic writing and the other is the competition of the performances and sometimes the competition part can overwhelm the other part.

I was really, really lucky when I was involved with the slam teams and as an individual competitor in the Nuyorican Poets Café in the early '90s. The people who ran the café and who were the killers of the café were really, really, really good poets. They knew a *lot* about poetry. They were not trying to find something interesting about poetry. Steve Cannon, rest in peace, was a wonderful mentor of mine and many other people like Paul Beatty and Willie Perdomo. Steve knew everybody and he knew a *lot* about poetry. He was an experimental poet, he was a Black bohemian. [Laughs] He was also blind. He was part of Umbra. He was close friends with everyone from Amiri Baraka to Miles Davis. I mean, he knew *everybody*. And when he would critique your poem, even when he used to drink a lot at the end of the bar, he would be very specific and clear with his comment, but the critiques would sound like a heckle. Like I said, that's one of the ways I developed my thick skin. All the "cats" had thoughts. It was also really, really pointed. Miguel Algarín taught Shakespeare at Rutgers. Astounding poet. He was very much connected to bilingual and multilingual poetics, and performance art, and queer art. I was really lucky that I was hanging out at a place that was founded by people like that. It encouraged folks who went through that process to develop their own voices.

Some of the experiences I had with the slam scene outside of New York, I didn't realize it was different at the café until I started going out with teams – that people sounded exactly like the person who was the most popular. They all wrote like the person who was the most popular. Sometimes, rumour had it, the person who was most popular was writing for other people pretending that each person wrote their own work, [laughs] which is another politics of the slam, which is ridiculously put in a sentence. (The slam scene is like hip hop in that people give a sidelong glance on those who don't write their own work.) We would just be like, "What *else* y'all say?" When we were going to these competitions, none of us sounded anything like the other person. Maggie Estep, who passed away, was known more as punk, riot grrrl. And even though I was/am also a feminist, our styles were totally different, and they were nothing like Willie, and nothing like Mike Tyler. All these people were completely different. Dana Bryant and Dael Orlandersmith. They were all really, really different.

I think that's when it can become a little bit of a challenge, when the poetics are not front and centre.

Another thing that I resist is the term "spoken word." That term – people have struggled to try to make that term a thing and I'm just absolutely not gonna make it a thing. It doesn't mean anything except talking. So that could be anybody. The reason that it developed – I remember when it developed! [Laughs] It was because folks didn't want to say poetry because they didn't think it was marketable. So they just said "spoken word" to brand a range of speaking/talking/entertainment. I still don't know what *that* market is, honestly. Because you don't *have to* have any specificity, right? I mean, it could be stand-up comedy, it could be storytelling, it could be preaching, it could be poetry, it could be singing – you know, like styling. It could be a million things! So I'm like, "What is that?" People say, "Oh, Tracie is a spoken word artist," and I'm like, "No, I'm not a spoken word artist!" This isn't to say there isn't any hybridization of genres with me and other folks. But that's not a generic branding "wash" of "spoken word." One can trace the influences and the development of the hybrid forms.

CM: I agree with that. I've also found that it can often be used pejoratively. When I first started my PhD, I remember speaking with some senior colleagues about my project, a few of whom repeated a similar refrain of: "Well, you don't really just want to work on *spoken word*, do you?" As though it alone is not an object of study, or that there were better types of poetry that one could be working on. So I think, especially in the academy sometimes, it can also be used to denote something that's not poetry. Like a popular kind of poetry that people perform that's maybe not very complex or "poetic." Like it's not poetry – it's *spoken word*.

TM: Yeah, well! That's the other side, right? On the other side are the academics who can't read well in public and want an excuse to read in public. [Laughter] One of the things I do is teach voice. I'm like, "I can't hear you. Why should I come see you if I can't hear what you're saying? If you're mumbling into the microphone and that's supposed to show me that you're sincere about your writing, I could just read your book in my house. Why am I out here?" I don't expect people to be like actors. I think acting is a very different thing and actors need to know that. [Laughs] The idea that people who, well, are not to be taken seriously, especially if they're topical, is oftentimes people feeling defensive because they don't read well, and they can't galvanize an audience with their voices.

But, in my humble opinion, the beginning of language precedes writing. The beginning of poetry is the beginning of the utterance. So, to say that it's not related to performing aloud or it's not connected to community, saying something out loud in a way that is a mnemonic device that tells a story of the times, *that* is what poetry is predicated on. Before even that community responsibility, it is the utterance, the *need* to convey. That is the beginning of language. So when people say, "the spoken word," I'm thinking about the beginning of time, the beginning of humankind. That's not getting points on a scoreboard. It's the beginning of human being-ness. That's where poetry starts for me. Whether it's the cloying, bad poetry screaming that has nothing whatsoever to do with technique, or the people who say it's not to be taken seriously because all serious poetry is written on the page and only for a select few. Both of those positions, to me, are extremist positions that have nothing to do with why I love poetry and what I think poetry fundamentally is.

DF: This reminds me of a quotation from *Who Do With Words*. You write, "We resist because *we know better in our spirits and we utter this perception. The uttered voice collaborates in this resistance.*"[2] That's very much what you're talking about. The actual origin of the word *poiesis* – "to make" – this uttered voice, this poetic voice that precedes writing, *makes the world around it*. I wanted to ask you how this uttered voice – this resistant voice, which is embodied, which is performative – has served as a world-making act of resistance in your own work?

TM: It's resistance but it's also embrace. It's not just against something, it's *for* something. With *Who Do With Words*, with my performances – whether as an actor, a vocalist, singer, or as a sound poet or as a page poet – I'm embracing things as well as resisting other things. I feel like they have to work together. I feel like being against something all the time or that that's the real motive can be a trap. I think there's danger in that. I think that people can be pushed in certain directions because they feel like their art is bound up with misery of some sort. Even if it's righteous misery. That's why I want to make this point. Whereas I think, not to be too corny, but love and joy and affirmation of what people have managed to do before you to make it possible for you to do the things that you're doing is something to be embraced. That you stand on the shoulders of people who can tell you how it's done, and to tell you that you're part of a community and you're not by yourself. Even when you are by yourself. I resist the notion that I'm by myself. I resist the notion that I can't win – [laughs] you know – win in my resistance!

A lot of times, Black people say, "If we can get through slavery we can get through this." And it's not because whatever "this" is at the moment isn't hard. It's because to be denied the status of humanness, for your existence in a place to be predicated on the fact that you are an object, you are not a person – to resist *that* thing, legally, but also by what you choose to embrace – that is probably the most profound existential challenge that maybe humanity has ever experienced. I'm not saying people haven't been bigoted and cruel and murderous and rapacious and everything before. I'm just saying that *that* thing, that this example of African American ethics, power, and affirmation, is something to be aware of and that people have managed to get past that. To get through that. The existential nature of that. The conceptual nature of that. Nothing that you face can be as hard as that. Because you're with people who showed us ways to do that. I expand that idea to anyone that I see is suffering because they're part of a vulnerable group. It makes me hopefully less small but bigger because of that grounding. When I think about children separated from their parents, I understand that story. I don't understand their story right now because I wasn't separated from my parents. But I understand what that story can mean and feel that I want to speak to that story. The poem shows up to speak to that story. And yes, I can find examples in my history to understand that story of migrant families being separated, but the particular aspect that they're dealing with is specific and theirs. Yet a poem shows up because it's my job to not just sit by and say it doesn't matter. The poem demands I speak up, or that it speaks up, or channels. Or whatever it is. I can't always describe it.

It's interesting because there's another element to the resistance part. Sometimes I don't want to do that because it's not fun to be a vehicle for those kinds of ideas. But one of the things I can do as a sound poet through my performance is step my ego to the side and say, "It's not about my feelings." I can step to the side and say, "This is the thing that needs to be said," and then channel the audience through that. I remember, I only had done that poem one other time before I was invited to a performance at the 92nd Street Y here in New York. I thought about the magnitude of me performing there but also other things about that venue which I wrote in a commentary to the 92nd Street Y, which I won't get into now. But, the idea that I was there made me feel like I had to tell that story because the 92nd Street Y is an institution that was built on people feeling isolated and wanting a community. So I had to tell that story and other stories that I feel like are connected to the Black experience in connection with other types of suffering. I feel like there's ways to resist and there's things to embrace and we can feel power in both and we don't have to choose.

DF: Hear, hear. That's amazing.

CM: Just as a tiny sidebar, since you were talking about Shakespeare earlier, you said, "bound up in misery" at some point in that answer and there's echoes of a *Julius Caesar* quotation in there: "bound in shallows and in miseries ..."³

TM: Well, that's the thing about Shakespeare. I really like him and he's always showing up in things. Part of that is because of his unflinching commentary on the human experience. So I want to say one thing about Shakespeare – even though I feel like I'm talking about him a lot. But I do talk about him a lot [laughs] and that's why I became a Shakespeare fan – especially after my British acting training. It's because he did one really good thing besides write really well: with the exception of *The Taming of the Shrew*, all of the characters that were displaced, for the most part, spoke to their own experience, on their own terms, in the play in their particular time. That actually changed my life when I understood that, even though I appreciated his writing. When the nurse in *Titus Andronicus* says we have to kill this Black child – the queen had given birth to a Black child, Aaron's child, her child. The nurse basically says this child is ugly, look at this ugly Black child. And Aaron is like, "Who are you to say that my child is ugly – first of all because he's *my* child? But second of all, who are you to say this child is ugly because he's Black? Who are you to say a child is ugly because he's Black? Who do you think you're talking to?"

I just think the fact that the whole soliloquy is predicated on his fatherhood is extraordinary – and the fact that that child is one of the few characters to live. I just think he didn't have to write that. Two of Shylock's soliloquies, when he addresses the hatred toward him because he's Jewish in his beliefs, and that he looked different, Shakespeare didn't have to write that. He was speaking to Marlowe, you know? Why did Shakespeare write those things? The racism in *Othello* is not something that he shied away from. He's just like, "You let your daughter marry that Black guy?" But then he put Othello in a place where he was noble savage, naïve, okay – problems maybe with all of those characterizations. But it was because he trusted his environment that he thought somebody who had been in battle with him, had killed with him, that they shared blood with, would be on his side. He didn't have to frame it like that. There are a lot of interesting stories there – especially with the tragedies where he didn't have to say things the way that he said it, but he gave those characters a voice. You might say the superstructure of the play itself was problematic or whatever but *that* is one thing I took away.

I remember seeing Harry Lennix play Aaron and I just said, "This is a Black man's story." He's the mastermind of this entire play even though he's not the central character. And he says, "Who are you to say that I'm base or my child's face is base because I'm Black?" These are the ideas of someone who's speaking outside of his own moment. He's speaking in the past, in terms of the Moorish influence on Europe. But he's also talking about the present and the future and critiquing the ideas of race. And even though Shakespeare put Shylock in a terrible box and a coffin, if you will, the character still got to speak his truth in those stories. Is that a resistive act? I don't know what that is. But I embrace the fact that he told the truth of those characters as he saw it. That was pushing the envelope back in the day.

DF: So, Cole definitely is more knowledgeable about the slam scene. My jam is the avant-garde sound poets. One of the ideas that you come back to often in *Who Do With Words* is Austin's idea that an utterance needs to be meaningful in order to perform, which you trouble in so many ways. From Bruce Lee's high-pitched screams or James Brown's count-in or onomatopoeic language. All language has a performative function because it makes us – it fashions us in the world. For me, I did a lot of work on the Zurich Dadaists: Hugo Ball, Tristan Tzara, and Richard Huelsenbeck. It seems to me that in their sound poetry, it's very much like they're trying to find some sort of Ur-language that's before meaning, or behind or – I don't really know what the spatialization would be, but something that's *not meaning*. So, I think what you're talking about is even when language doesn't necessarily make sense in a linguistic or semantic way, it always has inherent meaning because it has an agency to it. Agency that is evident in your dialogue with Kurt Schwitters's *Ursonate*, for example. I was wondering if you could tell us a little bit about your relationship to historical avant-garde sound poetry.

TM: I gotta send you a poem I wrote. Somebody asked me to be on a panel talking about Dick Higgins. It made me think about a few things. What is this conversation between Black people and the avant-garde? One of the things that I didn't realize until a few years ago was that the first year that I did my first couple of sound poems, 1996, was the same year that I performed for the first time for the Vision Festival in New York. It's a festival for innovative musicians. I was reading my little poems and I think it might have been the very first time I read by myself. I'm not sure if the time I read with the pianist D.D. Jackson – I think I read by myself. That was in the spring and I did my first sound poems in the fall of 1996. I think what happened is, the relationship to sound was changing in the back of my head. I was waiting for it to come through and it did and I think it was a culmination of a whole bunch of things.

The first person to introduce me to Schwitters was my long-time pal Edwin Torres. I had taken a workshop with him, just because I was curious about who Edwin was into. He was really pushing the envelope then and had a unique voice even then. So I checked out his workshop and Schwitters. I had taken a workshop with him. I was like, "Who's *this* guy?" Then I saw Edwin do a performance of some of Schwitters's written texts from *Ursonate*. I was like, "Oh! Okay. This is strange stuff." I think it sat back there. I just think it sat back there waiting for me to catch up. To move itself to the front of my head. Then, before that, I had gone to a conference on Black people in the penal system and one of the people who presented at that conference was Sonia Sanchez. I didn't see her perform, I was actually helping out with the thing – activist helper. But I heard this sound. I was like, "What is that sound?" and "Oh, that's Sonia Sanchez." So that stayed in the back somewhere. Leon Thomas and Babs Gonzales, just sitting there waiting. And my relationships to jazz. My family, my mom and my uncles, all of them loving jazz. That's somewhere back there. Especially Miles Davis. It was just waiting for me to catch up.

I think it's not a coincidence that a lot of this Dadaism work was emerging in the 1920s, when you saw this expansive influence of Black art in Europe in various art forms. I just think it's not separate that we're all having a similar conversation but I think it's important to affirm Black influence on what's considered European high art. Not because I feel like we have anything to prove, but it's just factually the case. Since I talked about Shakespeare it's like, the quintessential notion of what it means to be English is also something that he was creating in these stories. So our perception of a lot of things is tied up with English not being the language of the Podunks over there or on the island. It affects what we consider suave, sophisticated, smart, high art – that's bound up with English-ness in a way and French-ness in a different kind of way. It's just that we all are influencing each other. But often when you're with a marginalized community, acknowledgment of that influence is also marginalized. It's made to be nothing by those invested in presenting "high art" narrowly. In a lot of ways it makes the myth that people who create that marginalized influence are nothing. One of the things I wanted to say with *Who Do With Words* is not only that I love J.L. Austin to pieces, but because of my experience as a

AN INTERVIEW with TRACIE MORRIS

Black person, I love J.L. Austin to pieces. You know? I think that J.L. Austin is relevant not only to my Black experience, but that his work, his philosophy, is a tool that can help free people because of his generosity of spirit. I think a lot of people play that role. But with Austin it's a particular thing.

The meaningfulness of what he's saying is that the language of everyday people is profound and worth philosophical investigation. When I realized *that* was what he was saying, that's when I fell for the guy and I applied that to every other lens that I had experienced in my life as an artist, as a little baby growing up in a Black neighbourhood, and all the other things I've seen since then. It's like, "Oh, this is the key of everything in my life that I love." He just said *the thing*, you know? [Laughs] He uttered the thing and that's why I wept when I heard his voice in the British Library. I was just like, "That's what he sounds like! [quietly] Oh my God!" [Laughter] And then I emailed Fred Moten. [Laughs] "I just heard his voice for the first time!" You even hear the chalk squeaking. You hear the chair on the wooden floor moving around. It was the RCA with the little puppy. The master's voice.

DF: And all that sound *means*, too. It has agency.

TM: Yes, because the thing is, he was a teacher first. He didn't write any books. He wrote one book, a translation. All the books of Austin's that we are aware of are collections that his students lovingly put together from his notes and theirs. To put into the world. Talk about collaboration. He cared more about their writing and their development than his ambition. Yes. He did well – we're talking about him – but that wasn't the focus. That's almost impossible in American academia because you gotta publish or perish. But he knew the most important thing is the *student*. And I take that with me with my pedagogy. Remember Austin: the most important thing is them.

NOTES

1 The term "perlocutionary" was conceptualized by J.L. Austin in *How to Do Things with Words* (Cambridge: Harvard University Press, 1962) as words or speech acts that have "effect on the person who receives them," as opposed to the two other forms of speech acts, *locutionary*, that is, "words-phrases-actions

that mean something", and *illocutionary*, "those that have a specific intention for being said" (26).
2 Tracie Morris, *Who Do With Words: A Blerd Love Tone Manifesto* (Tuscon: Chax Press, 2018), 75.
3 William Shakespeare, *The Tragedy of Julius Caesar* (New York: Penguin Books, 2000), 4.2.273.

8

"It's resistance but it's also embrace"
Tracie Morris's Collaborative Ear, an Open Letter

Nicole Brittingham Furlonge

Dear Tracie,

There is a moment in your rich conversation with Deanna and Cole that I keep returning to. It is the moment when you speak of when you learned that Edgar Allan Poe was pro-slavery. You share, "When I found out that Poe was a pro-slavery person – which means that he was a bigot – I had such a strong opinion about Poe's relevance to my life, and his core meaning for me as a creative person, that I could not and chose not to dissociate myself with his importance ... I have to say, 'Yeah, he was a racist and he was important to me and those things are both true.'"[1] This capacity – this willingness – to hold two deeply dissonant things as true strikes me as vital as we live in a world of hyperpolarization. Especially as we think about racism and racial reckoning. And I wonder – both as I listen in print to your thinking and as I engage in listening work with students and educators in the classroom – how do we create the conditions that might allow for such willingness to listen into a space of both/and? "[T]here's ways to resist and there's things to embrace and we can feel power in both and we don't have to choose."[2] And, in doing so, how do we hold our students – those who you name as "the most important thing" – central to a pedagogical choice to risk listening? "It's resistance but it's also embrace. It's not just against something, it's *for* something."[3]

I hear in your conversation a possible response to that question: "I came to [J.L. Austin] as Fred's student, so I trusted the context in which I approached him but, in a very grad-student way, I still was: *harrumph*. But I figured there was some reason for me to bother. There was a reason for me to get to know this person, at least to learn something. The only reason I took that class was because Fred was teaching it. I knew nothing about Austin. Nothing. So that had something to do with it."[4] Context matters. This makes me think about the ways in which the classroom and the teacher present preconditions that invite the complex engagement that is listening: if there is trust, then the assumption is that there is value there, and that context and relationship motivate listening – and cultivate a willingness to take a risk to listen.

In spite of your sense that J.L. Austin is dismissive of poetry, I appreciate the ways in which you are able to hold his thinking relevant to your creative and Blackness-amplifying project: "One of the things I wanted to say with *Who Do With Words* is not only that I love J.L. Austin to pieces, but because of my experience as a Black person, I love J.L. Austin to pieces. You know? I think that J.L. Austin is relevant not only to my Black experience, but that his work, his philosophy, is a tool that can help free people because of his generosity of spirit."[5] Listening to his work, you are able to discern what resonates vibrantly for you as a poet and through your own work: "the language of everyday people is profound and worth philosophical investigation. When I realized *that* was what he was saying, that's when I fell for the guy and I applied that to every other lens that I had experienced in my life as an artist, as a little baby growing up in a Black neighbourhood, and all the other things I've seen since then. It's like, 'Oh, this is the key of everything in my life that I love.' He just said *the thing*, you know? [Laughs]"[6] I have yet to read J.L. Austin. But I will. Thank you for the introduction.

I wish I knew about your work while I was writing my book *Race Sounds*.[7] In that project, I coined the phrase "listening in print" in order to describe listening practices that work to allow "print" and "the ear" to coexist and contribute to each other's expressivity and possibility. Key to the practices of "listening in print" is the work of unmuting print in order to listen – or tuning in to the other side of printed language – a tuning to an interior acoustics made public, allowing print to perform. Akin to your inside/outside work involved in living performatively: "sound engages with viscera in a way that compels physical interaction. Sound is something that works beyond the 'brain barrier' and directly intersects with the body."[8] Both/And. Fully embodied practice and performance.

Your interest in listening to the art of others as a ground for your own sonic compositions and improvisations strikes a deeply resonant chord – especially *Handholding: 5 Kinds* and in your work with Kurt Schwitters's *Ursonate*, where you listen to a recording of his performance and then improvise your own vocal response to what you hear. A dynamic activation of call and response! You've got me thinking about the ways in which your work aligns with what I wish for my work: that it invites readers as listeners to it, and compels them to sense and engage in ways that generate collaboration and new ways of listening and being in cocreation together, whether through resonance, inquiry, or counterpoint.

I hear this listening also as a kind of collaborative and generative thought-partnership. You spoke about your practice of an ethics of collaboration and the possibilities you find in collaborative endeavours: "[T]he ethics of collaboration is assuming that your collaborator knows what they're doing, that they're going to teach you something, and you're going to hopefully teach them something, and then something new will come out of that ... For collaboration, understanding that you're coming from a particular point of view and that you're making something new is helpful. It also helps in finding where you intersect ... There's a conceptual foundation and then we can both come to it in our perspectival ways."[9] What a powerful framing of collaboration. This captures, for me, an ethics of collaboration as well as the ethical work of listening. I wonder: how do you come to know and understand the perception of another? How does doing so create the conditions for authentic engagement and collaboration?

Along with collaboration as a kind of listening, your metaphor of handholding as a figure of listening grabs my attention. Handholding "takes different shapes but I want to encourage the visualization, care, and intimacy that this gesture references ... I'm only thinking of it as caring. I care about these works, these creatives. I want to delve into their meanings."[10] It was such a sensory-full experience to listen in print to *Handholding:*

5 Kinds. Your engagement with Kurt Schwitters's *Ursonate*, Gertrude Stein's *Tender Buttons*, John Akomfrah's *7 Songs for Malcolm X*, John Cage's *4'33"*, and Stanley Kubrick's *Eyes Wide Shut* models throughout the book the kind of holding you describe in your relationship with Austin's work. As I read, within each space of engagement, I felt invited to listen anew. Toni Morrison's invitation and admonition at the end of *Jazz* comes to my mind's ear as well: "Look where your hands are. Now."[11] Now, I am thinking about listening as a kind of handholding, an intentional choice and intention to engage with another and their way of thinking and expression. Or, as Charles Bernstein describes in the foreword to the collection *Handholding: 5 Kinds*, "a display of the possibilities for poetry."[12]

This shape of connecting, handholding, also makes me think of making space to listen as sensorially expansive beyond hearing. For instance, musician Evelyn Glennie:

> Hearing is basically a specialized form of touch. Sound is simply vibrating air which the ear picks up and converts to electrical signals, which are then interpreted by the brain. The sense of hearing is not the only sense that can do this, touch can do this too. If you are standing by the road and a large truck goes by, do you hear or feel the vibration? The answer is both. With very low frequency vibration the ear starts becoming inefficient and the rest of the body's sense of touch starts to take over.[13]

Handholding leads me to wonder: How does poetry frame the way that you listen? Or another way of saying it: *Why* and *how* poetry as a form of listening?

Back to Moten. Your discussion of Moten makes me think about his pedagogical impact on me though I have never had the privilege of being in his classes. Reading his work, though, is a sort of instructive, learning opportunity. An opportunity, certainly, to *listen in print*. As your poetry that you've recorded in print provides. As do the works of Morrison or William Shakespeare, which remind us again and again that the canon is both lofty and low, both timeless and timely, curates a world of relevance in print, and is an ongoing series of historical and often contentious choices.

They remind us through their literature that learning is about developing a capacity to consider the nuances, richness, and complexities in both/and, and that it is essential not to default to polarized thinking or reasoning.

There seems to be a socializing in this, a pedagogy of the artistry that instructs and socializes one in certain ways. I wonder not only about the pedagogical impact of a professor and thinker like Fred Moten, but also about the role artist collectives like Cave Canem have played in your poetic emergence – about the collaborative energy and focus that come through such intentionally offered spaces and how you enter the space to be embraced and simultaneously embrace that community of makers, that space carved for poetry, for care, for excellence, for brilliance to develop and shine. (There is a question in all this!) How does that community provide an apprenticeship space, a space to make, play, and learn, a space to hone you as a poet? Who have been the poets in those spaces that you've informed and that have informed your art?

Even in your performance work, speech functions as both an act of community and the site of embedded divisions, contradictions, and long histories of hate and violence. I listened recently to "Africa(n)" where you take this phrase – "It all started when we were brought here as slaves from Africa"[14] – and cut, twist, stop, stammer, repeat, reshape, and reconstruct the language so that we hear new possibilities of expression, the reality of fracture and disrepair, and the urgency of historical witness. Your performances unsettle the layers of power and history embedded in the sound of speech. Your poetic utterances invite and compel us to engage complexity.

This is not to say that listening is easy. Certainly, the idea that you raise in this interview that listening can result in disappointment is an idea I want to sit with for a bit. What does it mean to walk away from a listening session disappointed? Is there a problematic expectation that listening is always fulfilling, full, resonant? Is there a way we orient listening toward an engineered perfection, enjoyment, fidelity? Or even in our twenty-first-century playlists, do we architect pleasure in our listening? Where are the spaces and capacity for dissonance? Or for the admission that we have heard wrong or not enough? I think, too, that your poetry sounds in ways that invite in its repetitions a listener to listen *again*. Such repetition can also be challenging as while the thing said might be the same, the meaning of the utterance shifts with each repetition. As Christine Hume observes in her essay on your work, "Morris employs the kind of fierce, active repetition that might make even veteran Stein readers dizzy, but she does so with electric phrasing, lightning-fast tonal shifts, an uncanny sense of time, and a stampede of ligatured sounds that provides a literal vocal bridge between musical improvisation and poetry."[15] I think of Gertrude Stein. I also hear Harryette Mullen. In listening to your "My Great Grand Aunt Meets a Bush Supporter," you create a skipping effect with vocals, playing on words and sounds of words that morph with each repetition into a slightly different sonic shift or slip. To my ears, the underlying gravel in the throat turns to sonic sound skipping, or even sound sticking, or sound being stuck. The piece reminds me of / rewinds me to Mullen in print, but instead the performance explores the kinds of sonic and verbal shifts/slips that Mullen records on the page.

Listening, as your poetry simultaneously and resoundingly demonstrates, is essential. As I listen in print to your conversation with Deanna and Cole, I can't help but hear Claudia Rankine's response to a question I posed during a Zoom event, where she was discussing her most recent book, *Just Us*: "How might listening help us navigate our polarized world?" Here is part of Rankine's response: "Nothing can happen if you're not willing to listen. I think we are sometimes held back by our commitment to be right. And we need to understand that being right is only good if you want to stand in the same place. I am not interested in listening to people who are not interested in listening to me. Discourse is give and take. I am willing to engage in order to move forward if you are willing to engage to move forward." Rankine asserts the vital role listening plays in merely the possibility – let alone the realization – of a healthy democracy. As I listen, I wonder about the slips between media – page, performance, recording – that also allow for listening's repetition in the rewind and replay. "My Great Grand Aunt Meets a Bush Supporter" reminds me, too, of a powerful question Deanna asked you: "I wanted to ask you how this uttered voice – this resistant voice, which is embodied, which is performative – has served as a world-making act of resistance in your own work?"[16] I love this notion of the performative – and, by extension, of listening for and with the performance – as a world-making act of resistance. Your performance insists we remember that listening and poetry are intertwined as embodied and inspirited practices – practices that compel us to listen in ways that assert our embodied, inspirited humanity while embracing the humanity of others.

Your comments on an ethics of collaboration resonate here as well. During your conversation, you explain collaboration as more than an interaction between two artists meant to create something new. Your notion of collaboration emerges as a relationship that allows for a practice of coming together to create anew through the different ways of knowing. Your question struck a chord: "How do you come together to make something new based on these different perceptions?"[17] Differences in making sense.

Your ways of listening and sense making – what I think of now as your *collaborative ear* – lean into the uncertainty and possibility in the space of different perceptions. "Then seeing how you diverge from your point of view and what you have in common."[18] Your collaborative ear is what we need right now. It activates a dynamic, ethical listening practice that resists absolutism and embraces what it could mean for the poet, and for us all, to be listeners to and for each other in a fractured, polarized world. Your listening poetics and practice offer not a promise or a utopian remedy, but a *possibility* for repair out of this polarization: that a vibrant community might emerge through shared artistic praxis and exchange. I like the idea of vibrant community – as an ideal emergence created through a community that listens.

Thank you for listening,
Nicole

NOTES

1 Tracie Morris, "'It doesn't mean anything except talking': An Interview with Tracie Morris" by Cole Mash and Deanna Fong, in this volume, 140.
2 Ibid., 149.
3 Ibid., 147.
4 Ibid., 140.

5 Ibid., 153.
6 Ibid., 153.
7 Nicole Brittingham Furlonge, *Race Sounds: The Art of Listening in African American Literature* (Iowa City: Iowa University Press, 2018).
8 Tracie Morris, "Journal, Day Five," Poetry Foundation, 31 March 2006, www.poetryfoundation.org/harriet-books/2006/03/journal-day-five-56d34c690b825.
9 Morris, "'It doesn't mean anything except talking,'" 138.
10 Tracie Morris, "An Interview with Tracie Morris," by John Melillo, *Kore Press*, 27 March 2017, https://korepress.org/archives/2363.
11 Toni Morrison, *Jazz: A Novel* (New York: Vintage International, 2004), 229.
12 Charles Bernstein, "Forward and Backward," foreword to *Handholding: 5 Kinds*, by Tracie Morris (Tucson: Kore Press, 2016), 1.
13 Evelyn Glennie, "Hearing Essay," Evelyn Glennie: Teach the World to Listen (website), 1 January 2015, www.evelyn.co.uk/hearing-essay/.
14 See Tracie Morris, "Africa(n)," PennSound, 28 October 2008, https://writing.upenn.edu/pennsound/x/Morris.php.
15 Christine Hume, "Improvisational Insurrection: The Sound Poetry of Tracie Morris," *Contemporary Literature* 47, no. 3 (Autumn 2006): 428.
16 Morris, "'It doesn't mean anything except talking,'" 147.
17 Ibid., 137.
18 Ibid., 138.

9

"What is being resisted is our 'yes'"

An interview with Tawhida Tanya Evanson, El Jones, and Erin Scott

Cole Mash, recorded over Zoom
TRANSCRIBED BY MEGAN BUTCHART

Cole Mash: So, hello, it is Friday, October 16, 2020. I'm here with Tawhida Tanya Evanson, El Jones, and Erin Scott. I am Zooming in from unceded Syilx Okanagan territory in Kelowna, British Columbia. I don't know if you all wanted to say where you're Zooming in from today?

El Jones: Halifax/Kjipuktuk in unceded Mi'kmaw territory.

Tawhida Tanya Evanson: Tiohtià:ke/Montreal, Kanien'kehá:ka territory.

Erin Scott: I'm also in Syilx Okanagan territory in Kelowna, British Columbia.

CM: The four of us were supposed to do an event back in March, right before the COVID shut-down happened. I had already been working on this project with Deanna. When Deanna and I were talking about who we might want to interview, I thought it would be a great opportunity, since the four of us missed out on having the event, to get us all in a room together and chat about poems, practice, and community.

So, as a way of beginning here, could you each just talk a little bit about yourself and your art practice generally. Maybe we'll start with you, Tawhida Tanya?

TTE: I am a poet, an author, performer, producer, and arts educator. I was born and am based here in Tiohtià:ke/Montreal. I am Antiguan Québécoise. I've put out about six artist books and I've also had two collections of poetry published. My first novel will be coming out next year in early 2021 with Véhicule Press. It's called *Book of Wings*. I also publish a lot of work in anthologies and journals. But my primary practice is spoken word performance. I do a lot of touring internationally at literary festivals and arts festivals. I've been doing that for almost twenty-five years now, but I've been full time for the last eight years. So, since 2012, I've been a full-time, professional artist. I've presented work in maybe a dozen countries or so and I've put out four spoken word albums and six video poems. I graduated from Concordia University Creative Writing. I didn't learn that much, but ... [all laugh] I learned "don't be afraid to edit." And I'm a board member of the Quebec Writers' Federation, the QWF, here in Tiohtià:ke and also I am on the board of directors for the Black Speculative Arts Movement, or BSAM, which focuses on speculative arts and Afrofuturism. I also moonlight as a whirling dervish. It's not really an arts practice, but some people say that it is. I disagree. [All laugh] That's all!

CM: Awesome. Thanks so much, Tawhida Tanya! El, how about you?

EJ: I'm a spoken word artist, journalist, and essayist – I guess now we call that non-fiction writing – and then obviously I do a lot of teaching. Not in creative writing – they won't hire me [all laugh] – but in sociology and in the Social Justice and Community Studies Department. I've done some teaching in journalism at King's University, Women's Studies. Everything except English. So, yeah, I don't know. I don't have as much of an extensive thing to say. I mean, I just write things that are very much embedded in a political viewpoint. So it's very much in continuum with my political practice as well.

CM: Thanks El. Erin, how about you?

ES: I'm a poet and a performer and a community producer. I just released my very first chapbook, *Atrophy*, with Kalamalka Press. It won the John Lent Poetry/Prose Award here in the Okanagan. That just came out in spring 2020. It looked like it wasn't going to come out because of the pandemic but, yay, it did! I've put out a couple of spoken word albums over the years and I also hold a Master of Fine Arts and Performance, so I do a lot of interdisciplinary and highly audience-participatory performance work that engages community as one of the main components of the creation of the art form. I'm co-executive director of Inspired Word Café here with Cole Mash in Kelowna. So I've been doing a lot of community arts-based work over the last twelve years. And I'm a mother. So I'm pregnant with my fourth child, which seems really fucking crazy to me! [Laughs] I don't know how I got here! But also it's pretty crucial and integral to who I am both as a person and as an artist – this kind of caretaking and generative sort of interchange between people.

CM: Awesome. And for the record and in the interest of academic integrity, Erin is also my partner, but I hope that listeners or readers of this collection in the future will not hold that against her. [All laugh] Okay, so to move into the next question here, I thought I would ask how the three keywords of this collection – resistance, community, and sound – might resonate with your poetic practice in some way?

TTE: El, do you want to start?

EJ: No, I don't! [All laugh]

TTE: Okay, I'll start then! [All laugh] Well, okay, there are three really powerful words: resistance, sound, and community. Well, the first thing is, when I think of resistance, I think of the word "no." A very powerful word that also unites us in many ways. But I think it's also a word that can open the door to "yes." But it has to come first. [TTE chuckles] I mean, babies are born, everything is "yes!" I think "no" is a very useful word to learn how to use wisely. When I was first starting out doing writing and performance, I accepted every invitation that came my way – while I had my day job at the same time. It took a lot of contemplation and also experience to start to say no and not just do every kind of performance that was put forward. But it extended beyond that.

I realized that having an arts practice, especially full time, is something really amazing and if I'm going to do that, I'm going to have to say no to a job. That's why I quit my day job; at the time I was doing project management at a language school. So the first big "no" for me was saying no to a salary. That was, for me, a big aspect of how I move forward in the world, through "no." So I quit my job, I also don't have a mortgage, I don't have a car, I don't even have a driver's licence. I would like to think that if I live with resistance and every step is a quality of resistance then that will come through in the work, even if the work is about surrender, and about "yes," and about healing – it's still coming through the tunnel of "no." And so I feel very blessed to be in this space now, because it is an honour to be a full-time artist. But you have to go through a lot of no's before you get there.

The other thing I would say ... The other one is sound. So when I saw that word I thought, "Well, you know, everything is sound; even if I shut up there's sound." There's this thing called an anechoic chamber, and it's this room that you can go in and when you go into this room it's completely soundproof. So the only sounds that you bring into it are you in your body. And even if you don't make any sounds, apparently you hear two sounds: you hear the blood coursing through your veins, and your spinal fluid. Like, not even your heartbeat! You hear the liquid, the water, moving in your body. We're on this planet that's spinning, that's spinning around the sun, just because there's no oxygen for sound to be transmitted, it doesn't mean it's not happening. This planet has a hum, and all planets have a hum, and all stars have a hum, and our own bodies have that hum. So, that's where I am with sound.

Let's see, what else ... Community. Well, I'm part of the community of human beings, first and foremost. I'd like to think that the work I do is trying to bring a quality of unity to the world community. But it's really hard to do that, and you have to start in small pockets. So you start with family, your family community and your friends. And then cultural heritage, so then Black community, and then for me Sufi community. And also the literary community. And then your neighbourhood, your city, Turtle Island, and the world. So that's how I see community, my place in it, and also the place of my work. I'd like to think my arts practice is meant for all human beings, which is why I test it out when I travel. When I present it to people

AN INTERVIEW with EVANSON, JONES, and SCOTT

all over the world. Then I can see if it has the same punch that it would in the community of the city I live in, for example. So far it has been pretty good [TTE and CM laugh]; so far it has been pretty successful. So those are my thoughts on those three words. I could say a lot more, but you know, I'll shut up now. [TTE laughs]

CM: No, that's great. Thanks so much. Erin or EJ?

EJ: Go ahead, Erin.

ES: Yeah, I can jump in. I like your ideas about resistance coming in the shape of "no" and I immediately thought of how that connects to surrender. It's funny actually you said babies come out and it's all "yes," but they say "no" way before they say "yes." [TTE laughs] They just become obsessed with it. But I think it's exactly what you've pointed to, which is that there is power within that word, and there's power as an autonomous being, but also as a being who is in relation to others. That expression of no and of resistance that often leads to what we actually need and what we actually desire. So there's this chain of events that has to happen. In my own art practice, I've found that over the years people, when they engaged with my art, they dubbed it with things like satirical – so that was kind of a resistance to the normative – that I was often writing about motherhood and maternity, which was also resistant to this patriarchal mode that was so dominant in the literary arts. So without really thinking that I was actively creating a practice of resistance, others were saying, "Well, you're resistant to all of these things that are kind of at the hegemonic centre and therefore that makes your practice resistant." Which really it was just a practice like we talked about the other day, Tawhida Tanya, which was coming out of my own lived experience and the ways that I mythologize that in art practice.

So I think resistance is this wonderful, empowering thing, but I also think a lot about surrender. It's something that comes up so much in my journey both actually labouring children out of my body and then engaging with them as they form themselves into whoever they are going to be in the world. You just have to surrender constantly and sometimes that surrendering to others' no's and to others' resistance towards your own identity, your sense of self, what you're putting out there, and accepting that that isn't always a negative thing – that resistance kind of feels like a dichotomy in some ways.

Sound has always been so important to me in all these different ways. I love the different sounds of the world and of language. Quite quickly when I started writing it became clear that I would favour sound over other elements in my writing – like, over narrative, or even things having continuity. The sound was always something I absolutely adored to play with, and that of course when spoken through an actual voice became something different than when it was sitting there alone on the page. I still feel that way, even when I was reading from *Atrophy*, my new chapbook. Quite a few people said, "This is just so different when you read it!" It's like, "Yeah, well, that's kind of the point." [All laugh] So, it lives within this voice; voice is always really important for me. It's important to me in story and that's often what I think of with sound.

Community is such a funny one. Cole has been working through his PhD comp exams and his first one was about community. Both of us work extensively in "community arts," which is a hard thing to define. But it starts to feel like community is this really positive thing, and he began doing all this research that pointed to the way that community is also kind of a way for us to exclude while we're trying to include. Again, it's not all that dissimilar to the idea of resistance, where it holds these two very different things within itself. So that's been something we at Inspired Word Café have been investigating: how do we open up our community to try to make it more accessible while simultaneously cutting off access to other people? This new mode of COVID-19 existence has been a big one. We have got people in our community who don't have internet access, who live on the street, who have different types of cognitive abilities, and so going on Zoom five times a day is out of the question for them, and so suddenly our community has been separated because we can't get in this physical space with one another. So it has been this really interesting thing to navigate. How do we continue to create a sense of community while creating barriers for others? That's why I think community is really complex and empowering, but can also be kind of damaging at other times.

EJ: So as far as resistance goes, I think there also can be, or is, a "yes" in resistance, but usually what is being resisted is our "yes." I think about this moment where basically everything I've been saying and doing for my entire adult life has become true after all this time of people telling me I was crazy. But we will always be in this process of shaping that, you know? Our resistance was always a positive shaping. It was always perceived as a negative thing. It was always perceived like we were hateful and angry, but it was always this work that we've been doing towards reshaping something different in the world. Abolition is about removal, sure, but it's actually about building something new and coming into a new relationship. Defunding has that piece that's the "de-," the removal, but the part we are talking about is the "and": giving those resources elsewhere. Reliance on care, new and different kinds of support. So I think what we're resisting actually is a negative, sick, cruel society, and we're imagining and bringing into being, and acting on something else that is a resistance to society – that is actually a "yes." So, I think it is also important to frame it in those generative terms as well. I don't necessarily think we are living in a negative space and resisting; we're resisting the thing that phrases itself as normal and mainstream and is, in fact, the thing that is radical. It is radical to live in the world that we live in now that puts billions of dollars into policing and can't even give long-term care for a senior in a home. That is a radical act. Saying that that is wrong, and that we should redistribute those funds, is actually common sense and not radical at all. It's just phrased as "radicality" because we live in a sick society. So, I also just wanted to inject that realm of the "yes" into our conversation on resistance.

As far as sound goes, I was in the Writers Program in Banff over last Christmas where they have readings. It occurred to me that I never describe things visually. I don't think I ever, in writing anything, set the scene visually. I just never do. I never describe what people look like. All my work, I realized, is based around conversation. In the book that I wrote in Banff, *Canada Is So Polite*, which is gathering essays and stuff, I realized everything revolves around conversation. Because I'm always having conversations. I mean, part of it is a mechanism: I'm always talking to people in prison over the phone. So I'm usually starting in a place where it is something that someone said to me, but so many essays open with somebody talking to me or me talking to them, or I'm like, "Desmond [Cole] says this," and I realize that everything revolves around the conversation and nothing is visual. Like, I'll never say, "Fatouma is a petite, brown-skinned woman ..." It just never occurs to me. But I'll be, "Fatouma tells me this ..." [TTE laughs] So I realized that all my work is constructed around that oral space. I do spoken word, that's oral, but I think my orientation in writing is towards the oral, towards the conversations, towards the relationship that takes place in a conversation. If I ever finish the edits on my book [EJ laughs], if it ever comes out, the whole book is in some way about the relationality of doing this work. It's a lot of conversations with people in prison and then building analysis, building what I'm talking about. So, I'm just not a visual person; I pick up people's language very quickly, the wording that people use. I've always picked up the language or the phrasing right away and then it becomes incorporated.

I also think of that when I think of sound, in terms of orality not just as, "Okay, you wrote an oral poem," but as a particular kind of orientation to the world, a particular practice, a particular being through conversation. What it means to listen and be in conversation. I often say that advocacy is 90 per cent listening; it's literally like you're just sitting on the phone talking to people and then you're like, "Oh, that's a thing we should probably do something about." People telling you stories, being able to listen to people, being able to hear that. People feeling listened to. It's much more listening than the action, I would say. I think that's part of a kind of aural orientation toward the world as well.

Community is about that relationality as well. What do we mean when we say community? We talk about the Black community, but not everybody in the Black community is in the community in the same way. We're often meaning something quite specific. There certainly is a prison community of people who do this work. There's an abolition community of people. There are only fifty to one hundred actual abolitionists in Canada who have been working long-term in abolition. There's more now because we hit this summer, now there's like ten thousand abolitionists, but people who have been doing the on-the-ground, front-line work with abolition, there are very few. So those are actually closed communities where everyone knows people; there's a history there. Then there are questions like: Are we all a community of writers just because we all write? Do we share the same goals? Are we actually in community? Are you just part of a community? Does it require a kind of commitment of being? Acts of kinship, acts of belonging? Who determines who is in the community or out? These are actually political questions that sometimes just go unasked and then sometimes become fraught, like at moments when self-identification comes into the picture around a prize or a grant – who is Indigenous, or who is Black for these purposes. That's when it becomes fraught. But it's also active in other places as well. Who do we think of as our community? When I'm writing, my first level of community is people in prison when I'm writing about those issues. They read things first, they hear things first, they give permission for what is said or not said. So that's certainly action that's taking place in community. Who do I imagine I am writing to in my head? That sort of imagined audience. That's in a sense the community I'm writing to. Obviously Black people I'm writing to, Black women specifically. Political Black women more specifically. What I'm saying is that is an actual act of *active* constitution.

Community isn't necessarily a passive thing; it's something that we actually have to take part in and invest in. Especially as we have these conversations that are political conversations – like, put resources in community, but whose community? I don't even agree with everyone that's standing with me on the front lines. I think there are a lot of sellouts [ES laughs] that are right now claiming a lot of politics that they don't really live. So, are they my community? What happens when I want to reject them, or say that publicly, or if I don't share their politics? That becomes difficult. I think that these are actually political questions: who is your community? Who do you actually trust? Who have you been sharing these things with? Who holds your voice? Who do you trust to stand beside you when things get hot? Who do you trust to actually have your back? Who do you trust to actually be able to bounce ideas off of? I think we also have to be clear on that, because when we start saying, "Give resources to the community," do you mean to Kamala Harris [EJ laughs] or do you mean to an actual Black woman that doesn't put Black mothers in jail? Because I want to know the difference when we're talking about community.

TTE: Can I add one quick thing, just in response, because it was really lovely what you said, El, specifically with regards to active listening and sound, which is really important. I find working outside of literary communities really helpful in developing that. For example, musicians are much better listeners than writers. [CM laughs] I include myself in the writing category, so I'm always working really hard toward active listening. I read this really good book called *Ritual* by Malidoma Somé and he was talking about the arts and community and how it always was that: everyone in the community, which would be basically a village, like a small group of people who all live in one geographical area – and we're on the African continent here – and so everyone was involved in the arts. It wasn't just for one specific person who was like, "Well, I'm the painter here." No. Everyone was involved in that; there was never any separation. Which is why some things like slam and open mics I think bring that back: it's a return to arts in the community where everyone can participate, and everyone should be participating because all human beings are creative and artistic. You may not decide to be a full-time artist and that's fine, but I still believe that every human being is creative and artistic. I mean, look at Trump. [All laugh] That's creativity in action. It's just that the hardcore ego gets in the way and this is what we are left with. [TTE laughs]

CM: I was reading recently about the movement in health care toward "narrative medicine." What they are finding is that if doctors take ten minutes with a patient instead of two minutes and just let that patient talk about their life and about what's going on, that doctors can diagnose things much, much quicker by actually doing some listening. It saves the medical system millions and millions of dollars on tests and all these interventions which cause other issues, by actually just listening to the patient first instead of this [CM snaps fingers] get-them-in, get-them-out-quickly mentality.

Okay, so my next question, as Tawhida Tanya brought up deals with spoken word and slam a little bit. Spoken word and slam are polarizing modes of writing. Vancouver poet George Bowering has been quoted as calling slams "abominations" [all laugh] and adding of slams and spoken word that "[t]o treat poetry as performance is crude and extremely revolting, akin to dogs who walk on their hind feet."[1] [All laugh] He took a lot of flak for that, but he went on in a different interview to clarify that what he was referring to there is poetry that is performed for self-glorification rather than simply poetry and performance generally.[2] Literary critic Harold Bloom has called slams "the death of art."[3] However, other scholars such as Corey Frost have written about the "highly social, community-based" nature of spoken word and slam.[4] El, I know that you've written in the past about the way that Black slam poets face discrimination and exclusion in both local and national slam scenes. So to direct this question more toward Erin and El, as people who have a long history of competing in poetry slams – I know Tawhida Tanya you haven't done much slamming – I was hoping you could speak to their potential to either glorify the individual or create community, which as we've been talking about can be both an act of inclusion and exclusion.

EJ: Well, I think first of all it's one of those things in which everyone who does slam criticizes it, but if you haven't done slam then that's a different kind of criticism. So I think everyone who has slammed has particular critiques of how the audience engages. Like the racial content of the audience, the kind of poems that do well, the whole process of it, certainly. But then you also get people who aren't slamming and just want to be like, "Slam does this, slam does that." But do you know what slam does? Have you been part of it? The good things about slam, are that it definitely teaches you to sharpen your work within a time limit, even dealing with your nerves and lasering in on performance. I think for young poets it's definitely a good experience. I'm always like, "I think you should slam once and then you should walk away from it." [All laugh] I feel like people should experience it.

But now so much of slam is team-based. So, in Halifax, when we were winning the slams, I think we did one team poem the entire time. Now everything is team. That's interesting in terms of the ways that it weaves in choreography, the ways that it weaves in collectivity. On the other hand, I don't know necessarily as an individual poet whether that supports your own vision of poetry, your own voice, which I think is, in the end, what we as writers want to cultivate, is our strong internal voice that survives through pushback. Are you going to have a voice? Do you know what you're doing? Are you clear on what you're trying to say? There's that line that someone said about Samuel Taylor Coleridge, if you saw a line of his poetry going by you in the desert you would know it's Coleridge's line. Do you have that sense of your work or are you subsumed into this team-piece voice, which is perhaps more theatre? There's nothing wrong with that, but it's interesting in the sense that the work is both more collective and often theatrical or using choreography within team pieces – using the full body, using space – all of which I think is innovative and interesting. It certainly moves away from the idea of poetry as a linear thing that is expressed in one way – in the same way, always – and then only is supposed to change or have depth upon repeated rereadings rather than in the living self. But what that means then for individual work, I suppose, is an open question.

I haven't slammed in years, so I'm not the expert on it. It has changed a lot. A slam generation is like three years. OG's in slam are people from like five years ago. [CM laughs] It doesn't have a lot of longevity in that sense. It is always fresh and new. So that's a bad thing in some ways. We always say this: there's no history in slam. People don't remember what came before them. You have young people coming that don't know their own histories and don't know the political battles that were being fought over membership, or what was going to show up on stage. There isn't a lot of preservation that way. There isn't a big archive in Canadian slam that allows people to access the history of their own art form. When that happens there's always an erasure of Blackness. The result of that is a massive erasure of the Black presence and always the white-ification and claiming of slam as some kind of white history. You have young Black poets coming up who can't believe when we tell them that in the 2008 finals there was one white poem on the entire stage. Black poets used to absolutely dominate. Now you have Black poets coming up that are changing the work because they're like, "Well, you know, you can't really do Black work so I just write for a white audience." I'm like, "Wow, we were having entirely Black slams." So those things change, and when you don't remember where you come from I think that's always what happens – it defaults towards whiteness. So those are the negatives.

But the positives are, I think, that dealing with nerves is important. I think showing presence is important. I think being able to be in the moment has important skills: practising together with teams, perfecting something in a particular way. Even getting something in under time. These, I think, are particular skills that slam offers. It's what you do with it in terms of how you take that work and run with it later. It's not inherently negative or inherently positive. It provides a space to do a certain type of performance. Nobody who does that performance thinks it's the only way to perform or even the only way they in themselves perform. It's a particular kind of performed work that you select for this space. Then hopefully you have a broader work beyond that and you can also move into those spaces beyond slam, and move back and forth between them. I think there's a lot of critique of slam that assumes slam as a kind of non-changing, parody kind of space that people say, "Oh, so like everyone just kind of gets up and yells and there are points."

Actually, that's not really what's happening in the space. There are many, many critiques to be made of that, but that's not necessarily the one. A critique I would make is the specificity of Canadian work that has, I think, gone down. There used to be very clear regional styles, very clear regional differences that were interesting. What you heard out of Vancouver was nothing like what you heard out of Halifax. Halifax was always deeply political, always about the police – before this was cool, you know what I mean? Before everyone was talking about social justice issues in poems, that was always us. Vancouver was totally different. The gestures were different. How you sat on stage was different. You got a sense going across Canada of the different regional styles and the different ways that history and culture developed. Then when everyone started going down to the States for the National Slam, you got this importing back of more of an American hegemonic style. Like, "What killed it at the American slam last year, let's do that." So I think that's something, as in all arts, that you're always fighting: the development of a dominant voice, and how, within that, do people hold on to different cultures and different ways of being, or different ways of presenting yourself that may not be the of-the-moment thing?

A few years ago everyone wanted to do poems in voices of people like, "I'm in a coma." Kind of weird. [All laugh] I mean these trends that you will see because something did well and people will do it. But that's part of it. It's not different in a slam space than in a literary space. It's not like essays don't shape each other, editorials don't pick up what is being done on the page of the *New York Times*. That's kind of how people are. So, yes, that exists in slam. I think there's been a bleed-in from the United States more and more, which I find somewhat unfortunate in terms of the kinds of different voices that could exist, but again, that's not specific to slam.

So if you haven't slammed, you probably don't know much about it and you should probably shut up, and if you have slammed you're going to have all kinds of critiques because everybody has both good and really terrible experiences, and fights with their teammates. The scene always falls apart eventually and then has to remake itself, much like any political space. A lot of what I carried into political activism was, "Thank God for slam" because I had to suffer so much bullshit in the slam space, that when it came to standing up to the Minister of Justice and stuff I'm like, "Yeah, I can do this." [ES laughs] But you learn through the conflict. It's not good, but I'm saying in a way it's just a microcosm of any world where you get up and speak. It's going to look like that if you're an activist, it's going to look like that if you engage in the media, and so I think it gave me skills for dealing with that. I think it gave me skills in my job interviews, or in terms of just being able to get up and deal with my nerves. So there are a lot of things you can bring out of slam for yourself, whatever that is, and then there's obviously negativity because it's human beings and no matter what, human beings are human beings.

People like to attribute the frailty of human beings to specific spaces, like "the left" or "slam" or "poetry." I'm like, "No, that's just humans." Like, the Beatles broke up, right? Like, conservative people beef with each other over whose definition of the Bible is correct [all laugh] and it just happens that people on the left beef with each other over particular other things, and people in poetry beef with each other over other particular things. It's not something unique because it's poetry and therefore it's a failing of us as poets or as slam artists. People have egos, people are frail, people have follies, and all of that will be played out on a slam stage times ten because it's all the flaws of actors and writers combined together. So you're going to get all the neurosis of performance and the neurosis of writing in the same place. Plus then you add the pressures of scores and it's going to be a shitshow in a lot of ways. But that's human life. I don't think it's caused by slam.

I think that's just caused by being human. I mean, laughing at human follies never did go stale. That's the entire eighteenth-century genre of writing, and slam basically is that writ large. But I don't think it's a failure of the writing as such, I think it's just a space where there's a lot of human stuff going on behind the work that I think influences how people experience the space. Because you're like, "Oh man, everyone hated my poem and then I went to my hotel room and cried," you know?

ES: Yep.

EJ: And then there's drama about it, but that's human drama. And people are young too.

CM: Erin, how about you?

ES: Yeah, I agree with a lot of what you say, El. I think that it's really easy that there's this strange divide in the literary world, that if you're a spoken word poet or you participate in slam predominately, that that removes you or separates you from poets who are coming out of academic traditions and/or the CanLit publishing world. But we know that Can Lit is the biggest shit-show out there and so it's a funny thing to hear critiques coming from it about this enclosed community of slam when CanLit is just brimming with all of this same type of self-glorification and egotistical bullshit that leads a lot of writers to continue writing and pursuing, not just writing for the sake of writing and for publication and connecting to audience, but for the sake of big awards and prizes and validation in and amongst a group of peers that they deem acceptable, or capable, or whatever becomes that kind of classification. I always find that to be really comical. It's just so *not* self-reflexive. It's like, who are you kidding right now? You participate in all of the same types of bullshit.

But in a lot of ways, to further what El said, they do it behind a book. They do it at home and then they hide, and they go well, "That fucking asshole wrote that review about me and I hated it." When you get on a slam stage, you can see in people's faces when they hate your poem. There's no hiding. There's something that's really powerful about being willing to put yourself in that situation. I know that, personally, as El said, I've had amazing experiences with various slam communities and also really shitty ones. You end up learning about who you are and what you value and how you participate in the creation of your own self-identity as you put that out to the world. Because that's a big part of what we're doing as artists. We're saying, "Hey, this is a piece, or a part, or a presentation of who I am. What do you think about that?" And that comes back to us and has all of these implications that in a lot of ways do tend to lead towards ego or self-glorification. So, you have to be constantly critically pulling apart what matters to you in the creation and publication or presentation of your art. Is it your peers who matter or is it the panel of judges who are going to give you the Nobel or the Pulitzer? Or is it random audience members who are half-drunk giving you scores out of ten, you know?

For me, I brought slam up into the Kelowna community. There was no poetry slam happening here. There were only open mics and I really wanted it because at first I was really young and I thought that this would allow Kelowna to get on the map, kind of like what El was saying. What we are doing here is not the same as what is going on in Vancouver. It's not the same as Toronto. This is Kelowna: there's barely any people, there's a whole bunch of conservatives, and then this weird underground hippie movement. It's a strange orchard town. What people are presenting is not anything that I had been hearing at any other poetry slams and I had lived in LA for years and been in that slam scene as well. So it became this motivation for me to put us on the map. And then the more I started going to these outside slams, the more I was like, "Oh, no, we must insulate, we must hide from them, we must protect what is ours here because it's beautiful and it's not full of bullshit yet." So we do slams in this really casual way where it's an open slam, anybody comes down and we give out cash prizes and that is it. The night ends when the night ends. There's no sort of, "We're going to create a team and we're going to put them into the Canadian Festival of Spoken Word." None of that ever came to be for us in our slam community. Part of that was this conscious formation of our community as something that people would ask for if they wanted it, but really it was about getting the audience involved and having some type of interaction and engagement that promoted the type of active listening that we've been talking about. We said to the audience, "You're here; you're just as much a part of this as those who are standing on stage and have prepared." How can we engage in that exchange and continue that dialogue so that this is about everyone in this space, not just about the person who feels valuable enough to go on stage and recite? Kind of like what Tawhida Tanya was saying about everybody in this room is a performer even if you don't get on stage and perform. Even if you don't say those poems out loud.

I think sometimes when we get these big, canonized writers reflecting on that it feels really intrusive to their sense of identity as special, as talented, as a poet who has worked to commit to themselves as a poet. What does that mean if everyone else is also allowed to be a poet? How does that minimize the work and this sort of commitment they feel that they have put forward in their life? I think that's a great thing to do. I think we cut down all of these boundaries that we build up and allow people to be artists as professionals, or amateurs, or audience members. That actually we're all holding that space together. That to me is one of the greatest powers of slam, is that you're putting that energy back into the audience's hands.

EJ: I think what also offends the sensibilities of the poetry establishment is these ideas that poetry is slow. If you've ever gone to the Governor General's Awards ceremony everybody makes this speech in the slowest, most boring way, you know? [All laugh] But legit, this is one of the essays in my book and I talk about going to the Griffin Prize readings because I wanted to watch Dionne Brand. I'm sitting there – it's me, Desmond Cole, and Reed Jones – and we got there at half-time so we didn't know what was going on, and this woman started speaking and I legitimately thought it was the poetry. It opened like, [EJ speaks in soft, slow voice] "poetry." [All laugh] "Strong. Foundational." I thought that was a poem! And then the minute she said the name of the poet, I'm like, "Oh my God, this is the intro!" And I turn to Desmond and I'm like, "I legitimately thought that was the poem!" [All laugh] Then we both started laughing so hard. And you know who we were with? David Chariandy. He had snuck us in, and we were howling with laughter. Embarrassing.

So the point is here: that is performance. "A good poem rewards frequent engagement." So I think it bothers people, the idea that a poem can just be like that [EJ snaps fingers]. I think it bothers people when I say, "I don't know, I just wrote it," because it removes this idea of a particular kind of very Europeanized, intellectual exercise, and the ideas of improv, the ideas of ephemerality, the ideas of, "I just did it because it sounded good and it was what I wanted to do in this moment." Those run very counter. So, it's sad. It's very threatening not only to people's own roles in the literary establishment, but the very idea of literature, which has always excluded things that involve youth poetry, queer poetry, feminist poetry, Black poetry, Indigenous oral traditions. We're never included anyway, and then people just get angry when we dare to assert that this is actually a space and maybe their stuff is laughable, you know? [ES laughs] Maybe it's funny when you go to the Griffin Prize and people feel the need to talk in this really low poetry voice and then when you start laughing, not even to be a dick, but because I genuinely thought that was the poem. How am I supposed to tell the difference? Then I was like, "Maybe there should be a game. Is this an intro or a Canadian poem?" [All laugh] And that's not to say the poetry was shitty! It was the Griffin Prize and the poetry was good, but it's the thing around it all. A slam is not the only performative space, as has been pointed out. Everybody is constantly performing themselves. Constantly. We live in a fucking performative world. Hello, social media. Tawhida Tanya, you might want to say something. I'm going to drink from this huge jug of lemonade. [EJ laughs]

TTE: I just wanted to say that, by George Bowering saying what he said, he removes any understanding of the roots of spoken word and the roots of poetry, the griots of West Africa, the djelis, the storytellers, the troubadours, the wandering dervishes who went around telling stories. That is all removed, or maybe he is just ignorant of the history of poetry, which is oral [TTE laughs]. It is not written. It is pre-literate.

CM: Now that we're thinking through this, the label "spoken word" is a contentious one, and not always deployed in the same way. In her book *The Cultural Politics of Slam Poetry: Race, Identity, and the Performance of Popular Verse in America*, Susan Somers-Willett defines slam and spoken word poetry not as genres so much as a body of work with a range of styles and tones, etc. But not every poet feels it is a word that describes their practice. In the interview that Deanna and I did with Tracie Morris, Morris pushed back against the term, noting something along the lines of "spoken word could be anything" and that "everything is spoken." So to ask a really large question, and you may have touched on this in some way already, but what is spoken word and is this a movement that you consider your own art practice to be a part of? Where do you stand in relation to that as a keyword?

TTE: Are you asking me? Shall I jump in then?

CM: Yeah, this is kind of to everyone, but please, jump in!

TTE: Yeah, I can call myself a spoken word artist. Some people say "performing writer" or there's all these titles for it. I consider it more like a vast umbrella and many things live or can take shelter underneath it. Hip hop is spoken word. Clowning is spoken word. Storytelling is spoken word. Dub is spoken word. So there's just a vast umbrella, and I'm okay with that vastness. I'm okay with it and I dig it. I think that goes back also to the griot tradition where the griot has like fifty different job titles: you're the poet, the storyteller, the dancer, the ceremony participant, the village librarian, the genealogist. You have all these titles. I think spoken word is just perhaps a more modern version of the griot. So I'm okay with calling myself that. I also think we're kind of this group of folks where if you don't belong anywhere else, if you're a monologist or something, you belong with us. We'll accept you! And if you start to make a list of anyone who falls under this umbrella of spoken word it will be extensive, more extensive than you can possibly imagine. I've done this in a workshop setting. I forgot to mention also that I work at the Banff Centre every couple of years doing the spoken word residency program there. We had a workshop where we said, "Okay, write every job title for someone who could call themselves a spoken word artist." The list ... I mean, we had like a hundred different people. Like, an auctioneer is a spoken word artist. It just was an exhaustive list. And I'm cool to be in there because there's a lot of us in there. And it means there are a lot of us out there.

I'm really outside of academia. Like I said, it didn't do much for me when I was in it, even when I was putting on events. No one from my classes would attend them because they were all spoken word events and I guess it just wasn't literary enough for them. But, in fact, we work twice as hard because we are writers and performers. So we're actually interdisciplinary artists. So I think that also is something that should be recognized as far as what spoken word is. We are interdisciplinary artists. From writing and performance we can go anywhere we want; we can go into film, we can go into dance, we can go into music, we can collaborate with all these different other art forms. We can publish if we want to, we can self-publish. We can get our stuff published by publishing houses. We can put out an album. It's just incredible; it lends itself to experimenting and I'm really happy to be part of this kind of genre that is so wide open to experimentation. Also, that is specifically from a West African oral tradition. I take great pride in that.

ES: It was kind of similar to how I was talking about when I first started to form my identity as an artist, a similar sort of thing happened where people just started saying that I was a "spoken word artist," which I always found interesting. They used the word "artist" as though they were saying, "Well, you're not really a poet; you're an artist." Which again, odd. But sure, whatever. But it was that kind of thing where I actually, before I became a writer, was always performing. Acting was my jam. Being on stage and having an audience was kind of my lifeblood through my teenage years. So when I went into the university I wanted to shift towards writing, but I wanted to write plays. I still do write a lot of plays and writing for that mode is really important to me, but I've always said, and will argue vehemently, that poetry and playwriting are just sisters and so they share a lot of the same DNA, and a lot of the same structures in the way they are formed, created, and then actually delivered. So, spoken word is just to me some mini poem-ologues, as I have called them in the past as well. They are some kind of tenuous thing. They are this hybrid, wonderfully beautiful thing, but I think what happens often is we are just in that Eurocentric thinking of what is the box, and how do we categorize this? When things don't accept that – when they're holistic, and they're shifting, and they're malleable – it creates some kind of resistance from a lot of these types of bodies who say,

"You can apply to the BC Arts Council, but you can't apply to write a book, because you're a spoken word artist and therefore you will create a CD and that's all you'll create for the rest of your life." I think sometimes we just come up against classifications.

So, I really love Tawhida Tanya's interpretation and understanding of it. That it's actually an empowering thing and an incredible thing that we have this group of all of these creators who are making just vastly different, and strange, and unique creations under this umbrella term of spoken word. There's sort of this limitlessness. Again, that's challenging to those who want to keep some semblance of control. When I don't discipline my children in typical ways and the whole world goes, "What the fuck are you doing?" it's like, "Well, they're their own beings. They're going out there!" That's what spoken word is; it's the same kind of thing. It's this acceptance of some sort of chaos that isn't predetermined but has an incredible path to follow at the same time, you know?

CM: Yeah, you kind of speak to the boxes of BC Arts Council, and places like that, and the way that the arts are affected by the takeover of neo-liberalism in the academy, and outside of the academy as well. That there is less and less funding for the arts and maybe that speaks back to some of the animosity between spoken word and page poetry: the pie for arts is getting smaller and so as a practitioner of a particular field you are sort of forced to define yourself in distinct or aggrandizing ways in order to access opportunities and funding that is more and more going to STEM or other fields.

So, Tawhida Tanya, I wanted to turn to you for a moment. We heard Erin and El speak to some of the slam stuff, but one thing that seems particular to your work is that both dance and music are constitutive elements of your performance practice. In academia, and especially literary sound studies, so often performed poetry is highlighted for its textual or sonic qualities, but not always its corporeality. So I was wondering, how important is the body to your performance poetry and what is the relationship of music and dance to your work? And then maybe as a little bit of a question at the end, if you want to speak to this as well: when you were working on *Nouveau Griot*, which collects earlier performance poems from your career as text, how was the process of translating those poems – specifically the elements of body and sound – back onto the page?

TTE: Well, everything came out of the page, so it wasn't that hard. I just went back to it. I think I can name maybe two or three spoken word artists who don't write first and who can conceive things in their mind and perform, and this is outside of hip hop, outside of things like a cipher and stuff like that. I am a writer first and foremost, so everything starts on the page. After that, the work will tell me how it wants to live. Does it want to stay on the page? Does it want to be a song? Does it want to be something that is shouted, or something that's whispered, or something that's said very quickly, or something that's said [TTE speaks slowly] very slowly? [CM laughs] In a way, I've tried to get out of the way.

The same is true when it comes to what the body will do when the poem is embodied. If you can memorize it, then all of that process of writing and memorizing will inform how it is presented through the body. So I use lots of different physical aspects from my tool box. I used to study ballet and West African dance. Even doing Buddhist sitting meditation. I remember once seeing Ian Keteku doing a spoken word piece on his head. He was standing on his head in this yogic posture and had the mic on the ground! [TTE laughs] It was beautiful! So it just depends on what is in your tool box when it comes to your body. Sufi whirling is also in my tool box, it is a kind of active meditation; I just happen to do it a lot in public which not a lot of people do. That's okay.

Everyone has different things in their tool box. El, you're a runner, I remember; you're a jogger. You know? Those kinds of things, they're all in our tool box. Who knows in the piece that is coming out, what aspects of that tool box are going to emerge? And I think we just let that happen. Because my practice is full time, I think I have a lot more time and space to focus on that. And so I just do. I'm also interested in performance, and when I go to a show, it doesn't matter who is on stage, I want to know how close that artist can get to dying without actually dying. Like, that for me is a good show. And so I want to see that in any kind of performance, right? I want to see that in music, I want to see that in theatre. That's what I dig. So that's what I'm trying to do. I might fail, but that's okay because I'm trying really hard to push this body. I'm trying to push my understanding of language, my understanding of sound. So that's where the body and this work come together.

Music is, well, I always just wanted to be a musician and I just wasn't. I slept with lots of musicians. So I had a good time, but it didn't get me closer to being a musician. [TTE laughs] Until I moved from Tiohtià:ke/Montreal to Coast Salish, to Vancouver, and I met Sufis. And in a Sufi practice music is encouraged, and music from inspiration is encouraged. It's like gospel in church. You know when a lot of singers will say, "Oh, where did you learn how to sing?" "In church." Well, I learned how to sing with the Sufis. So I learned how to become a musician just by being with other people who allowed everyone to sing. You don't have to "be a singer" or "be" this or "be" that, just hit the drum! Fucking let your voice cry out. And so sitting with the Sufis is what allowed me to also become a musician which means that if I wrote a piece and I'm like, "Hmm, what is this? Oh, maybe it's a song." So it allowed some of my work to become more musical, and then made me feel more confident in collaborating with musicians, which I still think is a really great way to interact with spoken word – through music. If I think of my ultimate spoken word artist, it's still Saul Williams, and pretty much everything Saul does is with music as well. I've always been in that school where I want spoken word with music, and so I'm just trying to do my best within that realm with what's in my tool box.

CM: Thanks so much. Yeah, you were talking about just letting that sound out, and we've talked a little bit as well about the way that people are kind of taught what writing is and what writing isn't. Watching my kids grow and do things, kids haven't learned what music isn't yet, or they haven't learned what writing isn't yet and so they just *do*. Our one-year-old just finds any two things he can and smashes them together and then he claps and dances a little bit, and in no way is it a beat [TTE laughs] or anything that resembles traditional kinds of musical measures, but he's loving it. So I love that you uphold just "hitting the drum," or *doing* art for art's sake, outside of an artistic economy.

TTE: You asked me about *Nouveau Griot*, but I just wanted to mention that that book, all the work, just came from the original writing of all those poems. I didn't write a script so that you could visualize what I would be doing on stage while you're reading the poems. If you want, you can listen to the albums while you're reading the book, but also the voice in your mind is enough. If I can transmit this mind [TTE touches head] to your mind [TTE reaches toward camera] then I did my job. Nothing else really matters – gestures, or sound. It's just about mind-to-mind transmission and that can happen on the page, or it can happen through headphones, or it can happen through our eyes. Through all our senses – how we interact with the world. So I just wanted to mention that.

CM: Yeah, I actually did an experiment – I work in the digital humanities where we try to use computers to do traditional humanities work. I used this coding language called the TEI, the Text Encoding Initiative, and I tried to do a TEI markup of "Temple Exercises" and mark up what your body was doing in a YouTube video in relation to the words on the page. It actually didn't really work out. [TTE laughs] But it was cool! I learned a lot about my own scholarly work and I listened to that poem like eight thousand times. [All laugh]

Anyway, so I'm going to turn to you, El, for a moment. You're an activist, and a poet, and an educator. You've done radio work. You've done so much. I read recently that you were appointed to a Halifax police commission to help them find what defunding the police might look like. So I was hoping you could maybe talk about the way that your poetic practice, activism, and public service intersect with and/or inform one another. As a more general, overlay question: what is art's potential for resistance or to effect change, whether directly or indirectly?

EJ: Going back to people's hostility towards Black people, we just do shit. When I wanted to be a journalist, I just started writing articles. Like, I didn't have to go to fucking journalism school. [All laugh] When I wanted to go on the radio, I just started talking on the radio. That doesn't mean that we don't have an intellectual practice; we have an extremely strong intellectual practice, but it's just fucking life. It's not that deep, in some ways. Tawhida Tanya was talking about running. It's not like if someone sees you run, if you've been running your whole life, like, "Oh, you have a really nice and easy stride." It's easy because every day of my life I go out and run, but in the moment I'm not thinking about it; it's just running.

Writing is just like that to me. I don't sit around and be like, "Oh, what word would be perfect here?" Either I'm writing it or I'm not. If it's not working, I'm not doing it. Unless it's for school or something, it ain't happening. So either it sounds right or it don't. Jessica Care Moore said on the spoken word thing, "We're poets. I can't help it that it falls out of my mouth and it sounds good just because I'm Black," you know what I mean? [All laugh] It's like, kind of! I'm not essentializing Blackness here, but what I'm saying is that there are very European ideas around what an intellectual discipline is and this fetishizing of particular forms of labour and production. It must look hard in these particular ways, and we must be thoughtful in these particular ways, and fetishize a particular form of slowness.

When you have practices outside that, it's shocking to white people that you're like, "Yeah, no, I just wrote that on the bus." Because it is like, life just flows. I don't got the time to be precious about my work. I've probably got to present it in an hour, and it's just got to be written the way it's written, and I'll figure it out. That doesn't mean I don't have a sharp analysis. I'm thinking 24/7. Desmond Cole and I spend absolute hours on the phone. Desmond, me, and Idil Abdillahi: that's our practice. Our artistic, activist, and life practices: we talk everything out for hours. Like, when we were doing the Abdoul Abdi campaign, it was twenty hours on the phone. You would see Desmond calls Idil, Idil calls El, and it was hours. That was how we built consensus in our actions. That was how we built tactic and strategy. We don't disagree, because when we disagree we are talking it out so we don't have fights over ego or who wants to go in what direction when we're working on something together because we just talk about it. We know each other, and we trust each other, and we talk constantly. Desmond and I will go through articles together and just tear them apart word for word. But that's the practice, because then when it comes to us writing we're internalizing that.

I'm not the kind of learner or writer where somebody could tell me what to do. If someone's like, "Go and move your arms like this," I would feel stiff and awkward. I have to internalize it for myself and watch other people do it and then I'll adopt it and just do it. So that's just how I learn. I learn the law by sitting in court. That doesn't mean I could go be a lead lawyer on a murder trial, but I could certainly help you do your habeas because I can absorb it that way. I do think that's culture, and I think European culture is very much against that because it is a culture of credentialing, and a culture of siloing, and a culture of expertise in particular ways. I think that for a lot of Black people and in Black arts, that hasn't been the case. Poetry is protest. Your life at home is your political work in reading. So if I'm doing a poem, the analysis in that poem is also my academic work, is also what I'm going to present on the police board in defunding. All of that is because I am always thinking about Black liberation 24/7, and strategy, and tactic. Whatever I'm doing, it's just going to come out in that. But I also just don't think it's that deep. So in one way I'm always like, "I hate talking about poetry because I just kind of write it." A lot of it is off the rhyme, like you pick a word and then that's going to be the first line and then everything else is just going to sound like that line. It's going to be in that rhythm; or you're going to break that rhythm; or it's going to rhyme, or you're going to split that rhyme; or it's going to come off the vowel sign; or you're going to move to something else; and it is either going to sound right or it won't. If it ain't sounding good then I'm going to stop doing it after about twelve lines, if this ain't working. I guess I'll do something else. I just don't, in that sense, find it that hard. I don't think it needs to be.

Same with writing an article. I think you have to be centred in what you think, and know what you think, and know your own voice. That's an ongoing process to fight for your voice back from other people, to fight for yourself back from other people, the way people always contain you, the way people constantly critique you, the way, if you're a Black woman, that you're not allowed to live, and be, and think. You have to claw yourself back from that. But once you've done that, the process of saying things just isn't that hard. If I have to wake up today and write a terms of reference for a defunding panel for the police board, it will let me do public hearings, and then that's also a poem. These things flow together. I think that's part of African practice as well.

Even when we talk about spoken word, there's a difference between spoken word in mainstream Canadian culture and spoken word if you go to Jamaica, which is an oral culture and totally different. People are picking up so fast on what people are saying and the refrains. Jamaican is a totally separate language in English, how people are speaking it. They're hearing a refrain once and they've got the whole chorus because they are from an oral country. Their respect for oral work is on a completely different level. When I went to Garvey fest in Ocho Rios there were thousands of Rastas in a tent, and everyone coming up and asking you questions about, "You did this poem about Malcolm X and in this line you said this ..." All from memory. It's totally different – it's an oral culture, and it's a culture that respects oral arts and understands a particular form of decolonial life through these arts that's nursed through Rasta culture.

It's just totally different than when you speak in Canada, which is "sit on your chair and clap politely." I mean, in mainstream Canadian society. It's just different, because orality is an actual culture, it's an orientation to the world, it's an orientation to other people. It's not just that you wrote something and now you're saying it, which is what the Canada Council wants to say it is, which is literary performance. If you write something and then say it, that makes it oral. It does, but not in the same way as orality, which is engrained in a practice. My mom taught me orally. That was my mom's study thing. I had to say all the spelling to her orally and repeat all the science books to her orally. She would quiz me on it. That was a form of oral learning, which is how she learned too. It's an oral pedagogy. No one put it that way. Ten years from now some white person will name that and be like, [EJ speaks in a British accent] "Oh, you know, best practices in education pedagogy ..." [EJ laughs], you know? Then it will be called something and then they'll be like, "Hey, this white person invented this." And it was like what your mom had been doing to you because her mom did it to her. It's just how we talk, and how we learn, and how we pick up. I don't want us to move into the discourse of the "natural." Oh, so Black people just "naturally" do these things, because that's how we're dis-intellectualized. This is always how what we do can be dismissed and excluded because that's just Black people – they just happen to be good dancers, they just happen to have good memories ... We don't. We've just been practising this and it's a specific pedagogy and practice. We just don't go around calling it a pedagogy and practice. We just call it life. But it is actually a practice. So I can think of all kinds of ways in which these things were just practised.

My grandfather was a political artist, and he was a trade unionist, and a Calypso artist, and a chemist, and he made fireworks, and that was just all part of life. So I don't like to separate it in that sense, and I think there's a preciousness about art that is very post-Romantic as well. Tawhida Tanya's been saying this as well. This notion of the "role of the artist" in Western society as opposed to just the person that walks around and tells you your history and shit. So, yeah, for me it's connected and it's part of life. That doesn't mean I don't also see the cursor blinking on the page and be like, "Fuck!" I don't mean that writing just falls out of my mouth, but I mean I don't fetishize the practice, I guess. This idea of like, "What is the writers' desk? Let us see what you have on your bookshelf!" [All laugh] I just find that stuff laughable. I just find that stuff funny. Writing is sitting at your computer in your pajamas unshowered and you're like, "Fuck, it's 8:00 a.m. and I've got to get this shit in by 10:00." It's like [EJ mimics typing very fast.] [All laugh] If I want to make it into something else to justify the labour – which is very capitalist, because capitalism wants us to believe that we always have to be productive, and busy and performing, and labouring in certain ways – the only way we can justify these things we do is by being like, "It's so much labour," instead of just being like, "It's life." So I reject this kind of capitalist idea of what art has to mean for us. I resist that.

CM: I love what you say about when you have an hour, you have to write it in an hour, and that is what it is. I think sometimes especially when you look at the types of writing that are rewarded in Canadian literature, that things can be so over-conceptualized. There are these really predictable kinds of structures of like, "Okay, I'm going to show you an orange or something and then I'm going to talk about my grandmother, and then I'm going to bring the orange back at the end and the orange is going to be charged up with all this grandmother meaning." It can start to feel predictable in unproductive ways, and I think that when writing in a quicker or more improvisational way it can result in work that feels more fresh.

EJ: Bring me your orange grandmother shit. Like, I'm all for whatever writing, but I mean, it's at the point where it becomes valued differently. If what is important to somebody is slowness and conceptual writing, I'm not critiquing that. I'm not saying that's lesser. I'm saying the difference is that it becomes, "This is what poetry is, and this what intellectuality is, and this is what meaning is, and this is what the hiring of a Creative Writing department is." That is what I reject. But I'm all for your conceptual orange grandma, [all laugh] you know what I mean? Thank God!

CM: I've always found in my own writing practice that I have a really hard time – just with poetry, not so much with fiction – with editing. Whenever I start editing something it becomes worse and worse. So a lot of the poems that I write, 80 per cent of it is like there on the first go and I like that freshness of it, or that you can tell that things aren't tied together as neatly as maybe they could be.

EJ: I also really like the idea of writing a parodic thesis. Like, if I ever wanted to get a really conventional dissertation done, I always thought that if I did it as a satiric act, I'd probably get it done, and it wouldn't be really a dissertation it would just be me fucking around and making up citations and stuff and then I'd get expelled or something. [CM laughs]. But I think there's also this element of play, right?

Sound is play, when we go back to sound. Rhyme is play. Sometimes I'm just like, "How long can I stretch this rhyme just to see if I can do it? How long can I flip this word around?" It doesn't have to be that serious, is what I'm saying.

ES: Yeah, I totally agree. I often find in my own art practice that there's this big tension between my identity and role as a mother, and my identity and role as an artist, as though those two things actually can't work well together. There's this idea that I vastly and intensely must separate them. I've often talked about how that's just not how it is – that actually, what it is for me is like a residency in motherhood. So now I just have all this fucking amazing material every single day of my lived life whether or not I'm actually writing or sitting down and doing it. It's happening as part of my existence. My mom is a Scottish immigrant and so she comes from this long line of Gaelic traditions of song. The other day she was singing a song to Cole and I that she would sing when they would play kick-the-can, which I was just like, "You guys just have songs for everything." [All laugh] But they do! It's part of it, you know? So I agree that I think there's so much more of practice that's just living, that often when we talk about life as artists it's this very delineated thing of like, "Well, now when you go and do that thing of making art, and that's set aside and separate." When I think they're actually all just meshing and melding together. For me that's one of the most fruitful things when I'm not writing. I'll go years. When I first had my kids I went three years without writing anything. I was writing things, I just wasn't sitting down and writing things. I was always creating and always thinking through and working on that practice in ways that are not that sort of traditional, Eurocentric "sit down at your writing desk," you know? [All laugh]

TTE: It comes from a life well-lived though. I mean, you're living. The writing comes from living, so you actually have to live, and engage, and collaborate, and be in service to human beings if you're going to write about anything. Then there's no difference. There shouldn't be a difference between your living and your writing. The only difference would be opportunity. Those who have an opportunity, or a space to share it, and those who do not. That's where we can shift our responsibilities and make sure we support those who need to be supported so that we can all get to this concept of unity, of all of us in community as a species on this planet that we're killing. [TTE laughs] [ES laughs] So we can't even deal with that if we can't even be together in small communities or even with ourselves and the work that we do. It can't be separate. For me that would be the opposite. You know, I hold artists to really high standards, and if you call yourself any kind of artist or writer or whatever, you better tell the truth. I don't want to hear any overt lies because then you're out. Why do this work? Go and be an accountant where lying is part of the game. I don't want to be in this game where lies are part of it. That's why we're doing this work. Because we're interested in clarity and in seeing things clearly. This is the Sankofa idea of looking to the past so we can build a better future for ourselves. As we hopefully dismantle what's going on now, we can replace it with something beautiful that did not exist before. If we can all access our Indigenous selves, we would know that. I'm not angry; I'm just angry. [CM laughs]

CM: Of community-art organizations, scholar Claire Bishop writes, "it is a difficult task to be countercultural while asking for state approval and support."[5] Erin, you're the executive director of the Kelowna poetry non-profit Inspired Word Café and you've been doing lots of community arts organizing for years and years. I was hoping maybe you could speak to the way that, as a community organizer, you have to navigate this tension between creating radical and inclusive community art, but also the demands of event production and funding and all these sorts of things under late capitalism.

ES: Yeah, [ES laughs] that's a big one. It's kind of like I was pointing to, it crosses the boundary from my work in the arts non-profit world, which is essentially just going around trying to validate your existence to people with money, and then being an artist, which often times actually feels very fucking similar. I do have value. I will make something that is important, and here's how many people it's going to reach. Suddenly we kind of get into all of these sort of quantitative ways just like Tawhida Tanya was just saying with the accountants, where they want artists and art to generate these types of outcomes that I don't really know how we're supposed to ever express the outcomes of what art does because it's about feelings, and it's about perceptions, and it's about things that are often not tangible or are at least not able to be turned into metrics. So it's really challenging.

It's really challenging. Most of all because a big part of what we have done for ten years at Inspired Word Café is put people on stages who would never otherwise get up and do it. They wouldn't send their work out for publication. They're not going to universities for schooling for this type of art practice. We've got a member who comes out to every single event and reads, and he has serious brain damage and was told he would never write, and yet here he is creating and memorizing and reciting poems every single month for ten years. How do you quantify that into a grant where you say, "This has these values" and they turn to you and they go, "Well, it has value for one person, so what does that matter?" So it's always a challenge; it's a challenge because a lot of these councils or bodies who have funding also get their funding from other bodies and so it becomes this chain of command.

Just like El has talked about a lot, with any type of political system that we're existing within where what's deemed as valuable is ever-changing, and is dependent on a whole entire series of policies and different political underpinnings. So it becomes a game in a lot of ways, and that game gets really exhausting and challenging to continue to participate in all the time. But it also feels fucking great when Mark gets onstage every single month and recites his poems and feels community that maybe he never would have felt in his life. People come in off the streets and say, "I don't have money to come in," and we say, "come in and sit down." By the end of it they share poems and suddenly it's like, this is what it's about. But it just feels like sometimes I'm a wizard and I'm trying to cast spells on corporate people to give me money to put on events, which I often don't get paid to do. I think my kids don't really know what it is that I do for a job. They always say that I'm the weird mom. So I don't know if that's a good thing or a bad thing. [CM and ES laugh]

But, yeah, I think it's a really big struggle, and as you've pointed to in the conversation earlier, it's changing in terms of how funding is getting doled out and what's being valued. I was going to apply for a grant the other day. It was for our open mic, which is all amateur poets – well, not all. We have a wide range of people who come out; some professionals with lots of books and whatever. It said, "Who is on your creative team?" And I was like, "I don't know? Fuck, half of Kelowna is on my creative team!" [All laugh] "Any poet that gets on the stage is on the creative team! What do you mean?" What they're looking for is four professional artists who I can write about their bios and send proof of their work. So I was just like, "Fuck it, I'm not writing this grant. I'm going to find money in other ways." Part of my art practice has shifted both as a producer and as an artist to being hyper-local. There's this woman in Kelowna – well, she's not in Kelowna, she's actually in Grindrod, which is a tiny little town outside of Kelowna – and she runs this art non-profit, and everything is about the people in Grindrod. There's like four thousand people in Grindrod, and she gets huge funding, but she's an amazing puppeteer and she's committed her life to the people of that community and those artists, who are also nurses and are the welder in town and all these things where maybe their lives wouldn't have art. So I've been trying to really actively shift my own sense of where my art goes and how I put my time and who I'm bringing into the fray of supporting and funding the operations or the art that I'm trying to put out there.

NOTES

1 Charles Leroux. "Filling Chicago with Poetry," *Chicago Tribune*, 1 April 2003, accessed 15 July 2021, www.chicagotribune.com/news/ct-xpm-2003-04-01-0304010013-story.html.
2 Corey Frost, "Border Disputes: Spoken Word and Its Humble Critics," *Liminalities: A Journal of Performance Studies* 10, no. 3–4 (2014): 3.
3 David Barber, "The Man in the Back Row Has a Question VI," *Paris Review* 154 (Spring 2000): 379, accessed 4 December 2018, www.theparisreview.org/miscellaneous/780/the-man-in-the-back-row-has-a-question-vi-david-barber.
4 Corey Frost, "The Omnidirectional Microphone: Performance Literature as Social Project" (PhD diss. New York University, 2010), iv.
5 Claire Bishop, *Artificial Hells: Participatory Art and the Politics of Spectatorship* (London: Verso, 2012), 188.

10

The Whatever-icity of Spoken Word
Community, Identity, Performativity

Corey Frost

After more than a year of pandemic lockdowns and semi-lockdowns, including a year of reluctantly teaching writing and literature classes via Zoom, I thought I'd be tired of listening to rectangular virtual people. In much of what I've written about spoken word in the past, the thesis has been that physical presence is paramount, that the real performance lies in how we coexist in a room. Being at an event and observing the ways that performers and audience interact in real time, in real space, is central to both spoken word performance and scholarship, and I've been missing it. But deprivation can sharpen certain senses, and it seems that physical absence can make one more attuned to the pleasures and complexities of digital presence.

This essay is, mostly, a response to a conversation between Cole Mash, Erin Scott, Tawhida Tanya Evanson, and El Jones, which happened originally through synchronous online video, but which I experienced as a video recording. Some important ideas came up in this conversation, and I'd like to splice together and amplify a few comments found therein: I touch on how communities are defined, the distinction between popular and avant-garde, race and poetic communities, and the performative nature of identity. But let me begin with some observations about degrees of distance and mediation.

Acousmaticity

A computer screen is not a room, and a Zoom conversation is not a stage performance, but the virtual can be as full of complexity and performativity as the non-virtual. Using Zoom is like watching several performances at once, through several tiny windows, looking onto several small domestic stages where the performers are also the set designers – while you also perform on your own tiny stage. Even in a recording, another degree removed from live conversation, so much of the substance of in-person oral communication is there: the timbre of voices and the rhythms of overlapping rhetorical patterns, smirks and raised eyebrows, gestures that reveal half-glimpsed tattoos, the non-verbal and nearly imperceptible evidence of a joke landing or missing, the mysterious dimensions of virtually inhabited spaces, the background wall art, the cameo appearances by people, animals, and plants. It's not an unmediated, embodied experience, but it is an uncanny representation that, in its difference, shows us something about the nature of performance itself; T.L. Cowan has referred to this difference as *transmedial drag*,[1] and it has never been more apparent than in the online audiovisual era.

The digital-presence technologies made ubiquitous by our unfortunate virtual reality are something new, but they are also just the latest step in a long technological revolution. As I have written before,[2] the spoken word movement itself could be seen as a by-product of the invention of the microphone and audio recording technologies, in the same way that abstract painting was arguably a response to the invention of photography. The microphone and the radio and the phonograph (and later the tape recorder and the MP3 and so on) enabled literature to expand into the realm of *acousmatic* sound – sound heard without seeing its origins, the realm of voices beyond bodies – and this had a significant impact on poetry in particular. It ended the millennia-old monopoly of writing as a technology for recording speech, and, I argue, it provoked a gradual performative turn in literary culture.

To use terminology developed by film scholar Michel Chion, in an audio recording the poetic voice becomes "acousmatized." Yet, an earlier technology – writing itself, long the dominant medium for poetry – effected an even more radical deracination and disembodiment of the poetic voice. Even though writing doesn't require sound, it was in a sense the first and most thorough acousmatization of poetry. A poem by its nature is an oral artifact,[3] and when we don't have the actual voice of the poet in our ears, we still have the disembodied sound of the words in our head. The audio recording, from this point of view, partially *de*acousmatizes the text by restoring a vocal echo, a clue to the source's identity; the video recording is a further (but not complete) deacousmatization, giving us a virtual apparition of the source itself – and a Zoom call brings us to the brink of actual presence.

"Deracinate" is a particularly apt or provocative term in this context – it means uproot (from the Latin *radix*, meaning root), but it's tempting to read it also as a synonym of "deracialize" (even though the two stems are etymologically unrelated). When a voice is acousmatized, either literally as an audio recording or more figuratively as written text, it becomes harder to identify the source, to assign an identity – including a racial identity. Conversely, the closer we are to the live utterance, the more we assume we know about the identity of the speaker. Words on a page, most of the time, do little to signal race or gender or age or ethnicity – but voices are subtly racialized, as are faces.

This is the subject of Nina Sun Eidsheim's *The Race of Sound*, which interrogates the social production of race through voice and vocal qualities. A key premise for Eidsheim is that the sound of a human voice provokes a fundamental question – *who is speaking?* – which she calls the acousmatic question. But, she explains, it's a question we ask even though we can't answer it; we continue to ask it *because* we can't answer it: "We ask the acousmatic question because it is not possible to know voice, vocal identity, and meaning as such; we can know them only in their multidimensional, always unfolding processes and practices, indeed in their multiplicities. This fundamental instability is why we keep asking the acousmatic question."[4] It's not that we are bad at recognizing voices (we are in fact very adept at it, as with faces) – the epistemological impossibility lies in the indeterminacy of identity, in its constructed and contingent nature.[5]

The assumption persists, of course, that hearing the human voice does allow us to perceive the essential and authentic identity of the speaker. It is reflected in long-standing metaphors and clichés about the voice being the pure expression of an inner nature, the notion that voices *are* identities, identities *are* voices. It's an assumption that is prevalent in spoken word discourse, which is why this analysis is so relevant. It may be why spoken word, especially slam poetry, has been so often associated with the expression of identity and "identity politics": because it is seen as one of the least acousmatized, most embodied (therefore least deracialized) literary forms. It is also related to why, when we talk about spoken word, we so often end up talking about community. I do think that community is the most important attribute to discuss in studying poetic genres – *performance literature as social project* is the frame I favour – but, if spoken word is a social project, it is one with the potential to subvert rather than reinforce identity as a principal of social organization.

Community

Community is the topic that stood out most for me in the Scott-Evanson-Jones-Mash conversation. El Jones makes a very direct connection between sound and community, especially when she talks about orality as an orientation to the world. Speaking and listening, after all, are fundamentally how we form communities. With her sharp, fast, funny style, each minute Jones is on the screen seems to do an hour of work, and that work is not just intellectual but social; she draws us in to a spontaneously created circle. She talks about how, in the work she does toward prison abolition, listening is vital ("advocacy is 90 per cent listening"),[6] and how conversation, the working out of a shared reality through oral communication, is an essential constituent of community for her. There is undoubtedly a way in which oral culture is beneficial to community formation – something we perhaps lost in our millennia-long drift toward literate culture.

But as all the participants in this conversation point out, community also has its discontents. "How do we continue to create a sense of community while creating barriers for others?"[7] asks Scott. "Who determines who is in the community or out? These are actually political questions,"[8] says Jones. These are the problems and pitfalls: that every act of community inclusion also entails an exclusion, and, furthermore, that there are power dynamics within communities – they can end up reproducing the same hierarchies that the community may have been intended to defeat. The word "community" is often deployed as a kind of thought-terminating cliché, representing a vague ideal seen as an almost universal good, but its invocation can also support a range of oppressions. Miranda Joseph in *Against the Romance of Community* argues (based on the work of many scholars including Étienne Balibar and Judith Butler) that "communities seem inevitably to be constituted in relation to internal and external enemies and ... these defining others are then elided, excluded, or actively repressed."[9]

Poetry communities are notoriously factional in ways that illustrate the dangers of community formation: fearing that the greater society has no love for poets generally, they tend to become territorial, and they mark their territories according to various protocols of style, politics, or lineage. In other words, they generate identities. To understand how spoken word communities tend to be defined, it is useful to think about the distinctions that have long been applied to poetic communities, such as "popular" and "avant-garde": how those distinctions are related to identity, why it might be useful to redefine or avoid defining them, and how that might be possible.

Popularity

Analysis of spoken word, both friendly and critical, has often been concerned with distinctions between low and high culture. Whether it's then Poet Laureate of Canada George Bowering referring to performance poetry as "crude and extremely revolting,"[10] or Harold Bloom calling slam poetry "the death of art,"[11] there are always numerous notorious naysayers that attempt to create a hierarchy of poetry based on some unspoken but transparently elitist criteria. Sometimes the distinction is one that spoken word proponents are happy to buy into: spoken word is defined as a *popular* (and therefore *more* authentic) form, against either academic or avant-garde or literary poetry. These broad categories are obviously not comprehensive, even though they are often framed in binary or relative terms. A lot of poetry – maybe most – is neither avant-garde nor academic nor popular. Rather, each of these categories is exclusionary – the popular excludes everything that is not accessible; the avant-garde excludes everything that is not innovative – and poets who align themselves with either category often consider themselves marginalized by the "mainstream." Susan Somers-Willett, in *The Cultural Politics of Slam Poetry*, implicitly makes opposing aesthetic categories of popular and official (dominant) poetry, with slam poetry on the "pop" side of the binary.[12] She specifies, for example, that avant-garde poetry is not popular (in the sense of widely appreciated). To be fair, if we just go by the numbers, we can't justifiably say that spoken word is *popular*, either. But perhaps this conception of a popular/avant-garde dichotomy isn't about the size of the audience so much as the authenticity of the form – with each side considering itself to be more authentic. What exactly does it mean to claim to be popular?

If it doesn't mean "widely appreciated by people in general" then maybe the usage means "of the [common] people" – plebeian, in other words. It's an odd usage, suggesting that while some poetry is "of the people," other (avant-garde or academic) poetry exists beyond people, beyond the social. All poetry is, of course, by people and of people.[13] This sense of the term "popular" is both a slight to the poetry it excludes and a diminishment of the poetry it means to justify. It has the same double edge as terms like "folk art" or "outsider art," similarly used to demarcate cultural boundaries. "Popular" art is marked as ephemeral, contingent, naïve, non-canonical, marginal, "other," while at the same time the term implicitly creates and privileges another category that is seen as permanent, universal, knowing, canonical, central, dominant (and of course "unpopular," which is empirically accurate, if unflattering). This othering of the popular is a political problem that leftist theorists such as Raymond Williams and Stuart Hall recognized when cultural studies first began to examine mass culture. "There is no fixed content to the category of 'popular culture,'" Hall points out, and as much as dominant culture may try to define one, "there is no fixed subject to attach to it – 'the people.'"[14] It is not possible, nor should it be, for "the people" to be a subset of society.

To mythicize spoken word as the poetry of "the people" is a bit eyebrow-knitting, then. Who exactly are "the people"? Do they realize that poetry slams are being conducted in their name? That the form arose from and represents marginalized people is certainly a part of spoken word's popular history. The mythos of slam suggests that its combativeness is born of the struggle to survive oppressive circumstances – most memorably embodied by Saul Williams in the movie *Slam*, where rhyming saves his character from a prison-yard confrontation. I have no doubt that poetry is a saving grace for many incarcerated people – El Jones can speak to that. But Saul Williams, the slam poetry star, as talented as he is, is not one of those people; he's an NYU-educated actor who portrayed one of those people in a movie. We should affirm that spoken word is, among other things, a manifestation of Black oral culture, and we should affirm that spoken word is more inviting to marginalized people than "official" poetry. But when defining it now, we should recognize that spoken word also trades on *representations* of marginalized people. When we say, "of the people," which people do we mean? The people talking, the people being talked *to*, or the people being talked *about*?

Arguments about the status of popular culture raged in the twentieth century – the debate between the Frankfurt School's false-consciousness view of popular culture and the Birmingham School's more activist consumer-as-producer view, for example, formed much of the theoretical ground on which contemporary spoken word studies can be situated. That debate was about the post-industrial, mass-produced culture vilified by early twentieth-century intellectuals and avant-garde artists, described by Renato Pogglioli as "fabricated (indeed 'prefabricated') on the lowest intellectual level by the bourgeoisie itself."[15] He contrasted this with the "popular" culture celebrated by Romanticism, a "purely ethnic" folk culture, which he believed had virtually disappeared. When Pogglioli wrote *The Theory of the Avant-Garde* (in 1949–51, translated in 1968), he was covering well-worn ground, but coming to different and interesting conclusions: for him, avant-garde movements were best seen as social rather than aesthetic groupings. In other words, it was not only because of stylistic or ideological affinities that avant-garde artists gathered to create communities; it was the communities that created the stylistic and ideological affinities.

This is an idea that can be usefully applied to other artistic groups, and, I think, to poetic communities in particular. A spoken word community could be fairly accurately described as "a social fact in a primarily psychological way, motivated by vocation and election, not by blood or racial inheritance and by economic or class distinctions."[16] Peter Bürger later corroborated much of Poggioli's views in his own *Theory of the Avant-Garde*, although his analysis, like that of the Birmingham theorists, allows us to conceive of a critical attitude toward mass culture happening *within* popular culture. It paves the way, in other words, for a recognition that popular cultural forms do not necessarily imply acceptance of hegemonic cultural norms. One implication is that avant-garde and popular poetry communities are not so dissimilar, both being primarily social phenomena and both producing poetry in reaction to a perceived poetic mainstream. However, consider the short list of qualities that Poggioli says do *not* motivate the "social fact" of avant-garde movements: "racial inheritance" and "class distinctions." To what extent is this true? Is it plausible that socially constituted art and poetry scenes could escape the pervasive social forces that shape other communities along lines of race and class?

Ethnicity

The development of artistic and poetic movements is, of course, deeply affected by social distinctions like race and class, and in the case of the twentieth-century avant-garde, it's clear that many celebrated movements drew aesthetically from the cultures of "othered" identities while being primarily socially constituted of white men – from the Dada artists with their interest in African sculpture and sounds to the Beat poets with their affinity for jazz. As Timothy Yu points out in his 2009 book *Race and the Avant-Garde*, despite the importance of these influences for avant-garde innovations, they were thought of as belonging to a different sphere, that of folk or ethnic art, and non-white artists were rarely acknowledged as peers. Something changed around 1970, Yu argues, when political and cultural shifts gave greater visibility to artistic and literary movements led by women and people of colour. Cultural innovation was no longer the proprietary domain of a single, white-dominated avant-garde, and as a result, "after 1970 the question of race became central to the constitution of *any* American avant-garde, as writers and artists became increasingly aware of how their social locations inflected their aesthetics."[17]

That doesn't mean that avant-garde poetry communities became racially integrated or even racially conscious, as clearly evidenced, for example, by the response to Cathy Park Hong's powerful 2014 essay "Delusions of Whiteness in the Avant-Garde," in which she asserts that contemporary avant-garde poetry scenes not only exclude writers of colour but do so by perpetuating a "post-identity" ideology at the expense of marginalized people, who don't have the luxury of ignoring gender, class, and race. According to this ideology, she writes, "[t]o be an identity politics poet is to be anti-intellectual, without literary merit, no complexity, sentimental, manufactured, feminine, niche-focused, woefully out-of-date and therefore woefully unhip, politically light, and deadliest of all, used as bait by market forces' calculated branding of boutique liberalism."[18]

The aesthetic and ideological bent of spoken word scenes is rarely described as "post-identity." Yet, I still think that spoken word is comparable to avant-garde poetry in this respect too. Timothy Yu describes a phenomenon he calls "the 'ethnicization' of the avant-garde,"[19] by which he means not desegregation, and not the absorption of some essentially ethnic quality, but rather the adoption of a position of marginality – that is, he's describing the process by which membership in a marginal artistic or poetic community itself becomes an identity. The major thrust of his book, in fact, is that Asian American poetry communities and experimental poetry communities (he focuses on Language poets, mostly white men) are engaged in very similar projects, and the terms "avant-garde" and "ethnic" might apply equally well to either. To a large degree we can say that spoken word has become – or has made itself – "ethnicized" in this sense. Whether this is a "post-identity" attitude, and whether we should see it as progressive or regressive, inclusive or exclusive – of this I am less sure.

I was struck by something El Jones said: that she has talked to young Black slam poets who perceive the slam scene – this tradition that has featured so much Black talent and showcases a form rooted in Black oral culture – as dominated by a white aesthetic. As Jones puts it, "When you don't remember where you come from ... it defaults towards whiteness."[20] There's no doubt some painful truth in their perception; spoken word has been described to me by skeptics as rap deracinated from its hip hop roots, or as one (white) poet described it, disdainfully, "skinny white teenagers talking like they are forty-year-old Black women."[21] Although the stereotypes are questionable, I think this is a subtly revealing characterization – and the phenomenon is perhaps unsurprising: a symptom, decades after the fact, of that shift of the revolutionary mantle from a largely white class-based literary avant-garde to a *de facto* political vanguard of writers and artists of colour, a shift to a new battleground defined by sexism and racism.

In trying to frame spoken word in relation to race and ethnicity, I think Yu's analysis of the poetic avant-garde is a promising model. He writes that, in thinking through what being "avant-garde" meant in the late twentieth century, "writers such as the Language poets had to acknowledge themselves as a socially as well as aesthetically delimited group, characterized by their own racial, gender, and class positions."[22] In turn, he calls on participants, critics, and theorists to adopt what he calls "a sociology of the avant-garde," which avoids the binaristic labelling that was the habit of earlier avant-garde theory and recognizes "the existence of multiple and even competing groups," with aesthetic programs that are "inflected by their differing social identifications."[23]

Performativity

The binaristic habit, as when a poetic faction defines itself in opposition to another faction, raises a fundamental issue: in doing so, a practice – like writing and performing poetry – is transformed into an identity. No one admits to liking labels, but we nevertheless are willing to call others slam poets or page poets, for example; we may be referring to what people *do*, but it also becomes a way of describing who they *are*. Unlike some communities, spoken word, for complicated reasons, has largely resisted policing identities, even the identity of "spoken word performer." It is a notoriously difficult genre to define, in part because there are few rules about what styles or practices it might include. Tawhida Tanya Evanson's expression of this lack of criteria for inclusion is direct: "If you don't belong anywhere else, ... you belong with us."[24] Critics, of course, often assume that this signifies a lack of *standards*, but that's not the same thing. To me, it signifies a prioritization of practice over status, or as Evanson puts it: "You don't have to "be a singer" ... just hit the drum!"[25]

It is this emphasis on practice that makes spoken word resistant to defining its borders: it is usually not conceived as an identity to which one can belong but as something one can participate in (by performing or by listening). Community formation can seem to operate in a loop: oppression leads to exclusion leads to identity-construction leads to solidarity leads to exclusion leads to oppression – and repeat. Various philosophers have theorized the problem, including Alphonso Lingis (author of *The Community of Those Who Have Nothing in Common*) and Giorgio Agamben (*The Coming Community*). Both were inspired at least in part by French philosopher Jean-Luc Nancy and his notion of "negative community." Agamben proposes an exit from the loop in the form of what he calls a "whatever" community, a kind of identity-neutral environment. Rather than building community based on identity, Agamben advocates community based on *whateverness*, which is not apathy or indifference but a kind of existentialist refusal to submit to essentialist categorization, "mediated not by any condition of belonging (being red, being Italian, being Communist) nor by the simple absence of conditions ... but by belonging itself."[26] This echoes but is subtly different from Poggioli's idea of the social fact of avant-garde communities – because it is more deliberate.

Spoken word poetry has been criticized as too intent on expression of identity as a political stance, which would be an impediment to the formation of a non-identitarian community if the multitudinous identities expressed at spoken word events had any coherence or authority. On the contrary, I think spoken word scenes exhibit precisely that quality of whateverness: the conditions of membership are indefinable except as simple belonging – maddeningly indefinable to some. Agamben describes the whatever-being as a threat to state power, but it could also be read as a threat to institutional authority: "What the State cannot tolerate in any way [...] is that the singularities form a community without affirming an identity, that humans co-belong without any representable condition of belonging."[27] Whateverness is at the heart of the discomfort caused by spoken word, because it allows the enactment of a community that, while not devoid of identity, accommodates multiple identities and is generally undiscriminating about the criteria of membership. The risk, in a white-dominated society like ours, is that any undefined social entity (in El Jones's words, again) "defaults towards whiteness."[28] And that is likely the case in many spoken word scenes, although the demographics of the larger community surely play a role in this. The relative inclusivity of a whatever community is really put to the test at the local level – who feels welcome at a spoken word event as compared to other poetry events in the same city?

Part of what makes spoken word a good candidate for whateverness is that, while it obviously involves performance, it is also *performative*, in the sense that it defines or redefines participants in ways that are assumed and contingent rather than inherent and unchanging. While the poetry may often seem to be about straightforward expressions of identity, the communal *activity* is a diverse, fluid environment in which participants experiment with different identities, passively and actively. This is precisely how I see spoken word as resistant to normative structures: not through fiery-eyed, forceful demonstrations of identity but through fiery-eyed, forceful *performances* of identity.

Parodicity and Hybridity

The performative nature of spoken word can be seen especially in the role that parody plays in the conception and execution of spoken word performances and events. It comes up in the conversation, when El Jones draws our attention to the specific appeal of parody, which (unless the assertion was parodic as well) seems to be a productive modus operandi for her. She says that writing becomes easier when you're doing it parodically, which rings true for me – and it's not just because you have a model to imitate;

there's also something freeing about it. Jones imagines herself having success writing an academic dissertation that is entirely satirical, where she is just "fucking around and making up citations" – playing with words and ideas, another way of playing with identity.[29]

For the average consumer of pop culture, of course, performance poetry is less parodic than ripe for parody. One episode of *The Good Place* has a jazz-backed spoken word performance as a torture that self-evidently belongs to "the Bad Place" ("No version of heaven for anyone would ever include three hours of this!") – and it's not the first TV show or film to make a similar joke. The performance poet is stereotyped as an embarrassingly earnest creature, willing to seize a microphone and inflict painfully cliché verse on a sparse and semi-interested audience, thereby exhibiting something that could be interpreted as egotism or self-abasement. What this portrait misses, though, is that parody is a quintessential feature of the genre: in performing the poetry, the performance poet performs "poet," explicitly or not, and credibly or not.

Spoken word as a genre and movement owes its origins to many sources, and many of them had a seriously ludic element. Black oral culture created scat and funk and hip hop – but it also created playing the dozens and yo mama jokes. The Beat poets cultivated and parodied the beatnik stereotype – Ted Joans for a while played the beatnik for a tongue-in-cheek "Rent-a-Beatnik" service, reading his poems at middle-class parties for cash.[30] Before the poetry slam in the '80s, there were punk-inspired poetry *bouts* in boxing gloves, with women in bikinis ringing a bell, making an arch and self-ridiculing commentary on poetry readings. The original poetry slam at the Green Mill in Chicago operated along the same lines as a professional wrestling match: it was an exhibition, a performance art piece arranged by the "contestants," who were in cahoots. One participant showed up with shoulder pads and studded leather gloves, while another one wore a camouflage-patterned tutu and called herself Rambolina. In New York, Bob Holman and Pedro Pietri featured dead poets such as Walt Whitman and Sylvia Plath in their onstage TV talk show. And in San Francisco, Gary Glazner created a carnivalesque slam with a barker and hot dog vendors, which he says was largely inspired by John Cage's ideas about aleatory art.[31] Later, the poetry slam became much more formalized, and the sense that the participants are actors in an ensemble cast was eclipsed by the sense of competition, but the element of self-parody persisted. In Montreal in the '90s, popular performers included Ed Fuller, whose act consisted of a lurid facsimile of a crooning lounge lizard; Dayna McLeod, known for her routine dressed as a giant beaver; and Les Abdigradationistes, who played wonky pseudo-New Wave music and read what they called "poésie pure."[32]

Parody in a spoken word performance displays various discourses in order to reveal the constructed nature of those discourses. Often spoken word texts are composed of a tissue of pop-cultural quotations: for example, the voice of a newscaster is used to convey incongruous emotional material, a snippet of pop melody is used as a refrain, and the metaphors used are drawn from TV shows and movies. This discourse collage is primarily a way of subverting the claim to "sincerity" of these pop sources. It's a kind of theatre that, rather than portraying characters, reproduces the interaction of discourses. A spoken word text, in other words, is what Mikhail Bakhtin called a hybrid utterance: a single voice employing multiple kinds of speech. That hybridity is enabled by the unique attitude of spoken word to community formation: the absence of identity requirements for membership, the fluidity of identity among participants, and the opportunity to experience multiple truths at once. It's a way of pushing back on the expectations of an identity-based community.

Some performances come straight from the gut and create a feeling of direct connection, a glimpse into the performer's deepest thoughts and emotions – especially in the blunt, first-person forms of the poetry slam. They do that, and the feeling is real. It's possible to appreciate and respond to artful performances of identity even if we know that's what they are, as long as we believe them. Spoken word is not acting, many purists will insist, but neither is it simply "being yourself." A spoken word or slam performance can perhaps be interpreted as a poetic drag act, where the line between good and bad poetry may become blurred or inverted, and in which the costume is never meant to fool anyone but rather to remind us of the costumes we all wear. There is a radical honesty to a drag performance.

Sincerity

There is a common perception of spoken word as a more direct, more sincere, even more true species of poetry – it is "one of the only art forms that still allows people to communicate truth in a world destroyed by the filth, lies, and disease that pass for truth in our deeply sick society" (says Montreal poet the one and only Fortner Anderson – in one of my favourite quotes – in a *Montreal Mirror* article by Juliet Waters). On the other hand, its very performative nature, and its tendency toward parody and camp, suggests something other than directness, something more complicated than sincerity. Could it be that spoken word involves a kind of role-playing, and that directness is just one of the "effects" adopted by the performer? Is spoken word not being *straight* with us? Which brings me to another comment from Tawhida Tanya Evanson that I want to highlight. She lays down what I think is the most fundamental dictum for anyone who dares to beat the drum: "If you call yourself any kind of artist or writer or whatever, you better tell the truth."[33] And surely the things we make are privileged as "art" when we believe them to be true, and when we don't, they aren't.

Maybe it seems like I've quoted my way into a contradiction, between the playfulness of parody and the absolute necessity of telling the truth: can spoken word possibly do both? If it is a contradiction, it's an interesting one. But I think the answer is that the two are closely related, that parody can be truthful – can be more truthful than sincerity, in fact. We are used to accepting sincerity as a marker of truth and locating that sincerity in a single, coherent identity. But we are suspicious of performances where identities become mixed or unstable, when the performance reveals to us the complexities and uncertainties of identity. And that is what often happens on a spoken word stage. Spoken word does still make some critics, academics, and gatekeepers uneasy. It undermines evaluative approaches to poetry and essentialist approaches to identity, complicating fundamental questions such as: What is good poetry and what purpose should it serve? What is a poetic community? Who is a poet? What is this voice? Who, exactly, is speaking? The nature of these questions means that we will never settle on definitive answers to any of them. Let's not try to figure out who the drummers are; let's just hit the drum and keep hitting it.

NOTES

1 See T.L. Cowan, "The Internet of Bawdies: Transmedial Drag and the Onlining of Trans-feminist and Queer Performance Archives, a Workshop Essay," *First Monday* 23, no. 7 (July 2018), which raises questions relevant to my argument here.
2 Among other places, in my 2011 dissertation, which is titled "The Omnidirectional Microphone: Performance Literature as Social Project" (PhD diss., City University of New York).
3 At least according to some schools of thought – Charles Olson's memorable articulation in "Projective Verse" (1950) being one example. Charles Olson, *Human Universe and Other Essays*, ed. Donald Allen (New York: Grove Press, 1967), 51–2.
4 Nina Sun Eidsheim, *The Race of Sound: Listening, Timbre, and Vocality in African American Music* (Durham: Duke University Press, 2018), 3.
5 Eidsheim's argument is against racial essentialism; it does not mean that voices never "sound Black" or "sound white," but rather that those perceptions are the product of acculturation (in both the speaker and the listener). For example, linguists working on Black English have detailed how the Black accent is produced; John McWhorter provides an outline in *Talking Back, Talking Black:Truths About America's Lingua Franca* (New York: Bellevue Literary Press, 2018). Accent is a dimension of voice that contributes to the construction of race – but that lies beyond the scope of this essay.
6 El Jones, "'What is being resisted is our "yes"': An Interview with Tawhida Tanya Evanson, El Jones, and Erin Scott," Cole Mash, in this volume, 170.
7 Erin Scott, "'What is being resisted,'" 168.
8 Jones, "'What is being resisted,'" 171.
9 Miranda Joseph, *Against the Romance of Community* (Minneapolis: University of Minnesota Press, 2002), xix.
10 George Bowering quoted in Alexandra Gill, "A Little the Verse for Wear," *Globe and Mail*, 1 January 2003, accessed 31 July 2022, www.theglobeandmail.com/life/a-little-the-verse-for-wear/article1333531/.
11 David Barber et al., "The Man in the Back Row Has a Question VI," *Paris Review* 154 (Spring 2000):379, accessed 4 December 2018, www.theparisreview.org/miscellaneous/780/the-man-in-the-back-row-has-a-question-vi-david-barber.
12 Susan B. Anthony Somers-Willett, *The Cultural Politics of Slam Poetry: Race, Identity, and the Performance of Popular Verse in America* (Ann Arbor: University of Michigan Press, 2009), 39–43.
13 I feel compelled to add a caveat here about certain computer-generated poetry experiments, or even certain algorithmic conceptual poetry, but my argument would be that even then the experiment must be launched by (human) people.
14 Stuart Hall, "Notes on Deconstructing 'the Popular,'" *People's History and Socialist Theory*, ed. Raphael Samuel (London: Routledge, 1981), 239.

15 Renato Pogglioli, *The Theory of the Avant-Garde*, trans. Gerald Fitzgerald (Cambridge: Harvard University Press, 1968), 123.
16 Ibid., 31.
17 Timothy Yu, *Race and the Avant-Garde: Experimental and Asian-American Poetry since 1965* (Stanford: Stanford University Press, 2009), 1–2.
18 Cathy Park Hong, "Delusions of Whiteness in the Avant-Garde," *Lana Turner*, no. 7 (2014), accessed 27 July 2023, https://arcade.stanford.edu/content/delusions-whiteness-avant-garde.
19 Yu, *Race and the Avant-Garde*, 17.
20 Jones, "'What is being resisted,'" 174.
21 Paul Vermeersch, "Rant: Why I Hate 'Spoken Word' Poetry," *Paul Vermeersch: Poetry and Such*, 2008, accessed 4 September 2010, www.paulvermeersch.ca/2008/05/rant-why-i-hate-spoken-word-poetry.html. Site discontinued.
22 Yu, *Race and the Avant-Garde*, 3.
23 Ibid., 4.
24 Tawhida Tanya Evanson, "'What is being resisted,'" 181.
25 Ibid., 185.
26 Giorgio Agamben, *The Coming Community*, trans. Michael Hardt (Minneapolis: Univeristy of Minnesota Press, 1993), 84.
27 Ibid., 85.
28 Jones, "'What is being resisted,'" 174.
29 Ibid., 191.
30 Dennis McLellan, "Ted Joans, 74; Beat Poet's Work Reflected Jazz and African Culture," *Los Angeles Times*, 13 May 2003, accessed 27 July 2023, www.latimes.com/archives/la-xpm-2003-may-13-me-joans13-story.html.
31 These excerpts from the history and pre-history of the poetry slam in the US are documented in Kurt Heintz, "An Incomplete History of Slam," e-poets.net, 2000; and Cristin O'Keefe Aptowicz, *Words in Your Face: A Guided Tour through Twenty Years of the New York City Poetry Slam* (New York: Soft Skull Press, 2007), particularly its interview with Bob Holman.
32 Much more on these and other Montreal performers can be found in Victoria Stanton and Vincent Tinguely, *Impure, Reinventing the Word: The Theory, Practice, and Oral History of "Spoken Word" in Montreal* (Wolfville, NS: Conundrum Press, 2001).
33 Evanson, "'What is being resisted,'" 192.

11

"A taking in, a holding with"
An Interview with Jordan Abel

Deanna Fong, recorded over Zoom
TRANSCRIBED BY DEANNA RADFORD

Deanna Fong: Thanks so much for taking the time to talk to me, Jordan. So the collection, as I mentioned, is going to be called *Resistant Practices in Communities of Sound*. A slight deviation from what it was called when it was a conference, which was "Resonant Practices." We decided that one of the themes that came out of the papers and creative works that were presented at the conference was about the ways that sound can resist in certain senses: to stand up against certain aesthetic practices, certain cultural notions of value; it can serve as political resistance; it can be resistance as a kind of refusal, resistance as a kind of endurance. There are all these different themes that we're trying to sound out in this collection. So as a super broad way of opening: do you consider your work – whether that's critical work, or creative work, or pedagogical work – a kind of resistant practice?

Jordan Abel: The short answer for sure is yes, especially with my creative work. I used to say I primarily work in appropriative conceptualism, except NISHGA isn't that [laughs] – which I'm sure we'll talk about later.

I definitely think I consider my earlier work a resistant practice in that it speaks back to settler-colonialism in a material way, and it seeks to deconstruct those logics of settler-domination. I think in my pedagogical practice, too, I mostly am thinking about research-creation right now in my teaching as a resistant space in which to create both creative and academic work, or whatever the intertwining of those two things might be. I think about it in part along the same lines as Natalie Loveless thinks about it in her work. She published a monograph a year or two ago called *How to Make Art at the End of the World* and she talks about research-creation as being a resistant practice to the kinds of regimes of truth that are produced within university structures.[1]

So, you know, I think definitely all of my major areas, pedagogical and creative, are resistant practices in different ways.

DF: Regarding the research-creation question, do you feel like you have experienced some *reluctance* in pursuing that as a method of scholarship? Or has your particular academic milieu been open to that as a form?

JA: It's so funny. I don't write on research-creation, really, but I teach it in a very similar way that I teach poetry. The resistance I face tends not to be from my students. It tends to be from colleagues that are skeptical, which I totally get. I think there's a real sense of distrust that it's a category that has been completely fabricated and/or co-opted by institutions like SSHRC. And I get that, too.

Tommy Pico has this great quote in his book *Nature Poem* where he says, "Poetry is a container."[2] I always understood that as a gesture towards the expansiveness in which poetry can contain all kinds of different work from different genres, and different directions, and different modalities. Research-creation, I think, is similarly a container. It's just a banner under which really interesting work can happen and it's work that often doesn't fit easily into certain kinds of mono-disciplinary logics. Or doesn't fit easily even within certain constructions of interdisciplinarity.

I think I'm really sympathetic towards work that doesn't easily have a home in part because I feel like I tend to always want to do that work in spaces that aren't accommodating to that type of work. So I feel like, as a teacher, I really want to try to create space for students who want to do stuff that doesn't easily have a home somewhere and that's when I'm the most excited.

DF: Yeah. It seems like the refrain of these various kinds of gatekeepers is like, "This is not *X*" – whatever the *X* is. This is not poetry. This is not research. This is not scholarship. All of these different mechanisms by which we maintain the status quo in elite cultural institutions, right? It's awesome to be able to – Oh! Is there a baby? [Laughs]

JA: Baby is back!

DF: Hi, baby! Hi! I see you! [Laughter] You've made a very beautiful human being. [Laughter]

JA: Yeah. [To Phoenix] You can go back to bed. Sorry!

DF: Yeah! So we'll mention for the record that Phoenix is now on the call. [Laughter]

So, following that, I wanted to talk to you about sound as a kind of poetic creative practice. So the last time I interviewed you, which I just realized was in 2017 and quite a long time ago now, we talked about your compositional practice and performing the appropriate works in *Injun* particularly.

We were talking about that relationship between the way that the text disintegrates on the page and sort of reformulates, twists upside down, and then the way that sound is distorted in your live performance using the APC Mini controller. The ways that those two practices are kind of analogous but not totally the same, right?

So I was just wondering how, if at all, has your relationship to the performance of your work changed since I spoke to you about it last?

JA: Well, I think it's changed in a couple of major ways. I guess the first way is that I've started writing new, different things that don't require technology to perform. So, in particular I've been reading a lot from my new project, *Empty Spaces*, which is a very different kind of performance where I read these endless descriptions of landscape, essentially. I've been really into that. I've been really into how quiet those spaces are. There's lots of repetition and it's a very circular piece. So, I'm really fond of reading that one in a mostly linear kind of way. That's one big change.

The other change is that I think my ability to perform that sound poetry the way I used to do it with the Akai PC Mini has diminished a bit because of Zoom. It doesn't make as much sense to me to do it on a Zoom call because part of the performative aspect of it for me was that I was physically in a room with people *not speaking* and displacing my position as an author. But through Zoom, there's this other layer that I think doesn't allow me to do that in the same way.

I guess the third thing though is that before the pandemic, when I was performing *Injun* still, I think that performance mostly remains intact. I still do it in a similar way. But I keep thinking there's probably a moment where I should retire it and move forward. I'm not sure if that's because I've gotten as much out of it as I want to get out of it. It's actually been a very long time since I originally wrote *Injun*. I wrote that book in 2013–2014. It was a while. I feel like I've grown as a writer and I have other things that I want to spend some time with. I don't know if that's a good answer to your question!

DF: That's a great answer.

JA: It's definitely an honest answer. [Laughter]

DF: Honesty is the best policy. Always.

Well, maybe that's a good place to jump in and ask, in NISHGA, there's an interview with Sachiko Murakami and one of the things that you say in that interview, "For some reason, some people – and here I want to say mostly white people but some racialized people too – project on us and/or expect us to perform their expectations of us"[3] – "us" in this case being Indigenous writers and performers. The question that I had originally around that note was in relation to the performance of *Injun* and other conceptual appropriative erasure works.

Does the mediation of poetry act as a way of defying what a white settler audience's expectations of what a performance of Indigeneity should be? And, sub-question, does it do that by deflecting the attention – maybe deflecting is not the right word – but focusing on the text rather than on you as the author who is often subject to these sorts of questions about racialization and identity, Indigenous experience, that sort of thing?

JA: That's really interesting. I think certainly that performance – the sound poetry performance for *Injun* – really does. I think it doesn't match up with the expectations that people have of me as an Indigenous author, and also doesn't match up with expectations of what poetry should *sound* like. Or be experienced as. I really love that part of it. [Laughs] It really felt like it shifted people out of their comfort zones and expectations, and that it also existed outside of people's expectations of how difficult art should be to consume.

That one in particular I'm very fond of because I always think that was a book that was about racism and really violent aggression against Indigenous peoples, and that those things are really difficult. They're difficult things and the art that I produce in response to that should also somehow try to address that level of difficulty.

I remember there was this one reading I did in Vancouver at some gallery – I can't even remember which one – where I did a sound performance of *Injun*. There was this old white poet there and he was really grumbly through the whole thing. [Laughter] He was asking the usual questions about, "Is this really poetry?" and was just not happy with it. My response at the time was just to continue to turn up the volume because, in part, it was a self-defence mechanism in that I couldn't hear him if the volume was louder.

DF: Wait, he was audibly heckling you and grumbling while you were performing?

JA: Yeah. And it was a small room so you could totally hear it and he was the only one. There were like twenty people or something in the room but it was small enough that it was uncomfortable for me.

But I really loved how uncomfortable it made certain people, you know? Some people, they experience some discomfort when they hear it but then they think about it and they understand the layers and continue thinking through it in a way that is productive and interesting. But for those who really dislike it and are not interested in it, I'm still very glad that I was able to perform those pieces in front of them and create this moment of discomfort where they at least had to confront that sound and that performance in some way.

DF: Yeah. And also just to take up some auditory space.

JA: Totally!

DF: But this guy! That this guy somehow felt *entitled* to speak even though you were the performer. Not baffling or surprising, but frustrating anyway to say the least.

JA: Yeah, it was *so* frustrating. I do think that performance did reflect the writing that I was trying to address or as you mentioned before. It's an interpretation of that book, although it wasn't exactly that book. [Laughs]

DF: Yeah. One of the other things that you mentioned in that interview with Sachiko is that oftentimes racialized writers are expected to have a kind of educational role in addition to their roles as performers. So answering questions about identity and experience in, as you mention, this particular way that an audience expects Indigeneity or race to be performed.

I have an example. I think it was at the University of Ottawa Congress and Leanne Betasamosake Simpson was performing. This sticks out in my mind because the offending woman was actually somebody I had just randomly met in the dorms that day and I was like, "You should totally come see Leanne Simpson, she's so great!"

JA: Oh my God.

DF: Yeah! So this woman comes to the event on my recommendation and feels compelled during the Q&A to stand up and admit that she's never read any of Leanne's work and then talk about her own work in classical Greek language or literature or something like that for a *super* long time and then her final question was, "So what can *we* as white allies do to support Indigenous books?" And Leanne just was like, "I don't care. I don't care about what white settlers do. You do you. I'm not responsible for that." Which I thought was such a great moment of refusal. [Laughter]

But to bring it back to what we were talking about, it seems kind of like you have to perform this doubly educational role on the one hand –

AN INTERVIEW with JORDAN ABEL

like having to answer these questions about experience and identity – but also having to field those questions of literary value on the other. All of those, "Is this even poetry?" questions, or your mentor in your MFA saying, "When are you going to start writing real poems?" So, are those two expectations of education related? Do they come from the same place, or a similar place, do you think?

JA: I don't know. The first thing that I can think of is that I recently saw Billy-Ray Belcourt do an interview with Emily Riddle.[4] Emily asked Billy-Ray a similar question about the role that education plays in creative writing and in Billy-Ray's work in particular, and whether or not Billy-Ray's work was purposefully didactic. And Billy-Ray's response was, "Sometimes the things we're talking about are too important *not* to be didactic about them and to purposefully try to educate."[5] I've been thinking about that since he said that. Now I'm thinking about that in relation to this question, and in the way that I've addressed education before.

I do wonder about it. As an educator, I do feel some obligation to do my best to try to help students out. But at the same time, students in that situation are different than you were talking about with Leanne – that's not a teacher-student relationship, you know? That is a very different setting and I feel very torn about it in some ways, in that it's difficult to turn off that part of me that wants to teach and impart knowledge – because I do think that that's the way that we can create change. But at the same time, I think that *time*, especially on the stage at a reading or a festival or what have you, is so precious and I would so love to talk about any other aspect of my creative practice.

DF: Rather than simply justifying its existence. [Phoenix vocalizes] Hi, you! [to Phoenix]

JA: Phoenix baby, do you want to say something?

DF: Yeah! Hello! We're not directing the conversation enough towards you, is that it?

JA: Yeah. [Laughs]

DF: Do you want a question? [To Jordan] Are you okay for a couple of minutes?

JA: Yeah. She definitely gets maxed out on me holding her sometimes. So I might put her in her little chair that's right next to me, which *maybe* will work. Hold on one second.

DF: All right. [Music playing in background] So, I thought maybe I would ask you some more specific questions about NISHGA, having just reread it.

JA: Sure.

DF: I did want to just mention that I was so moved by that opening note that gets at this weird temporality of the event, which is in that first note where you write, "I figured out later that I loved this band, but at the time it was just a band that I had heard of."[6] It's hard to even place what the time of this passage is. So, getting at this idea that these certain moments in time – or certain *events* – change things and make a split between a "before" and an "after," and that we come to understand that it *will have been* a moment of great importance after the fact. But not knowing it at the time. Throughout the book there are a lot of these moments of, "I will have come to understand" in this kind of weird retroactive temporality.

JA: Yeah, yeah.

DF: That specific note sort of makes a kind of parallel between hearing the song and then hearing your dad's voice for the first time. So I was just wondering, is there something particular about sound that is more prone or susceptible to this weird sense of time? This sense of retroactive feeling or memory?

JA: I think for me it was so strange, I guess, to have those two sounds have such intertwined but divergent impacts on me because the sound of my dad's voice for the first time through my flip phone was – I *still* can't even put into words what that felt like. I think that that section in the book where I attempt to describe it is not even adequate. [Laughs] I'm sure better writers than me could describe it in ways that might be more fulfilling, but I still am grappling with it.

All these years later, I still don't totally understand how to deal with that particular moment. Because it was – it was *just* sounds. I didn't have a picture of him. I didn't see him. It was just a sound object. That was such a deeply impactful moment that I guess I will continue to struggle to describe.

Pairing that with that really kind of uncanny moment where, not only was it Father's Day, I guess, but it was also that the band addressed that. There was this song that played at this particular moment that was just such a strange life moment. I think *that* was one of those moments where it was one of those hour-long moments in my life where I knew I really had to write about it at some point.

I didn't know *how* for the longest time. When I wrote about it in NISHGA, I still think that it's my first attempt to write about that moment in a way that made sense to me. I'm still not sure that really even captures all of it. You know? It's just this small sample of that moment.

DF: You know my next question – I have to! [Laughter] What was the band?

JA: I think they might even be from Montreal. Islands?

DF: Oh, Islands! Yeah, yeah. They're ex-Unicorns folks who I know from Campbell River, actually. That's weird.

JA: Oh my God!

DF: That's strange. Wow!

JA: I can tell you the song they played. It's off of *Return to the Sea* which is Islands' first record, which is I guess post-Unicorns. I'm pretty sure the song title is pronounced, "sucks-it." [Laughter] It's: T-S-U-X-I-I-T. It's the strangest song on that record, for them. But it was really such a bizarre sound to hear alongside all the stuff that was swimming through my head at that moment.

DF: Yeah, it's interesting. I think sometimes I feel like I, too, have had these moments of either perfect or just remarkable or arresting confluences of sounds where everything is coming into alignment for a second. That you're like, "Oh! I will always remember this."

JA: Yeah. That's a beautiful way to describe it. I think that's more or less exactly how I felt. Everything just clicked into place just in that moment.

DF: In a totally inarticulable moment. [Laughter]

JA: It's so weird to be confronted with that type of moment as a writer, I guess. There are so many moments that I can write about with … Not ease, because all writing is so difficult for me. But I think, with at least some degree of certainty, that I'm capturing the thing that I am trying to capture. But those moments, I don't know, I *still* don't know how to approach. That page of NISHGA was just my best attempt at that moment in time to try to capture this thing that's not capturable.

DF: I wanted to ask, too, because the book has so many visual components, right? Putting together artwork and text and photographs especially through overlay. Do you think maybe the visual impact of those elements is some way of getting at this thing that is otherwise inarticulable through language?

JA: Yeah, 100 per cent. I mean, I feel that way about most of my visual work in some way or another. That it's attempting to articulate a thing that language is incapable of articulating. There are moments in NISHGA where there's all these double exposures, photographs and text, and the literal shape of my father's artwork as well. I think all of those pieces are an attempt to address the overlapping incomprehensibility of my past in some ways, and of Indigeneity, and the intertwining of those things.

AN INTERVIEW with JORDAN ABEL

Intergenerational trauma as well. I feel like I'm attempting to address all those major themes in the book through the visual pieces in some way. As well as that layer of the family archive and archival materials as being the foundation of the project.

DF: Yeah. Definitely there's a substantial visual component to the book but then there are also *hints* towards a sonic element, too, in that a lot of the writing is taken from transcripts of events at which you've spoken. In fact, I happened to be at [at] least one of those events, which is the first transcript in the book from the TransCanadas conference at the University of Toronto – which ended up being kind of a shit-show! [Laughter]

JA: Totally.

DF: I think in large part because that space was so unforgiving and uncomfortable and drafty. Remember a bird flew in at some point? Do you remember that?

JA: I do! It's totally the kind of space that would have birds living in it.

DF: Yeah. Actually, I quite enjoyed the intrusion of the bird. It just sort of hit home how fucking ridiculous that space is, you know?
But, I just wanted to ask you a little bit about the role of transcription in that book – the act of gesturing to this live event that has the suggestion of a continuity before the event, and after the event. Why was it important to have it appear as a transcript and not just an essay? And how did you approach the creative act of transcription?

JA: So there are a couple of things. The first thing is, because it was written as my dissertation, there was a lot of pressure from the institution for me to finish this project in a timely way. When I was putting together the book, I realized that I had done all of these talks that were more or less what I wanted to say, but I didn't have the emotional capacity to actually return to, rethink and revise them, and construct an essay that was meant for print.

I originally put in those talks as placeholders. Because I'd always intended to go back and insert essays at some point or another and then I realized somewhere along the way that I had just *never* had that emotional capacity. It was just too difficult in many of those cases to return to those moments, to rethink them and revise what I had said.

So they ended up remaining as transcripts and once I'd come to that understanding, I was like, "Well, I think this kind of makes sense with my poetic." It fits with my poetic practice and now it's a found object. I'm just repositioning it in the way that I have repositioned other found textual objects. I guess the transcript is in part an act of self-care because, as I said, they were moments that I just didn't have the emotional energy to return to.

The transcription process was really basic. I had a script of what I had written, and I had an audio file of what it sounded like and I went through the audio file and I put in all the stuff that I had said verbatim on my script, and then I added in the stuff that I didn't have in the script that ended up in the audio file. Because I had a text file that I could work from, I didn't end up just retyping everything. I edited and readjusted that original file, and then also included all the time stamps from the audio file. I like the way that ended up working. It gives that dense prose some space to breathe.

DF: Totally. Especially with the time codes where there's just blank space.

JA: I mean, this is the follow-up question I have for everyone who's read it. I imagine in moving through those audio transcripts there is a sense of momentum perhaps between pages – that the way the white space works allows you to move through it a bit more quickly. [Phoenix sneezes] Or, it gives the reader some kind of sense of direction and momentum in their reading process.

DF: Absolutely. I've been part of this oral history reading group where we [are] talking about the velocity of speech and how incredibly important that is to how narrative and how testimony is recounted. That these shifts in velocity provide an affective road map to what a speaker is saying. So, the time codes instruct you on the auditory velocity of the way that the speech was delivered, which brought me back to the fact of it being an event and it having a voice – even if that was an imagined rather than literal voice, in this case.

JA: That's great. I'm so glad that it worked that way. I really wanted to connect that talk to a particular time and place and to locate it within certain spaces within ... I guess Canadian literature? Or, you know, whatever that is. [Laughter]

DF: Whatever that great hall is!
But I really appreciate that it's localized in space and time, too, because it seems like so much of the book, or the *whole* of the book, is just about how subjectivity is formed by an accumulation of all of these different moments, some of which are conflicting and some of which are really precise, and some of which are kind of hazy. I don't think it would have had the same effect if it were an essay, you know? Because it places it as a real moment in your life. So, I appreciated that and of course, obviously, the nod to the auditory is always good in my books, too!
So, another question I wanted to ask – one that's very dear to me and which I think is very important for the collection – is around that quotation from Samantha Nock on the act of witnessing. She writes:

> Too often we think that the act of listening is equal to the act of witnessing. Listening is passive. We can listen ... while making to-do lists in our heads, [while] thinking of what we are going to have for dinner, or what we are going to say next. When we witness a story, we are not only present physically, but emotionally and spiritually, to hold this story in our hearts. When someone tells us a story, that story becomes a part of us.[7]

You take up this quotation so beautifully in your work, too – thinking about witnessing in relation not just to stories that are told face to face in an oral sense, but also in literature. What does it mean to hold the story *as literature* as a part of you? One of the things that keeps coming up for the interviews in this collection is this question of how to feel alongside trauma that's not our own. Especially when that trauma, or the person who embodied that trauma, is somehow absent from us – we don't have access to that person or even a direct testimony from them.

Following on what Samantha Nock says here, is there an ethical way of witnessing in the communities that we are a part of, or apart from?

JA: This is definitely a question that I've thought around as well. I think one of the most difficult parts of writing this book for me is trying to grapple with other people's stories and how they may or may not have impacted my life in some way, and what it meant to ethically engage with those stories, or retell those stories, or even reference those stories – or to not do any of those things. I think this project could have been much different had I not attended to some of those questions and there's so many things that I left out of this book that I think have also impacted me that there's no ethical way of me *including* them. Or there was no way of including them without bringing up those questions about ethics.

I ultimately decided that I really just had to work with the stories that I was directly involved in, or was directly connected to, as much as I could. There's some stuff that was difficult to access because of that. The stories about my grandparents, for example, were always mediated through other people and that was really difficult. I wanted to include more of them. I think the only way I could access those stories *was* through other people, was through other stories that weren't my own.

I think, too, there's a question that comes up at the very end of the book about how much of these stories are really mine at all and where I come into it and specifically how to disentangle intergenerational trauma because it necessarily involves more than just me. It involves the generations both before and after me, in both directions. I think I don't know if I ever came to a firm conclusion as to what made the most sense to include or not to include.

But thinking back to Samantha Nock's quote, I think holding up those stories as forms of testimony, specifically the ones from my grandparents, is trying to think about how part of this book is actually my witnessing response *to* their stories. I think that the witnessing process is a really important embodied one that can also be a response. A taking in, holding with, and a responding to in some way or another. Hopefully that makes sense.

DF: Absolutely. And also holding space for uncertainty about whether or not we're doing it right.

JA: Oh, sure. There's so much uncertainty there. I think we ultimately have to be accountable for our own ethical engagements.

I remember talking to somebody years ago who was writing about their family. This person was writing a creative project and using the university's ethics board as a system to confront all of their ethical questions within. I think that's one way to do it, but I don't think that's the only way to do it. [Laughter]

DF: Yeah, that's something Karis [Shearer] and I have thought about a great deal: the difference between ethics and ... *courtesy* is not totally the right word but more consideration. Things that, if it were just a matter of ticking boxes in an ethics review, certainly would have been fine. But things like, if we're listening to a recording and all of a sudden there are two speakers on the tape and they're talking about somebody else that we *know* – before bringing that forward to a public, alerting that person and checking with them and making sure *they're* comfortable with being discussed in that way. Whereas the ethics review really only deals with the speakers on the tape, for example.

I was wondering how poetry might fit into the idea of witnessing. Witnessing and/or listening and if there's something in poetry that demands a certain sort of attention to form, attention to language, in a way that maybe prepares us for more receptive listening or possibly witnessing?

JA: I think that's a good question. Certainly, there are some types of poetry that can be witnessed. In that section that I talk about Samantha Nock, I also talk about Louise Halfe's *Burning in this Midnight Dream*, which is a poetry book about residential schools. An argument I make there is that that book, and other pieces of literature, can also be forms of testimony that can be witnessed. I think witnessing really needs to be not quite an active practice but a conscious one. A practice that requires a conscious effort on the part of the witnesser. To be responsibly engaged in some way or another.

My friend Melanie Braith, who I talk about in the book but I don't name, is doing all those kinds of work on witnessing practices. A lot of her research involves studying the drawings and sketches that have been made by people witnessing testimony. So I certainly think poetry can be a response to testimony. I wonder though, since so much testimony is oral or textual, if image is maybe a more natural witnessing response as it's often not literal.

DF: Well, this is the thing too, because I'm thinking about the role of difficulty in poetry and thinking about some of the conceptual appropriation work that you've done in your previous books. It asks for a certain kind of attention because it's not going to give you a certain sort of representative meaning, and so maybe it's demanding a different kind of engagement in that sense. Which does not *guarantee* that an act of witnessing will take place even if somebody has heightened attention. It's *possible* that would happen. But not necessary. The images in NISHGA are these sort of palimpsest overlays of different photographs and require both an imaginative reading but also very close scrutiny to make sense of what's going on. I think maybe that's also a very apt way of getting at that idea.

JA: I think the way that those images appear in the book are absolutely a creative response in some ways to the work as a whole. Especially those photographs that are the double exposures of black-and-white archival photographs. I think they have a place in the narrative, but I always imagine them as more thematically responding to the history of violence in residential schools more broadly, and then also to the history of my grandparents, my dad, and my dad's siblings.

DF: So the *response* part of the act of witnessing is important, then.

JA: I think it can be. The way Samantha Nock sets it out, she doesn't necessarily suggest that a response is part of it or that there's a more active role that the witnesser *should* take on. But, in my own definition of what witnessing is, I think that's totally part of it. In that same section too, I talk about testimony as a gift in some ways, when I say, "What gifts might I give in return?" In a very personal way, I feel very lifted up by other testimony from intergenerational survivors of residential schools, and also survivors of residential schools. I think they really help me figure out where I am in some ways within the larger narrative.

They also help illuminate certain kinds of stories that I don't have access to, and that even if my grandparents are still around, I may *still* not have access to. These things are so difficult to talk about. By that same token, I'm hoping that NISHGA is also a gift of testimony for others that need it in some way, or that could benefit from it, or could learn from it in some capacity.

DF: Yeah. Or maybe find some sense of reciprocity with. I was thinking of how, in the transcription of the lecture from Hart Hall, you discuss your first experience learning about Nisga'a culture coming through Marius Barbeau, which informs your work *Place of Scraps*. I interviewed Tracie Morris about a month ago now and she has a really lovely way of talking about works that are important to her but that are difficult, and also problematic. We had this conversation about the risk and reward of dabbling with these things that could be painful versus important to you. She has this great quote that says:

> By the time I had found out about that [i.e. Edgar Allan Poe's position on slavery] I had such a strong opinion about Poe's relevance to my life and his core meaning to me as a creative person, that I could *not* and chose not to dissociate myself with his importance. So then what do you do? I was like, "Well, I've got to balance that." I have to say, "Yeah! He was a racist and he was important to me and both of those things are true."[8]

JA: That's so great.

DF: I was wondering, does that ring some bells with your relationship with Maurice [sic] Barbeau's work?

JA: Oh, 100 per cent. I feel like the best way to describe my relationship with Barbeau is conflicted. So totally not unlike that beautiful quote! In part, when I describe it in the book, it's this process of first encountering Barbeau. In part because I have no familial access to Nisga'a culture at that moment and that my initial interest in Barbeau was ... I wouldn't say misguided, but I very quickly figured out what his deal was. I think it's very fraught.

It's such a fraught relationship to look towards Barbeau and try to *see* something underneath it that is so deeply distorted and shaped by his very colonial interests. But at the same time, recognizing that the reason I was able to see that totem pole from Kincolith in the Royal Ontario Museum was because of Barbeau. That's so conflicting to me. You know, I've still yet to actually go to Kincolith. I have not seen it because none of my family lives there anymore and having the means to get there has always been just outside of my grasp, which has been really deeply disappointing, you know?

But I think having *some* access by way of Barbeau has really profoundly shaped my life. And my art, which is messed up. I have to recognize both the positive and negative ways in which I've encountered Barbeau's legacy. I think it's so tempting to go one way or the other and to hyperbolize one's reaction to certain figures like Barbeau. It's much more complicated to recognize those murky grey areas that are kind of in the centre. That was always my interest in *The Place of Scraps*, trying to tap into that grey area a bit. To see ... I guess "both sides" is a terrible phrase. [Laughter]

DF: "There are plenty of good people ...!"

JA: Yeah! But I am legitimately trying to see the *whole*, I guess, whatever that is. With all of its complications and nuances and difficulties. After I published that book, I ran into some of my aunties and my cousins and we talked for a bit. One of my cousins said this thing that I'll never forget, which is, "I saw you wrote a book about Barbeau," and was like, "But why?" And then she read it and then she was like, "Okay, I get it." [Laughter]

That's always stuck with me and I feel like it makes sense to try to recognize everything, especially when it comes to trying to understand the far-reaching impact that Barbeau has.

DF: Absolutely. We're allowed to hold these things in our hearts as having a complicated relationship to them. That's what Tracie was saying, too. She says something like, "There are plenty of other works by problematic people that I feel totally comfortable just letting it go. This is not important, *I* get to decide what's important to me and I get to decide what I get to hold on to. No one else does."[9]

JA: Totally. It's so complicated – what people feel like *should* be cancelled and what *is* cancelled and what just slides under the radar.

DF: So, one final thing I wanted to ask you is about how NISHGA offers quite an extended meditation on community formations: the Nisga'a community, and the ties severed by the residential school system; and then also the academic and writing communities in which your work circulates, which we see over and over misreads your work, is baffled by your work – "But why?" [Laughter] That sort of thing. I was just wondering, given that we have so many failed instances of community, or disrupted instances of community, in the book, who *do* you see as the receptive community of your work and which communities have helped your work come to its fullest expression?

JA: To answer the second part first, the academic community at large has really helped lift my work up and circulate it, and supported me in sometimes very material and monetary ways. When I first started my PhD I had no intention of finishing it. Or, that was not necessarily a goal. It was more, "Here's a place I could hang out for a couple of years and get some funding and try to do some writing." That is a very happy accident I guess. Some of that community – it's tough to talk about these communities as whole entities – were extraordinarily helpful and really very positive influences in terms of supporting me and my work and helping me get my work to the right places.

I talk about this a little bit in the book, that my ideal readership for this book is in some ways a past version of me when I was younger. Hearing a story like this one would have been really helpful for me just to get that initial spark going – that this is not something that I'm experiencing entirely in isolation, but that other folks go through similar things.

So you know, I think ideally, I'm hoping that the communities that this book gets to are the communities of intergenerational survivors of residential schools, and communities of urban Indigenous peoples. I think those are fractured communities. I guess that's part of the problem. There are all these people who have very similar experiences of life but because of the nature of their experiences they're actually all disconnected and separated. Sometimes I think about it as a kind of diaspora of Indigenous peoples. I think there's been some work done in that area but I haven't read enough of it to say for sure what they're saying about it. I don't know if those groups are going to be receptive to this work. I just think that they're the ones that I wrote the book for and they're the ones who I *want* to read and to share my story with. It's such a difficult group even to think about in so many ways because they're all over the place and disconnected.

DF: The idea that someone would go into the library and type in *NISS*-GA and the computer would say, "Do you mean *NISH*-GA?" and find your book in lieu of or alongside Marius Barbeau. That's a pretty thrilling proposition.

JA: That would be ideal! [Laughter]

NOTES

1 Natalie Loveless, *How to Make Art at the End of the World: A Research-Creation Manifesto* (Durham: Duke University Press, 2019).
2 The quote in full reads, "why shd I give a fuck abt 'poetry'? It's a container." Tommy Pico, *Nature Poem* [Digital Edition] (Portland: Tin House Books, 2017), 80.
3 Jordan Abel, *NISHGA* (Toronto: McClelland & Stewart, 2021), 12.
4 Billy-Ray Belcourt, "In Conversation with Billy-Ray Belcourt," Litfest Alberta, 20 October 2020, https://litfestalberta.org/presentation/in-conversation-billy-ray-belcourt/.
5 Ibid.
6 Abel, *NISHGA*, 9.
7 Nock, quoted in Abel, *NISHGA*, 185.
8 Tracie Morris, "'It doesn't mean anything except talking': An Interview with Tracie Morris" by Cole Mash and Deanna Fong, in this volume, 140.
9 Paraphrase of Morris, "'It doesn't mean anything except talking,'" 140.

12

Can We Think of Sound (or Voice) without Sight (or the Gaze)?

Lacanian Theory and the Horror of Community

Clint Burnham

Introduction

Lacanian theories of the gaze and the voice – specifically, as objects, that traumatize the individual, in which this trauma is necessary for a coming into subjectivity – have much to offer the contemporary practice of sound.[1] Particularly, viewing the voice as a traumatic, partial object unyokes the act of listening from its associations with benevolence, altruism, and intimacy, moving it toward more disturbing registers of alienation and abjection (from/of the Other). Conveniently, two recent horror films do us the service of separately working out this Lacanian theory via voice, or sound, and gaze. In *A Quiet Place* (John Krasinski, 2018), an American family struggles to survive in a post-apocalyptic world inhabited by blind extraterrestrial creatures with an acute sense of hearing. In *Bird Box* (Susanne Bier, 2018), a woman and her two children struggle to survive in, again, a post-apocalyptic world in which one cannot look at some unnamed (and invisible to viewers) creatures or risk insanity and suicide. In *A Quiet Place*, a deaf child is suddenly powerful, while in *Bird Box*, only the (already) psychotic and the blind are unaffected.

The serendipity of timing means that Hollywood film helps us understand Lacan's designation of voice and gaze as objects; that is, as Slavoj Žižek explicates: "they are not on the side of the looking/hearing subject but on the side of what the subject sees or hears."[2] For Lacan, seeing or hearing is not a matter of mastery (unlike the commonplace of the "male gaze").[3] In this chapter, I reference the two films as a way of arguing that we cannot think of sound without thinking of sight: the Lacanian subject exists in their dialectical relation. This dialectic, too, helps us work out the logic of this book's keywords: sound, practice, and community. If we cannot think sound without sight, we also cannot think practice without theory. Community is also (qua Lacanian "social link") predicated on the void of the subject. To reference Žižek, why do we listen to (community) sound archives? Not so much "*in order to avoid the horror of the encounter of the voice qua object*" but to a-void our own lack.

To put it more bluntly: *Bird Box* counters the feminist theory of the gaze of Laura Mulvey ("women as icon, displayed for the gaze and enjoyment of men"),[4] or the decolonial theory of Dana Claxton (which in turn distinguishes between the imperial, colonial, and settler gaze),[5] for in all these cases, the gaze is that which gives the seeing subject power. Rather, with *Bird Box*, we have the Lacanian argument (the gaze illustrates the limits of what we can see); in *A Quiet Place* we see a dialectical rejoinder to the ethics of listening with the, again, Lacanian argument that if you are heard, if you are listened to, you are in danger (in the extreme logic of the film, you will be killed). Or, to put it dialectically, *Bird Box* does not so much counter the feminist or decolonial critique of the gaze as enact it, castrating those who look; and in a "loser wins" logic, in *A Quiet Place*, it turns out that listening gives us (settler, men) power. I am not, it should be emphasized, discounting either the objectifying or otherwise toxic valences of the look or the gaze: to be sure, cinematic and other apparatuses are designed to present women, and to limit them, in certain reified ways. Nor do I wish to minimize the importance of those victimized by personal or structural violence being heard, of their stories being told. Rather, I am arguing – I am suggesting these films make the argument – that the gaze is not unproblematically a position of power, and that, on the other hand, listening can itself be a subject position of power.

CAN WE THINK of SOUND without SIGHT?

Two Films

I begin with two critical accounts of *A Quiet Place*, the first perhaps laudatory, the second arguably political. As befits our post-theory age, the first comes from amateur reviewer Jake C. on the website Rotten Tomatoes, and the second from the *Still Processing* podcast:

> As taut a thriller as it is lean, Krasinski's debut exemplifies the acousmatic horror of the ever vulnerable ear, which we can never close, and the always blind eye, which never finds what it searches for – that's a Lacanian reading, at least. Yet, from a more Derridean perspective, it is a family drama that illustrates the hauntological, how the traces of our past trauma dangerously, inescapably echo into the present. What is more, from a Foucauldian vantage, the film also exemplifies the modern surveillance state – ironically represented in a rural farm, rather than a more standard high-tech urban setting – here seen not as panoptic, but as panaural: The gaze can only land on one thing at a time, but the ear hears everything, the ear is always listening.[6]

If Jake C. finds in the film a confirmation of theoretical readings (and a warning not to impose same), Jenna Wortham and Wesley Morris's *Still Processing* podcast argues, in an episode titled "We Watch Whiteness," that *A Quiet Place* explores dystopia in a way that reveals submerged white fears of a brown invasion, touching on the role of place and rural nature (where are the Black and Brown workers? and cornfield as site), where the monsters are a racialized other. The film, they argue, is a veritable Caucasian *Get Out*, replete with white entitlement via an Etsy/crafty hipster lifestyle (canning fruit and vegetables), analog dystopianism of soft toys and board games.[7] The logic, according to Wortham and Morris: pioneer aesthetics are white privilege on the run (or even pioneer = post-apocalypse of slavery/native genocide; see also Lindsay Brown).[8] The white characters may think they're not making noise (withdrawing from capitalism), but they are still taking up space. Their rural *habitus* connotes the hippie or rural retreat as a space emptied of brown bodies.

The film foregrounds the role of a sound archive qua surveillance control centre – like diagramming boards in cop or espionage thrillers, such a space or representation constitutes the film's unconscious qua cognitive mapping.[9] But it is the white protagonists' attempts both to outwit (or elude) the other *and* their eventual triumph that are most symptomatic. Thus they plan to keep their newborn in a soundproof crib (every new parent's dream, the quiet baby) – *they do not want to be heard, they are refusing representation*. But they are able to defeat the monster with deafness as a McGuffin. For the film notably features the deaf actor Millicent Simmonds, playing teenaged Regan, who discovers that a hearing aid her father is tinkering with makes such a piercing sound that it disables the monster. This plot device is essentially the cinematic version of what in politics is called the "dog whistle," or a coded reference to whiteness that appears innocuous and yet signals maleficent meanings to the initiated (crime, immigration, "old stock Canadians"). The logic of the film: voice/sound are deadly. You do not want to be heard. But we also might want to consider the trope of dog whistle as interpellating the listener as split subject. That is, such coded sounds or signifiers allow the listener to disavow their racism, or that of their favourite politician.

But this excursus to the political reminds us that in the film, the hearing aid also makes evident how listening/being listened to function in necessarily uneven ways. The white protagonists do not want to be heard – they do not want their story told. This is the subjectivity of the racialized or colonized other who seeks to remain silent as a decolonial subject. And then the ethics of listening – in danger of descending into the extractive logic of what Dylan Robinson calls "hungry listening" in his book of the same name – are a demand for the subject to listen. No matter how harmful. This is the important counter-argument that the film presents as a corrective to a facile alignment of speaking with power and listening with passivity, in a political sense: listening can be, and is often, an act of exercising power and privilege.

In an episode of the *SpokenWeb Podcast* titled "Listening Ethically to the Spoken Word," hosted by Deanna Fong and Michael O'Driscoll, I expound upon this point in an interview:

CAN WE THINK of SOUND without SIGHT?

I want to say, listen, if listening is not great, it's also not, not great ... I want us to consider how listening is often the activity of the powerful. Think of the judge in a courtroom who listens to testimony, or a priest who listens confession, or a therapist who listens to a patient. The structure of listening actually bequeaths a kind of master position onto the listener, who then decides what to believe, what to do with this knowledge. We put too much trust in listening. We think the listener is a good person. It's good to listen. We have an entire repertoire of neoliberal, therapeutic listening, active listening. "I hear what you are saying" ... Lacanian psychoanalysis proposes a different kind of listening ... That ethical call to listen is what I think really has to be thought about because it puts the listener into this position of the master, of the beautiful soul.[10]

Self-reflexivity about that position of power ought to be at the forefront when we consider political calls for audition, such as the Truth and Reconciliation Commission on residential schools, or the #MeToo movement, that we risk re-entrenching the listener in a master position. I think it's no coincidence that this film was produced in the wake of the momentous upheaval produced by these calls to listen.

When we turn to *Bird Box*, consider the murderous gaze at work: here, it is not that seeing or looking at something kills or damages that which is seen (in the Foucauldian or panoptical sense that Joan Copjec and Todd McGowan have criticized)[11] – this is not the male gaze theory that cinema stages or frames women as desirable or fatal subjects. Rather, this is the Lacanian gaze, the gaze of lack or castration, of the stain or the side-glance. When we see, in *Bird Box*, we do not have power over what we see; when we see, we die. Or, rather, we kill ourselves. What we have seen is so horrible that not only can we not "unsee it," as our present-day vernacular has it, but also it is so traumatic, that we will repeat the trauma with our action, with our suicide. What we are seeing is our drive, is our anamorphic death drive, akin to the distorted death's skull in Hans Holbein's painting *The Ambassadors*.[12]

This premise of the film results in any number of plot points: Sandra Bullock's character Mallorie and others hide out in a house with paper over the windows, but then need to get groceries, so drive to a store in a car with its windows covered, using GPS (this reliance on the digital is important, as we will soon see). At a certain point, Mallorie learns that there is a refuge of sorts and so heads out down a river, *à la Deliverance*, in a boat with her two children, everyone blindfolded. So now we have the two iconic shots of the film: first, the image of a blindfolded family (iconic for media representations, including the film poster), and second, the shot through the blindfold, which, reproducing the veiled gaze of Marlene Dietrich in Sternberg's *The Scarlet Empress*, updates Mary Ann Doane's theory of the same in *Femmes Fatales*.

These two shots have to be considered dialectically: first, the shot of a blind/blindfolded woman (Mallorie) tells us justice is not *blind*, it is *blindfolded*, for it cannot bear to look at the American state, *which will kill justice*. This is one of the logical conclusions of the film: America kills justice, America is fundamentally *unjust*. And then the shot of what Mallorie can see – light through the grain of the fabric, a blindfold or a blanket – suggests a screen in the sense of that which we see through, like a screen window, and the screen a film is projected onto. A screen that is akin to the sheet between Clark Gable and Claudette Colbert in *It Happened One Night* – which Stanley Cavell describes so well as both film screen and that which separates the noumenal and the phenomenal in Kant.

What is interesting about the shots of the blindfolded Mallorie/Sandra Bullock is how these went viral, how people tried to emulate those shots IRL. Such acts that "digitize the real" are always problematic, or even traumatic, in our present-day milieu: as with *Pokémon GO*, when people playing the game outside would bother other folks just going about their day, or "do it for the 'Gram," where foolhardy Instagrammers would endanger themselves or simply clutter up natural environments with their picture-taking. The "*Bird Box* challenge" was traumatic because it posited that online culture would not be kept on the ghetto or reserve of the digital and instead would bleed into the everyday. And, further, this entailed emulating not simply blindness (or ableism) but also the gaze as lack. The ultimate embrace or acceptance of castration.

But what the change in film industries means from classic Hollywood cinema – of which Cavell was writing – to the incoherence of the post-classical period[13] to today's algorithmic gaze, is that in the media ecology of *Bird Box*, the post-apocalyptic monsters that make you kill yourself are the algorithms of streaming cinema. On the one hand, *they cannot be seen* – they constitute the "black box" of plot generators (as Ed Finn argues in *What Algorithms Want*[14]); they are the unconscious of cinema; they are the subject qua Lacan's algorithms of desire, sexuation, or the sinthome. On the other hand, if we see them, like Medusa's head or Sodom for Lot's wife, they kill us – or we kill ourselves – we are, in ways that Neil Postman could only dream of, "amusing ourselves to death" via late-stage capitalist demand to enjoy. In *Bird Box*, the premise is that if we see the (mostly invisible) monsters (that we nonetheless can *hear* as they rustle leaves, as birds chirp), we will commit suicide: one of the first images is of a woman bashing her head against a glass wall. In *A Quiet Place*, the premise is that if the alien monsters hear us (we do see them, in particular their slimy, vaginal ears), they will kill us. In a less dramatic way, the monster that kills us if we see it illustrates, as Gautam Basu Thakur and Jonathan Michael Dickstein write, "the psychoanalytic theory of the subject as suspended in the Other ... When the subject sees the Other, it also envisions itself in relation to the other, such that there is already a picture from which it, the Subject, is absent"[15] – or, in the *mise en scène* of the film, has killed itself.

From Doane to Jameson

Here we should visit Doane's commentary in *Femmes Fatales*. In the chapter "Veiling Over Desire," Doane considers the close-up in classic Hollywood cinema, arguing first that this signifies the "generalized social exchange of women ... established as the possession of the gaze of a man through glance-object editing."[16] But then the conundrum she immediately turns to is how often, in that same corpus, the close-up must be, in her words, "masked, barred, shadowed, or veiled."[17] The veil simultaneously makes the woman's face more alluring – because it stages a disruption – and renders her own gaze interfered with. So far, standard theories of the male gaze. But there are also moments in this analysis that suggest a post-male gaze critique (which is to say, of the Copjecian school). Already we can see that women's beauty is phallic (hence the close-up as enlarged cinematic image – Doane refers to *Blade Runner*) and so must be veiled (or barred in the form of the subject). As well, Doane refers, tantalizingly, to a minor character in Fritz Lang's *Secret Beyond the Door* (1948), who "uses a scarf to veil a facial scar obtained when she saved the male protagonist's son from a fire,"[18] enacting an emotional hold/debt on the father. Of course, it turns out there is no scar: the veil conceals nothing or, rather, in Doane's fine phrase, it "functions to hide an absence, to conceal the fact that the woman has nothing to conceal."[19]

Finally, Doane points out the very important role of the veil as simultaneously opaque and translucent: it facilitates vision *and* blocks it, "allows and disallows vision" and thus "the magnification of the erotic becomes simultaneous with the activation of objects, veils, nets, streamers ... which intercept the space between the camera and the woman, forming a *second screen*."[20] Doane goes on to produce some fine readings of Marlène Dietrich in two Sternberg films in particular, *The Devil Is a Woman* and *The Scarlet Empress*. She concludes these readings by inviting us "to imagine what Dietrich's return look might be, from behind the veil."[21] So we can only conclude that where we find Doane's phallic close-up, necessarily barred, is *not* in film itself but in that other algorithmic spectacle of the face qua close-up: social media, Facebook, and so on.

Consider the closing moments of *Bird Box*, when Mallorie and her children have reached the sanctuary: she and we learn that this is a school for the blind, and that many of the inhabitants are not sighted. This is akin to the plot device of *A Quiet Place*, where it is the deaf child who saves the family from the monster who can hear them. But it also recalls Alenka Zupančič's argument in "Philosophers' Blindman's Bluff" that the blind subject is the ideal "ontological condition."[22] Like the algorithmic subject who leaves the digital for the real, the blind subject groping their way in the world, the blindfolded or veiled subject is a condition we should all aspire to. This argument takes seriously what otherwise might be dismissed as a social media trifle. Only by taking the *Bird Box* challenge can we encounter the real.

Now we can see how the two films form, as Adorno puts it, two halves that do not make a whole. For in *Bird Box*, we see Sandra Bullock's character, Mallorie, walking around with her arms in front of her, with a blindfold on. Here the visual is toxic: if the first film is acousmophobic, now we are in an iconoclastic society. Blindfolded, but listening, Mallorie is akin to the monsters in *A Quiet Place*, that is, both the gaze *and the voice* as lack ... Or, rather, in a similar logic to Žižek's parable of the frog with the beer bottle, now we should have the two monsters fight it out, and yet they cannot – it is only humans who can fight each other.[23] Each is defined by the lack in the other. And what holds for the subjects holds true for the two films, for it turns out that the sanctuary toward which Mallorie and her children flee in a boat on a river is a school for the blind, and the students of course are impervious to the monsters. Blindfolded in a boat, Mallorie's journey is akin to Homeric oarsmen with their ears stopped-up, bringing together the visual and the aural.

The aural version of the veiled gaze in Doane's analysis and in *Bird Box* would be silence, or what Ed Pluth and Cindy Zeiher call the "apophatic tradition," a matter of negation, but also the proposition that "[a]t every moment within language, we have the sense that there must be some sort of absolute silence on the other side of it, some sort of pre- or non-linguistic noiseless, pristine realm."[24] Further, they argue, "the only silence available is not one that is beyond language, but one that is available only within language."[25] We might draw a parallel between Pluth and Zeiher's observations here and Dylan Robinson's commentary on Peter Morin's silent drum piece in our interview in this collection: this silence is anything but asignifying; rather, it presents itself as an oversaturation of linguistic/symbolic structure.[26] If silence is what is produced by language, then the silence of the characters in *A Quiet Place* is called into being by the language of the monsters, of the others.

Is this the decolonizing argument about the film, that the white characters' silence – when they are trying to *avoid* being heard by the monsters – is a proper response to the Other's discourse? That when Indigenous or Black people speak, white people should be silent? Perhaps, although I am loathe to reach for such pat and simplistic ethics and instead return to the double-negation of listening as not, not good. What if Pluth and Zeiher's logic is attentive to the demands of the film, that is, on the one hand, the characters' silence is created by the monster's discourse, but at the same time, it is a way of hoping not to be heard by the monsters? And what are we to do with how the characters attack the monsters – with a malfunctioning hearing aid, a media object?

Do gaze and voice as objects mean we can think of them as media objects? Consider what Fredric Jameson dubbed the first postmodern French film, *Diva* (Jean-Jacques Beineix, 1981). Shot in a vertiginous style that foregrounds artifice, mirrorings, the mutability of the image (from postal-employee Jules's loft with its photo-realist mural of American-style cars – next to actual, demolished vehicles – to a shoplifter's skirt printed with an image of the Paris Opera House), the film's plot concerns two tape recordings: one of a reclusive opera singer, another of a prostitute's accusation of police corruption. Describing the look of the film, Jameson comments that we never see the mural whole, and that "like the ... eponymous being of *Alien*, it never did (does) exist as a completed thing, an object that could be represented."[27]

Blogger Royal S. Brown has justly called *"Diva*, a masterpiece not just of the *cinéma du look* but also of what could be called the *cinéma du listen*."[28] If the film's look, in Jameson's argument via *Alien*, is akin to that of horror, so too is its "listen": for the voice has been reified into media objects, which, as reel-to-reel and cassette tapes, are now properly the object of an entire new academic discipline – media archaeology. And this has happened against the opera singer's wishes: thus the horror at the voice's reproducibility. The mediated voice qua *objet petit a* structures our desire, or at least that of the film's characters. First it functions as acousmatic signifier, so we hear the opera singer both "live" in performance and then as diegetic sound when Jules plays his pirated recording. But the mediated voice also works as McGuffin, when colonial French mobsters – *les Antillaises*, who are after the cassette – cross paths with Taiwanese executives, who are after the reel. Finally, it turns out, late in the game, that a third recording has been made, by the corrupt police officer.

Conclusion

Examining how the gaze and the voice function in three films via Lacanian theory, I have sought to counter theories of the gaze as powerful and listening as a gesture of solidarity. In *Bird Box*, seeing kills you. In *A Quiet Place*, being heard means you are dead. Or at least, these are the premises of the films: the blind turn out to be powerful in the first, and the deaf in the second. In calling for a psychoanalytic approach to listening, we reject the standard notion that listening either secures power for the person enunciating, or that a frictionless act of communication takes place whenever we "add dialogue."[29] Indeed, as Jordan Abel points out in his interview, there is value to be found in the "difficult" listening demanded by sounded avant-garde poetry – one that lines up more productively with the analyst's agnostic position as auditor. Not "this is the master signifier?" but "why is this the master signifier?" (to take a cue from the hysteric). But what does it mean to offer a historical argument, and of what interest can such interpretive strategies as, on the one hand, talking about commercial film, and on the other bringing the visual together with the aural, be to the larger project of this collection of essays?

There seem to be three issues: first, an assertion of commercial, or pop-cultural, media forms as sites for inquiry; second, a critique of normative notions of listening as an inherently respectful or empathic practice; third, an argument that the aural and the visual are intertwined not only in cultural objects but also in the constitution of the subject. What does my reading mean for this project's shift from "resonance" to "resistance"? Perhaps we can think of Paul de Man's argument that the resistance to theory was already a part of theory: "It may well be ... that the polemical opposition, the systematic non-understanding and misrepresentation, the unsubstantial but eternally recurrent objections, are the displaced symptoms of a resistance inherent in the theoretical enterprise itself."[30] So, too, a resistance to listening, as argued in my chapter, is already baked in to the DNA of the listening project.

NOTES

1 See Mladen Dolar, *A Voice and Nothing More* (Cambridge: MIT Press, 2006); and Todd McGowan, *The Real Gaze: Film Theory after Lacan* (Albany: SUNY Press, 2007).

2   Slavoj Žižek, "'I Hear You with My Eyes': or, The Invisible Master," in *Gaze and Voice as Love Objects*, ed. Renata Salecl and Slavoj Žižek (Durham: Duke University Press, 1996), 90.
3   See McGowan, *The Real Gaze*.
4   Laura Mulvey, "Visual Pleasure and Narrative Cinema," in *Visual and Other Pleasures* (London: Palgrave Macmillan, 1989), 21.
5   Dana Claxton, "Wisdom for All Through Identity Politics: A Hopeful Idea," in *In the Wake of the Komagata Maru: Transpacific Migration, Race and Contemporary Art* (Surrey: Surrey Art Gallery, 2015), 46.
6   Jake C., "Review of *A Quiet Place*," on Rotten Tomatoes, 16 November 2018, accessed 15 September 2020, https://rtv2-production-2-6.rottentomatoes.com/m/a_quiet_place_2018/reviews/ (site discontinued).
7   Jenna Wortham and Wesley Morris,"We Watch Whiteness," *Still Processing* (podcast), 26 April 2018, accessed 15 September 2020.
8   See Lindsay Brown, "When Hipsters Dream of the 1890s: Heritage Aesthetics and Gentrification," *Briarpatch* online (May–June 2015), accessed 31 July 2023, https://briarpatchmagazine.com/articles/view/when-hipsters-dream.
9   See Alberto Toscano and Jeff Kinkle, *Cartographies of the Absolute: An Aesthetics of the Economy for the Twenty-First Century* (London: Zero Books, 2015).
10 Clint Burnham, "Listening Ethically to the Spoken Word," on *SpokenWeb Podcast* s2, ep 7, 5 April 2021, hosted by Deanna Fong and Michael O'Driscoll, https://spokenweb.ca/podcast/episodes/listening-ethically-to-the-spoken-word/.
11 See Joan Copjec, *Read My Desire: Lacan Against the Historicists* (Cambridge: MIT Press, 1994); and Todd McGowan, *The Real Gaze*.
12 See Jacques Lacan, *The Four Fundamental Concepts of Psychoanalysis*, trans. Alan Sheridan (New York: W.W. Norton, 1998), 85–90.
13 See Robin Wood, *Hollywood from Vietnam to Reagan* (New York: Columbia University Press, 1986).
14 Ed Finn, *What Algorithms Want: Imagination in the Age of Computing* (Cambridge: MIT Press 2018).
15 Gautam Basu Thakur and Jonathan Michael Dickstein, *Lacan and the Nonhuman* (London: Palgrave Macmillan, 2018), 5.
16 Mary Ann Doane, *Femmes Fatales: Feminism, Film Theory, Psychoanalysis* (New York: Routledge, 1991), 48.
17 Ibid.
18 Ibid.
19 Ibid.
20 Ibid., 49.
21 Ibid., 75.
22 Alenka Zupančič, "Philosophers' Blind Man's Bluff," in *Gaze and Voice as Love Objects*, ed. Salecl and Žižek, 56.

23 Slavoj Žižek, *The Plague of Fantasies* (London: Verso Books, 2008), 90–1.
24 Ed Pluth and Cindy Zeiher, *On Silence: Holding the Voice Hostage* (London: Palgrave Macmillan, 2019), 21.
25 Ibid.
26 Dylan Robinson, "'Songs are so much more than songs': An Interview with Dylan Robinson" by Clint Burnham, in this volume, 344.
27 Fredric Jameson, *Signatures of the Visible* (London: Routledge, 1992), 57.
28 Royal S. Brown, "The Jean-Jacques Beineix Collection (Web Exclusive)," *Cineaste* 35, no. 2 (2010), accessed 31 July 2023, www.cineaste.com/spring2010/the-jeanjacques-beineix-collection-web-exclusive.
29 Robinson, "'Songs are so much more than songs,'" 347.
30 Paul de Man, *The Resistance to Theory* (Minneapolis: University of Minnesota Press, 1986), 12.

13

Transcript of *Lesbian Liberation Across Media: A Sonic Screening* Podcast, Introduction

Felicity Tayler, in consultation with Mathieu Aubin

This podcast transcript uses a citational composition method that deliberately blurs the boundaries between documentary audio recording and collage narrative. The voices that are printed before you have been remediated several times from archival video recording, to online broadcast and gathering, to podcast, to digital text, to printed page. Following Judith Butler, this remediation engages a citational politics, "by which discourse produces the effects that it names." Each time these voices shift the context of their mediation, there are parallel shifts in meaning in the context that you, the reader or listener, will receive them.

These ambiguities of mediated communication are deliberate, and they mirror the ways that lesbian and wider queer communities have historically formed counterpublics, as shared practices, languages, and knowledges are communicated and reinvested with meaning across generations. When this podcast began with an online event held through the Zoom platform, with a smaller attendance of about thirty people, we knew more or less who would be there. We screened clips of the film *Labyris Rising* (1980) and two other rarely screened documentary films of feminist and lesbian historical significance. *Labyris Rising*, a film by Margaret Moores and Almerinda Travassos, appropriates its format from Kenneth Anger's iconic gay film *Scorpio Rising* (1963). Neither film includes dialogue, only a pulsing desirous musical score set to a collage of erotic visuals. We see and hear how citation through visual and sound editing is a form of care in the film produced by Moores and Travassos. This mode of film production and reception is labour-intensive for both the producers and the viewers. To become part of the lesbian community depicted, you have to understand the visual and musical codes that operate as a kind of secret language.

The clips of *Labyris Rising* generated so much desire in the first smaller audience that there was demand to watch the entire film. We organized a second event, an online film screening, again on Zoom, for a larger audience of over seventy people. We didn't know who would attend this second event, but we knew we wanted to make a podcast that would resonate with our shared experience, and that would mean making our intentions to record and remediate transparent to our listening audience. How would we cite and remix the sounds of people's voices, echoing the films we enjoyed together by splicing together our shared enjoyment and co-production of intergenerational community and counterpublics?

And here is where (and why) the editor(s) have asked me to address the role of consent or of feminist ethics in this process of care, citation, and a collage aesthetic that deliberately blurs the boundaries between the documentary genres of public event recording and oral history transmission, as the transcript is remediated further away from the audio space of the podcast and onto the printed page. To publish the podcast transcript in an academic book shifts both its context and receptive network. Despite both contexts being public – the watch party was free to attend, publicized, and open to all – most of those in attendance at the watch party were already part of a community who shared history, values, and common frames of reference (despite how contested and/or multiple these might be).

Publishing the transcript in a book opens it up to a community of outsiders – one which has the potential to forge new relationships of solidarity and allyship, but also one that comes with a certain level of risk, as T.L. Cowan and Jasmine Rault have identified in their essay "Onlining Queer Acts: Digital Research Ethics and Caring for Risky Archives." There, describing the archives of trans- feminist and queer performance that they work with in their scholarship, they write: "Academic researchers who mine, quote, and re-publish parts of an online conversation/thread, of which they are not active participants ... are technically following recommended ethical research practices, but are also (potentially) disrupting the scene (and potentially exposing it to harm) whether or not that is their intention."[1] Despite the fact that the text makes its move in the opposite direction – from a text that is openly accessible on the Web to a print journal – the ethical implications of shifting receptions contexts remain an important consideration. How do we ensure that participants are cared for in the event that a context-shift exposes them to unforeseen risk? How do we balance the potential benefits of connecting with new audiences with the care work of ensuring participants' consent and safety?

In response to this editorial address, what I am enacting here is a feminist principle of transparency of the labour involved in the processing of digital audio files, all the while acknowledging the incompleteness of it as a gesture in communicative space. We began with the principle that the film screening was a public event; that is to say, with a clear message to participants letting them know that the session was being recorded and that we would use this recording in future publications. We encouraged them to use the chat or to speak as part of the film discussions, but we also made it clear that they were free to alter their screen names or turn their cameras off, if they wished to remain anonymous. Some people used pseudonyms, and others had more than one person on camera, or turned their cameras and mics off. We also embraced the principle that if we were transmitting these voices in remediated form into the future, that the speakers should be acknowledged as contributors to the podcast. Moving from the video recording to the audio-only track when creating the podcast audio collage produced an ambiguity as a lack of visual context separated voices from their names and faces. This is why we added a list of contributors as acknowledgments at the end of the podcast. Moving from the audio space to the transcript asked us to match the names of the speakers back up to their words, which was a challenge because of pseudonyms and the doubling-up of people on camera. We marked some voices as "unidentified" but an acknowledgment of their contribution was preserved in the transcription of the list of names and pseudonyms spoken at the end of the podcast.

When the podcast was ready to launch, we sent out invitations to all attendees of the film screening, explaining our process and thanking them for their contributions. This way we made sure to distribute access to the podcast to contributors before the public launch event. Because the recordings were made at a fairly large and explicitly public event, and we had listened very closely in our editing process for the sound collage, our judgment was that the content was safe to share. Any retroactive editing at this point would be significant because of the collage format. These gestures were our way of extending the principles of care central to the communities at the heart of the discussion: making sure that contributors could listen to the episode and respond to us before the launch, as well as the discussion session during the launch event alongside the formation of another listening counterpublic. We hope that this extra layer of remediation will continue the work of intersectional and intergenerational dialogue occasioned by the multiple events that preceded it.

Lesbian Liberation Across Media: A Sonic Screening

Transcribed by Kelley Cullen
Edited for print by Deanna Fong

Hannah McGregor: [Instrumental overlapped with voice] What does literature sound like? What stories will we hear if we listen to the archive? Welcome to the *SpokenWeb Podcast*: stories about how literature sounds. My name is Hannah McGregor, and each month I'll be bringing you different stories of Canadian literary history and our contemporary responses to it created by scholars, poets, students, and artists from across Canada. This episode of the *SpokenWeb Podcast* is a little different from episodes you've heard from us before. What you're about to hear is a kind of feminist memory work; an audio collage, a method, an approach to community building that aims to honour lesbian feminist collective histories and renewed public attention to lesbian feminist culture.

In this episode, producers Felicity Tayler, Mathieu Aubin, and Scott Girouard cordially invite you into their sonic memory world: a three-part audio collage of "Lesbian Liberation Across Media," a virtual film screening and discussion held in summer 2020 in partnership with SpokenWeb and featuring three iconic lesbian feminist films: *A Working Women's Collective*, *Labyris Rising*, and *Proud Lives: Christine Bearchell*. Through a weaving together of the voices of over seventy participants in attendance, along with original music scores, archival clips, and more, we ask: how do we listen to Canadian lesbian liberation movements across media? Whether it's a feature-length film or a spirited virtual chat session, this audio collage episode invites you to experience a citational politics that makes audible the intergenerational relationships, conflicting concerns, nostalgic reveries, and a sense of togetherness-while-apart in the pandemic-related time of crisis. Here are Felicity, Mathieu, and Scott with "Lesbian Liberation Across Media: A Sonic Screening.".

Voiceover, Emma Middleton: On June 10, 2020, following the extreme social isolation of the first COVID pandemic winter, over seventy people gathered over Zoom to watch three lesbian liberation films: *A Working Women's Collective, Labyris Rising,* and *Proud Lives: Christine Bearchell*. In this podcast, we've created an audio collage record of the sounds of watching these films together.

May Ning: [Zoom entry chime] I'm excited to see what it's going to look like with a hundred people.

Unknown speaker: I know. Yeah. [Instrumental music] When we were watching *Bound*, there was one person who hadn't seen the movie before and she had her camera on, so everybody was getting more excited about watching her reactions. I mean, they were excited about the movie too, but it was like her reactions were the best version of the show. [Laughs]

Rachel E. Beattie: It's so different when you're doing an online thing, because if you're at a talk or something, you can see people smiling at you and responding to stuff that you'd say. I just feel like doing Zoom stuff is like speaking into the void. For the trivia night that I've been doing for the ArQuives, we had to turn off the comments and also people's videos, because we had Zoom-bombing and people doing offensive stuff. So, it's like I'm literally speaking into the void. I have no idea if people are enjoying the material or if they're laughing at my jokes or anything.

Michelle Schwartz: What time is it?

REB: 8:26.

MS: When should I start letting people in? [Instrumental, drums] I just let them in at 8:30 or earlier?

Felicity Tayler: I'd let them at 8:30.

MS: Yeah.

REB: How many people are in the waiting room?

MS: Seventeen.

REB: Cool. How's it going, May?

MN: Good. I'm excited. I haven't seen the films yet.

REB: Yeah. Mathieu sent me the Press Gang one, but I haven't seen the other two. So, I'm really looking forward to watching them.

MN: I know, I wanted to save them to watch it with everyone else.

REB: Yeah.

FT: It's 8:30. I guess we can –

Various Voices: [In unison] – open the doors.

Mathieu Aubin: It's funny because I imagine when you would open the door in a real office and then thirty-six people came in at once, it'd be like –

MS: Much louder.

MA: Yeah.

FT: And also more visually obvious. [Laughs]

MA: All the bodies.

Constance Crompton: It is sort of wonderful watching like everyone arrive and roll in –

MA: Yeah.

CC: – I haven't hosted a lot of Zoom meetings, so I don't get the waiting room feature very often. It's just very nice.

Elspeth Brown: Nice to see many friendly faces and names in the list of participants, even if a lot of people don't have their video on or their audio.

CC: It's so true. Yes. Hi, to everyone who is sort of disembodied at the moment.

VV: [Laughter]

MS: Hi to everyone who we might've usually seen in the summer conference season that we've missed.

MA: Yes.

MS: Our annual hangouts were cancelled.

CC: And now with the combination of theatres being closed and bars being closed, I think this would be the kind of event that could blend both of those things, even if everyone's in their own living room.

REB: Yeah, totally.

CC: That's great. Also, I think we had been expecting a much smaller event and we could be like, "Oh, we can go around." Well, shall we dive in with official programming?

FT: Zoom says you're the host so I guess you get to make the decisions.

CC: Yes, indeed. In which case, I would say, "Take it away, Michelle."

MS: Oh, no, you're first Connie. You're supposed to welcome everybody.

CC: Ah! Welcome, everybody. We are definitely touched by how many people have taken up the screening just from the last week and a half. It was put together by several organizations: the Humanities Data Lab at Ottawa U, SpokenWeb, the University of Toronto Media Archives, Lesbian and Gay Liberation in Canada project, which Michelle and I co-direct together, and the ArQuives.

MS: We, as the organizers of this event, are participating from Toronto. So, we have the University of Toronto and Ryerson University, from the University of Ottawa and from Concordia University in Montreal. We acknowledge that our respective institutions are located on the traditional lands of many Indigenous nations, including the Algonquian, the Anishinaabeg, the Haudenosaunee, the Wendat and the Mississaugas of the Credit. Just as Toronto has been a gathering place for many people for thousands of years, we are grateful to be able to provide a space for people to gather together tonight. We ask you to think about the land that you are on and how you can show solidarity with the Indigenous caretakers of that land by talking about what traditional people are from the land that they are on. So, if anyone wants to share their traditional land with us, we would love to know where you're all coming in from.

Voiceover, EM: This screening of 1970s lesbian liberation films was organized in response to a clamorous demand to watch these films from the audience of an earlier event. We wanted to ask an intergenerational question: are we doomed to have these same fights forever?

MA: What I would love is for me to stop talking and to hear from people that we've been wanting to hear from. Go ahead.

REB: Hey, did you see that Ontario had a plan about students going back to school today? I couldn't find anything in it about libraries. Like we're not important. Nobody gives a shit about us. The press release for the Ontario government said nothing about university libraries ...

FT: Just to go back to the listening session that Mathieu and I led with these films in April for an audience of around thirty people. So, we knew more or less who was going to be there, and that we're able to put on this other event that is reaching a much wider audience. So, for me, this kind of comes back to this question of gaining access to media that we see in the first film, and that we'll see continuing through in the other films.

MS: The screening was based on a SpokenWeb event that Mathieu and Felicity hosted where they showed clips of *Labyris Rising*, which is a film that we're going to watch tonight. I've never seen a 1970s lesbian short film that I haven't wanted to see the entirety of. There was a great clamour in the chat of that Zoom asking to see the whole movie instead of just the short clips. That was the birth of this screening tonight, where we get to watch the whole movie as well as two other movies. So, we have three short films to watch and we have a few panellists who will take turns introducing each one. We'll have a time for discussion and questions at the end. So, you can use the chat at any time, but we'll hold the questions until the end.

Baylee Woodley: I just read an email from Connie from earlier. I would love to hear about Michelle's experience visiting the installation *Killjoy's Kastle* if you're willing to talk about it and your thoughts on how it engages with this lesbian feminist history. Also, maybe it's another way to facilitate these sorts of intergenerational conversations.

MS: I just went as an attendee and it was a huge amount of fun. You went into this house and there was the graveyard of lesbian organizations past, which were all these gravestones painted with these lesbian organizations that had broken up due to in-fighting or the cause getting - well, I don't know, potentially they solved the cause. I believe there was a menstrual cup reading with a diviner of menstrual blood. There was smashing truck nuts - [Sound effect: campfire crackling]

REB: There was a lesbian singalong in that campfire room with all the little wood stools.

MS: Yeah. It was a really wonderful experience and it did provide another version of watching these films for me, as someone who didn't live through the time period - a nostalgia for something that I missed or felt not fully part of. Being able to experience the history in a certain way, and also feeling very strongly the gaps between the generations. So, I loved *Killjoy's Kastle*. I don't know if anyone else was there.

REB: I went on opening night, actually. It was with Michelle and a bunch of other people -

REB: Yeah, some other people on this call. Like Stark [inaudible]. So, for opening night they had all of these lesbian feminist theorists - or I don't know how everyone identified. But because it's the last room in Killjoy's Kastle was the processing room. So, after you've gone through this whole experience, of course, lesbians have to process, so literally you could not leave without talking to famous feminist theorists. It was amazing.

FT: But what I do remember is that there was kind of this double narrative of like, "Oh, that's just like white feminism." Then inside Killjoy's Kastle there was this trying to atone for, or come to terms with, or critique of whiteness at the same time as having this intergenerational smorgasbord of experience. I think that that's just part of what comes with this.

REB: Yeah. I remember they had the lesbian singalong room. There were all these quotes on the wall from various lesbian feminists. And then there was an accusation made that they were sort of appropriating without bringing in more diverse voices into the making of it, so it was like essentially these white feminists that were using the voices of feminists of colour, and that kind of thing.

FT: It doesn't mean that the history that we have access to has less value. It just means that there are other histories that we can now look to as well.

MS: I wanted to say how odd it was to watch that Press Gang film, and then hear people restating debates that we hear so much now in the movement. Like that woman who was ranting about how she doesn't know what's politically correct and so she doesn't know what she can say because now everything she says is wrong, and so she's not going to say anything. It's just so frustrating to hear the same things eternally return within these kinds of communities. It was fascinating to hear that particular kind of iteration of political correctness from so far in the past. [Beat] I always wonder whether we're doomed to have the same fights forever. Is that too dark? [Laughs]

FT: No, but I do think it's worthwhile embracing it, or learning to live with the discomfort – learning to live with that affect. So, there's this question of nuancing intergenerational conversations and tempering your fandom for something like *Killjoy's Kastle*, right? I always kind of had this FOMO relationship to *Killjoy's Kastle*, 'cause it was never in the city that I was in.

REB: Yeah. I think it's a very important point that you raise and I think that sort of came out before: that for all of these movements there's never just one thought. People have really big, serious fights about very specific points of ideology and very specific things like, "Where are we going?" Movements have always been like that – they're always going to be like that. And so, looking back, you can look at both of those things. There was this wonderful thing that was achieved by the movement and this great togetherness, but then also you argue day and night, but then you love the people at the end of the day, but like, "Oh my God, they made me so mad and we had a big argument" kind of thing. I think it seems like a thing that is sort of evergreen. I've certainly noticed that in organizing spaces now and in the documentaries that you see about various different groups organizing.

MS: We also just wanted to thank everyone that donated towards the screenings. Because we were able to source additional funding for the screening rates we were able to donate all that money to The 519 and to support our youth in Toronto. So, thank you so much. We raised almost $400 for those organizations for queer Black and trans youth in the city. That's just a really great thing that we can do for our community. So, thank you all for donating.

EB: I mean, it's so nice to just watch these fabulous films without leaving my house, I can't even begin to tell you. I probably never would have gone, frankly, because I'm such a homebody.

Voiceover, EM: The first film, *A Working Women's Collective*, opened a discussion of lesbian feminist film aesthetics and printing collectives. In listening to a cacophony of lesbian liberation print sounds we wondered what these sonic resonances told us about how printing collectives lived their politics through their work and loves.

MA: So, I just want to quickly introduce Press Gang. Press Gang was a feminist collective with a strong lesbian constituency that were a publishing house and printing press in Vancouver, British Columbia. I'm happy to say that some people here are from that area. It started in 1970 as a mixed collective, but in 1974 it became a women-only collective and it would go on to publish several books that were integral to the lesbian liberation movement, such as *Stepping Out of Line* and *Still Sing*, and print many, many documents, flyers, and posters for lesbian liberation organizations in the city. The video we're about to see is called *A Working Women's Collective*, and it was produced by the Media Mothers organization. It is currently housed at VIVO archives in Vancouver. What's exciting about what you're about to see is that it does document the origins of the collective and their values as they stood in 1974.

MA: You get to hear from the members of the press, but what you also get to see is what the site looked like. So, what I want to encourage you to think about is: what does the relationship between sound and visual do in the film? What does the relationship between diegetic and non-diegetic sound mean? What you can see and hear at the same time, and whether you can actually identify the source of the sound. If you can't do that, I encourage you to think about that with the rest of the videos as well. Finally, really just a general question to ask yourself, which is: when you're watching this, what can you see in the documentary and what can be heard in relation to lesbian feminist culture production? That's really what I've been thinking about collaboratively with this wonderful collective.

REB: First off, with Press Gang, I love the lo-fi look. [Sound effect: film reel] It looks like it was shot on some kind of magnetic video that is rapidly deteriorating. As a person who works on analog media, I really loved that. When we were talking about doing this session, there was a lot of talk about the sound of the film, so I was really listening to that. The thing that I've been sort of obsessed with for a while is the way that voices sound different from the past, like there's a different ... I don't know, not like an "audio person" [Audio: background chatter from film] I don't know the exact word, but there's a different tone to those voices. That's on display when you're looking at the beautiful printing presses and then hearing those voices in your ear. So, Mathieu, I wonder if you had any thoughts on the prominence given to the sound of the voice.

MA: [Sound effect: film reel] What's interesting about the voices is it cuts because of the editing. It's a bit choppy. It's not just the way that they're articulating their politics and their relationship to the press, but also the way that they sounded doing so. And also the sound of the machines. They don't sound like the printer we have at home producing these books. Like, it's really loud and that's part of their daily sounds, right? So, in thinking about that, I think we have a cacophony of sounds in the video. Part of what I'm interested in thinking about is not just what we can see and where the sources of the audio are, but how they inform each other. So, when somebody is talking about taking over the means of production [Sound effect: printing press] and then all you see is a machine just pumping, you're like, "Oh, okay. Like this is literally it." Then I'm thinking, "Oh, step back. Let's look at this video that they produced, and the choppiness of that." As they're explaining something it almost cuts out and you're like, "Oh, okay, well, we might have missed the message." The best way to describe it at this point in terms of that video is like is a cacophony of lesbian liberation print sounds. [Instrumental music]

Audio from A *Working Women's Collective*: Why I was a printer and why all this had happened to me was because women don't have access to the media and that women have to be printers or have to be publishers to – [crackle] [new voice] – fell into it, too. You know, I was working, designing posters and things, and I came down and I thought, "Oh, there's this press." I knew one of the men and he was doing darkroom stuff. So I went in and he showed me how to do all the darkroom stuff. So, I developed the negatives of my own, like my own artwork. Then he was starting to print it and he said, do you want to do this? And I said, sure. [Laugh] I was really afraid, but I thought, "There's this big press. I can't drive a car and I've never run a machine." I had this mental block and I thought, "Now's the time." [Instrumental music]

FT: I had a follow-up on that. I've seen the film in different contexts now a couple of times, but the thing that struck me in this listening is there's this moment where they're talking about how it's about gaining the skills and being really good at what you're doing. You see them working with wrenches and fixing the machines. Then they're talking about how they're having this conflict with somebody who's like, "Who cares if you can do stuff? You just have to say things!" It's like this big production-versus-content sort of false binary.

Maureen FitzGerald: Hi, hi. Yes, I was connected with Press Gang through feminist publishing because I was involved in the Women's Press Collective, and I actually –

Amy Gottlieb: You're here in Toronto?

MF: – I am in Toronto. I'm speaking from Toronto, but there was a year that I spent in Vancouver because I was lovers with Pat Smith. It was wonderful to see those images. I knew and know Sarah. The skills debate in '81 was very interesting. The way I worked at Press Gang, I suppose I volunteered once a week and they taught me how to do layout. I'm an academic. I was on leave from U of T for the year, because that's where my lover was. But the raging discussion was around skills. Some people thought that everybody should do everything. That there should be no division of labour and no acknowledgment of the skills that some of the people who had been working in the presses had and were very experienced at. As Marusya just said, it was a very sophisticated operation. By then it was also publishing books, a lot of books. So, Press Gang publishing, I think probably didn't outweigh the flyer printing and printing for other organizations, but it became more predominant. When I was there, it was more predominant. I remember this discussion around skills where some people thought, "Well, we should all do everything, and all be able to do everything. There should be no specialization."

Rachel Epstein: It's Rachel Epstein. Yeah, I worked at Press Gang in the early '80s just after Maureen – maybe '82, '84 or something like that. I don't actually remember that skills debate so much, but I started out working as the production coordinator and then I actually learned to run a press. I remember that being one of the most empowering things I ever did, was actually learning how to run that printing press and how to fix it and all of that. I was also lovers with Pat Smith at the same time that Maureen was lovers with Pat Smith. [Laughs] That's how Maureen and I met each other.

So, that was going on too. Unfortunately, I came in late and I missed the film. I think I may have seen it a long time ago. So, I can't really speak to that, but just not to romanticize totally what it was like there. We were also struggling with working collectively and I have some harsh memories of how we treated each other – how, in the process of trying to be fair, we were very unfair. I know lots has been written on post-feminist collectives, and what we did was amazing in so many ways; the skills that we developed, the political causes that we supported. But there were many things going on there in that attempt to work collectively.

Voiceover, EM: [Instrumental music] In the second film, *Labyris Rising*, we hear no dialogue, only an Eros-propelled musical score, set to a collage of visuals built through mimesis and citation. We see and hear how editing is a form of care. If you want to be part of the community, you have to understand the codes.

FT: So, when Mathieu and I first looked at these two films together, what we were listening for was the sound in the films, and how that sound worked with the visual [Instrumental, percussion] to show us how community is created through different kinds of cultural institutions that produce a common language and a set of shared practices. It's a video made by Margaret Moores and Almerinda Travassos, who are two former members of the Lesbian Organization of Toronto (LOOT). It was filmed in the basement of the LOOT building. [Sound effect: printing press] What you don't see off-screen is a printing press where the newsletter was published.

In *Labyris Rising* we hear a continuous soundtrack of folk rock and R&B. I saw a comment go by while we were watching where somebody was trying to guess the track. I have to say, that's kind of my experience of the film as well, trying to situate the sound while I'm watching the images. [Instrumental, trumpet] So the musical landscape helps the flow of the non-linear narrative structure throughout the film and the collage, but, as you saw between the two clips, the collage aesthetic of the video, and also the sonic composition are borrowed from the iconic film of gay culture, *Scorpio Rising*. There's a lot that's borrowed from the film, but there's also a lot that's kind of worked at redefined in relation to that film.

jake moore: We all know the soundtrack from *Scorpio Rising* and that's even many years after the fact because Kenneth Anger was able to draw from very known popular culture to find the representation of this so-called outlaw. That outlaw is fully coded as what we accept as a masculine identity. The idea that travel was going to happen and this gathering that would become a Hell's Angels gathering ... Whereas in the Michigan Womyn's Festival, you have people riding bicycles and all of the coded things that you're describing, but the soundtrack, most of us are not as familiar with. And, well, Joan Armatrading. Until we see Janice Joplin, it really doesn't enter into a contemporary imaginary. I think the outlaw status is still much stronger for the lesbian woman. It still doesn't enter into the same kind of accepted social practice.

FT: Another parallel between them is that both opening clips also point to fashion as a signifier of community belonging. For the woman fixing her bicycle, we can look at the embroidered patch that you see on the hip of her jeans, so what you see there is the line "woman identified woman." So, in the context of fixing the bicycle, it echoes that popular saying that people would wear on T-shirts and protests at the time: "A woman needs a man like a fish needs a bicycle." But it also has an organizing function. Historian Becki Ross, when speaking about LOOT, talks about this term as a political category. She says, "A true feminist is a lesbian by definition in the political sense." This is further explained by a Vancouver journalist, Judy Moreton, that all women fully committed to the cause of freeing themselves and all other women from oppression are lesbians.

Marusya Bociurkiw: So, I was interested in the sort of warning at the beginning around different ideas of gender in second wave feminism, that there were no "non" – I mean, the word "non-binary" didn't exist. Transgender existed, but it was identified, I think, in different ways. Certainly, there was gender-bending. We see that in the clothing and the embodiment of female masculinity.

FT: So, this of course is an articulation of an ideal that's easier said than done, because there are tensions. There are always tensions in social movements, and so there will be tensions in this time period between gay and straight feminists, and also between feminist organizing and male-identified gay liberation organizing, for example. This tension within the gay liberation movement is alluded to in Moores's appropriation of *Scorpio Rising*. When I looked at this film, I looked at it as kind of a semantic structure: so, the different scenes are being put together as if the visuals themselves and the soundtrack are a narrative structure that's built through mimesis or citation. It's repeating motifs that come from somewhere else. And there's no spoken dialogue, so it's not as direct or explicit as the last film that we saw. You have to kind of imagine yourself into the scene and draw on your knowledge of what you know about the scenes that are being portrayed, the kind of community that's being shared with us, and the music that's being played to imagine yourself into it, depending on what your existing experiences are. So, this ambiguity of origin contributes to the sense that to be part of the community, you have to know its references or codes, which include specific genres of music as a cultural institution. In *Labyris Rising* you'll see that those genres of music lead to this heady dream of the outdoor music festival. [Sound of concert cheering]

jm: The Michigan Womyn's Festival was this iconic, though clearly specific, gathering site. It's telling that it was known as the land where people gathered, and my exposure to it as a musician was as a punk rock musician that they invited there. But we were very much interlopers in the warm, fuzzy kind of breakdown of feminist status. And what was outlier? What was allowable outlying? I think you get into really interesting territory thinking about when a rebellious figure can be fully embraced by a larger dominant culture, like the masculine biker that is still embraced today. We still see this in contemporary film and television. It gets a lot of play. It's a very common association of a powerful and often militarized understanding of how to achieve power.

FT: You learn a lot about the world of LOOT from the movement of the camera around the scene in *Labyris Rising* and I'm going to read an excerpt that describes the scene from historian Becki Ross's book:

An inventory of 1970s, lesbian feminist lifestyle is richly detailed in the 1980 film *Labyris Rising*. A deliberate feisty send-up of the urban gay male style captured by Kenneth Anger and *Scorpio Rising*. This lesbian cult classic was shot on location at 342 Jarvis Street and the Fly By Night Lounge by former LOOT members, Margaret Moores and Almarinda Travassos. The half-hour super eight film is full of clues: the double-headed axe. The Labyris or cunt beads on a chain. The famous maxim "woman identified woman" embroidered on the back of blue jeans, pinky rings, interlocking women's symbols, pink triangles, and suspenders. While reading the Washington-DC-based feminist journal, *off our backs*, the protagonist drags deeply on her marijuana joint and drifts off to remember scenes from the Michigan festival to the music of Be K'Roche, Heather Bishop, Joan Armatrading, and Janis Joplin.[2]

If you think about *Labyris Rising*, then taking the vocabulary from that film, what's interesting is noting what they keep, right? So, the scene that we all love with the cat and somebody named Mars on the bed ... there are some comments going by, like maybe people knew the name of this person in the bed.

MA: Oh, we have a comment from Amy Gottlieb that says the person on the bed is Marcia Cannon known as Mars.

FT: But in *Labyris Rising* you have somebody on the bed, they're smoking a joint, they've got all the music festival kind of paraphernalia all around them, they've got a cat and they're reading *off our backs* right? So, it's like –

Raegan Swanson: They're reading *off our backs*! All I could think about was how I was about to watch a movie about Chris [Bearchell] and how much work she did around censorship. That was one moment where it all felt very tied together.

MA: There's the sound of the music and the voices as they are connecting, which are mostly non-diegetic then become diegetic. I think at a certain point, if I'm not mistaken, there's a poster referenced, and that's where you're like, "Okay, here's where there's a whole community." They're not just trying to leave the music production. It's there. Here it is. Right?

MB: I was published by Press Gang, but I worked more in feminist video collectives, Emma Productions and Women's Media Alliance, which Nancy Nicol was part of. I remember when I first joined Women's Media Alliance there were no roles. There was no camera person. There was no sound person. We just rotated those roles, which was part of that notion of collaboration and of circularity. I think that it created a kind of aesthetic, actually, which results in those kinds of interesting audio choices or editing choices. I remember the video we worked on, *Our Choice*, about teenage mothers and we edited that entire thing by committee.

REB: Wow.

MB: What resulted was also long swaths of talking that weren't edited and that kind of editing was a form of care. It was a way of caring for our interview subjects and working against the grain of television and mainstream cinema.

Voiceover, EM: The third film, *Proud Lives*, featured a significant force in Toronto's local communities and Canadian lesbian and gay liberation at large. We heard how a singular figure could be part of a generative field of queer cultural production and galvanize a movement to shift the terms of the world, our bodies, and our relationships.

RS: Hi everyone, so the next film we're going to be watching is *Proud Lives: Christine Bearchell*, which was directed and produced by Nancy Nicol. It was a commemoration video that was shown at Chris's memorial in 2007 after she passed. For those who aren't aware, Nancy describes her as a towering figure in the history of gay liberation in Canada, and I think that's a fair assessment. She began writing for the *Body Politic* in 1975. When you look at the pictures of the *Body Politic*, she's the woman, and everybody else is the guys. She was one of the founders of LOOT. She worked for the

Coalition for Lesbian and Gay Rights of Ontario (CLGO). She was a part of Gay Alliance Toward Equality (GATE) in Toronto, but she also did organizing in Edmonton when she was a teenager. When the *Body Politic* was charged, Chris was right along there and so there's this really great picture of them celebrating after they've won the court case.

A lot of people, when they think of Chris, they think of her yelling, "No more shit!" [Audio clip: People chanting "no more shit"] as part of the bathhouse raids. That's a picture of her that sums her up in an interesting way. She's definitely one of those people that I really wish I could have met in person, especially reading about her and seeing all of her work. If you look at the material that we have at the archives, she's got her fingers in all the pies, you see her stuff in the CLGO, you see her stuff [in?] the *Body Politic*. You see it everywhere. We have a small collection of her material, and one of her fonds at the archive as well. And she's a part of our national portrait collection. I really love the portrait that we have of her. She's done a whole bunch of stuff that I know some of it's going to be in the film, but you should definitely look up more about her, especially if this video piques your interest.

FT: There are so many things that I love about that film. In the work that I do, I've been really interested in the work that Chris did with Pink Type as the typesetter for so many different magazines, so sort of like an arm of *Body Politic*, but also typesetting *Fireweed* and all these other magazines. It becomes kind of this really important sub-layer to all the kinds of cultural production that were coming out of all the different edges of this lesbian-gay feminist press movement in Toronto. That's kind of where my personal desire comes from in relation to this film, but there are so many other aspects of it that pull on those emotional threads. But I guess the biggest takeaway – the thing that I think about from that film in relationship to *Labyris Rising* and the questions about how do you see or hear these institutions that lesbian and gay liberation produce for themselves – is when she's talking about how the lesbian-gay rights movement is not just committed to rights as an end in itself, but that the political protests and the boots-on-the-ground efforts to change legislation are just one way of generating community. The cultural institutions that are the actual movement, or the bigger part of the movement, form this multiple multilayered push towards shifting the terms through which your body interacts with the world and that you, in your identity, interact with the world and others. Both are important, but there is this much larger force that's taking place alongside this kind of challenge to the law.

CC: Not to put anybody on the spot, but I do see in the chat that Amy Gottlieb - amazing - has a comment about working at Pink Type. Amy, did you want to talk about it? [Instrumental, piano]

AG: Sure. I worked at Pink Type. We typeset - I mean, I remember typesetting the *Body Politic* and *Fireweed*. At that time, we were on Duncan Street near Queen and University area. Gabe Bell worked there with me as well. I remember all sorts of people in the office and I remember our wonderful, beautiful typesetting machine, which we took great care of and felt quite privileged to be using to typeset all these incredible magazines and all sorts of different kinds of publications. People came in and there was a space for people to do the layout. You got to hang out with people and learn about what these different publications were all about. And, yeah, there was lots of discussions about the content of the *Body Politic* about the personal ads in the back. That was another interesting, and at times difficult tension that I think I certainly felt, and I think that Gabe might have felt as well. Yeah, it was a time.

FT: Were you ever tempted to change what the type was going to say?

AG: In terms of the ads? [Laughs]

FT: [Laughs] Or, you know, editorial copy. Who knows?

AG: I don't think so. You're working at such a fast pace when you're typesetting [Sound effect: printing press] and it's just so many of us trying to get it out there so that it can be proofed and pasted up. There were some crazy hours as well. And so no, we didn't organize in that way. Good idea though! [Laughs]

MA: Thank you for listening to "Lesbian Liberation Across Media: A Sonic Screening." Welcome to the epilogue. My name is Mathieu Aubin and I am here with Felicity Tayler, and we wanted to take a moment to reflect upon the process of making this episode. [Instrumental music]

FT: In designing this audio collage, we have proposed a reflexive remix, an aesthetic that Eduardo Navas describes as a sonic collage that blurs the origin of the sounds that we appropriate while relying on your allegorical recognition of the many sonic codes embedded within the soundscape, their larger meaning, and how they are received by members of LGBTQ2+ communities. We've remixed the sound space of the "SpokenWeb: Lesbian Liberation Across Media" listening practice held in April 2020, and the watch party of the same name held later in June. We think this produces a new sonic space as a continuation of what Judith Butler calls a citation politics, and that we honour the sounds of feminist press and lesbian liberation films shown during these events. We consensually cite and remix the sounds of people's voices co-producing these events.

MA: This episode cites and further circulates a queer language that acknowledges rich and complex lesbian histories. It makes room for intergenerational discussion and listening. In the virtual space of the watch party, attendees from different generations came together to watch lesbian liberation films, and listen to each other's responses to them. The event highlighted the importance of earlier community building, while challenging romanticized notions of what that community meant. It also enabled members of more recent generations to reflect critically upon that time period, and to identify shared, lived experiences across generations. All this to say, the event built a virtual space that created rich intergenerational dialogue.

MA: So, with that being said, I want to take this opportunity to reflect upon the whole process of making this episode with you, Felicity. You and I have been working on this project for months now. Time flies by even during a pandemic. I remember when you originally asked me to co-lead the listing process with you [at the] beginning of the pandemic, and it's kind of surprising that we're now here with a podcast episode capturing all the Lesbian Liberation Across Media events. So, my question is kind of broader and it's this: what surprised you the most about the process of producing this episode, given where we started and where we are now?

FT: I think what surprised me the most was how easy it was. How smoothly it went. But I feel like it's because we've been establishing an underlying trust for so many years. Our work around feminist presses, and this sense that the communities used these presses as an apparatus to produce their own kind of alternate world, is something that brought us together in the beginning. So, we're starting from a space of queer affinity in order to be able to continue to speak about these things and draw a wider narrative around it. Now we're thinking through it in relation to sound.

MA: Yeah. I still remember when we first met at that Concept of Vancouver conference and you were like, "You! You do queer things. I'm going to come and talk to you." That was, what, 2016, I think? So, four years this month. Wow. Time flies by.

FT: Yeah. So, I guess I can follow up on that with my question. This is a question that other people have asked me as I continue to work on this material. The question that I get asked is whether or not this is about identity. So, is this about identity and if so, what does that mean to you?

MA: That's a tough and good question. I think that, for me, it's strange because I've come to these materials through – Well, let's just say I identify as a man and I'm interested in queer materials in general and the sounds of that period. So, for me, it's not just an idea of identity, but also community building and solidarity, and thinking about what that type of solidarity work looks like. So, one of the things that was really powerful for me was being invited by you to not only participate in that listening practice with our past relationship and amount of work that we've done together, but also being invited for that launch party and being asked to contextualize some of those materials and to give some of my reflections. So, the word that I think that comes to my mind is privileged to be able to be in those spaces with the identity that I have, and also knowing when to perhaps limit the amount of space that I occupy when I'm invited to be in those spaces.

MA: Being invited there means that I have to be responsible and be respectful. So, I guess going back to your point about the easiness of all of this work, I'm feeling not only an enormous sense of respect for you but also feeling that this respect is mutual. I think that is grounded in our shared queer affinities. That's probably the best way to put that. At the end of the day, I think that it has something to do with community building and identity, at least at the level of producing and collaborating together, you and I. So, in short, yes, it has to do with identity.

FT: [Laughs] Yeah, that's what I always say. I mean, of course it has to do with identity, even if it doesn't pivot on it. But it is always about creating a sense of self in relationship to the idea of communities and their production. In this sense, it has a temporal dimension, as it often does in queer spaces, because we're always looking for a past that isn't always necessarily available to us.

MA: Yeah. Exactly.

FT: But what we were talking about earlier today about this clip that we wanted to revisit and the editing kind of illustrates where these questions are going. In an earlier edit, there was a mistake where your voice was overlaid on top of one of the other participants' voices and so you kind of produce this typical stereotype of mansplaining – not making space. So the ease with which we were able to address that and to smooth it out in the final product I think is a really great example of how working together has worked.

MA: Even though it's a tiny glitch in our process over logic, I was listening to that and I was thinking, "This is egregious if we let this be, because this is just bad."

FT: But also funny that there was an ambiguity as to whether it had actually happened in real life or not when we were working in the collage space – which it didn't. It did not happen in real life. [Laughs]

MA: This is great. I'm super thankful that I've had this opportunity to collaborate with you on this project and for all the other collaborators as well.

FT: Yeah. Well I thank you for your thoughtful ways. With that in mind, here are some other thank yous for all the voices that you hear in this podcast. And also for the institutions that we were able to wrangle to make this series of events possible. So, we'd like to thank Stacey Copeland, Hannah McGregor, Jason Camlot, Katherine McLeod, Scott Girouard, Constance Crompton, Michelle Schwartz, Rachel E. Beattie, Raegan Swanson, May Ning, jake moore, Becki Ross, Amy Gottlieb ...

MA: Rachel Epstein, Maureen FitzGerald, Emma Middleton, Marusya Bociurkiw, Baylee Woodley, Elspeth Brown, Stark, Humanities Data Lab at U Ottawa, SpokenWeb, Lesbian and Gay Liberation in Canada Project, University of Toronto Media Commons Archives, ArQuives, vtape, and vivo archives. All the proceeds from the event were donated to supporting Our Youth of Toronto and their Black queer youth and Trans crew and The 519 Trans People of Colour project.

FT: We couldn't have made this podcast without you.

HM: [Instrumental music] *SpokenWeb* is a monthly podcast produced by the SpokenWeb team as part of distributing the audio collected from and created using Canadian literary archival recordings found at universities across Canada. Our producers this month are SpokenWeb team members, Mathieu Aubin of Concordia University and Felicity Tayler of the University of Ottawa with guest collaborator, Scott Girouard.

Voiceover, EM: And additional voiceover by Emma Middleton.

HM: Our podcast project manager is Stacey Copeland and a warm welcome to new podcast research assistant Judy Burr. To find out more about *SpokenWeb* visit spokenweb.ca and subscribed to the *SpokenWeb Podcast* on Apple podcasts, Spotify, or wherever you may listen. If you love us, let us know. [Theme music] You can rate us and leave a comment on Apple podcasts or say hi on our social media @SpokenWebCanada. From all of us at SpokenWeb, be kind to yourself and one another out there. We'll see you back here next month for another episode of the *SpokenWeb Podcast*, stories about how literature sounds.

NOTES

1 T.L. Cowan and Jasmine Rault, "Onlining Queer Acts: Digital Research Ethics and Caring for Risky Archives," *Women & Performance* 28, no. 2 (2018): 132, https://doi.org/10.1080/0740770X.2018.1473985.
2 Becki Ross, *The House That Jill Built: A Lesbian Nation in Formation* (Toronto: Universtiy of Toronto Press, 1995), 92.

14

Listening to LGBTQ2+ Communities at the Lesbian Liberation Across Media Watch Party

Mathieu Aubin

On 10 June 2020, during the first Pride month of the COVID-19 pandemic, the Lesbian Liberation Across Media (hereafter LLAM) digital watch party gathered over seventy attendees from across Canada to shed light upon and discuss Canadian queer history. As attendees logged onto Zoom in anticipation of watching lesbian liberation films, they were greeted by hosts Rachel E. Beattie, Constance Crompton, Michelle Schwartz, Reagan Swanson, Felicity Tayler, and myself. While the hosts could be seen and heard, some attendees arrived with their cameras on, showing squared glimpses into their personal spaces (e.g., displayed Pride flags, family photos, cups of tea), some vocally said hello, others wrote their salutations in the chat, and several remained quiet with their videos off.

At the same time, attendees could see a larger looped slide show describing the event and warning:

> Before watching these films we'd like to provide a note about their content. Ideas around gender and sexuality are constantly in flux. These films all come from a time when thinking, specifically around gender, was not as inclusive of the many gender identities as it is today. We just want to make you aware of the lack of trans and non-binary representation as well as the absence of people of

colour in these films and in a lot of these historical spaces. These are important issues that we can return to in our discussion after the screening.[1]

Despite the isolation of the pandemic, the beginning of the event created a feeling of connectedness and encouraged attendees to think critically about queer history, especially in terms of trans discrimination and racism.[2] How, then, did this type of event create space for dialogue where community members could learn and critically reflect upon the ways in which earlier activists imagined an alternative and more equitable world for LGBTQ2+ people?

The LLAM brought together archivists and scholars who worked on queer culture (i.e., Aubin, Beattie, Crompton, Schwartz, Swanson, and Tayler) to watch and discuss three films. Attendees viewed *A Working Women's Collective* (1974) – a documentary about Vancouver's Press Gang Publishers and Press Gang Printers Ltd – alongside other lesbian liberation films *Labyris Rising* (1980) and *Proud Lives: Chris Bearchell* (2007) over video chat. Press Gang Publishers and Printers (1974–2002), one of Vancouver's original lesbian collectives, became integral to the development of lesbian liberation movements during the 1970s by printing and publishing lesbian materials that made homosexuality and feminism visible. After showing the documentaries, attendees were invited to reflect upon the films, ask Press Gang members in attendance questions about their lived experiences, and respond to each other. The two-and-a-half-hour event resulted in a rich dialogue between members of Press Gang and other attendees, including many queer people from across Canada, that amplified polyvocal, intergenerational perspectives and contributed to recent LGBTQ2+ debates.

With a specific focus on the LLAM event, this chapter examines the activist potential of the watch party as a queer community-building practice that relies on audio-visual (AV) materials and oral histories. LGBTQ2+ communities have historically come together based on a shared sense of sexual and gender identity and lived experiences in a heteronormative world. In her work on lesbian communities, Sara Ahmed argues, "lesbian bonds can involve orientations that are about shared struggles, common grounds, and mutual aspirations, as bonds that are created through the lived experiences of being 'off line' and 'out of line.'"[3] That is, queer bonds can be generated by shared lived experiences of being "out of line" with a heteronormative society's practices and create grounds for new social formations.

While they bring people together based on those shared experiences, LGBTQ2+ communities are not homogeneous. Rather, they have multiple valences that are grounded in other identity markers such as gender, race, class, and political ideologies that form part of these communities' living conditions. To better understand these communities, queer oral historians often use physical materials (e.g., photographs) in interviews to elicit personal stories that make previous silenced histories audible, disrupt heteronormative histories, and create space for critical discussions of queer social relations.[4] That is, in turning to queer oral accounts, oral historians can not only create space with queer folks to discuss collective histories but also critically reflect upon one's role within those communities.

LLAM was originally conceptualized as an event that would bring together members of LGBTQ2+ communities to watch lesbian liberation films, learn about the histories that these materials reflect, and share personal accounts during the discussion period that followed the screenings. Crompton, Schwartz, and Tayler invited experts on the lesbian liberation movement to situate the videos and generate dialogue about the films through a discussion period.[5] Unexpectedly, by viewing the materials, former members of Press Gang were compelled to share their reflections on the documentaries and about their time working with the anti-homophobic, anti-sexist, and anti-racist lesbian feminist publishing and printing collective. These oral histories formed what Nan Alamilla Boyd and Horacio N. Roque Ramírez call "bodies of evidence"[6] because they brought "personal affect, individual significance, and personal memory to bear"[7] on the materials presented during the event.

This dialogue then led younger queer people in attendance to reflect on their own positions within this lesbian history. In this chapter, I argue that this LLAM event formed an intergenerational, dialogical space in which queer people could examine the multiple valences of their communities, build intergenerational bridges, and reflect upon moments of dissonance between members that illustrate gaps in memory, time, political values and identification, and communal concerns. At the LLAM event, attendees collectively listened to members from earlier generations discuss their original values and disrupt romanticized notions of intersectionality, thereby challenging the whitewashing of earlier movements discussed further below. Attendees also listened to members from younger generations critically reflect upon inherited lesbian histories and consider how earlier issues within queer communities continue to affect them today. Thus, this LLAM event produced what current LGBTQ2+ activists have called for in their critiques of liberation movements: an intergenerational dialogue that both recognizes rich queer histories and critiques long-standing issues within them to generate more equitable LGBTQ2+ communities today.

Reconstituting the Community

Through the LLAM watch party, the organizing collective recreated a virtual version of some of the material conditions that made Press Gang a physical space for queer dialogue in Vancouver. During the 1970s and 1980s, Press Gang's offices provided collective members and the larger community a space to produce books and discuss politics. As former Press Gang editor Nancy Pollak recalled in a personal interview,

> it was actually a kind of remarkable building at 603 Powell. The building is still there, it had been built in the Post War period by some guy who used timbers from the Burrard Dry Docks in North Vancouver, a huge building and you walk in and it's a mess because it's a print shop for the most part, there's printing presses, there's the bindery, there's the archaic guillotine, the paper cutter, and then upstairs were the offices and it was just a fascinating environment. It actually changed my life ...
>
> It's also where we would be participating in collective meetings where we would discuss very important political questions.[8]

Pollak's description of the press's physical location reveals how it offered a "working ground"[9] to the community where collective members could not only produce books (i.e., the printing presses and the bindery) but also a discursive space in which to hold meetings to discuss queer politics. As Pauline Butling indicates in her feminist analysis of the importance of experimental and activist small presses and literary magazines, small presses "exist to encourage dialogue, to support risk-taking, to generate argument and debate, and to foreground work in process … they have sustained the social/material/discursive nexus that enables radicality."[10] That is, these types of small presses create an opportunity for like-minded people to come together to radically experiment with publishing and thinking to create a movement that challenges restrictive publishing and social practices. As such, they depend upon sociality to facilitate a process and potential for radical intervention.

The LLAM watch party's digital social space temporarily recreated the press's material conditions by functioning as "a space to gather,"[11] where people could hold discussions and debate about lesbian liberation print and activist history. Although the spaces described by Pollak and Butling were mostly physical, thereby offering intimacy by enabling people to meet in person, during the LLAM event, the dynamics were transformed.[12] Attendees in various locales logged in through a Web link and password that brought them to a video chat room in which they were able to view the films and communicate with other attendees. Whereas in-person events would have previously been available to people in proximity, LLAM was available to people anywhere who had access to the internet. People joined from major cities such as Halifax, Montreal, Ottawa, Toronto, Vancouver, and Winnipeg. Also, queer people from more distant regions, such as the interior of British Columbia, were able to join the event. As such, people from different localities with their own rich histories came together and held a dialogue that reflected different geographical experiences and perspectives.

Through the video chat software Zoom, they could communicate visually with their cameras, orally with their microphones, or textually with the chat function. In this way, rather than meeting in a public space, many attendees opened their personal spaces for the first time by making it visible through their video camera, thereby creating a new form of intergenerational intimacy. Whereas in-person meetings would have limited the location to one physical space, the LLAM event created a virtual space in which everyone was able to see each other's personal spaces, including personal objects, which frame their everyday lives. Attendees could also identify themselves by writing their name when they logged in or remain anonymous by choosing a pseudonym and staying off camera. However, the ability to use a pseudonym and to be off camera while attending the event created a dynamic during which not everyone was fully aware of who was present and listening during the event, echoing the possibility of RCMP surveillance at literary events in the 1960s–1980s.[13] Moreover, given that Zoom's use was in its infancy, resulting in some events being "Zoom bombed" by people who sought to disturb events, including a Pride event held by Beattie that month, measures were implemented to protect the event.[14] Attendees needed to sign up for the event to access its password, which led to no one disturbing the event. In this new space, the LLAM functioned as a "working ground"[15] in which to engage with LGBTQ2+ concerns in which attendees could listen to each other, communicate their questions about lesbian history, discuss their lived experiences in relation to the AV materials presented, and reflect upon their communities' histories.

As part of the event's exchange, members of Press Gang engaged with the documentary to frame the dialogue by discussing the collective's many personal and intimate relationships and reconstructed the community's history. For instance, when *A Working Women's Collective* was playing, members of Press Gang actively responded to the film by identifying in the text chat the names of collective members (e.g., Sara) who were appearing on screen. These responses constituted a form of activism by writing those members back into the public's memory and enabling attendees to learn contextual information about the communities portrayed in the documentaries. Similarly, when asked to share their reflections on the Press Gang documentary, former members, Maureen FitzGerald (MF) and Rachel Epstein (RE), situated themselves within the community by discussing how they became involved with the press:

MF: Hi, yes, I was connected with Press Gang through feminist publishing because I was involved in the Women's Press Collective in Toronto ... but there was a year that I spent in Vancouver because I was lovers with Pat Smith and it was wonderful to see those images [in the documentary] because I know Sara.

RE: It's Rachel Epstein and yeah I worked at Press Gang in the early '80s, maybe just after Maureen in '82, '84, or something like that ... I was also lovers with Pat Smith at the same time that Maureen was lovers with Pat Smith.
MF: [Laughs]
RE: [Laughs]
MF: You go Rachel!
RE: That's how Maureen and I met each other. [Laughs][16]

The humorous moment between Maureen and Rachel illuminated the collective's history: while the press had strict policies that discouraged collective members from dating each other because it often led to inner conflict,[17] Maureen and Rachel shared with event attendees the open secret that many women were romantically involved while working at the press. Sharing this secret helped create a sense of community between attendees and also positively affected Maureen, who contacted me via email a few days after the event to share the following: "I am one of the two women who identified ourselves as having worked at Press Gang in the conversation after the Lesbian Liberation Across Media films. Thank you so much for helping organize this event. Many trips down memory lane for some of us. LOL Could you please tell us how it would be possible to see the Press Gang film again and potentially share it with others [sic]."[18] FitzGerald's email speaks to the watch party's importance as it enabled her to reflect upon her role within Press Gang's community (e.g., "Many trips down memory lane for some of us") and to continue some of the discussions' laughter. Moreover, as her email suggests, the watch party encouraged her to circulate the documentary to other community members, potentially leading to further discussion. In short, the event was not only helpful for attendees to learn about the press's communities but also beneficial to original community members who revisited their collective past and strengthened their bonds.

The LLAM event's discussion period also created an opportunity to critically think about the ways that lesbian communities were portrayed in the films. Nostalgic commemorations of literary communities' events and histories in Vancouver – as feminist scholar Karis Shearer indicates in her analysis of *The Line Is Shattered*'s retelling of the 1963 Vancouver Poetry Conference – have at times erased historical power structures.[19] Similarly, *A Working Women's Collective* is focused on women's history; it does not necessarily address the many conflicts that divided the printing collective. However, in response to an attendee who spoke about what she perceived to be intersectional practices at Press Gang, Rachel Epstein (RE) troubled homogeneous, romanticized interpretations of her former community during the discussion period.

> RE: [j]ust not to romanticize totally what it was like there. We were also struggling with working collectively and I have some harsh memories of how we treated each other – how, in the process of trying to be fair, we were very unfair ... what we did was amazing in so many ways; the skills that we developed, the political causes that we supported. But there were many things going on there in that attempt to work collectively.[20]

Epstein's personal account does not dispute Press Gang's contributions to Vancouver's lesbian liberation communities, but it challenges romantic ideas of how this work was conducted. As she suggests, although they worked together to promote political causes, many members treated each other "unfair[ly]" because of inner political divides. Some of those divides included the press overrepresenting middle-class white women's values, publishing work that appropriated Indigenous voices, and disenfranchising more marginalized members within the community.[21] Although she does not name these conflicts, Epstein provides space for critically assessing power dynamics within the lesbian community, which is necessary when returning to earlier movements' histories. Thus, by challenging nostalgic interpretations of the community, Epstein's personal account invited attendees to critically reflect upon the city's multiple lesbian histories and the politics of belonging within the lesbian community at the time.

Intergenerational Dialogue at the Event

During the discussion period, other attendees who form more recent generations of LGBTQ2+ communities also explored the larger complicated lesbian histories that they have inherited, and what they mean today. Specifically, following Epstein's discussion of the difficulties of working collectively, some of the attendees discussed the lesbian history art installation *Killjoy's Kastle*. The Kastle installation was exhibited in Toronto, London, Los Angeles, and Philadelphia during the 2010s, and explored the ghosts of lesbian liberation movements and their complicated legacies.[22] While several attendees spent part of the discussion period reflecting on and sharing their experiences of exploring the art installation, Felicity Tayler (FT) reflected upon what she called "bad affect" and lesbian genealogies. "Bad affect" in this case entails sitting with what Sianne Ngai calls "ugly feelings"[23] that stay with us, prolonging the potential for critically evaluating social issues and encouraging us to reflect upon "aesthetic and political ambiguities."[24] Tayler suggested:

> I do think that it's worthwhile to be kind of embracing it or, I don't know, learn to live with the discomfort of living with bad affect. Like this question of nuancing intergenerational conversations and tempering your fandom for something like the Killjoy Kastle, right? ... But what I do remember is that there was kind of this double narrative of like, "Oh, that's just like white feminism." Then inside Killjoy's Kastle there was this trying to atone for, or come to terms with, or critique of whiteness at the same time as having this intergenerational smorgasbord of experience. I think that that's just part of what comes with this.

Listening to Tayler discuss the Killjoy Kastle's representation of "white feminism" and the importance of engaging with the uncomfortable histories reflected by the installation generated a collective moment of reflection about the stakes of the watch party. While the watch party could generate good affect by celebrating lesbian history, it was also an opportunity to reflect upon the more complicated aspects of lesbian liberation movements and their communities. That is, intergenerational dialogue during the event was not only about celebrating lesbianism but also about "coming to terms" with the more problematic aspects of these lesbian collective histories. As such, the watch party's discussion facilitated a critical exploration of intergenerational dialogue and community building.

The watch party's dialogical space also built bridges between different generations of activists that were present at the event by creating opportunities to listen to each other's concerns and reflect upon their shared experiences. For instance, Michelle Shwartz (MS) noted how, in *A Working Women's Collective*, a member of Press Gang discussed the ways in which she felt at odds with other members of her community over the proper use of language to address social injustice because she did not know what was deemed politically correct. In her reflections, she indicated:

> I wanted to say how odd it was to watch that Press Gang film, and then hear people restating debates that we hear so much now in the movement. Like that woman who was ranting about how she doesn't know what's politically correct and so she doesn't know what she can say because now everything she says is wrong, and so she's not going to say anything. It's just so frustrating to hear the same things eternally return within these kinds of communities. It was fascinating to hear that particular kind of iteration of political correctness from so far in the past. [Beat] I always wonder whether we're doomed to have the same fights forever. Is that too dark? [Laughs][25]

Schwartz's moment of critical self-reflection illuminates the long history of issues currently affecting LGBTQ2+ communities and the difficulty of overcoming these challenges. Rather than reproducing a distanced and homogeneous understanding of earlier generations' issues, she highlights her shared experience by identifying with the woman's concerns, thereby creating an intergenerational bridge. Moreover, when she says, "I always wonder if we're just doomed to have the same fights forever," Schwartz both indicates her frustration with issues within her community and suggests a need for change. More broadly, as this moment illustrates, in this LLAM event, more recent activists were not only able to better understand the long-standing histories of issues affecting their communities but also to ask questions that speak to the present and suggest a need for change.

After Party Reflections

In this chapter, I have argued for the establishment of a virtual space where attendees can explore LGBTQ2+ communities' concerns through collective listening, watching, and intergenerational dialogue. As I have suggested, by relying on AV materials and oral histories from attendees, the Lesbian Liberation Across Media watch party virtually recreated the type of dialogical space that earlier collectives offered to their communities. The teleconferenced watch party joined the private and public by giving attendees an opportunity to see each other in a public context and hold discussions in their private spaces. For instance, whereas some Press Gang members could be seen in their current homes discussing their lived experiences alongside their partners and personal objects such as family portraits and art, younger community members could be seen in more youthful spaces such as their bedrooms and apartments. The breaking down of the public and private divide was equally reflected in the watch party's documentaries, which showed the private lives of lesbian liberation collectives who sought to transform what constituted public sexuality.

While there is now serious video chat fatigue four years after the beginning of the pandemic, the "anywhereness" of this type of event is difficult to recreate given the larger obstacles of being dispersed across Canada and the globe, which create mobility restrictions grounded in financial capabilities, and the often inaccessible spaces of physical small presses. The virtual accessibility of the event made it possible for some people to see each other for the first time in a long time and for some to access an event that would have maybe been inaccessible to them otherwise, perhaps addressing a key issue of ableism within LGBTQ2+ communities.

In the watch party's virtual space, members of earlier generations could engage with the films and share knowledge about the history of lesbian communities while benefiting from the event's social space by solidifying their communal bonds. The event also gave them space to be self-reflective of their communities and dispel romanticized understandings potentially created by the documentaries. At the same time, the watch party gave more recent generations of LGBTQ2+ communities space to critically respond to the documentaries and consider their complicated, inherited histories. Moreover, some younger members discovered how much their current experiences reflected those of earlier communities, consequently bridging generational divides. Therefore, the LLAM watch party offers an important and much-needed model for how to virtually create grassroots events that facilitate much-needed intergenerational dialogue within LGBTQ2+ communities today.

NOTES

1 Rachel E. Beattie et al., panelists, "Lesbian Liberation Across Media Watch Party," 10 June 2020, Zoom, video. 1:32:04.
2 As an example, on 7 April 2019, members of Vancouver's LGBTQ2+ communities gathered in downtown Vancouver to respond to the pressing question, "Has the LGBTQ movement failed?" During the event, a panel composed of gay and trans politicians, sex-work activists, and two-spirit and lesbian scholars shared oral histories about their experiences as members of the city's LGBTQ2+ communities. By sharing personal accounts, each speaker questioned the movements' legacies, suggesting that their communities had failed their most marginalized members, including First Nations, disabled, racialized, homeless, and trans people.
3 Sara Ahmed, *Queer Phenomenology: Orientations, Objects, Others* (Durham: Duke University Press, 2006), 103.
4 Sherna Berger Gluck and Daphne Patai, "Introduction," in *Women's Words: The Feminist Practice of Oral History*, ed. Sherna Berger Gluck and Daphne Patai (London: Routledge, 1991) 2; Kevin P. Murphy, Jennifer L. Pierce, and Jason Ruiz, "What Makes a Queer Oral History Different?," *The Oral History Review* 43, no. 1 (2016): 8; Gary Kinsman and Patrizia Gentile, *The Canadian War on Queers: National Security as Sexual Regulation* (Vancouver: UBC Press, 2010), 14.

5 My role in the watch party was event co-organizer, presenter, and, most importantly, listener. Following a SpokenWeb "Listening Practice" event that Tayler and I curated (using Zoom) during which we listened to and discussed short clips from *A Working Women's Collective* and *Labyris Rising*, Crompton and Schwartz decided to spearhead a public event that would showcase the films in their entirety.
6 Horacio N. Roque Ramirez and Nan Alamilla Boyd, "Introduction," in *Bodies of Evidence: The Practice of Queer Oral History*, ed. Nan Alamilla Boyd and Horacio N. Roque Ramírez (Oxford: Oxford University Press, 2012), 1.
7 Ibid., 17.
8 Nancy Pollak, personal interview with the author, 10 April 2017.
9 Pauline Butling and Susan Rudy, *Writing in Our Time: Canada's Radical Poetries in English (1957–2003)* (Waterloo: Wilfrid Laurier University Press, 2005), 37.
10 Ibid., 41.
11 Beattie et al., "Lesbian Liberation Across Media Watch Party."
12 The web event was open to the public, who could attend from anywhere in the world, with the caveat that no homophobic, sexist, or racist remarks would be tolerated. In doing so, the purpose of the discussion group was to create an open dialogue while respecting people's diverse backgrounds and identities.
13 Gary Kinsman and Patrizia Gentile, *The Canadian War on Queers: National Security as Sexual Regulation* (Vancouver: UBC Press, 2010), 247.
14 Zoom-bombing entails showing up to a Zoom meeting unexpectedly and disturbing it.
15 Butling and Rudy, *Writing in Our Time*, 37.
16 Beattie et al., "Lesbian Liberation Across Media Watch Party."
17 Nancy Pollak, "Press Gang Policy from the Sagging Memory of NJP" (Press Gang Printers and Publishers, 1983).
18 Maureen Fitzgerald, "Press Gang film," email received by the author, 3 July 2020.
19 Karis Shearer, "'It's All a Curious Dream': Nostalgia, Old Media, and the Vancouver Poetry Conference, 1963," in *CanLit Across Media: Unarchiving the Literary Event*, ed. Jason Camlot and Katherine McLeod (Montreal & Kingston: McGill-Queen's University Press, 2019), 166.
20 Beattie et al., "Lesbian Liberation Across Media Watch Party."
21 The Telling It Book Collective, editors, *Telling It: Women and Language across Cultures* (Vancouver: Press Gang P, 1990), 16.
22 Allyson Mitchell and Cait McKinney, eds, *Inside Killjoy's Kastle: Dykey Ghosts, Feminist Monsters, and Other Lesbian Hauntings* (Vancouver: UBC Press, 2019), 3.
23 Sianne Ngai, *Ugly Feelings* (Cambridge: Harvard University Press, 2005), 71.
24 Ibid., 20.
25 Felicity Tayler, "Transcript of *Lesbian Liberation Across Media: A Sonic Screening* Podcast," in this volume, 256.

15

"It was an extension of the moment"

Five Poets in Conversation on Analog Audio Recording and Creative Practice

Karis Shearer and Erín Moure

Introduction

In the summer of 2013, seven senior writers were invited to UBC's Okanagan campus to take part in a poetry reading event followed by a round-table discussion about the ways that tape recording has figured in their poetic practices.[1] The two literary events marked the fiftieth anniversary of the 1963 Vancouver Poetry Conference and formed part of the Textual Editing and Modernism in Canada (TEMiC) "Poetry On and Off the Page" week-long summer institute.[2] Co-hosted by Karis Shearer and Erín Moure, the round table invited writers who had attended the 1963 conference, or worked directly with writers who had, to consider the role magnetic tape recording had played in their compositional practice, their apprenticeship as poets, and their literary lives more broadly in the 1960s and decades following.

The round table drew its initial inspiration from Jodey Castricano's 2011 gift to Karis Shearer of a box of audio cassettes and reel-to-reel tapes once belonging to UBC professor Warren Tallman (1921–1994). The collection had recently been digitized at UBCO, and by summer 2013 was in the early stages of being catalogued and transcribed by Lee Hannigan, who was then working as an undergraduate research assistant for Shearer. At that same time, the SpokenWeb project at Concordia University in Montreal was three years into its development, and Jason Camlot and his team of researchers there were digitizing analog recordings of the Sir George Williams University Reading Series (1965–74), making them available online for research and teaching. Both audio collections, and the work of Shearer and Camlot, frame the round table and are referenced throughout the conversation.

In the recorded panel discussion, we hear the poets trace out many of the concerns that occupied them in their past work, concerns that parallel those of contemporary literary audio scholars: the affordances of portable technologies; the production and circulation, collecting and archiving of tapes; textual authority, copyright, listening practices, memory work, gendered labour, and the voice. Significantly, the poets do this work in conversation with each other, allowing us to hear where some of the tensions arise, and how connections are made across view points and individual memories. We witness the writers, more than half a century after their first poetic encounters, still making space for each other, defying and questioning each other, and holding the line when they choose to.

Their conversation attends to the ongoing process of community building that takes place through the creation, production, and circulation of audio-texts. The arrival of compact (for the time), affordable (to some) recording technologies[3] in the late 1950s and early 1960s saw people such as Warren Tallman, Fred Wah, Gerry Gilbert, Daphne Marlatt, and Roy Kiyooka become prolific recordists whose practices included documenting different aspects of literary life – from classroom lectures to public poetry readings, to oral histories, to the daily life of the writer and their community. In evoking the role of recording in each of their practices, the writers at the round table, interestingly, trace the making of multiple copies of recorded conversations, lectures, and readings rather than valuing one official recorded version. The copies are what matter – there is no fetishization of "original" recordings – and they matter because of the community they build by sharing thinking, questions, arguments regarding writing practice.[4] In uncovering and examining this process of community building, it is important as well that the critic or literary historian bear in mind *whose* voices are reproduced in the act of copying.

The recording technology itself has a corporeal relation. Physical aspects of the technology are highlighted in the poets' conversation: the colour of the machines, the changing dimensions of equipment over time, the smell of the wires, or Fred ("Inky") Wah's love of machines that persisted throughout his working life – machines always played a role in his poetic practice. Recording equipment and writer familiarity with it enabled those who primarily identified as poets to engage as well in other community writing projects that lent themselves to the use of recording equipment, such as Marlatt's and Robert Minden's *Steveston* (1974 and still in print today) and Marlatt's social memory collaboration with Carole Itter, *Opening Doors: In Vancouver's East End* (1979). Both these projects, steered by writers who recorded and attended to the voices of people who were fishermen and fishery workers, not writers, motivated new understandings of social issues such as immigration, racism, forced relocation and internment of Japanese-Canadians, and made these understandings public.

Each of the writers invokes different ways that the body interacts with recording technology. All speak eloquently of various qualities and conditions that affect voice, making mention, for example, of the "drunk poets" whose alcohol consumption marked their voices. Daphne Marlatt reminds us about the body and its hormonal responses audible in the recorded voice. At another point, Marlatt emphasizes: "We're talking about *sound* but I think the stillness, the silence, the pauses, and the breaks are very important aspects – they are part of the *texture* of voice."

The round table also raises important questions about the authority of the audio-text, and the tension between print and audio. Although American literary historian Michael Davidson notes, "[f]or poets of the 1950s and 1960s, a new oral impulse served as a corrective to the rhetorically controlled, print-based poetry of high modernism,"[5] George Bowering makes it clear that, for him, print remained the ultimate medium in which the vocal impulse was to be materialized. In contrast, Fred Wah speaks to his own focus on sound, and his training as a musician, which fed his desire to record poetry to capture aspects of it that print could not: "I'm fascinated by how language works as music. I come to language as I come to music; that is how I compose with it."

In the discussion, it is apparent as well that certain recordings became touchstones of group cohesion; we hear how specific recordings can act as communal reference points of listening and influence development of poetics. In the early decades of portable magnetic tape recording, the tape clearly served, on many occasions, as primary reference material for discussion, and for scholarship, without an intervening print text. Frank Davey emphasizes the importance of the personal archive of "tape[s] in private possession" that were primary points of reference for his doctoral dissertation. Bowering recalls writing an early critical essay called "How I hear *Howl*" in response to an LP recording of Allen Ginsberg's *Howl*.

Listening practices come to the forefront of the discussion, in particular with regard to the physicality of transcribing recordings. Sharon Thesen, for example, speaks of Daphne Marlatt's voice and says that it was passing through her ears as voice and out her hands as transcribed text – with her body as conduit. She was listening to what Daphne was saying, and learning. Memory work is shared: Sharon Thesen also recalls working for George Bowering when she was a student at SFU, transcribing taped conversations. Most revealing, perhaps, is the palpable sense of "liveness" held *in* the recordings: someone could go to an event, tape the proceedings, and this tape is later still considered to be "alive." People listening to it later receive it not as an archival record but as an event. Frank Davey points out as well that because the recordings could be replayed, over and over, the voice was given a quality of iterability that it did not have if it were just remembered. Marlatt notes later on that Roy Kiyooka received that iterability – the fact that the conversation could be re-experienced "live" – as an "extension of the moment." It is as if the iterability of the voice lengthens time.

This period of magnetic tape recording also marked a new stage in literary history, wherein the intricate webs of lived/living relation within a community (i.e., non-institutionally instituted and kept) took on a material form that could later on be archived and discussed.[6] The material record thus created would, however, eventually become difficult to access, even by those who created it, as the technologies used to make recordings became obsolete and the media formats began to degrade. Today, the material recordings are approaching or past their manufacturers' anticipated shelf life of twenty-five years[7] and are difficult for writers, critics, or any listener at all to access and engage with without remediation into a digital format such as WAV or MP3. The temporal shift in the material meaning of the tapes as they have been moved from their original communities and writers' personal archives into institutional archives is now one of the features that affects their study. And with it comes an uncertainty that Wah and others express several times in the conversation – "I hope I'm not talking too ahistorically here" – about whether the media and poetics reference points resonate with the round table's contemporary audience, many of whom are several generations younger. As such, the opportunity for audio researchers, archivists, students, and poets to hear writers speak on the 2013 round table about their own conversations and recordings from the context of writerly memory is unique and represents an event of literary history worth recording in itself.

So many moments in the 2013 writerly conversation at the round table anticipate the research questions that later emerged in the SpokenWeb project. It was a conversation in which much history was condensed, and that opened and opens possibilities for further scholarly research into archive, sound, body, gender, labour, and community.

Transcription[8]

Friday, 2 August 2013
Co-Facilitators: Karis Shearer and Erín Moure
Panel Speakers: George Bowering, Frank Davey, Daphne Marlatt,
    Sharon Thesen, Fred Wah
UBC Okanagan

Karis Shearer: I think we'll get started. This is a slightly more intimate setting than yesterday's big extravaganza: this is our long, rectangular "round table" on audio recordings. I wanted to give you a bit of background on how this came about: when I first arrived at UBC Okanagan in 2011, I'd come from Concordia where Jason Camlot, who is in the crowd, is working on a spectacular project called the SpokenWeb Archive and it has a number of recordings from the Sir George Williams Poetry Series from the '60s.

I was really excited by that project and wanted to imagine what kind of sound archive I might produce here. I was talking to my colleague, Jodey Castricano, about this idea and she said, "Just a second, I have to get something for you," disappeared into her basement, and came back with two boxes of magnetic tape recordings. Warren Tallman had given them to her saying, "One day you'll know what to do with these. Here they are." [George Bowering chuckles] And so I took the boxes and hired Lee Hannigan – who's in the crowd – who helped me find the tape deck and the reel-to-reel player so we could listen to these, and they were fascinating. And I began thinking about this culture of recording – this moment when tape recorders were suddenly portable: what did it mean to be the person recording these conversations? What did it mean to be a young poet at the time? What did it mean to have these tapes and listen to them retrospectively? All these questions emerged and I wanted to pose them to the people whose voices feature on these tapes and who are with us participating in this round table today. Erín Moure, who is here with me co-facilitating, and I have already had a lot of conversations about these questions.

It shouldn't surprise you that I have a tape to play for you. It's the cassette tape that I happened to pluck out when I first received the box and on it, we hear Warren Tallman describing his project and his relationship to the university. You can also hear the hiss of the tape recorder.

[Plays tape]

Warren Tallman: *Oooookay, this is Warren Tallman, in my Bellavista sitting room with all my poet photographs, some new Kiyooka camera studies, some new bill bissett paintings, and my new wooden floors, and all my poet books around. It's December 14, 1986, and I'm about to explain the contents and purpose of this tape.*

[Cut]

WT: *And this little announcement will get it started.*

[WT reads invitation to retirement event as follows]

November 17, 1986.
3504 Bellavista Street, Vancouver BC, Victor-Five-N Three-W-Nine.

Dear blank:
Today this Scorpio turns 65. Having spent 30 of them at UBC, I suddenly discovered I forgot to reform either the place or myself. So, I thought I would tidy up this oversight with a quick fling at both on November 27, 1986, at 3:30 pm in Buchanan A 100 –

[Cut]

George Bowering: Oh, God. [Chuckles]

KS: He's about to introduce his retirement speech. What strikes me about Tallman's recordings is that he is certainly imagining someone like myself coming along. Many of the tapes are narrated like this. He's an amateur recorder but also a compulsive, serial recordist. [Panellists chuckle]

I've asked the five writers on the panel today – poets Sharon Thesen, Frank Davey, George Bowering, Daphne Marlatt, and Fred Wah – to think through this question of what it means to have poetry recorded or events recorded. Sharon, do you want to start?

Sharon Thesen: Sure. Just hearing that excerpt now, I can see those big beige reel-to-reel recorders of the time that required physical splicing. As time passed, they became sleeker and blacker. I'm remembering Gerry Gilbert, too, at poetry readings always at the front of the room with his tape recorder. But the recorder and the person recording were always very *present*. Nobody had anything in their pocket. There was never this sense of ubiquitousness or invisibility. It was "that was the recorder." I don't remember ever signing a waiver or there being any copyright issues. Who knew what happened to these and, really, who cared? They were just recorded. I guess the sense that this was an occasion worth recording must have been there. There must have been a sense already of posterity. I know Gerry did some recordings for Co-op Radio,[9] that program he had. But Warren had projects. You know, the Astonishments project. He had a much more project-minded approach to recording. But what I wanted to say for this part of the discussion was that, as a young writer, before I'd really done much writing at all, I was doing a little job for George at SFU.

GB: Oh God, yeah. [Chuckles]

ST: I was a really good, fast typist and had for many years done a lot of Dictaphone work.

GB: Did you have a foot thing to stop it?

ST: I had a foot pedal. And I know I transcribed a number of tapes but the one I remember most is Daphne's. And Daphne was talking about *The Vancouver Poems*, I'm sure.

Daphne Marlatt: Oh, really?

ST: Yeah. So, I had one pedal and another pedal to turn it on and off, backwards, forwards. And these headphones and out would come Daphne's voice through my ears and through my hands. So, my hands, my feet, my ears were all involved in creating Daphne's voice on a page. I couldn't help but feel the annunciatory quality of it. Through the ear, the voice, then the word becomes flesh.

GB: Do you know whose recorder they were taped on?

ST: Whose?

GB: George Woodcock's.

ST: Oh, for heaven's sake. But I do remember being absolutely amazed by Daphne's prose, her sentences, the way she talked about those poems. It was marvellous. It was marvellous for *me* as a young writer to have that intimate a connection with your voice, Daphne.

DM: That's amazing, Sharon.

Frank Davey: I was thinking just how fortunate we were to begin our writing careers right at the time when tape recordings became available. I'm not sure where I was at the time tape recorders were newly available, but it was clear that until 1955 there were no domestic tape recorders and when they appeared they were very expensive. The kind that we used, which were four-track stereo tape recorders, only came on the market in 1959 and '60. My college roommate[10] was working in a radio and television repair store and bought one and brought it to our writing workshop, before there was TISH, and recorded some of the sessions with George and Daphne at the Writers Workshop, which was the amateur writers' club at UBC that I was president of and [Gladys] Maria Hindmarch was secretary of in 1960 or '61.[11] These machines meant that oral and verbal events were now preservable by amateurs. Previously you would have to go to the CBC to be taped [sounds of poets' agreement] and the recording equipment was massive, like a piano. [Laughter] It was quicker and easier – although I don't think we realized this right away – to disseminate a recorded text than a printed text. Just like today, you had to wait a couple of years for a magazine to print something. And it created equal what Derrida calls "iterability" – equal iterability to a printed text. I could listen to the 1961 Robert Duncan lecture at Tallman's over and over again. And I probably listened to them through earphones six or seven times along with the tapes of the Creeley lectures in 1962 and the seminar lectures in 1963 with Duncan and Charles Olson. And the tapes of the [1965] Berkeley lectures and readings. So, the tape recorder was absolutely invaluable to the first ten years of my writing career. I just kept listening to these tapes and hearing different things and being reminded of things that I might have forgotten. And much of that material still hasn't been published in print; the only way you can approach the 1961 Duncan or 1962 Creeley lectures is still through audio.

It also meant, I think, probably that a lot of alternative poetry and poetics got more scholarly attention right away than it would have otherwise. That is, a lot of early scholarship on, say, the Black Mountain poets was on the basis of the tape recordings that were circulating. I couldn't have written my PhD thesis in '68 on Duncan, Olson, and Creeley without this enormous tape archive. It was interesting that my supervisors at University of Southern California had no problem with this. We just had to document it. And a lot of it says, "tape in my private possession" in the bibliography, because where else was it? No university library held these tapes. [Sounds of poets' agreement] Only the private archives of myself or Fred or Warren.

I've used tape to prepare for many of the scholarly books I've written, starting with taping Earle Birney in 1970.[12] I taped the 1986 Long Liners Conference and had someone transcribe the question periods and we published them in *Open Letter*, transcribing them with the use of headphones and a foot pedal much like Sharon has described. And I think that the interview book that you [Bowering] published in *Open Letter* with Daphne and myself and Audrey Thomas – I think that must have been taped.[13]

GB: Oh, they were all done on George Woodcock's tape recorder. And they really went on for hours and hours. I must have talked to Daphne for six weeks in a row, once a week or something like that. I think yours, Daphne, was the longest of the three and it was over a hundred pages.

FD: And in the early '60s, I actually had critics approach me by mailing a tape to me with a written set of questions that they wanted me to answer on the tape and then I would mail it back to them. [Panellists' chuckle] I suppose it's similar to the kinds of email interviews one has today. I haven't over the years encountered much curiosity about the tape residue that this period produced. It's only with Jason Camlot, yourself [Shearer], and the PennSound archive that there's been much attempt to make use of all this accumulated documentation.

ST: Yes, just to talk about the Olson-Creeley thing. Ralph Maud had me transcribe Olson's 1965 Berkeley lecture, if you can imagine –

FD: The lecture, not the reading?

ST: No, the lecture, which was then published as *Causal Mythology*. That was very difficult because, well, it was a very amateur recording and there was noise and there was a lot of hemming and hawing. It was unintelligible, mostly.

FD: It's interesting that it was a very amateur recording because it was such a professionally produced event –

ST: It was a bootleg, I'm sure.

FD: And the recollections of it, there's complaints that it was such a disciplined –

GB: And a drunk poet.

FD: Well, a disciplined proceeding and a drunk poet, yes.

GB: When I think back on people in our early days, we've mentioned Inky: Fred handled anything that had to do with machines when we were running TISH. He ran the printer and that's why we called him "Inky" because he'd always come out of the back room covered with ink. [Laughter] Every time a poet came around to talk or speak, Fred would be dangling a microphone in front of them. He had a big archive – these are *amateur* archives. And then, as Sharon pointed out, Gerry Gilbert – many years later with a much smaller machine – because Fred's machine was this big, right [gestures], and Gerry Gilbert's machine was this big [gestures] but he would always tape it with tape that had been used twelve times before and then with a microphone, away you go. [Laughter]

But every time you went to a reading or an art gallery or a discussion or a lecture or a party [sounds of poets' agreement] – The other person who had a tape recorder going, and sometimes you didn't know it, was Roy Kiyooka. [Laughter] You would be sitting at a party and Roy would be peppering you with these questions and you had no idea it was all being taped, right? [Laughter] But Roy was a polymath – he was a great painter, and sculptor, and poet, and he thought he was a musician. He knew what he was doing, he knew what he was looking for all the time. That's just something that popped up. But despite all the TISH poets' proclamations, and Lionel Kearns – Lionel would always say, "Poetry is a *vocal* art." That was news to the world at that time. [Laughter] Which was kind of almost true because whenever there was a poet travelling across the country doing poetry readings, it was always a kind of circus act. Like that drunk English poet, what's his name? Dylan Thomas! Or Walt Whitman and Dickens, or like E. Pauline Johnson, it was a show. But I've always placed – and still do, personally – online poetry, and recorded poetry, movie poetry and all that stuff as secondary. As far as I'm concerned, it's just the dessert. I still think of the poem that's there in that lovely paper, especially in the olden days when the ink, when the thing [slaps hands together] would make a depression in the paper, when ink was down lower than the paper. That gorgeousness of it. Like, you can't do this with a tape recorder. [Sniffs loudly]

DM: So that's the real meat. [Laughter]

FD: You can smell the *wires* burning inside it. [Laughter]

GB: Curiously – in parallel with what Frank said – when I was a young guy thinking, "Okay, part of your job as a poet is to write articles about other poets." I did one on *Howl*. I think I had one of the first essays anybody ever wrote on Allen Ginsberg's *Howl*. I think it's called "How I Hear *Howl*." And it was done not from the book *Howl*, from Lawrence Ferlinghetti's press, but rather from an LP. There are many, many, many Ginsberg LPs and I have a big collection of them. But this was the first one and it's really curious: when he comes to part three of *Howl*, he's doing it in a studio instead of out there, and you can tell he's drunk, as he later admitted, when reading that part. But all the references, all the footnotes, in my [essay] were to that LP.

We haven't mentioned *The Astonishment Tapes*.[14] Those were Warren, eh? Even though they were made in my house, I always thought it was a Robin Blaser thing. And I was not allowed to come anywhere near the room at the time, if I recall, though *you* were –

ST: – no, I wasn't.

FD: We were both at one of them, because we're both on record on one of them.

GB: I think they might have let us in one time.

FD: It was probably a mistake! [Laughter]

GB: So, I haven't heard those tapes. I've known that they've been in a box somewhere. Cassettes.

FD: I've heard the one we were on.

GB: I've never even heard that one!

ST: They're being published.[15]

GB: I've also recently had the experience – and this is still ephemera, kind of, although it's really enjoyable – of having movies made of my poems and you can find them online, which is kind of interesting. But then *how* do you keep them in your little record thing? You know, this is what I've published, these are my books, and so forth. So, you say, "Okay, I'll just let them do it." They're all on the *cloud* somewhere! I have one that's all about women putting on brassieres. And there was "Lost in the Library," which was a lot of fun: me in a tuxedo, which doesn't have the bowtie because I dropped it into the toilet while I was changing into the tuxedo. It's really enjoyable. They were professionally done by a guy named Elvis Prusic in Toronto.[16] He also did two of my short stories put together into a little movie. But I'm not devoted to those things. And probably less so than are Frank and Fred, I think. Like, when somebody says, "Can we do something of yours online?" I say, "Yeah go ahead, just don't bother me." If somebody says, "Can I make a film out of this?" I say "Yeah, but don't ask me to help out; I'm just not interested in that." I'm *really* interested in what's done on the page.

But I couldn't have enjoyed my writing life, if that's what you call it, unless I had heard those old recordings of Ezra Pound, William Carlos Williams, and for me especially H.D. [Sounds of agreement from the panel] And then the later collections of Ed Dorn, Robert Duncan, and Ginsberg. I've still got all those LPs, I just can't make my machine work to play them. [Laughter] That's the other trouble: we keep producing things on some technology and then later on, well. But a *book* that was produced in 1775, we can still read it! That's the problem there. So that's why I'm really interested in what Jason's doing at Sir George Williams – at Concordia. What were the years again? '69 to –

Jason Camlot: '65 to '74.

GB: Okay, I was involved from '67 to '71, I think. Wonderful collection. The best poetry series I was ever involved in or ever heard of. And the *best* set of tapes of that series. I think almost everyone here was involved in that series. We had put people up at the Ritz Hotel.

DM: That's right.

GB: We got artists to make –

FD: You didn't put *me* up at the Ritz Hotel! [Laughter]

GB: Well, we put up every poet there except Frank Davey! [Laughter] And we took them out to a big fancy dinner. And then we had a big party for them at somebody's house afterwards. And then we made tapes on reel-to-reel. And then I got a personal collection from the years I was there. They made me a copy of these tapes and then I gave those tapes to Simon Fraser University Library so I don't have them anymore. Now Jason and his gang have digitized all these things, treating it as seriously as any print archive, anywhere, which I think is the important thing. Then was it this winter or last winter they started bringing the poets who are still alive to Concordia and doing an event in which the audience gets to hear both the recordings that were made in, say, 1970 and the poets who are still alive now also reading. The event I was at was with David McFadden. I still remember: he gave his reading in the faculty club, I think, and at the end of the reading, he said, "I made them laugh. I wish I could make them cry." [Laughter] It was beautiful. I'm hoping that somehow people are going to be able to tap into this without going to Montreal, right? That's gonna be the beautiful thing about it.

That was enough said and more. And now Daphne has twelve pages.

DM: No, I don't! [Laughter] But I'm glad you recalled Roy because he was such a chronic recorder –

GB: Oh, God!

DM: And I remember being with him at Christmas at his mother's place in Calgary and he recorded *everything*! All the nonsensical conversations that went on, the TV that was playing. I said, "*Why*? What did you do that for?" He said, "I just liked having it around and listening to it again." It was for him an extension of the moment. There were also some wonderful staged occurrences that were extensions of the moment. Because he was very into improvisatory music toward the end of his life. His daughter Fumiko has made a very interesting film about her father called *Reed*. And there's a beautiful sequence – I think that's where I saw it – of Roy reading in the basement of the old Museum of Anthropology, in the basement of the library. Remember? With those pillars?

GB: Yeah.

DM: It's all empty, there's nothing left in it. There was Takeo [Yamashiro] playing the shakuhachi with him and there's a sense of distance and space coming in through the performance. I wish there was more of it in the film.

So, I am going to read something but first of all, I want to say something that isn't in what I'm going to read, which is that for me, the advent of the cassette recorder was extremely important. Even before I was living with Roy, the cassette came into my life through oral history. And it was so incredibly portable. I remember doing an interview on a net float in Finn Slough with Inez Huovinen who was the only woman fishing on the Fraser River at that point. This was in the early '70s. There's the sound of the water and she and her brother-in-law are mending their net. I was just standing there asking her questions about her life with my little cassette recorder. And it formed the basis of one of the poems in *Steveston* (1974).[17] Now, one of the things I was working with in *Steveston* was the interface between my voice in poetry and their life voices – the voices that came out of their lived experiences. There are a lot of quotes in those poems because I had the good fortune of having a cassette recorder. And, of course, there were actually formal interviews that Maya Koizumi did that I ransacked for some of those quotes.[18]

Okay, so what I want to do is trace a little journey that Karis sent me on: she sent me two very short excerpts from a July 1969 tape recording Warren made of my reading from my very first collection of poems *leaf leaf/s* (Black Sparrow, 1969) and I think it was made in the Tallmans' living room because you can hear a cat meow in the background at one point. I seem to be haunted by cats lately. It was remarkable, first of all, to hear Warren's very distinctive voice, so familiar to me from the years of his teaching, the years of so many conversations with him during the '60s and '70s. So, the first pleasure was: "Ha! Warren comes alive in this room through my computer in the resonance and characteristics of his voice." I want to make a point of that because the voice, it seems to me, is almost as distinctive as a fingerprint.

Everybody's voice is unique. That's part of pleasure, actually, of the lived occasion of a reading – an actual reading – to an audience. We're talking to you [audience] now and nothing can replicate that except a tape. So, talk about extending the moment – a tape can take you way beyond that event. So there, George talked about the pleasure of hearing the voices of people long gone, long dead through recording devices. But it was also remarkable to hear my *own* voice from forty-four years ago. Still with the trace of an English accent which I don't believe I have anymore, but some people say I do. [Laughter] A voice that sounds so incredibly level to me, cool, very clear in its enunciation, and a higher register than I think my voice has now. And as I thought about that voice, I remembered I had given birth to my son only two and a half months before and so I was still in that pre-birthing, nursing, hormonal storm. There was a distanced quality to it; I think that was the effort hidden in it to keep the voice level. I want to bring that up because I think we often overlook the physical state of the body at the time of the recording. I mean, you both made references to drunken poets. [Laughter] But that's gross compared to the hormonal changes women are constantly having to undergo and that play into their vocal characteristics of a reading at any given moment.

GB: The body.

DM: Yeah, the body. Now, it was interesting for me to hear some of the statements I made at that reading forty-four years ago about poetics and language. It was curious how many of them made sense to me, even though I wouldn't put them in the way I put them then. So these were prompted by Warren's questions: I mentioned that when I was living in Bloomington, Indiana, and in Napa, California, and having many conversations with the remarkable poet-linguist D. Alexander, who unfortunately died quite young so no one remembers the legacy he left through *Audatala*, the magazine he published out of San Francisco, and his books. But he gave me a sense of clarity, I said to Warren – a clarity of language. I probably meant clarity of the *structure* of our language and how that enabled me to "dance with words," or move with them, meaning with their syntactic and melodic and semantic possibilities. I talked about words which were moving and not my will moving them, and Warren commented on how that sense of writing resembled Robert Duncan's sense of not being the master of language – that language was the master. That's still very much part of my poetics and, of course, Duncan was one of my very important poetic mentors. I started thinking about that image of the dance – that dance partner – and in the 1960s, a woman was still living that earlier concept of being led by a male partner in a dance. What I was talking about was much more collaborative than that and even more collaborative than Duncan saying language is the master, because, of course, it's always a collaboration between the infinite possibilities of language at any point in the writing and your own intelligence, your own shaping intelligence. They dance together.

Okay, so that's documentary value, historicity in a recording [inaudible] of poetry. But I'd like to talk about a more creative way of approaching those things. And that happened to me with Robert Minden and Carla Hallett coming to me, very generously, to say they'd like to make a recording of their music with my reading. Robert was the photographer for *Steveston* and he transformed into a remarkable composer-musician who uses a lot of found instruments – things like waterphones – that are quite strange to a Western audience. I mean, even then he was playing the musical saw. He and his partner, Carla, who has an amazing voice, do these improvisation soundscapes. They recorded two different readings of my poetry, five to six years apart, both in Richmond. Once, very fortuitously, right on the banks of the Fraser River in a little studio in Richmond. They did a lot of amazing editing work on it because you can't hear the difference between those two recordings. They worked on it for seven years from 2001 to 2008. And they brought out this little CD called *Like Light off Water* and these are *Steveston* poems.

What struck me when I listened to them again in preparation for this, was something that became apparent through my work with Japanese classical Noh theatre: I remember Richard Emmett, who was the musical director of *The Gull* and who composed the music to go with my playscript, kept talking about "mah, mah, mah" and, gradually, over the years I've learned with "mah" is. It's quite a beautiful concept: it's very strong in Japanese aesthetics. "Mah" is the space between sounds. It's also the space between words. It's the space between parts of a whole. And it contains the potential for all the possibilities that will arise from it. So when I listened to the recording – Bridget [MacKenzie] and I played it in the car on the way here – I was very much listening for how they use "mah." And they use it as a background space that is sometimes completely empty and sometimes holds the resonance of different sounds, slowly intermingling and dying into stillness, into silence, before a new rhythmic set, a new melodic series arises. We're talking about *sound* but I think the stillness, the silence, the pauses, and the breaks are very important aspects – they are part of the *texture* of voice. Even the characteristic way people will pause in their speech. That's not something we usually look at when we're thinking about recordings, so I just wanted to put that on the table.

So I didn't read it. You see, George?

GB: Have you noticed how us old farts still use the word "tape"?

DM: Ah, well, I know. [Laughter] That's our history! Fred? Over to you.

FW: It's kind of difficult to come after all this. There are so many layers involved in this work of audio poetry for me, and for these people too. The history, thank you for that, all of those reminiscences. I've always been involved, as George says, with techy stuff, tools, printers, mimeograph machines, tape recorders. And I'll talk about my own history there. But one of things that came up when they were talking was that we came out of the world of LPs in the '50s. Everyone knows what an LP is, right? [Laughter]

GB: It was a 33⅓ album. [Laughter]

FW: We all had collections of LPs and I had a wonderful jazz collection from Pacific Jazz. I was studying music, so there was this wonderful connection between music and poetry that occurred, for which the audio recording became very central, very useful. We also came out of the early '60s – since we're hearing about the '63 thing – we also came out of Olson's poetics. I was just realizing when we were talking that a lot of our interest in voice and the body was coming out of that sense of proprioception that he talks about in "Projective Verse." I hope I'm not talking too ahistorically here. You all know what "Projective Verse" is? LPs? "Projective Verse"? Charles Olson? [Laughter] It just occurred to me that Charles Olson – and maybe one of the scholars here can tell me where this comes from – but in one of his poems he says, "The quickest, finest tape recorder is a lie of what we know went on." So there's this kind of paradox that's going on for Olson and Dorn and Creeley, etc. At the time that the portable tape recorder came in, there was also this sense of poetics – at least in terms of Olson and Duncan – very much as George says, that says print is the most authentic place for the poem to occur. This becomes a bit of a problem for me as a young poet: I'm fascinated by how language works as music. I come to language as I come to music; that is how I compose with it. Not at the level of semantics and meaning, which are frankly fairly secondary for my interests.

All of us, I think, here, or most of us were in Ron Baker's linguistics course at UBC in the early '60s and we got interested in poetry because of Duncan's insistence on paying attention to elements like the syllable, like tonal leading of vowels, the very particles of language. We got very interested in the use of linguistics, and particularly, for myself, phonetics and phonology. And Lionel Kearns developed a form of verse called "stacked verse," which paid attention to the primary stress and intonation patterns. It was a very interesting and useful gesture into investigative poetics for Lionel and for us. So we were interested in things like juncture, pitch, intonation pattern, the voice - everything around the voice became very important because here we were with a poetics that was proposing the "voiced poem" - that is to lift the poem off the page. Whereas we had grown up in the tradition of the poem on the page and quite silent. Ginsberg, of course, was major in bringing this to our attention.

Then most of us became teachers, and there was this kind of combination of pedagogy and practice going on. At least for me, there was. Probably the most useful poem I ever used in my teaching career, which was fairly lengthy, was a recording of Allen Ginsberg reading "Wichita Vortex Sutra" that was made in Seattle at a radio station. They added little cymbals and gongs and Bob Dylan singing in the background - it's a beautiful landscape of that poem. I found that poem to be extremely useful. For my own use, I was very influenced by William Carlos Williams. And to hear Williams's voice, the kind of authenticity of voice. [Imitates Williams reading aloud] The whole question of authenticity I don't think came up and I don't think we were concerned about the differentiation between print and voice very much. The audio was something that went alongside print. For me, it happened when Creeley came to town and he had a Wollensak tape recorder. I was playing trumpet and vibes and I traded in my trumpet and vibes for a Wollensak.

GB: You offered to sell me your vibes and I didn't have the money to buy them! [Laughter]

FD: You left them in my basement and blocked the bathroom door! [Laughter]

FW: It's impossible to be around these guys with our history. [Laughter] But I was very impressed with this young poet Robert Creeley in his early thirties, showing up in Vancouver with a *beautiful* Wollensak 4-track tape recorder. Creeley had been recording interviews with poets for a radio show in Albuquerque, New Mexico; I think most of these recordings were with Louis Zukofsky, Witter Bynner, [inaudible] Dawson, Ed Dorn, and so forth. They are all on PennSound. So Creeley was already into it. This was in 1961, I think he first showed up at UBC, maybe '62.

FD: No, it was '62, I think. He was here one year just before the conference [of 1963].

GB: That's right. He was at that spring festival.[19] In February.

DM: He taught '62 and '63. [Laughter]

GB: It doesn't matter.

FW: Then why did you mention it? [Laughter]

GB: It wasn't me! You know, I think he was led to doing that by Paul Blackburn. Paul Blackburn was sort of the American Roy Kiyooka. He never went anywhere without a shoulder bag full of tapes. He started doing it at ... What was that reading series at that church down at the bottom of Manhattan? That famous series.

FD: St Mark's.

GB: Yeah, and it was the most famous, for me anyway, American reading series. And he taped every single reading there and then when he travelled around the US. He taped everybody. He came to my house in Montreal with a tape recorder and I wouldn't let him turn it on. But he had a bag full of these damn tapes. For me, Paul Blackburn is the hero of taping.

FW: This is true, but it's not just Paul Blackburn. It's something that came out of Black Mountain. John Cage was very much into audio. His performance he did at UBC in the spring of '61 [February 1962][20] was putting a radio on the stage in the auditorium and then walking off the stage. That whole sense of inserting the machine and audio into a creative performance was new. Also poetry and jazz was happening. Kenneth Patchen read at the cellar. [Inaudible] played bass. This was new. To have poetry and jazz. So, spoken word stuff was going on.

GB: Did you go to the Kenneth Patchen event? Did you get to hear him?

FW: Oh, yeah. I went to that.

GB: That was electrifying, I thought.

FW: One of the things that's come up recently – I still use my tape collection, which is still in the basement, but a lot has been digitized now. On my website the other day, I was doing a thing on George Stanley's book *After Desire* which is also about buses. So I made a note about this and I said, since George's book is also about buses, have a listen to Kenny Tallman in August 1963 read his bus poem, which was part of Robert Creeley's reading at the 1963 poetry conference.

[Plays recording of young Kenny Tallman reading his poem]

GB: This is Warren Tallman's son. How old was he then?

FW: He was about nine. Anyway, in terms of my life as a writer, the audio was there as much as print. I use audio almost every day. I use it for my thinking. I was doing some work on Ed Dorn recently and I had this poem on tape which I couldn't find in print. So that resulted in a search for the print poem. John Latta in Chicago gets on the internet and says, "Here it is, it was published here." So it adds to the community or the sharing of text. The debate between privileging print or audio is really interesting now: Jason [Camlot], Steve Evans, and Al Filreis have got some very interesting things to say [about audio]. Steve Evans, or was it Al Filreis, was talking about a course they'd like to teach in poetry with no text, just audio. Because the experience of a student just having audio is provocative and interesting to explore. We all know, those of us who have taught, that there's this response: "Wow, the poem is fantastic and it has become more humanized for me" or "God, I used to like that poem until I heard George Bowering read it!" [Laughter]

There's another aspect I just want to mention from my notes here. Pauline and I were talking on the car ride up here [to Kelowna]. Pauline mentioned the difference between the public reading and the studio reading. Pauline's done work on Phyllis Webb and her studio recordings of Olson, Duncan, and Creeley for *Ideas* that were never produced or allowed to be aired. We were talking about how you hear Olson reading on these studio recordings that Webb did in Toronto [for the CBC]. And it's good but it's not as vibrant as hearing Olson at the '63 conference with the audience there; there's a kind of dynamism. [Panellists respond affirmatively] We had this wonderful reading Duncan made as a wedding gift to us because Pauline was working on Duncan for her MA thesis. Duncan sat at his desk and made an hour-and-half-long recording of his poetry and it's the most boring reading. He's just reading these poems into a tape recorder. We have most of these poems in different readings he's done.

For me, in the '60s, the big thing was recording the '63 conference, sitting there with a single mic – the Wollensak – because Warren's tape recorder had broken down. And that's all we have from that '63 conference. All through the '60s people were after those tapes. And Berkeley came along, the Berkeley '65 conference. I was in Buffalo as a graduate student, and to be able to hear Olson's three-and-a-half-hour reading at Berkeley, [from] Buffalo! I remember we had a big meeting in our basement in Buffalo just to sit around and listen to this tape.

FD: And we could hear it almost instantly, within weeks of that reading.

FW: Yeah. Oh, it was! There was an immediacy to it. I'm also fascinated by what Daphne was talking about: the notion of documentation and history. One of my peeves right now is the whole question of memory. I mean, listening to us here, there is a whole lot of "memory" going on. [Chuckles] The notion of voice as memory is worth thinking about. My mother is suffering from dementia and has lost language. Voice is lost in terms of memory is lost. I'm fascinated by that and I'm wondering about how much of the ubiquitousness of audio now is entering into our cultural awareness.

FD: I'd like to add something about what George and Fred were saying about the page and the oral record. I was quite interested in the University of California collections of Olson's poetry.[21] Was it George Butterick who edited those volumes? The editor went through all of the tapes of Olson's readings where Olson would actually alter the lines of his poems as he read them. For Olson, the reading was a moment of composition. The poem for him was always an act of the instant and the reading was a new instance. And so the editor went through those tapes and regarded those moments on those tapes as editions, as variants. The same way you'd go through all the editions of Shakespeare's plays and accumulate the variants and make a footnote or list at the end of your edition about the various variants. And so in the University of California Press definitive Olson editions, you have all the variants that Olson created during those poetry readings that were taped. And of course that couldn't have happened without tape. One of the very earliest tapes I think I heard was a 1957 Olson reading which was probably a professional recording, because I don't think the equipment existed for amateur tape recordings, and then was copied onto amateur tape and then mailed to Tallman. I think you have a copy, Fred, in your collection, and it was "Olson reading from Gloucester" Warren called it, although I think it was actually recorded in Boston. That's an instance which complicates our discussion of which is the "real" text: the tape recorded [poem] or the one on the page? It probably depends a lot on the poet. We decide.

GB: I've been thinking about this for twenty minutes now. We often assume that the tape is secondary to the printed thing. There's the printed thing and then there's a taped version of it.

FW: That's what *you* said! [Laughter]

GB: But the opposite happens all the time. With Fred it happened in terms of composition. His syntax was a musical syntax, and if you want to read his early poems especially, you got to forget about everybody else's syntax. All those breath poems. But one of my favourite moments in or after the '63 conference was Olson had these two unpublished poems that he read over and over again because we forced him to: "Maximus 27" and "Dogtown II." And "Dogtown II" is about five pages long? Dan McLeod listened to the recording of it and wrote it down, trying to see if he could get Olson's notation right from what Olson told us how notation worked. He sent the typed-up version of it to Olson, and Olson wrote him back and said, "you got it absolutely right except for maybe two or three occasions in which this word should have been at the beginning of this line instead of the end of this line." That was an attestation to Olson's greatness in terms of his notation and Dan McLeod, who's now the millionaire owner of the *Georgia Straight*, how incredibly attentive his ear was as taught by reading Charles Olson. And I don't know if Olson decided to use his own handwritten notation before he published the poem or used Dan's. Maybe he thought Dan got a couple of them a little bit better than he had. But he agreed with him, is the important thing. And I think that happens a lot: that we work from the spoken/tape to the [page]. And Lionel Kearns used to stand at the podium while reading his poems and change the notation because he was speaking them out loud and noticed what was wrong. The tape recorder was absolutely a gift when it came to learning notation.

FW: Yeah, well we were hung up on notation.

GB: We were. Because we heard people reading poems as if there weren't any. And occasionally you still can, I think. As if that stuff on the page is just words and you can read them whatever order you want. [Laughs]

FD: I don't know about the rest of us, but I always read my poems aloud after I've written them down to find if I've written them down right. And so I will actually change the written text as a result of trying to read the poem. And sometimes I'll tape record it to listen to myself having read the poem.

DM: Roy used to compose vocally. I always knew when he was writing because I would hear this mutter from his room. It was the voice first and then the page.

FD: Me too, yeah, me too.

GB: Writing is another version of reading.

DM: No, he [Roy] was sounding possible alternatives at every point as he was going along.

GB: Yeah, that's reading. [Laughs]

DM: No! It's not reading. [Laughter] It's listening!

GB: That's what I mean. It's the same thing! [Laughter]

DM: One you do with your eyes, the other you do with your ears.

GB: Really? [Laughter]

Erín Moure: It was really a privilege for me to be here listening to all of you talk about recording and those early recordings. I was wondering if there was kind of a Vancouver strain to this whole focus on recording and creating archives? My own experience as a developing poet would have been a second-generation experience, and through writing not through hearing things. There were always interviews in the *Capilano Review* and many of them were not the formalized interviews you would find elsewhere all printed and edited. It was really clear that a bunch of people were sitting around in a living room. And they always bore the trace of whoever transcribed it. There was a conversational ebb and flow. Poetry is a conversation. I learned so much from those conversations. But I didn't *hear* them; I read transcripts of them. For me, those were very important adjuncts to reading the poetry itself. It was in those interviews, those exchanges, that I learned a kind of manner of thinking. Seeing Daphne talk on the page, or Robin Blaser, or Sharon. Knowing their words were not just written; they had listeners, they were spoken in a community. I don't really have a question specific to that comment, but, Sharon, you've had the most involvement in the *Capilano Review*, maybe you have a comment?

ST: I don't remember if I was involved in transcribing those interviews.

EM: But even from a point of view of editing and giving a place of privilege to those interviews in the magazine, they seem to be an important ethos of the magazine itself.

DM: I'd like to say something about that, Erín! When Pierre and Bill and I started doing that in the three years that I was working with them, I did transcribe several of those interviews, and I brought to it some of what I'd learned from oral history because it's really important to convey in a way you punctuate – and that's a major decision at every point – how the voice is moving.

EM: I would excitedly go and find these issues of the *Capilano Review*. And I also avidly read *Sound Heritage*, which is where I first encountered some of your projects, Daphne. That was another case of my [encounter with] sound recordings being through transcription.

DM: Yeah, that was a great little oral history magazine.

FW: I just wanted to add something. Sharon mentioned translating *Causal Mythology* for Ralph and I remember that Ralph stole from my study some of the Olson tapes. He didn't tell me he took them. This was in the '60s, '70s. He took the tapes back to Simon Fraser where he was teaching and he got Karl Siegler to transcribe the "Place and Names" session we had at Vancouver in '63. One, I was outraged that it was in print. And there was a sense, all of a sudden, that there was an invasion of privacy or an invasion of intellectual property, maybe? I was really bothered by this. I think Olson had already died. How could Ralph do this, I thought? He had done it as a class thing and was handing it out to people. So that bothered me. I don't think it would bother me as much now. But there was a moment when the transcription of audio into print changed it. It's an interesting aspect.

GB: And it makes it interesting to see that difference: to hear that and then see it, to see that difference.

FW: It kind of captures it and puts a stamp of authenticity on it that the audio wasn't claiming somehow. But when it's in print, even when it's mimeographed for a class, it belongs somewhere.

GB: Because we were brought up people of the book. Authenticity is in terms of print. "It says right here in the bible."

FD: There's another aspect to it too. Canadian copyright law and US copyright law for tapes is quite different. In the US the performer or the speaker or the reader has a share in the copyright. Whereas in Canada, copyright law rests with the recorder. So Fred actually has copyright on the 1963 tapes that were made at UBC. Bill Walker, who was my roommate, has copyright on the Duncan tapes that were made in 1961. I can't remember who made the Creeley tapes in '62. I think it was Warren.

ST: Warren's estate has copyright on the *Astonishment* tapes.

FD: Yeah, not Blaser's estate.

GB: That would suggest that the spoken word is not as important as the printed or recorded word.

ST: Or the guy that turns it on!

FD: Although there could be complications. In the '63 conference tapes, if Fred was employed by Warren or by the university that could alter the copyright. Not that anybody has worried about it over the years.

FW: We offered UBC a copy of the tapes. And they said, "We don't want them." [Laughter]

EM: I just wanted to open the floor to questions. I'm sure some of you have things you would like to ask the five panellists. Anybody?

[Audience member 1]: I wondered what aspects of the fingerprint are recorded in the text? [inaudible] I'm wondering what parts of the author are authenticated by the text and the voice. And what parts of the environment are [inaudible].

ST: I'm very interested in voice anyway, and I know how contested the idea of voice has been recently in avant-garde and postmodern poetics. And the voice as fingerprint, I think, exists anyway in any tape recording of any voice; there's an almost supernatural quality of the presence of the person if you listen to a tape recording of someone who has died or someone who was once close to you. It's eerie to hear their voice again and it brings them back. A voice, to me, brings a person's presence much more than a photograph does or even a video of them walking across a room. And I think partly because it involves the breath, it involves in that sense something spiritual. It involves the body. And so the imprint of the voice on the page is part of the decisions that a poet makes about notation, about line break, about rhythm. And usually can be heard more clearly after you've heard the poet read. Then you hear as well as read the poem on the page. Once I've heard Olson or Creeley, I still have the echo of their voice when I read on the page.

A very interesting experience for me was listening to Basil Bunting read Wordsworth in what would have been Wordsworth's Cumbrian accent. It was astonishing. And that was like three ghosts back. I can never read Wordsworth the same now because that is the way he would have read his work. And so then the question becomes: in a text in which voice is contested in some negative sense for whatever reason (and there are plenty of them ... we won't go into metaphysics and presence and all of that), then is the personality available on the page? Is the fingerprint, the uniqueness in a world swirling with language, what is unique, what is original, what is a fingerprint? I don't remember what your question was really. [Laughter] But when I was thinking about the future of voice recording and the ubiquity of it at the same time that the very presence of voice is contested in Flarf or conceptual poetry or whatever. So is the disappearance of voice, presumably to make a better world, actually going to accomplish that? I don't know.

FD: Well you can read Flarf aloud.

ST: Yeah, but it's collective and anonymous. It sounds very different from an Olson or a Creeley or a Davey.

GB: If somebody phones you, you say, "they're *on* the phone." But if they text you, it could be anyone texting you. You can identify hundreds of thousands of voices even on the telephone.

FD: In law there's now the concept of voiceprint, which is parallel to fingerprint. And engineers can produce audiographs or whatever of the voice. [Panellists express awe] Just like they used to be able to do from magnetic tapes. You could have an identifiable and unique picture of a magnetic field on a tape that a voice was producing.

ST: Can I read what I wrote about this?

DM: Do, Sharon! [Laughter]

ST: I just wrote a note about my sense of things: the sense of sound recordings as historical is going by the wayside or changing. I expect a blending in or de-emphasizing of the sense of the occasion of the voice. As far as voice in general goes, I have noticed the general aspiration in the public media is to sound like a five-year-old or maybe a ten-year-old. There's a diminution of voice in poetry that began with the LANGUAGE writing in the '80s and its distrust of presence. So if there's no voice in poetry, what is there to record a bunch of words in a row? So that's just a note I made, it's not developed at all. Well, you've been doing this in the conference too; coming together to talk about these things.

[Audience member 2]: I'm interested in technological transitions and the way in which they have impact with the way we interact with sound. Funnily, you can still buy *new* LPs. I actually just got a new pre-amp for my turntable last year. So you can still buy that as well, for those of us who love old technology. But my question has to do with my sense that throughout your story there's been something rather revolutionary about the ability to use tape to reflect voice and sustain memory. Sharon got into a conversation that really interests me: how does that change with the digital universe, how does it change your sense of what poetry is and what poetry does, and how does it change your sense of how that relates to memory?

GB: I think it has mostly to do with what Fred was talking about before: the *availability* of machines. Because when Ezra Pound and William Carlos Williams and Gertrude Stein were taken into a studio and recorded it was so that they could record their voices. They had no, I'm pretty sure, no sense of using it themselves or that it would have something to do with how they wrote poems. It was just to get their voices recorded. That has changed now. Part of the compositional act is the recording of sound. What happened later on when they took the Beatles' records and came out with that new version of them a few years ago where you can now actually hear everything? What did it do to their voices? Did it make them less authentic or more authentic or more available or what? I don't know. But I'm sure that a musician is saying, "I'm going to do that from now on." It's going to become part of the compositional act.

FD: When we're talking about music and you're talking about your LP collection, the missing word here is *performance*. When Charles Bernstein gives the poetry reading and it's framed by his feeling that the oral poem doesn't exist or is less important than the written poem that reading is a performance. What I would add to the little discussion we were having about Flarf is that when someone reads Flarf it's a performance. Now I suppose there might be theorists who would suggest that the readings we gave yesterday were also performances. So this is something that is up for discussion.

FW: Another missing word, I think, here is *production*. Making poetry, it seems to me, has always been: how to make it public? Jason's SpokenWeb is much like the emergence of a small press. It's an instance of production. And one of the aspects of the technology and the machine thing is that it has allowed us to – and certainly this was something we were very conscious of –

GB: – We seized the means of production!

FW: We wanted our hands in our own work. We were not interested in having it homogenized out into some kind of distant public sphere; we wanted to be present to it all. That's part of tape recording and the printing and the small press work that's very important. I'm glad you can still get an LP machine, by the way, but try to find a good reel-to-reel tape recorder these days so I can digitize my tapes. [Laughter]

ST: Sound editing, too. I think one of the best books for teaching poetry is *The Conversations*, which is Michael Ondaatje's interviews with Walter Murch, the editor of *The Godfather* and all those films. Where do you make the cut? Where do you jump? It's just brilliant.

DM: But we are talking about authenticity in the voice, and in terms of your question, there seems to be a lot of interest in automation. How do you make a voice automatic? How do you do all the reverbs and so on that distort the voice so you get something creative, new. But it's not something I'm interested in. I can't stand it when I phone a company and all I get is an automatic voice. It's not even a human recorded voice.

GB: But your call is very important to them. [Laughter] [Applause]

DM: Yeah, exactly! [Laughter]

GB: I don't know if this is pertinent, but my best friend from childhood is blind and so he goes through all kinds of ways of reading. He has this machine for two years that I didn't know existed. We were over at his place saying, "Okay, we got to do something with your official papers. We'll put them in an envelope." He said, "Okay, I'll get my little gadget." I forget how it works, but you know those little address things you get on the corner or your envelope? Well he makes them this way: he's got a little machine that he puts up to the corner of the envelope and he says "my important papers" or something like that and the machine prints on the envelope: "my important papers." And the next time he can put the machine in read mode and it will say aloud to him, "my important papers." I thought, "Why didn't we have that!?" [Laughter]

FW: Our papers weren't important enough. [Laughter]

DM: Yeah, there is a program like that for people who have visual disabilities and I remember talking to somebody who was having trouble and using one of those programs and the person said they couldn't stand the automatic sound of that voice.

GB: Oh this one sounded just like Willie.

DM: Well that's good! They've developed it then! [Laughs]

KS: I want to pick up on something Fred said. You said, "we seized the means of production." And I've been thinking how yesterday we had Jentery Sayers from UVic in here talking about historical audio and how recording came out of ham radio. And he used the word "masculinist" at one point and it got me thinking about the gendered nature of recording technologies. And what has come up a little bit in this discussion is that, Sharon, you transcribed and typed, and typing has a gendered history. I wonder if I could hear from Daphne and Sharon about the gendered nature of recording.

DM: I did my share of transcription for the oral history books we did. I think that one of the reasons, aside from that I needed a job and was offered a job, that I moved into oral history was that there was a chance to record more of women's life experiences, women's life stories. And the different natures of the voices that we recorded was so rich texturally. Women's voices, I don't know, there's something about women's voices that is very appealing. There seems to be a greater range of vocality in a woman's voice. Sharon, what would you say?

ST: Well, most of my transcription jobs prior to the work I did for Ralph or whomever in aid of poetry were working for bosses in an insurance thing. I would have to correct the grammar and put in the punctuation. And it was terrible because all day long it was about why someone's insurance claim couldn't be paid out. [Groans] [Laughter] For me, I'm a listener and I love listening to the way people talk. And I was actually very happy doing those jobs because I could be inside voice. And I could be kind of musically conducting; it would be flowing through me and I would be able to punctuate and get into the rhythm and nuance and knowledge of that voice, even if it was someone I didn't know. I didn't mind that work, but I did do a lot of it.

FW: Could I follow up on this? Because implicit in your question of something around the machine being gendered, I just wondered for you two women if the typewriter was important? I mean, the typewriter was probably a bit more important than the tape recorder at least in the early '60s. And most of the writers I knew valued the kind of typewriter, its font, etc. Was the typewriter important for you two?

DM: Oh yes, the typewriter was fantastically important because it could keep up with the pace of your thought. And my handwriting has always been very bad because I was taught to write as a child in English style - sort of backhanded. And then coming to Canada I was forced to write forwards - the MacLean method of writing [laughs], if anyone remembers that. And so it was the speed of the typewriter that I loved. And my first typewriter was one of those big old office typewriters that my father got for me where the keys all stand up on these little stems. And you have to really use your fingers hard to make any imprint. And then there's the heaviness of the carriage, you know, the clang and then whoosh! [Laughter] But there was such a rhythm to it! [Laughter] I loved the rhythmic quality of it.

GB: This was true of not just us but a whole pile of other writers. When I lived in Kitsilano I loved that summer day you'd be walking down Yew Street and you could hear typewriters coming from all windows. [Panellists respond affirmatively] Everybody was writing a novel! [Laughter]

ST: Well, Pauline has written a book about the means of production, women in transcription and typewriting in the production of the little magazines at that time. A very valuable contribution.

Pauline Butling: Well, I'm looking at the role of women. There was a pattern in the women's editing work. But it was certainly not all [inaudible]. Frank and George [inaudible] TISH.

GB: And Audrey Thomas has always had someone else type her stuff.

PB: What I was looking for was the kind of support. Not so much what women did. Did all of the back-end work and got none of the credit.

ST: Yeah, none of the credit.

PB: So I referred to her as being like a [inaudible] in those days. So there was no [inaudible] of a gendered factor in the production, but it was not clearly categorized. Especially in alternative production spaces where some might *think* [inaudible], but I think when there's less power involved, the categories are less fixed. Not that you guys had no power.

DM: Yeah, no, that's true. In those days that's very true, Pauline. I'm really glad you've written about that. But it's interesting just listening to the conversation up here. It's always the men who are doing the recording. I don't remember women going around with a tape recorder.

ST: Yeah, I don't remember doing any recording.

FD: Phyllis Webb.

DM: Yeah, but that was part of her job for CBC.

GB: I think when they became portable us guys got to write with the typewriter – despite your experience – when the typewriter became portable. Because typewriters before that were in an office, and all kinds of people – not us – would say "this needs typing" and take it to a woman sitting in an office with a gigantic typewriter. Now, we could carry it along with us.

FW: But right now, in my mind, it's women who are working with audio: Oana Avasilichioaei, Kathleen Brown ... These are young women writers who are playing with the technology. Oana has all of these foot pedals and wires and things. She knows more about it than I do. So I get your point, Karis, about the gendered thing of techy boys and their toys, but I think it does flatten out a bit so that it's not that distinct. It kind of works all around. But I don't think I remember anyone except Daphne and Carole [Itter] going out taping.

FD: But then they were using cassette recorders, presumably.

DM: Yeah, we were.

FD: It would be difficult for women to lift the early tape recorders. They were quite heavy because they often had attached speakers.

DM: We had to have a cassette that was small enough to sit on a coffee table. We'd often be sitting with whoever we were interviewing in the living room. We finally figured out that in order to stop the reverberation from the mic, because it was a handheld mic, nobody wanted to talk to a handheld mic, so we put it in a knitted woollen glove inside a glass and that was perfect. [Laughter]

NOTES

1 These writers included George Bowering, Frank Davey, Gladys Maria Hindmarch, Daphne Marlatt, Sharon Thesen, Fred Wah, and Phyllis Webb. Hindmarch and Webb were not able to attend.
2 The SSHRC-funded TEMiC Summer Institute was co-organized by Karis Shearer and Dean Irvine.
3 Frank Davey, "Tape-Recorded Poetry in the 60s #mediaarchaeology #poetry," *London Open Mic Poetry Archive* (blog), 22 July 2013, accessed 27 July 2023, www.londonpoetryopenmic.com/frank-davey-blog/tape-recorded-poetry-in-the-60s-mediaarchaeology-poetry#comments.
4 Cf. Deanna Fong and Karis Shearer. "Gender, Affective Labour, and Community-Building through Literary Audio Recordings," *SpokenWeblog*, 21 April 2022, https://spokenweb.ca/gender-affective-labour-and-community-building-through-literary-audio-recordings/; Karis Shearer. "Copy, Copy, Copy! Community-Building through Reproduction and Circulation," *AMP Lab* (blog), 15 February 2021, http://amplab.ok.ubc.ca/index.php/2021/02/15/copy-copy-copy-community-building-through-reproduction-and-circulation/.
5 Michael Davidson, *Ghostlier Demarcations: Modern Poetry and the Material World* (Berkeley: University of California Press, 1997), 196.
6 At their time of initial production and circulation, mainly in the 1960s and '70s, these collections might have constituted an analog version what Abigail De Kosnik has called a "rogue archive": they are made and maintained by the volunteer labour of community members and not, at the time, shared with official archives; they are circulated without the expectation of payment; and there is no regard for copyright restrictions. See *Rogue Archives: Digital Cultural Memory and Media Fandom* (Cambridge: MIT Press), 2. From the outset, these rogue archives had considerable cultural capital in both literary and scholarly communities.
7 Chris Mustazza. "Les archives sonores de la poésie: production – conservation – utilisation," *Transatlantica* [online], 1 (2016), posted 7 February 2017, accessed 29 August 2022. URL: http://journals.openedition.org/transatlantica/8185.
8 Edited for clarity. This transcription was co-produced by Karis Shearer and Megan Butchart.
9 The name of the radio show was *radiofreerainforest*, which aried on CFRO-FM Radio.
10 Bill Walker.
11 See SoundBox Collection, Davey Fonds.
12 Ibid.
13 "Three Vancouver Writers: Interviews by George Bowering (including Audrey Thomas, Daphne Marlatt and Frank Davey)," *Open Letter* 4, no. 3 (Spring 1979), accessed 27 July 2023, https://publish.uwo.ca/~fdavey/c/4.3.htm.

14 Robin Blaser, *The Astonishment Tapes*, ed. Miriam Nichols (Tuscaloosa: University Alabama Press, 2015); Robin Blaser, "The Astonishment Tapes, Vancouver 1974," PennSound, accessed 25 July 2023, https://writing.upenn.edu/pennsound/x/Blaser.php.
15 Blaser, *The Astonishment Tapes*.
16 This was a videopoem produced circa 2002 and shown at the Calgary Spoken Word Festival, 2006. See Elvis Prusic, "Lost in the Library," vimeo.com, 3:57, 31 August 2009, https://vimeo.com/6359731.
17 Daphne Marlatt, *Steveston* (Edmonton: Longspoon Press, 1974).
18 Cf. Daphne Marlatt, "Interview with Maya Koizumi," 1974, BC Archives AAAB0258, https://search-bcarchives.royalbcmuseum.bc.ca/maya-koizumi-interview.
19 UBC Festival of the Contemporary Arts.
20 His performance was part of the UBC Festival of the Contemporary Arts.
21 Charles Olson, *The Collected Poems of Charles Olson, Excluding the Maximus Poems*, ed. George F. Butterick (Berkeley: University of California Press, 1997); Charles Olson, *The Maximus Poems*, ed. George F. Butterick (Berkeley: University California Press, 1985).

Curatorial Agency at Véhicule Art Inc.
"Openness was a guiding spirit to VÉHICULE"

Klara du Plessis

Curatorial Agency at the Poetry Reading: Curating versus the Curatorial

Broadly speaking, and in terms of the promotional or academic poetry reading[1] that has systematically come to define this literary form over the past half-century in North America, the poetry reading has been less deliberate than the visual arts exhibition[2] in theorizing its status as a critical vehicle for the presentation and dissemination of creative work. In contrast to the literary event, the visual arts field has a long-standing and diverse tradition of conceptualizing the collection, preservation, and presentation of visual art in a variety of private and public museum and gallery spaces.[3] Moreover, the visual arts are more finely attuned to the key mediating role of curators as "translators, movers, or creators" in this process of displaying work.[4] Arguably, the visual arts have a more fully theorized awareness of the inherent relationality of how a curator brings an artist and their creative work into dialogue with a venue, its context, and its public.

My current research aims to shift the critical nexus of the poetry reading away from literary and performance studies in isolation and to merge it with curatorial studies, a mode of thinking both practically and conceptually interested in the presentation of creative output. This implies that the poetry reading as a formulation of literary work is amplified as a sonic art form through the structural formation of curating. By means of this disciplinary cross-pollination, I aim to highlight the literary curator's deliberate resistant labour and responsibility in the aesthetic and ethical shaping of an auditory field for listening to and experiencing poetry, and to move toward a more nuanced understanding of the poetry reading as an intentionally curated form.

This umbrella project is informed by an engagement with curatorial and exhibition studies and museology. Narrowing the scope for this paper, though, I'm advancing the term "curatorial agency" – the degree to which the literary curator (or the poets themselves, or any other instigator) are involved in the creation of literary presentation, and the level of responsibility they shoulder as a mediator between literary work and audience within the relational performance space. Curatorial agency is indebted to a useful distinction theorized by practitioners of the visual arts and museum studies, namely between *curating*, as practical, organizational concerns, and the *curatorial*, as the dynamic, interactive space which is created at an exhibition or, by extension, a literary event. Scholar and curator Irit Rogoff expands upon this rift: "the distinction [is] of curating as professional practice, which involves a whole set of skills and practices, materials, and institutional and infrastructural conditions ... Developing the concept of the curatorial ... has been about getting away from representation ... and trying to see within this activity a set of possibilities for much larger agendas in the art world ... The curatorial then defines the larger frame."[5] The degree of intentionality or conscious harnessing of the codependence of curating versus the curatorial shapes both the process and product of organizing an exhibition or literary event. I call this self-awareness "curatorial agency."

Articulating curatorial agency in relation to the poetry reading as sonic event makes discernible the often invisible or neglected labour of decision-making, organizing, and structuring inherent to the literary reading. Curatorial agency thus works to resist false assumptions of non-intentionality in relation to the shaping of the poetry reading as a site of constructed, public performance. Applying curatorial agency to Véhicule Art Inc. as an initial exploration of the relevance of this new concept shows, in turn, how a reading series can model a stance of openness in order to oppose traditions of gatekeeping, literary elitism, and concomitant assumptions of authorship and literary value. While celebrating this openness of diverse literatures and experimentation within modes of literary production, my analysis likewise questions a rote equation of openness with a democratic performance space, calling for a revaluation of agential and intentional curatorial practices.

Curatorial Agency as Openness: Véhicule Art Inc.

I focus on Véhicule Art Inc. – a bilingual, interdisciplinary artists'-run centre and exhibition space that intermittently hosted a weekly poetry reading series and quarterly open mic marathon events in Montreal, from 1972 to 1983 – as a case study for a preliminary investigation into curatorial agency in a poetry reading series environment. In particular, I argue that while Véhicule maintained a firm hold on curating, it entrusted curatorial agency to the poets presenting work, aligning itself with a laissez-faire curatorial strategy that provided space and moderate resources to explore a set of conditions without much intentionality towards the outcome. Indeed, in a comparative study of artist-run centres of the 1970s and 1980s, Diana Nemiroff finds that "Véhicule had never been dedicated to a single direction but had seen itself, rather, as a conduit for the newest forms of artistic activity ... this did not constitute as it did in the United States, an alternative to an active art market; here it was a passive rather than an active factor."[6]

Arguably a fair modus operandi, this passivity in the face of curatorial agency, or this division of domains of authority between curating and the curatorial, has significant consequences for the ethos of the Véhicule poetry readings. Articulating itself as a space of superlative acceptance and openness to diverse literary traditions and experiments, Véhicule also had to contend with the cultural climate inherent to the time and place, and which informed the kind of work being performed under the auspices of open and experimental. As Felicity Tayler convincingly argues about Véhicule as temporally positioned at the political aftermath of the October Crisis, and ongoing federal and provincial language debates in Canada and Quebec, the "material and social relations that produced this free space worked as a countermeasure to the link between language, territory, and social identity in political programs."[7] Tayler likewise illustrates with ethnic and sexist slurs in examples of personal journaling from Véhicule members that "uncensored thoughts indicate how the linguistic space at Véhicule Art was not so much free from these pervasive cultural restraints."[8] While Véhicule articulated its space around politics of liberation as identified with individual freedom – a creative space where people could do as they pleased – this openness was itself informed by a nominal bilingualism predicated on political language debates, and subject to the ventriloquizing of implicit (and sometimes explicit) sexism, racism, and other discriminatory gestures. Véhicule's valorization of exploratory, non-traditional literary engagement and spontaneity of participation, while simultaneously remaining shackled to both the political and socio-ethical concerns of the time, translates retroactively as a laxity of curatorial agency and evaluation in terms of the literary content presented.

Centred around the seven so-called Véhicule Poets – Endre Farkas, Artie Gold, Tom Konyves, Claudia Lapp, John McAuley, Stephen Morrissey, and Ken Norris[9] – Véhicule Art Inc. aimed, according to a document of incorporation from 5 October 1972, to "establish, maintain, and operate a center for the promotion, development, encouragement, and exposition of the arts, and to act as agents and promoters of the arts and artists ... To establish periodicals and publications ... To arrange for exhibitions and performances by artistic groups."[10] Clearly all of these intentions are to provide the material necessities for creative promulgation, to provide the physical platform, along with any subsidiary organizational necessities, on which art and literature could be played out. So, for example, from the date of its establishment, Véhicule had a fixed address at 61 Saint Catherine Street West, Montreal, previously a night club and a location which Nemiroff feels "served as a sign of difference, distinguishing Véhicule philosophically from the west-end galleries. In situating itself physically on the margins of downtown Montreal in the underbelly of the city's commercial activity, Véhicule announced its own marginality and made an anti-establishment gesture."[11]

Initially, Véhicule was financially secure, receiving $103,000 from the Local Initiatives Program, and another $12,000 from the Canada Council for the Arts, in the first year and a half of their existence alone.[12] Sifting through the meticulous archive of Véhicule's paperwork now housed at Concordia University, it is significant to note the consistently rigorous nature of its administration. Every invoice is on record. Rough brainstorming notes, formal funding applications, and forthcoming events' advertisements alike are all on file. Véhicule held frequent meetings, which were formally structured with board members making motions that were voted for or against, and detailed minutes were typed up and recorded, outlining decisions on grant-writing strategies, progress on new advertising prospects, and intentions to purchase better audio recording equipment, among many other conversations. Tayler suggests that the quantity of administrative, archival materials was "conceived of as a work of conceptual art,"[13] but whether managed ironically or in earnest, it is safe to say that Véhicule took its organizational duties seriously. This was not an improvisational endeavour. The locational, financial, and supervisory structure of Véhicule, as a collective effort to promote and showcase art and literature, was, by all appearances, methodical and efficient.[14] So in terms of curating, the organizational, and practical dimensions of administering an artists' centre, gallery, and reading series, Véhicule was focused and businesslike.

This acuity of curating is particularly salient when contrasted with the apparent unsystematic hosting of poets and their literary output at both the weekly poetry reading series and the quarterly open mic marathon events. Whereas Véhicule's organizing body appears to have deliberately constructed a resistant space open to new work, as evidenced in the bulk of administrative archival traces, the wide range of performers suggest a loosening of that insurgent resolution instead. On the one hand, scheduling rosters, posters, and communication records name numerous established North American authors such as Kenneth Koch, Anne Waldman, Constance DeJong, and even Marina Abramović. On the other hand, seemingly indiscriminate scores of undergraduate and high school students, only beginning to hone their craft, were likewise welcomed to the mic for readings, which occasionally exceeded four or five hours, extending well beyond midnight.

Caroline Bayard interprets this diversity of billing as a compression "within less than a decade [of] the major aesthetic explorations, concretism and post-modernism, which their older counterparts in Toronto and Vancouver had spent twenty years upon."[15] Differently put, this vast discrepancy of acclaimed and amateur writers implies that the curatorial ethos of these literary events was defined through a radical acceptance of varying professionalism, aesthetic difference, experimentation, and novelty. In fact, in the minutes from a meeting held on 15 September 1972, the board members collectively voted that "openness was a guiding spirit to VÉHICULE."[16] Openness can imply access, welcoming a diverse range of authors to share their work, but openness can also mean a lack of articulated and implemented intention as to the kind of work presented. One might think of Jo Freeman's writing from the 1970s about the dangers of organizational openness or structurelessness in relation to the Women's Liberation Movement. Freeman argues that a fetishization of "a myth of [structurelessness] ... becomes capricious" by denying institutional regulation, but not checking the power imbalances formed around charismatic individuals and informal elite groups either.[17] Regarding Véhicule, openness or curatorial structurelessness asserted itself as aesthetic promiscuity, in a way that both reaped the rewards of a superlatively supportive environment for writers to try out new literary approaches and outputs and led to the unquestioning acceptance of the new, as I illustrate in the next section.

Véhicule was uninterested in directing a unified expression of a certain school or movement or corpus of poetry. The collective was also indifferent to the notion of regulating or defining literary value. As articulated by Tom Konyves at a reading on 20 November 1978, the series focused more on "what is new than on what is good," purporting to support any literary experiment, disregarding the relevance of its final product.[18] In fact, in a series of essays about Véhicule and "Montreal English Poetry in the Seventies" more broadly – initially published in *Contemporary Verse 2* in 1978 and 1980 – Ken Norris admits candidly that there was a consciousness among the Véhicule Poets doubling as poetry reading curators that "some [work presented] was quite bad."[19] He continues, "The poet was never meant to create art objects that become 'literature' ... The Véhicule poets have no intention of blunting their own shafts so that the reader [or the listener] can play the part of the happy consumer and have a gay old time, or so that you, as critic, can have that secure feeling of being happily ensconced in the hallowed halls of Art."[20] In terms of an expression of curatorial agency, this is perhaps as close as Véhicule gets. For Norris, the purpose of Véhicule is to make its audience uncomfortable, to challenge their expectations of what "good literature" is, to present itself as a countercultural space, and to resist the sanctification of literary tradition, priding itself on an arguably anti-capitalist acceptance of all literary production instead.

Poets Retain Curatorial Agency: Performances of Sexual Liberation, Interdisciplinarity, and Radical Politics

To illustrate the range of work presented at Véhicule Art Inc.'s poetry readings, I zoom in from the overarching curatorial ethos of openness to the granular level of work presented by three poets. The first will exemplify the manipulation of curatorial openness to posture a countercultural stance through sexual liberation, most frequently translating in contemporary terms to an objectification of women through a performance of machismo. The second example presents an interdisciplinary crossover between the literary, visual, and performance arts, and uses Véhicule's curatorial openness to expand the definition of "the text" from the limits of the page to the canvas of the body. The final example typifies a handful of readers who employed the series as a platform for radical politics, representing timely yet timeless issues, such as feminism, Indigenous rights, and environmental conservation. It is important to note that none of these examples are from the Véhicule poets themselves, but rather from poets presenting work at an open reading. This distinction is important because it positions the three poets as guests presenting work, but not as invited, featured performers. They thus exemplify the difference between curatorial labour, which could have deliberately selected poets to present particular works, and Véhicule's curating, which offered an open space for literary experimenting but did not necessarily support or take aesthetic or ethical responsibility for the work. Even this lack of curatorial agency in relation to the poets in question has implications for the climate of the broader series, however.

When engaging with Véhicule Art Inc.'s poetry readings through its archival fonds decades after the fact, it is important to take the gaps and lacunae of the archive into account. Many events remained undocumented, even though additional recordings in individual poets' repositories or private collections are slowly being uncovered and might eventually challenge or expand this current research. However that may be, the audio recordings preserved in the archive today, and that I have had access to, provide an unsystematic and selective perspective for understanding the range of readings hosted. Documented communication with poets, posters, and other advertisements offer traces of events with authors that are missing from the audio archive itself.[21] Moreover, whether or not an event was recorded seems to have been the result of chance circumstance.

Nemiroff confirms that documentation of events was only "supplemented when borrowed equipment was available by videotape recordings"[22] and that once a Portapak video camera was purchased in the mid-1970s, interest had shifted toward the creation of video art over documentary audiovisual reels. This haphazard approach to audio recordings of Véhicule's complete literary scheduling limits contemporary access to the sound of the events, skews an understanding of Véhicule's curatorial agency away from the organizers themselves, and underlines the porous authority of the archive when viewed as a static window and soundtrack onto the past. I must acknowledge, then, that my analysis of curatorial agency in regard to Véhicule's billing is informed by this audio record, which is itself slanted toward the large group or "marathon" events that included predominantly younger, Montreal-based student poets rather than many of the smaller feature events of more established, visiting poets that I know took place, but cannot retrieve to hear again.

The first example, then, is from the Fourth Annual Poetry Marathon that took place on 20 November 1978. An open mic event, each poet was introduced only by name and then allowed to read work of their choosing for five to seven minutes. Here a poet identified as Dan Hastings reads, in his words, "a series of three poems and they're from the point of view of three different girls from the ages of pubescent to 16 or 18 or 20 maybe."[23] To paraphrase (with a content warning for misogyny and statutory rape), the first poem details a young girl puncturing her hymen with a tampon, while the second and third poems continue to develop imagery of pain, blood, and suffering on the part of the girl as she mutilates herself in order for her male lover to feel powerful when he is too weak to break her hymen and to break her in the process. What I would like to emphasize about this presentation – beyond the sexualized underage girl, the appropriation of a fetishized female voice, and the overt violence of objectifying female affect in the service of male ego – is simply the fact that it was given space to be performed.

Véhicule's articulation of curatorial agency as openness and uncritical acceptance meant that any sharing of creative output would be applauded – and this performance was, in fact, generously applauded by the crowd. While Véhicule's organizational mandate presupposes an oppositional stance to notions of canonicity or tradition, the live and archival sounding of Hastings poems operate as a tension between curatorial openness itself as a form of agency and the irresponsible voicing of abusive sentiments. In an enactment of countercultural sexual emancipation at a historical moment when constrictive social practices were being systematically reconfigured, Hastings is provided access to a platform and an audience to recite poetry which has aged from what was apparently deemed bold and experimental in the 1970s to an unredeeming expression of abuse and pedophilia.

The second case study is from the same Marathon reading of 20 November 1978, and features francophone poet Daniel Grimaud's "a body text and a bloody text," to quote his introduction.[24] The recording proceeds to play two minutes of silence, including a performance piece of self-mutilation framed as a non-standard cast of text; as Grimaud himself phrases it, "It's simple. All you need is one writer and people to watch ... you need razor blades ... and you just need to cut yourself." Tom Konyves, who MCed the event, was clearly very excited about Grimaud's contribution, explaining that he brought something truly new to the night. Konyves then continues to formulate a manifesto of novelty: "Somebody has to move forward, so I appreciate that there are people who make the effort to do the kind of thing you've just seen because we'll always have poets who will read what we call regular, ordinary, traditional poetry, but this is 1978, so you have to bear with the future."

Here curatorial openness unambiguously adopts the guise of the new, an inclusion of the experimental to the extent of futurity and as resistant to the past. Poetry is excised as a print-based medium and reframed through physicality and pain; in particular, poetry is lauded as a vehicle for the unexpected. Véhicule claims to stand for an acceptance of work which might seem unpalatable to an audience of its time as it reaches beyond the already experienced to alternative, raw expression that will find its true niche in years to come. This avant-garde rhetoric of Véhicule being ahead of its time adds a potential amendment to Véhicule's apparent lack of interest in canonicity and literary value, suggesting that while work presented might appear to be extravagant in the moment, it is expected to age into vintage.

The final example features work that embodies a very different expression of novelty in the form of feminist, political consciousness. At a reading from 5 March 1978, Janet Kask alludes to her job as a news reporter, reversing Konyves's call for newness by acknowledging that, politically speaking, there is "nothing new really under the sun."[25] She then continues to narrate the urgent innovation, at the time, of second wave feminism and her participation "in the surfacing of women's consciousness back in 1968." She declares poignantly that when "you've experienced your own revolution, you've experienced a kind of exhilaration that is very exciting ... a new kind of relationship that is going on between men and women at this point in history." The zeal that Kask expresses in her preamble is assimilated into and communicated through her poetry. In "Imitation to the Waltz," she pronounces, for example, "waltz with me soldier, generalissimo, king of hearts, show me this dance with all its paramilitary turns, civilized as lilies." Framing her reading in a discourse of women's rights activism and an acute awareness of current affairs, yet moderating her message with the lyrical indeterminacy of poetic imagery ("civilized as lilies"), adds an integrity of novelty to Kask's work that goes beyond salacious content, shock value, and transgression of generic borders.

Both Kask's poetry and sounded presence at the microphone rearticulate Véhicule's openness into a relevant critique of masculinist militarism, a discussion of feminist practice and gender equality, and ironically expose exactly the kind of sexist rhetoric represented in the example of Hastings's reading. While the politically engaged nature of her writing does not imply a reductively polemical or didactic performance, it is striking how she is able to embrace the curatorial agency provided to her by Véhicule and use it strategically in the service of a progressive and perennially pertinent subject. Kask's performance of openness still resonates now; hers is an expression of creative work that succeeds both in embodying its intended project and continuing to do so beyond the constraints and concerns of a single historical, sociological, and political moment.

As can be derived from the radically varying styles and approaches of the three poetry reading examples, Véhicule's curatorial tolerance of innovation for innovation's sake results in a shape-shifting literary forum, one that resists formal articulation beyond a kind of anarchic, deliberate lack of structure. There is, of course, less clearly acknowledged, subliminal curatorial messaging embedded in Véhicule's self-identification as an alternative, non-commercial, and interdisciplinary space, layering an implicit if unprescribed outline of the kind of work that would be welcomed. Openness as a structuring principle does not preclude curatorial agency and responsibility over the formulation of a public, sonic space either. Will Straw's exploration of the "scene" as "particular clusters of social and cultural activity [that do not specify] the nature of the boundaries which circumscribe them" is one way of visualizing an expansive substratum of curatorial savoir faire.[26] Nonetheless, Nemiroff insists that the "aesthetic direction ... [at Véhicule] was pretty much improvised,"[27] and Tayler reiterates that "[a]dministrative decisions at Véhicule Art were shaped by aspirations for a free space, just as this ethos encouraged the eclecticism of event programming."[28]

In other words, Véhicule's acceptance of poetry and poets uncircumscribed by any formal rules of engagement or formulated aesthetic, ethical, or political criteria – along with the overarching cultural and ideological climate of 1970s in North America – limited the series curators' concrete responsibility[29] to concerns of curating and shifted curatorial agency to the poets themselves. The idealized level of trust placed in the poets' individual preference in shaping not only the presentation of their own work but also, by extension, the accretive vision for the poetry reading and series as a larger, collective entity, points toward a conceptualization of the autonomy of art or poetry as independent from the interference of secondary direction or framing. Véhicule Art Inc.'s curatorial strategy is thus also suggestive of a space that negated the performance of literary value, as a shared assumption of transcendent evaluation, in favour of a default expression of an individual author's immediate aesthetic and ideological preference.

It is remarkable that this division of labour between curating and the curatorial – with the curator limited to overseeing the practical flow of the event and the poet controlling curatorial agency, the selection and presentation of creative material – is one that continues to be accepted by many, into the present, as synonymous with literary curation. Even as this hands-off curatorial stance is itself utopian and by default works to structure the sonic art form, which is the poetry reading, it is accepted by many as a form of resistance against curatorial control, against reproductions of larger-scale and directive institutional systems. This is a concern that formulates my continued research of poetry readings and curatorial agency, leading toward an attempted schematization of different modes of literary curation.

Acknowledgment

I would like to thank Ken Norris for reading and responding to a draft of this essay, and Endre Farkas, Tom Konyves, Claudia Lapp, Ken Norris, Stephen Morrissey, and Carole TenBrink for discussing Véhicule Art Inc. with me in a series of oral history interviews, which helped to inform my understanding of the reading series' importance to Canadian literary history.

NOTES

1 While it is contentious to generalize a definition for the recent and contemporary North American poetry reading – and while there is vast number of counter-examples to any norm – there is some precedent for a rote and depersonalized formal model that focuses on book sales and a performance of authorial presence rather than a consciously relational space of shared experience and

knowledge exchange. Karis Shearer and Erín Moure contend, for example, that the "current public readings paradigm ... might be called a flat model, largely driven by the administrative goals of the public readings program of the Canada Council for the Arts, which are two: to PROMOTE the work of writers ... to provide writers ACCESS to a live public audience." See Shearer and Moure, "The Public Reading: A Call for a New Paradigm," in *Public Poetics: Critical Issues in Canadian Poetry and Poetics,* ed. Bart Vautour, Erin Wunker, Travis V. Mason, and Christl Verduyn (Waterloo: Wilfrid Laurier Univeristy Press, 2014), 273. In conversation with Ashok Mathur, Smaro Kamboureli similarly notes, "we call such readings public, but they are really part of a promotional package ... consumption and commodification are a large part of public readings." See Mathur and Kamboureli, "On Public Readings and Pedagogy," *Open Letter,* no. 7 (Fall 2008):128. Lesley Wheeler prefers the term "academic poetry reading" and positions it as having "evolved largely from the model of the academic lecture rather than, say, the recital or exhibition, although it credentials the creative writer just as the latter activities serve as recurring qualifications for other artists employed by universities." See Wheeler, *Voicing American Poetry: Sound and Performance from the 1920s to the Present* (Ithaca: Cornell University Press, 2008), 128.

2 By the visual arts I imply an expansive field of knowledge creation and creative production, including the apparatus (and people involved in that apparatus) that generates new art, selects and presents it to a public, preserves it, and self-reflectively considers these different roles.

3 Hans Ulrich Obrist and Asad Raza describe a Western trajectory of the curator's role in the visual arts, starting with the Latin verb *curare,* already in circulation in ancient Roman times, as an act of caretaking for artworks and valuable objects; in the Middle Ages, curators were often priests occupied with archival labour, while the late eighteenth century saw the beginning of museum curators working to preserve, select, analyze, display, and arrange art, among myriad varying responsibilities. See Obrist and Raza, *Ways of Curating* (New York: Allen Lane, 2014), 25.

4 Carolee Thea, *On Curating: Interviews with Ten International Curators* (New York: D.A.P., 2009), 6.

5 Irit Rogoff and Beatrice von Bismarck, "Curating/Curatorial," in *Cultures of the Curatorial,* ed. Beatrice von Bismarck, Jörn Schafaff, Thomas Weski (Berlin: Sternberg Press, 2012), 22.

6 Diana Nemiroff, "A History of Artist-Run Spaces in Canada, With Particular Reference to Véhicule, A Space and the Western Front" (master's thesis, Concordia University, 1985), 171.

7 Felicity Tayler, "Linguistic Therapy c. 1973: Archival Traces from Véhicule's Press," in *CanLit Across Media: Unarchiving the Literary Event,* ed. Jason Camlot and Katherine McLeod (Montreal & Kingston: McGill-Queen's University Press, 2019), 198.

8 Ibid., 196.
9 Véhicule Art Inc.'s membership did, however, keep shifting and transforming over the years according to the organic conditions of life, as conflicts burgeoned, and people had to adopt different jobs and responsibilities of their own.
10 HA 367 – P027 Véhicule Art (Montreal) Inc. fonds, 1972–1983, Concordia University Archives, Montreal.
11 Nemiroff, "A History of Artist-Run Spaces in Canada," 124–5.
12 Ibid., 142.
13 Tayler, "Linguistic Therapy," 188.
14 As narrativized at length in Diana Nemiroff's "A History of Artist-Run Spaces in Canada," conflicts arose between different factions of the Véhicule Art Inc. members that stifled this initial efficiency.
15 Caroline Bayard, *The New Poetics in Canada and Quebec: From Concretism to Post-Modernism* (Toronto: University of Toronto Press, 1989), 111.
16 HA 367 – P027 Véhicule Art [Montreal] Inc. fonds 1972–1983, Concordia University Archives, Montreal.
17 Jo Freeman, "The Tyranny of Structurelessness," *Berkeley Journal of Sociology* 17 (1972–73): 157.
18 P027-11-0003 Véhicule Art [Montreal] Inc. fonds 1972à1983, Concordia University Archives, Montreal.
19 Ken Norris, ed., *Véhicule Days: An Unorthodox History of Montreal's Véhicule Poets* (Montreal: Nuage Editions, 1993), 15.
20 Ibid., 34.
21 A clinical research room at Concordia University allows me to view selected boxes from the truly substantial Véhicule repository. Only a pencil is permitted in the space and I must always wear white gloves, delicately paging through and observing folders of posters, photographs, typewritten and handwritten administrative notes, applications, and correspondence. The orderly nature of these institutionalized traces stand in contrast to the general ethos of Véhicule, but the quantity of boxes divided into folders subdivided into protective sleeves attests to more than a decade of administrative and creative activity. The audio recordings, with which I spend the most time, have been digitized from their original reel-to-reel technology, implying a mediated listening experience. All in all, I feel simultaneously excited about my investigation and unwelcome in the archive, as if my research will damage or destroy the precious remnants from half a century ago rather than helping to keep memory alive. I also experience my own listening as invasive, anachronistic, and an activity which I need to hone to a more humble agential position in relation to the past.
22 Nemiroff, "A History of Artist-Run Spaces in Canada," 149.
23 P0027-11-0003.1 Véhicule Art [Montreal] Inc. fonds 1972–1983, Concordia University Archives, Montreal.

24 P0027-11-0003.2 Véhicule Art [Montreal] Inc. fonds 1972–1983, Concordia University Archives, Montreal.
25 P0027-11-0009.2 Véhicule Art [Montreal] Inc. fonds 1972–1983, Concordia University Archives, Montreal.
26 Will Straw, "Cultural Scenes," *Loisir et société/Society and Leisure* 27, no. 2. (2005): 412.
27 Nemiroff, "A History of Artist-Run Spaces in Canada," 151.
28 Tayler, "Linguistic Therapy," 192.
29 Curating poetry readings at Véhicule Art Inc. was a collaborative venture, one which shared and shifted responsibility over the years. The first reading was organized on 24 June 1973 by Stephen Morrissey, Guy Birchard, and Artie Gold. Claudia Lapp formalized the reading series in fall 1973. From 1974 to 1975, Artie Gold and Endre Farkas took over, followed by Ian Burgess from 1975 to 1976. From 1976 to 1977, it was co-organized by Stephen Morrissey, John McAuley, and Robert Galvin. Tom Konyves concluded the series with the longest organizational stint from 1977 to spring 1983.

17

"Songs are so much more than songs"
An Interview with Dylan Robinson

Clint Burnham
TRANSCRIBED BY RAWIA INAIM

Dylan Robinson was scheduled to visit a graduate course that Clint Burnham was teaching in spring 2020 at Simon Fraser University (SFU). When this was interrupted by the COVID-19 pandemic, they conducted an interview on Zoom, including questions that Burnham had solicited from the students in the course.

Clint Burnham: Dylan, in your book, *Hungry Listening: Resonant Theory for Indigenous Sound Studies*, you mention the words of thanksgiving that Mohawk elders give on Haudenosaunee and Anishinaabe territories where Queen's University is situated, and I want to give some more here. First to you, for making time for our conversation when we're all under tremendous pressure from our employers, our universities, and our families, as we deal with this extraordinary pandemic. I also want to thank you for your generosity for passing on to the students so much from *Hungry Listening*. So, thank you on both counts, and thank you for writing this book; it's so rich, it gets me thinking, just to get my theory out of the way, of Theodor Adorno's essay on the regression of listening and psychoanalytic notions of the voice as object and the power valences of listening to soundscapes in our everyday life.[1] And I do like how you kick R. Murray Schafer to the curb at the start of your book. He's so venerated at SFU, as you know.

Dylan Robinson: Yes, it's true. Though I should also say that for all the necessary critique of the settler-colonial orientation of soundscape studies and compositional practice Schafer worked in, so much of my own formation as an artist, writer, and former student at SFU emerges out of a relationship with Schafer's work in inter-arts and soundscape traditions as well.

CB: Right, of course, right. It is worth remarking how you build into your book these "Event Scores," and in the first one, "xwélalà:m, Raven Chacon's Report," you write, "hear the word sound   scape / built upon the word landscape—"[2] The other day, when I was reading your book and I sent some quick message to you about me listening, it was early in the morning and the birds were chirping outside, and I sent that to you. Then later, I read where you talk about different listening to the landscape: if you're hunting, as compared to some leisurely activity of hearing birds in my little neighbourhood. There are so many weavings back and forth, but also in terms of what your book does with regard to the graduate course I am teaching and questions of reconciliation; the demand that settlers listen to the stories of survivors, the power structures, whereby judges, priests, or psychoanalysts listen, all that is thrown into new relief by your ideas of shxwelitmelh xwélalà:m. [Clint mispronounces]

DR: shxwelitmelh xwélalà:m; we'll work on it. [Dylan, laughing, corrects Clint]

CB: Okay, thank you.

DR: I'll have your whole class saying it by the end.

CB: Yeah. *Hungry Listening* calls for disciplinary redress and resurgent perception, analysis of structural refusal, and always a nuance of terminology, enriched not only by how you engage with such amazing and interesting examples as Peter Morin's and Tanya Lukin Linklater's performances and Jordan Wilson's territorial practice, but also your attention to critical, institutional, and auditory paradigms. All these things make this such an important book. But maybe, to start, we can look at some of those questions that my students sent. One of the first questions is:

I'd be interested to hear what Dylan has to say about the relationship between the performance of Indigenous music, such as a traditional welcome song, at institutional events, such as a university orientation or commencement, and the practice of performing land acknowledgements at these events, in relation to his idea of *spatial intersubjectivity*.

DR: Yeah, sure. It's an interesting question and there are a few different directions my answer would take depending on what is meant by a "welcome song." The kind of work such a song would do in this example is contingent on the specific song being sung, and the specific context it is presented in. It would mean something very different depending on who sings it, too, and where they are from. So, I'm not sure if there is a specific example that the student is thinking of, but it's a really important question for a number of reasons.

Firstly, the work that's often being done within welcome, institutional welcome, by universities, is of the kind – if it's done by an Indigenous person – that reminds settlers and other non-Indigenous folks the basic fact of whose land they are gathered upon. The primary addressees are settlers, non-Indigenous folks and "the university" in this context. The song, in a sense, like other welcome protocol, is a question: how will you proceed in the work you are doing today in relation with – and with accountability to – those who sing? But I wonder to what extent it is heard that way. Someone might say, you know, they're giving a welcome song, that's nice, they're being generous and extending welcome feelings. I do think such "welcomes" are often mis-heard as welcoming atmosphere, rather than the "Hey, you there!" of other kinds of address. So I wonder how the term "welcome song" already sets up the conditions for (mis-)interpellation.

But I think what is important in the question is also the way in which the student is referring to spatial subjectivity because in other instances those songs that Indigenous folks offer are not given for physical human presences – the audience and the attendants; they are given for our ancestors or for the land or for space itself. I talk elsewhere about this in terms of Indigenous languages offered at the beginning of events. I often speak in Halq'eméylem and begin a gathering or begin locating who I am with

Halq'eméylem, which is the language that Stó:lō people use and how we give welcome at home when we're in our communities, not because it's important from a perspective of linguistic sovereignty or asserting the fact of its vibrancy, both of which are important. Instead, I use it because I understand that action of speaking in Halq'eméylem as addressing my ancestors who are with me in whatever space that I'm gathering in. So it's important to think about the intersubjectivity of song – the relation between song and space – because this song's address might be oriented toward the lands, the waters, and other non-human presences of that space. We don't need to draw a line here between intersubjective relationships with so-called natural spaces. Perhaps the song addresses the walls, the floor, the ceiling, the lights – does it ask for an accountability there, too? There's a potential here, too. I'm really excited by the possibilities for thinking about how we, as Indigenous people, might create new songs that address non-human relationships or songs that address built environments, both the colonial and not, as doing a kind of work that is more than simply producing a song.

CB: Thank you. I was thinking of two things. In your book you talk about Musqueam/xʷməθkʷəy̓əm anthropologist Jordan Wilson and the work that he did for the *c̓əsnaʔəm the city before the city* projects – at the Musqueam reserve, at the Museum of Vancouver, but also at the UBC Museum of Anthropology, which is also on Musqueam land, of course – about the elders listening to each other and not just playing that game of waiting to get their thing in – not just what I have to say, but hearing what you're saying. (Wilson: "When one person was speaking, the rest of the group listened respectfully – as opposed to waiting for their turn to talk.")[3] But the welcoming is, if I can put it this way, weaponized by the university institutionally. I don't want to underestimate the agency of the group or the person doing the welcoming and what's going on in terms of intentionality and their subjectivity and what they're doing with their language in singing those words. You were talking about this in terms of speaking to the ancestors: the language as a living thing, all the histories of the recuperation of language. These conditions exceed any institutional intentionality to use welcoming and other land acknowledgments as a "get out of jail free card" for the university. Or when individual academics do those things in a good or shoddy way – those effects, however, cannot be predetermined.

The Métis lawyer Patricia Barkaskas, academic director of UBC's Indigenous Community Legal Clinic, came to our class as well. We were talking about things like the federal government's apology, and that even under the most instrumental forms we don't know where that's going to land, how that's going to be received by Indigenous people. I don't want to be too fancy or too dystopian about these possibilities. Also, I want to remember Marianne Nicolson, the Musgamakw Dzawada'enuxw artist, who talks about welcomes in the Kwak'wala language, and the welcomes were not saying, "You can stay here and extract our land."

DR: Well, there's also – and I talk about it in another section of *Hungry Listening*, on historical interaction between Indigenous and non-Indigenous people in Friendly Cove in Mowachaht/Muchalaht territory, where they are welcoming.[4] If I'm remembering correctly, the story is that they're actually going and getting the eagle down and welcoming Captain Cook's people to their lands because they understand this is a potential for trade. It's been said that the Nuu-chah-nulth repeated "ichme nukhta." Some say that the name, Nootka, comes from this phrase that was supposedly said to Cook's crew. But instead, what they're actually saying is "go around, our village is around the bay. Go around!" Of course, it wasn't heard that way. It was heard as, "Oh, this is the place that you are from."

CB: Right.

DR: I sometimes wonder about the word "Stó:lō" that we use to identify our twenty-six different communities along the Fraser River. "Stó:lō" actually means "river." We are Stó:lō not just because all of our communities are located along what is now called the Fraser River, but because everything we do is oriented in one way or another by the river. But, again, I imagine that early ethnographers that applied the term to identify our people because of the frequency they heard it spoken. It's funny in the case of Nuu-chah-nulth and Stó:lō that, first words, and frequent words become the names that stick, because if you applied the same logic to all nations and peoples it would likely not result in the same names of the nation-states we know today. There's something interesting about the assumption that the first words one would share in such an encounter would [be] the name by which one identifies the larger community. Wouldn't more practical things be shared? These are really interesting forms of misaudition based in settler-colonial logics.

CB: Ah, nice: "misaudition." Okay, another question about this talking around Indigenous listening resurgence, and to proceed from the intersubjective experience between the listeners and song life: would one be able to apply this intersubjective experience to Ayumi Goto and Peter Morin's "Hair," which is documented in *The Land We Are* collection? Goto and Morin write, "the drumbeats are writing. the drumbeats are living witnesses. living memory. writing a glimmer of the performance on their skins."[5] So how would you think of what Goto and Morin are doing under the terms you've developed in your book?

DR: For many Indigenous folks, this is a kind of everyday thing ... That is, it's possible to think of "drumbeats as living witnesses" as a kind of poetics that Morin works in to document his performance practice. But it's also quotidian in the sense of how Indigenous folks understand animacy, the life in and of the world. There is life to most everything. I think about conversations I've had with my friend Cheryl L'Hirondelle, a Cree-Métis artist and singer-songwriter, who talks about the way that Cree language brings life, which is a reason why one needs to be careful with the words one chooses. We want to make sure that we're animating the world in good ways, right? So, I want to say, yeah, a lot of Peter's work thinks about the animacy of what a Western museum would call "objects" and "artifacts" but that Indigenous folks understand as beings or ancestors, or having some aspect of life in their materiality. I've been thinking a lot these days about the museum as a carceral space. If that which museums are holding has life, then what they are keeping is life contained, incarcerated within these spaces. They are not just safekeeping objects but are maintaining a scenario where that life is not allowed to flourish.

AN INTERVIEW with DYLAN ROBINSON

CB: So, when you start talking about Tanya Lukin Linklater's work, and the discussion before then of museums keeping artifacts, objects on life support, and beyond ... they're not, on the one hand, allowed a chance to rest because they're always on display. Whereas, as I understand, say just for winter ceremonies in coastal nations, like the Kwakw<u>aka</u>'wakw, the mask and so on would be wrapped in a blanket and kept in a chest until it was brought out for another dance a year later and so on. And maybe after four seasons or five seasons, whatever, it would then be destroyed. This is from Kwakw<u>aka</u>'wakw carver and Chief Beau Dick's discussion of these things.

DR: Absolutely. Not treating life as interminable, you know? Understanding that beings need to pass on after a certain point because their work is done, or new work – or life – is needed. I think this is often a part of what Peter's work treats. I'm less familiar with Ayumi's practice. But Peter also mentions that the drumbeats *are* writing. I think that's really interesting because our songs are forms of knowledge – the ways in which we hold and continue our knowledge, historical documentation to the equivalent level of detail of a book. Perhaps it's actually better to say beyond what a book can do because songs hold not only the information but the feeling of that information. This is why, with the potlatch ban where winter ceremonies and longhouse work was made illegal, this was not just a banning song and dance as aesthetic practices, it was a banning of our primary form of historical documentation, of our forms of medicine, of our legal orders. Songs are so much more than songs. They are still songs – they don't cease to be songs, we can still think of their aesthetic qualities – but they do other things in the world. So, I like the way that Peter says that the drumbeats are the writing. Because we might conflate knowledge being carried by the linguistic content of a melody, rather than the rhythm. Of course, rhythm is so central to life – this is a pretty simple thing to say – but I like that way Peter emphasizes rhythm as knowledge. You can actually read and feel this in what Peter writes!

CB: Yeah, and just to stay with Peter's practice for a bit: in terms of his performance, or the collective performance that he was a part of at the church in London where an Inuit child brought back by Martin Frobisher had been buried ... Why do I remember Martin Frobisher's name? There is this colonial explorer's name there, you know, hardwired into my brain. At any rate, this sounds like an amazing performance, but also your writing of it seems to have a lot of care in it. And the nervous Anglican priest, who's trying every which way to sort of take no responsibility for the history and the legacy of this building that he's a temporary custodian for, but also representative of. And then his ... what's his remark about the response being, "Okay, as long as you can do it in your head"?[6]

DR: Yeah.

CB: You know, Peter was a student of mine twenty years ago at Emily Carr, so it's one of those cases we have where the student surpasses the professor, obviously. But he's had such genius in terms of how he takes what may seem like a very casual remark – the priest was just grasping at straws – and Peter makes that random comment the basis for the performance. So, the stick is not hitting the drum skin, I take it, right?

DR: Yeah, that's right.

CB: So, can you talk a bit about that – about the role of silence in that work, and how you're thinking about silence as something we listen to, or can't listen to, or whatever that means?

DR: I mean it's hard to speak about that work in terms of silence because my experience of it was *anything* but, even though to any onlookers – or on-listeners? – it was completely silent. So there is an important distinction in this work between what can be heard by the outside listener and what the participant or the subject performing, doing that work, hears. To anyone who happened to see the piece outside St Olaf's church in London, they would see the visual work: the drumstick striking the air above the drum. They would see a group of people walking. They would see a group of people holding a jar and putting their mouths up to the jar. But everything would be silent to them. But for myself as a participant in the event, it was very loud – the non-sound of the drumstick striking the air above the drum, there was something loud about that action. And singing into this jar: it increased the vibration of our voices reverberating with this jar as a resonating chamber. We felt our voices up against our skin, amplified. Then just the location, in this fairly busy public space – a lot of people were walking around and seeing this action. It felt like what we were doing was quite "noisy." So, it's important to question for whom something is silent, because, yes, for the priest it was silent literally, but for myself – and probably other participants – this was anything but.

CB: Yeah, perhaps silence or listening or not hearing flow back and forth between the actual and literal meanings of them, or metaphorical or conceptual ways of thinking about it.

Another question had to do with J. Martin Daughtry's work on the palimpsest, when you argue that this "work prompts further consideration of what it might mean for listening subjects to recognize our listening privilege and habits, and the responsibility of listening self-reflexively for our various – settler-colonial, heteronormative, patriarchal – tin ears."[7] Then the questioner asks if this work can be done alone, or if collaboration, dialogue, and communality are essential for recognizing "tin ears" syndrome.

DR: This is something that I have a couple of different answers for, and the first thing I should say is that these words "collaboration" and "dialogue" are words that often put me on edge. Since the end of the Truth and Reconciliation Commission, everything has been about collaboration and dialogue, and dialogue has been taken up by the state and institutions as an end in itself. That, in fact, there are instances where – and I think I gave an instance of this in the book – where dialogue is the thing that needs to be rectified. The problem in the first place wasn't that fact that, for example, violent video images of Inuit suffering are appropriated in a film by a Quebecois filmmaker. The problem was that the public didn't have an opportunity to talk about the use of these videos in the work. And so ...

CB: Yeah, you said, "To fix the problem, simply add dialogue."[8]

DR: Yeah, add dialogue and stir. So, I just wanted to note that those terms are things that put me on edge. I actually need to take a breath or more, to calm down and think about whether dialogue *is* what is needed. Sometimes that may be true. But I think for this particular question what I wanted to say is the opposite. That, in fact, for a critical listening positionality to occur, where one needs to begin is with oneself. This is something I've been working at with my students as well, really trying to identify those layerings of our individual positionalities, not as a static or reifying identity category, but as a practice. What is positionality when we think of it as perception, as something that we live and that orients the ways in which we are able to read and hear and see? It's hard work, but it's all work that we can do on our own and should be done on our own because I can't tell you or your students or anyone what your positionality is. Your lived experience of whiteness is very different from my experience of whiteness. So, we need to really become better attuned, I believe, to these layers and how these layers are in motion, in moments, and over the long term. Layers of our positionality are not static – they're not existing as a fixed thing over the course of our life or even in the course of a day, an hour, or a minute. I think it's important to have that beginning point to identify.

Firstly, how do we name those various aspects of our positionality and then name the ways in which they are forms of perceptual privilege and capacity? From this identification, perhaps we might better map our positionality in relation to specific listening acts or specific readings of things. If identifying positionality in layered, nuanced, and changing ways is the hard part, figuring out the kinetics of positionality is even harder alongside the movement of music and sound. But we also don't want to be overly deterministic about saying I am hearing "X" as such because I am a man or whatever it might be ... or I always hear "Y" sound in this way because I'm xwélméxw. It can easily slide into a kind of listening essentialism. I'm thinking about these forms of critical listening positionality as more of a hum or something that we can tune in and tune out in moments, that they can then deepen the ways in which we can start to identify our normative forms of listening. Because I don't also believe – and I try to make it clear in *Hungry Listening* – that we can't simply put on a listening filter in order to listen otherwise; we can't simply adopt a Cree, Inuit, Black, or xwélméxw form of listening. It's not possible and it's not what we should be attempting.

AN INTERVIEW with DYLAN ROBINSON

CB: Yes, thank you. Regarding "collaboration," "dialogue," and "communality": I think of when Sophie McCall has talked about how "collaboration" has these two meanings: working together but also being a traitor (in terms of World War II notions of the collaborator). She discusses collaboration in Greg Younging's *Elements of Indigenous Style* – such an important book. And this was taking up your idea of your critiques of inclusionary music and inclusionary performance, where Indigenous content fits in pre-existing structures. Tanya Tagaq – I think you quote her saying, "my voice would be used as an ingredient in someone else's stew."[9] So, the question sort of comes down to: how can these things change, do you think, the ways Indigenous singers, instrumentalists, and other performers take up space or restructure a musical event? Or, how would you imagine changing dynamics when it comes to Indigenous/non-Indigenous collaborations? I guess I would tag on to that if you want to talk about the *Against Hungry Listening* series that you curated, I suppose, at the Agnes Etherington Art Centre in Kingston?

DR: I think the problem, speaking in the most general sense, is around structural change. This is not a new thing in any sense. But what happens in inclusionary performance is that we don't even get to the beginning of what might be called structural change because the norms of the commission or the performance are so firmly embedded in classical music and new music, that they remain as the context in which all Indigenous performance must be made to fit within. The darkened concert hall, the conductor, the score as a way to transmit what should be played, applause. If we think about the ways that it might be possible to change these norms, this might then require that organizations or composers take a step back from what they think they are in the business of doing or in the business of offering, and identify the resources that they have to work with. Once those are identified, how might they be offered in such a way so that Indigenous artists are able to work with them, use them, or refuse them in ways that fit the cultural context of creation and performance?

If such an approach were to be taken, of not predetermining the end goal – the end outcome in terms of the place of presentation or the form of the presentation – then I think you might have some really exciting discussions and collaborations *beyond* mere inclusion. For example, what it might mean, if you think of our songs as forms of law-making, to use the orchestra as a resource to make new laws, to document history from an Indigenous model of doing so? How do we do that together? Or do we? It would allow things to just come together in a way where we're not saying, "We need a symphony," or "I want a public artwork," but starting from a different place entirely and beginning with, "We have this site," or "We have this orchestra as a resource. How would you like to use them?" It all involves taking a few steps back to think about new starting points and presumed end goals. And maybe sometimes we find that there isn't a synergy there, which is fine, too. The *Against Hungry Listening* series was – as the public programming series for the *Soundings* exhibition – a different take on that in the sense that it aimed towards providing space for artists, scholars, to guide a group of folks through listening to something. We would listen to the work together – a simple format actually. And then say, "What was that?" Not starting from the point that it was a song, of figuring out its structures and aesthetic qualities. We took as a given that the public experience of listening could be "doings" of different kinds. The presenter would often model how they heard the piece they were offering and how it intersected with their own positionality, but the conversation would turn in various directions to what the listening experience was.

CB: I heard Tanya Lukin Linklater speaking at the Indigenous summer intensive that Tania Willard ran at UBC Okanagan, where Peter Morin, Candice Hopkins, as well as many others visited, and I was there as a student. Tanya talked about a piece that she did at the Isabel Bader Centre for the Performing Arts in Kingston: a dance, a performance for an Inuit parka.

DR: Yes, that was her piece for the exhibition, *Soundings*.

CB: Ah, okay.

DR: And *Against Hungry Listening* was a public program within the *Soundings* exhibition.

CB: Right.

DR: So they are two different things.

CB: Yeah.

DR: Yeah. So, I can talk a bit about *Soundings*, if you want, because it is touring with Independent Curators International until 2023 at least, and will be in Vancouver at the Belkin Gallery at UBC. So this might be of interest to some of your students. *Soundings* is an exhibition that I curated with Candice Hopkins, who is Carcross/Tagish, and currently the senior curator of the Toronto Biennial. Candice and I extended an invitation to a number of Indigenous artists to create what I've been calling "art scores." These scores could take a variety of different forms: event scores which were a form used by Fluxus artists in the '60s and '70s, or object scores, instructions, videos, and an evolving number of forms as new commissions are realized. A starting point, for me at least, was a response to all the different kinds of recommendations offered by various commissions, from the Truth and Reconciliation Commission's ninety-four calls to actions to the recommendations from the Royal Commission on Aboriginal People.

In Canada, we are swimming in instructions and recommendations, mostly for institutions, about what needs to be done for redress to take place. But for me there is a lack in these calls to action of addressing the individual. So, a starting point for me was this question of how artists might offer instructions for actions to take place. A very direct action kind of thing. What do we want to take place? Who do we want to enact it? How can this happen through sound, but not exclusively through sounds in different kinds of performance forms? So, the exhibition started with thirteen art scores, but grew as it toured internationally in the coming years. In each of these locations on the tour, we've asked the gallery to commission at least one Indigenous or artist of colour to create a new instruction or score. This may be a visual artist, a composer, a poet, or any kind of artist, really. A number of the pieces are meant to be realized by the members of the public, but also by specific Indigenous performers and non-Indigenous performers that we bring in to have them perform.

CB: Great! Well, it looks like the time is rapidly closing, but Dylan I do want to thank you for having this time available for us and I hope your family is doing well and safe. I hope we can get your book launch happening whenever we're out of lockdown because I'm looking forward to that as well and I think a lot of people are. So, thank you very much for speaking with us today.

DR: You're welcome. It's nice to have the opportunity to do so.

Note: Thank you to Dylan for his time – including the time, months later, to edit the interview. Thank you to the students in the class – Michelle Allin, Jacob Goldbeck, Rawia Inaim, Matea Kulić, Amila Li, Saba Pakdel, and Kevin Spenst. Thanks as well to Rawia for the transcription and to Deanna Fong and Cole Mash for their interest in this interview for the book. – C.B.

NOTES

1. Theodor W. Adorno, "On the Fetish Character in Music and the Regression of Listening," in *The Essential Frankfurt School Reader*, ed. Andrew Arato & Eike Gebhardt (New York: Continuum, 1985), 270–99.
2. Dylan Robinson, *Hungry Listening: Resonant Theory for Indigenous Sound Studies* (Minneapolis: University of Minnesota Press, 2020), 107.
3. Ibid., 70.
4. Ibid., 119–21.
5. Ayumi Goto and Peter Morin, "Hair," in *The Land We Are: Artists and Writers Unsettle the Politics of Reconciliation*, ed. Gabrielle L'Hirondelle Hill and Sophie McCall (Winnipeg: ARP Books, 2015), 176.
6. "Morin asked the minister, 'what would you allow us to do in the church in order to honor this child?' To this, the minister responded, 'you are welcome to have a ceremony in your head.'" Robinson, *Hungry Listening*, 65–6.
7. Ibid., 60.
8. Ibid., 18.
9. Ibid., 8.

"Misaudition"

Kate Siklosi

If we listen closely, everything sings. In response to the interview between Dylan Robinson and Clint Burnham, "misaudition" investigates the idea that there is life, memory, and sound all around us, even in tired skeletons of leaves, peeled ribbons of birch, or snow-burnt reeds that lace a lake in early spring. In their discussion, Burnham and Robinson reference Ayumi Goto and Peter Morin's argument that "drumbeats are living witnesses, living memory, writing a glimmer of the performance on their skins." This work brings together the skins of decaying organic found materials, as well as reverberated fragments from Robinson and Burnham's interview, found paper, ink, watercolour, and Letraset. Collaborating with these found organic materials fosters a poetic of humility and deep listening; reanimating the memory of these items in concert with new sounds, shapes, and stories calls us into a practice of closer listening with our environment so we may hear, bear witness to, and act on their songs of beauty and warning.

– Kate Siklosi
8 April 2022

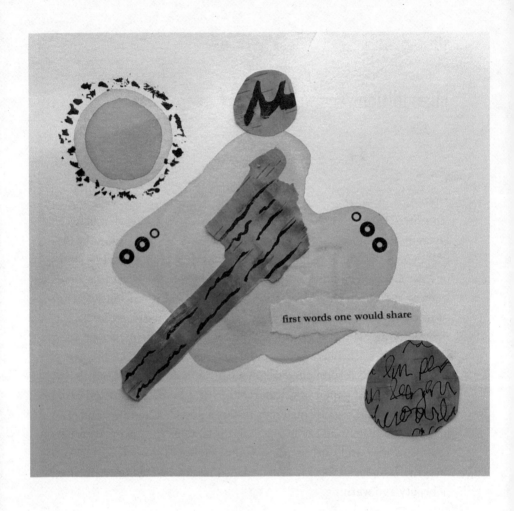

FIGURE 18.1 • "Misaudition 1," 2022, visual piece by Kate Siklosi in response to Dylan Robinson's interview with Clint Burnham, chapter 17

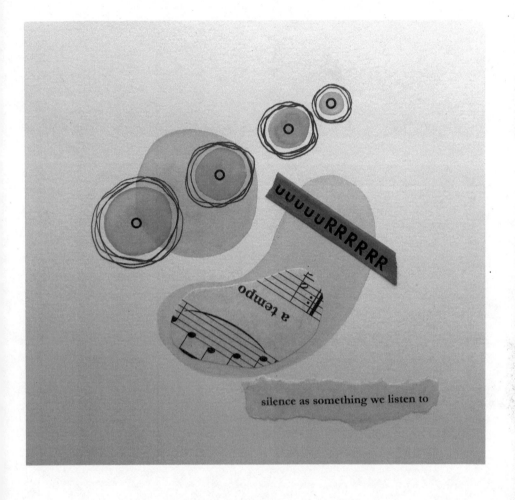

FIGURE 18.2 • "Misaudition 2," 2022, visual piece by Kate Siklosi in response to Dylan Robinson's interview with Clint Burnham, chapter 17

FIGURE 18.3 • "Misaudition 3," 2022, visual piece by Kate Siklosi in response to Dylan Robinson's interview with Clint Burnham, chapter 17

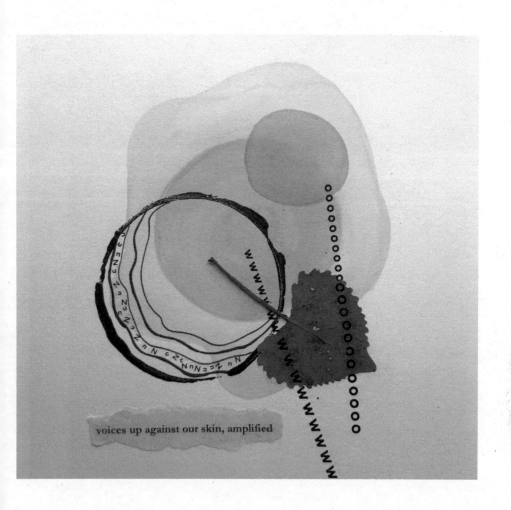

FIGURE 18.4 • "Misaudition 4," 2022, visual piece by Kate Siklosi in response to Dylan Robinson's interview with Clint Burnham, chapter 17

CONTRIBUTORS

Jordan Abel (University of Alberta) is a queer Nisga'a writer from Vancouver. He is the author of *The Place of Scraps*, *Un/inhabited*, *Injun*, and NISHGA. Abel's most recent book is *Empty Spaces*.

Mathieu Aubin (HEC Montreal) is a research affiliate in Concordia University's English department. His SSHRC Insight Development project Listening Queerly Across Generational Divides recuperates contributions of queer artists and activists to literary communities and social movements, and his work on queer listening was awarded the F.E.L. Priestley Prize. You can find his published work in *Canadian Literature*, *Journal of Canadian Studies*, and *ESC*.

Oana Avasilichioaei is a poet, sound performer, and translator based in Montreal. She has created many performance/sound works that mix electronics, ambient textures, noise, and vocal play, published six collections of poetry hybrids, including *Eight Track* (Talonbooks, 2019), and written a libretto for a one-act opera (*Cells of Wind*, 2022).

Clint Burnham (Simon Fraser University) was born in Comox, which is on the unceded traditional territory of the K'ómoks (Sahtloot) First Nation, centred historically on kwaniwsam. He teaches English literature at SFU.

Wayde Compton writes poetry, fiction, non-fiction, and graphic narrative. He teaches in the faculty of Creative Writing at Douglas College in New Westminster and Coquitlam, BC.

Klara du Plessis (Concordia University) holds a PhD in English literature from Concordia University. Her research focuses on curatorial structures in the context of twentieth-century and contemporary Canadian poetry, and she develops a research-creation component called Deep Curation. Klara is also a poet.

CONTRIBUTORS

Tawhida Tanya Evanson is a poet, author, producer, and Ashik from Tiohtià:ke/Montreal. Her collections include *Bothism* and *Nouveau Griot*, and her novel *Book of Wings* won the 2022 New Contribution Literary Prize. With a twenty-five-year practice in spoken word, her concert film CYANO SUN SUITE premiered in 2023. She moonlights as a whirling dervish.

Deanna Fong is the literary editor at the *Capilano Review* and a SSHRC-funded researcher at Concordia University, where she directs the digital archive of Canadian poet Fred Wah (fredwah.ca).

Corey Frost (New Jersey City University) is the author of *The Worthwhile Flux*, a collection of performance texts, and several other books. His published essays include "Border Disputes: Spoken Word Poetry, Community, and Identity." He is associate professor and chair of English at New Jersey City University.

Nicole Brittingham Furlonge (Columbia University) is a scholar, and professor of practice and director of the Klingenstein Center at Columbia University. Furlonge is the author of *Race Sounds: The Art of Listening in African American Literature* (University of Iowa Press).

El Jones (Mount Saint Vincent University) is a spoken word poet, educator, journalist, and community activist living in African Nova Scotia. She was the fifth Poet Laureate of Halifax. In 2016, El was a recipient of the Burnley Allan "Rocky" Jones human rights award for her community work and work in prison justice.

Cole Mash (Okanagan College) is a poet, scholar, teacher, and community arts organizer. As a spoken word poet, he has performed poetry locally and nationally for over ten years. His critical work has been published in *Scholarly and Research Communication* and the *SpokenWeb Blog*. His creative work has been published in CV2, *Pinhole Poetry*, *Forget Magazine*, and the *Eunoia Review*, and his lyric-memoir, *What You Did Is All It Ever Means*, was published with broke press in 2021. He is a founding member and the executive director of Kelowna-based non-profit arts organization Inspired Word Café, teaches English and Creative Writing at Okanagan College, and is a PhD candidate in SFU's English department.

CONTRIBUTORS

Erín Moure is a Canadian poet and translator with eighteen books of poetry, a co-authored book of poetry, a volume of essays, a book of articles on translation, a poetics, and two memoirs. She has translated or co-translated over twenty books of poetry and her work has received the Governor General's Award twice, the Pat Lowther Memorial Award, the A.M. Klein Prize twice, and been a three-time finalist for the Griffin Prize and three-time finalist in the USA for a Best Translated Book Award (Poetry). Her latest books are *The Elements* (2019) and *Theophylline* (2023), both from House of Anansi Press.

Tracie Morris (University of Iowa) is a poet, scholar, and performer. Her installations and performances have been featured at many national and international museums and galleries, and she has performed, researched and presented poetry, performance art, acting, academic addresses, talks, and live shows with music in over thirty countries. Her most recent poetry collection is *Hard Kore: Poems/Per-Form: Poems of Mythos and Place* (2017) and the expanded edition of her creative non-fiction work *Who Do With Words* (2019).

Reese Muntean is a visual storyteller and PhD candidate at the School of Interactive Arts and Technology at Simon Fraser University. Her research interests include the collaborative development of ethnographic media projects, including tangible computing, 3D scanning, and virtual reality applications focusing on cultural and environmental sustainability.

Deanna Radford is a Canadian poet, performer, and artist whose work examines how the tool of communication intertwines with our most personal and emotional connections. Her prose writing has been published with *Arc*, *Broken Pencil*, *Herizons*, *Musicworks*, *MUTEKmag*, and her poetry has been published by *Art + Wonder*, the *Capilano Review*, *carte blanche*, *Free City Radio's Art & Social Change*, the *Headlight Anthology*, *Occulto Magazine*, *Vallum*, and others.

Dylan Robinson (University of British Columbia) is a (Stó:lō/Skwah) artist, curator, and writer. From 2015 to 2022 he was the Canada Research Chair in Indigenous Arts at Queen's University. His book *Hungry Listening* (University Minnesota Press 2020) examines Indigenous and settler-colonial practices of listening and

CONTRIBUTORS

was awarded best first book for the Native American and Indigenous Studies Association, Canadian Association for Theatre Research, and the Labriola Centre American Indian National Book Award. His current research project xoxelhmetset te syewa:l, Caring for Our Ancestors, involves working with Indigenous artists to reconnect kinship with Indigenous life incarcerated in museums.

Faith Ryan (University of Victoria) (she/her) is a queer, disabled settler of European descent living on the lands of the ləkʷəŋən and W̱SÁNEĆ peoples. She is an educator who received her MA from the University of Victoria in 2021. Now pursuing a high school language arts certificate, she is a self-advocate who keeps dreaming of a world outside of ableism.

Eric Schmaltz (Dalhousie University) is the author of *Borderblur Poetics: Intermedia and Avant-Gardism in Canada, 1963–1988* (University of Calgary Press) and *Surfaces* (Invisible Publishing), editor of *Another Order: Selected Works of Judith Copithorne* (Talonbooks), and co-editor of *I Want to Tell You Love* by bill bissett and Milton Acorn (University of Calgary Press). From 2018 to 2019, he was a SSHRC Postdoctoral Fellow in the Department of English at the University of Pennsylvania. He is an assistant professor of Canadian literature at Dalhousie University.

Erin Scott (University of British Columbia Okanagan) is a poet and performer. She is a founding member of Inspired Word Café, a literary arts non-profit offering open mics, poetry slams, and workshops in the Okanagan Valley. Her first chapbook, *Atrophy*, won the John Lent Poetry Prose Award 2019 and was published by Kalamalka Press in 2020. Her second chapbook, *to make it whole again*, was published in 2021 with broke press. Her performance work has been hosted on stages across Canada.

Jordan Scott (University of British Columbia) is a poet and children's author. His debut children's book, *I Talk Like a River* (illustrated by Sydney Smith), was a *New York Times* Best Children's Book of 2020.

CONTRIBUTORS

Karis Shearer (University of British Columbia Okanagan) is an associate professor in English & Cultural Studies at UBC's Okanagan campus, where her research and teaching focus on literary audio, the literary event, the digital archive, feminist data studies, book history, and women's labour within poetry communities.

Kate Siklosi's work includes *Selvage* (Invisible 2023), *leavings* (Timglaset 2021), and six chapbooks of poetry. Her critical and creative work has also been featured across North America, Europe, and the UK. She is the curator of the Small Press Map of Canada and co-founding editor of Gap Riot Press.

prOphecy sun is an interdisciplinary performance artist, queer, movement, video, sound maker, and mother of three. Her practice celebrates conscious and unconscious moments and the vulnerable spaces of the in-between in which art, performance, and life overlap. Her recent research has focused on ecofeminist perspectives, co-composing with voice, objects, surveillance technologies, and site-specific engagements along the Columbia Basin region and beyond.

Felicity Tayler (University of Ottawa) is the management librarian at the University of Ottawa. She is an occasional visual artist and exhibition curator, and has published scholarly writing related to literary archives.

INDEX

Abdillahi, Idil, 187
Abel, Jordan, 5, 8, 9, 21, 41, 47, 55, 59, 74, 80, 243; *Injun*, 5, 74, 215–17; NISHGA (book), 21, 213, 216, 220–2, 228–9, 231
ableism, ableist, 92–4, 96, 98, 100, 100–1n3, 238, 284; culture of, 96, 101n5; ear, 15, 90–1, 93–5, 100–1n3, 101n5; ways, 95, 100–1n3
absence, 68, 70, 84–5, 111, 113, 196, 206, 209, 240, 273
absolutism, 20, 141, 161; aesthetic, 19
access: generating, 18, 98–9; physical, 97
Accessible Canada Act, 94
access intimacy, 92, 97–8
access listening, 100
acousmatic: question 7, 96, 100, 198; horror, 235; signifiers, 242. *See also* Eidsheim, Nina Sun
acousmatization, 197–8. *See also* deacousmatization
acoustic ecology, 63–4; environmentalists, 63
activism, activists, 22, 98, 100n1, 176, 186–7, 274, 277, 278, 283; disability, 92; political, 176; sex-work, 284n2; white, 103n35; women's rights, 333
Adorno, Theodor, 240, 339
advocacy, 170, 199
aesthetics, 17, 78, 92, 98–9, 122, 204, 235, 257; categories, 201; crip, 90; moralism, 63; promiscuity, 329; qualities, 345, 350
Africa, 159, 172; West, 20, 180, 182, 184

African: cultures, 72; music, 45; practice, 188; sculpture and sounds, 203
African American: ethics, 148; music, 52
Agamben, Giorgio, 206–7
agency, 19, 97, 109, 112, 115, 151, 153, 332, 342
Ahmed, Sara, 85, 93, 274
Alamilla Boyd, Nan, 275
amplification, 19, 33, 68–9
Anderson, Fortner, 210
Anger, Kenneth, 246, 262, 264; *Scorpio Rising* (film), 246, 261–4
appropriation, 13–14, 52, 332; conceptual, 213, 216, 228
archives, archivists, 57, 92, 174, 247, 249, 266, 274, 290, 296, 311, 331, 337n21; institutional, 290; personal, 289–90; rogue, 322n6
Armatrading, Joan, 262, 264
ArQuives, 251, 253, 271
artifacts, 132, 344–5
arts: community, 141, 165, 168, 193; folk, 201; oral, 189; outsider, 142, 201; popular, 201; visual, 12–13, 19, 107, 137, 144, 324–5, 336nn2–3
Astonishment Tapes, 292, 297, 313
Aubin, Mathieu, 10, 22, 250–2, 254, 258, 261, 268, 271, 274
Audatala (magazine), 302
audio collage, 249, 268
audio recording, 45, 48, 198, 290, 304, 331, 337n21; equipment, 328; technologies, 65, 197

INDEX

Austin, J.L., 138–40, 151–3, 156, 158
authenticity, 71, 80–1, 201, 305, 313, 317
avant-garde, 151, 196, 200–5, 314; movements, 202–3; poetry, 201, 204, 243
Avasilichioaei, Oana, 4, 18, 46, 59, 105–16, 119, 321; *Cells of Wind* (opera), 18, 105–6; *Eight Track*, 110–11, 114

Baker, Ron, 304
Bakhtin, Mikhail, 209
Ball, Hugo, 83, 151
Barbeau, Marius, 229–30, 232
Barkaskas, Patricia, 343
Basquiat, Jean-Michel, 143
Bayard, Caroline, 328
Bearchell, Christine, 264–6; *Proud Lives: Chris Bearchell* (film), 250, 265, 274
Beattie, Rachel E., 250–1, 253–6, 258, 265, 271, 273–4, 278
Beineix, Jean-Jacques, 242; *Diva* (film), 242
Belcourt, Billy-Ray, 219
Bell, Gabe, 267
Berne, Patty, 103n35
Bernstein, Charles, 158, 316
Betasamosake Simpson, Leanne, 218–19
Bier, Suzanne, 21, 233; *Bird Box* (film), 21, 233–4, 237–42
Birmingham School, 202–3
Birney, Earle, 295
Bishop, Claire, 193
Black: art, 142, 152, 188; Canadian writers, 8; community, 124, 166, 170; culture, 52, 56, 68–9; English, 211n5; experience, 52, 149, 153, 156; influence, 152; liberation, 188; music, 17, 52, 65, 68; oral culture, 202, 205, 208; oral tradition, 8; poetry, 174, 180; Speculative Arts Movement (BSAM), 164; women, 171, 188, 205
Blackburn, Paul, 306
Black Mountain poets, 294, 306
Blackness, 156, 174, 187
Blaser, Robin, 297, 312–13
Bloom, Harold, 200
Bociurkiw, Maryusa, 260, 262, 271
bodies, bodily: experience, 40, 80; particular, 18, 42–3; people's, 81, 101n5, 107; racialized, 67; speaking, 38
Body Politic (magazine), 265–7
Bowering, George, 23, 172, 180, 200, 288–9, 291–5, 303, 307–9, 320
Braith, Melanie, 228
Brand, Dionne, 179
British Columbia, 3, 9–10, 17, 22, 56, 62, 72, 163, 257, 277
Brown, Elspeth, 252, 271
Bullock, Sandra, 237–40; *Bird Box* (film), 21, 233–4, 237–42
Bunting, Basil, 314
Bures Miller, Georges, 119
Bürger, Peter, 203
Burnham, Clint, 13, 21, 23–4, 339–40, 353
Butler, Judith, 200, 246, 268
Butling, Pauline, 277, 308, 320
Butterick, George, 309
Bynner, Witter, 306

Cage, John, 116, 158, 208, 306
Camlot, Jason, 27, 271, 286, 290, 295, 299, 307, 317
Canada Council, 189, 327, 335–6n1
Canada's Lesbian Liberation Movement, 22
Canadian literature (CanLit), 7–9, 20, 177, 190, 225; history, 249; tradition, 76n23

INDEX

Cannon, Marcia, 264
Cannon, Steve, 145
Capilano Review (magazine), 311–12
capitalism, 17, 62, 63, 98, 100–1n3, 141, 143, 190, 235; late, 193; monetary, 141. *See also under* colonial
Cardiff, Janet, 119
Care Moore, Jessica, 187
Carroll, Lewis, 81, 83
Castricano, Jodey, 286, 291
Cave Canem (collective), 159
Cavell, Richard, 71
Cavell, Stanley, 238
CBC (Canadian Broadcasting Corporation), 294, 308, 321
Certeau, Michel de, 126
Chambers, Justine, 123. See also *Choreography Walk*
Chariandy, David, 179
Chion, Michel, 197
Choreography Walk, 122–5, 129
cinema, 237–9; cinéma-verité, 40
Clare, Eli, 103n35
Claxton, Dana, 234
Cleary, Emma, 69
Coalition for Lesbian and Gay Rights of Ontario (CGLO), 266
codes, 73, 236, 261, 263; linguistic, 72; musical, 247
Cole, Desmond, 179, 187
Coleridge, Samuel Taylor, 174
collaboration, 43, 66, 83–4, 107, 129, 136–7, 153, 157, 161, 347, 349; artistic, 38; ear, 20, 161; relationship, 19, 136
collaborators, 19–20, 106, 136–7, 157, 271, 349
collage, 24, 246–7, 261; format, 249; space, 270; temporal, 134
Collis, Steve, 84
colonial, 7, 70, 234, 242, 342; capitalism, 90, 99, 100–1n3; interests, 230

colonialism, 8, 14, 71, 101n5; legacies of, 8, 74
commodification, 143, 335–6n1
communal, communality, 207, 276, 347, 349; bonds, 284; relations, 122, 134
communication, 6, 15, 18, 90–9, 100–1n3, 101n5, 102n13, 102n16, 108, 243, 246; creative, 67; disability, 94; methods, 103n31; oral, 197, 199; styles, 92, 100–1n3, 103n31
communicators, 90, 93, 97–8, 102n11, 102n16, 103n31; disabled, 91, 101n5; and listener, 93
communities: artistic, 13, 144; disability, 91–2, 100n1; lesbian, 247, 274, 280–1, 284; literary, 23, 166, 172, 280; poetic, 196, 200, 203–4, 210
community: building, 22, 206, 249, 268–70, 282, 287; formation, 20, 199–200, 206, 209, 231; of listeners, 90
composers, 17, 105, 108, 118, 303, 349, 351
composition, 15, 18, 20, 63, 108–9, 114, 131, 309–10; of soundscapes, 63, 123
Compton, Wade, 15, 17, 51–63, 65–6, 68–74, 75n7, 75n13, 75n15; "Performance Bond" (poem, CD), 62, 70–2; "The Reinventing Wheel" (poem), 60, 73–4; turntablist poetics, 17, 65, 69, 74
Constante, Lena, 106
consumption, 90, 100–1n3, 335–6n1
Contact Zone Crew (collective), 17, 62, 65–8, 73
continuity, 22, 168, 223
Copjec, Joan, 237, 239
copyright, 73–4, 287, 313; issues, 292; law, 313; restrictions, 322n6
Corradi Fiumara, Gemma, 14
Coulthard, Glen Sean, 71

INDEX

COVID-19, 22, 163, 168, 273
Cowan, T.L., 197, 247
creation, 33, 66, 165, 178, 287, 325, 331, 349
creative output, 324, 332; creative works, 5, 7, 17, 19, 36, 213, 324, 334; process, 51
creators, 9, 63, 74, 183, 324
Cree, 348; language, 344
Creekside Park (Vancouver), 123–4, 128, 133
Creeley, Robert, 294, 304–8, 314–15
crip, 90, 99, 100n1; aesthetics, 90; futures, 89, 100n1; time, 92, 102n11; voices, 90, 99
critiques, 139, 142, 145, 175–7, 188, 243, 256, 276, 281, 340, 349; decolonial, 234; post-male gaze, 239; of slam, 175
Crompton, Constance, 252, 271, 273–5, 285n5
cultural: activity, 334; capital, 73, 322n6; heritage, 166; policies, 71; practice, 93; production, 5, 11, 265–6
culture: counter, 193, 332; dominant, 201, 263; of expertise, 188; lesbian feminist, 249; literary, 197; settler, 7
cultures, 13–14, 55, 65–6, 89, 96, 100–1n3, 142, 175, 188–9, 203, 291; mass, 201, 203
curatorial, 325–6, 335; agency, 23, 325–7, 330–2, 334–5; ethos, 329–30; openness, 23, 330, 332–3; strategy, 326, 335; studies, 324
curators, 22, 324–5, 335, 336n3, 351
cutting (DJ technique), 75n1

Dada, 81, 82–3, 151, 152, 203
Dance in Vancouver. See *Choreography Walk*
Daughtry, Martin, 347
Davey, Frank, 23, 289–90, 292, 294, 297–9, 315, 320

Davidson, Michael, 288
Davis, Bruce, 118
Davis, Miles, 145, 152
deacousmatization, 198
decolonial, decolonizing, 21, 24, 189, 241; subject, 236
de Couto, Jason, 7, 51, 53–4, 56, 57, 59, 60, 62, 65
De Kosnik, Abigail, 322n6
de Man, Paul, 243
deracination, 198
Derrida, Jacques, 116, 235, 294
Dick, Beau, 345
Dickstein, Jonathan Michael, 239
diegetic, 258, 264
Dietrich, Marlene, 238, 240
différance (Derrida), 15
difference, 4–5, 9, 15, 93–4, 107–8, 188, 191–2, 197, 303, 308, 313, 327, 330; aesthetic, 329; communicative, 93; vocal, 15, 94, 102n16
differentiation, 6, 305
disability, 35, 46, 89, 92–5, 102n16; culture, 96, 98–9; mental, 95; politics, 89; rights movement, 100n1
Disability Justice, 97, 103n35
Disability Justice Collective, 103n35
Disability Visibility Podcast (*DVP*), 89–90
disabled people, 14, 89, 92, 97–100, 100n1, 102n11; speech, 91–2, 95, 101n5
discomfort, 29–30, 79, 102n16, 207, 217, 256, 281
discourses, 9, 94, 160, 189, 209, 241, 246, 333; monster's, 241; public, 10
discrimination, 173; ableist, 94; trans, 274
disembodiment, 69, 111, 198
disgust, 93, 95
dislocation, 65, 69

· 368 ·

INDEX

disruption, 99, 239
dissonance, 7, 155, 159, 276
diversity, 71, 109, 328; of voices, 109
DJ Kentaro, 54
DJ Krush, 68, 74
DJs, 51, 55–6, 58, 72, 75n1; practices, 73; techniques, 62, 65
Doane, Mary Ann, 238–40, 241; *Femmes Fatales*, 238–9
documentaries, 84, 257–8, 274–5, 278–9, 283–4, 331
Dorn, Ed, 299, 304, 306–7
Drobnick, Jim, 118
drum, 185, 206, 210, 241, 251, 346
drumbeats, 344–6, 353
Duncan, Robert, 294, 299, 302, 304, 308, 313
Dunning, Brian, 66–7, 72
du Plessis, Klara, 22–3
dysfluency, 4, 81–2, 99; and speech, 101n5

editing, 38, 106, 111, 191, 258, 261, 265, 270, 312; choices, 265; glance-object, 239; process, 249; retroactive, 249; work, 303, 320
educators, 20, 155, 186, 219
Eidsheim, Nina Sun, 7, 96–7, 103n31, 198, 211n5; *The Race of Sound*, 7, 96, 198. *See also* acousmatic: question
elite, elitism, 55, 141–2, 215
elitism, elitist: aesthetic, 20; artistic, 141; criteria, 200; literary, 325
embodiment, 16, 23, 27, 29, 31, 37, 55, 114, 123, 157, 197
Emmett, Richard, 303
emotion, 85, 93–5, 209, 240
engagement, 8, 119, 122, 127, 129, 156, 158, 178–9, 325, 327, 334; authentic, 157; conscious, 18; creative, 133; ethical, 227; kinesthetic, 133; methodological, 118; sensory, 6, 122–3, 133
English, 105, 108–9, 152, 164, 189, 301; literary canon, 13
entanglement, 68–9, 73, 96, 132
ephemera, ephemeral, 8, 34, 60, 119, 129, 180, 201, 298
Epstein, Rachel, 260, 271, 278–81
erasure, 13, 85, 174
Estep, Maggie, 145
ethics, 5–6, 17, 73, 85, 115, 136–7, 161, 226–7, 241; of collaboration, 137, 157, 161; of listening, 234, 236; of ownership, 73; post-human, 19
ethnicity, 198, 203–5
ethos, 17, 20, 23, 312, 326, 334, 337n21
Europe, European, 8, 150, 152, 180; culture, 188; high art, 152; ideas, 187
Evans, Steve, 307
Evanson, Tawhida Tanya, 8–9, 15, 163–5, 167, 170, 172–3, 179–81, 183–6, 190, 192, 193, 196, 206, 210
exchange, 40–1, 46–7, 131, 141, 161, 179, 239, 278, 312; conversational, 38; sensorial, 128–9; symbiotic, 122; written, 28
exclusion, exclusionary, 20, 64, 89–91, 141, 173, 200–1, 206; practices, 65; of sound, 64
experience, lived, 98, 167, 268, 274–5, 278, 283, 301, 348
experimental: forms, 8; poet, 137, 145; writers, 8
experimentation, 8–9, 182, 326, 329; aesthetic, 23; literary, 62, 329; poetic, 65

False Creek, 124
Farkas, Endre, 327, 338n29
FAWN Chamber Creative, 105–6
feminism, 274, 330; second wave, 262, 333; white, 256, 281–2

INDEX

feminist poetry, 180; practice, 333; publishing, 260, 275, 279; theory, 234, 255
Ferlinghetti, Lawrence, 297
fidelity, 11, 16, 31, 159
films, 234–43, 246–8, 250–1, 254–5, 258–9, 261, 263–6, 273–5, 277–8, 280, 284, 285n5, 298, 300; feature-length, 250; first, 241, 254, 257; gay, 246; lesbian feminist, 250; short, 137, 254. *See also* lesbian liberation films
Filreis, Al, 307
Finn, Ed, 239
Fireweed (magazine), 266–7
FitzGerald, Maureen, 260, 271, 278–9
fitzpatrick, ryan, 86
flow, 11, 50, 64, 66, 124, 129, 131, 133, 187–8, 261, 311
fluency, 18, 77–8, 90, 94, 102n16; normative, 81; verbal, 79
Fluxus (art movement), 351
Fong, Deanna, 10, 16–19, 21, 27–8, 30, 43, 50, 65, 68, 77, 105, 119, 136, 138, 213, 236
forms: expressive, 10, 133; literary, 40, 199, 324; oral, 14, 45
Foucauldian, 235, 237
Fourth Annual Poetry Marathon (1978), 331
fragmentation, 51, 62, 66; of sound, 62
framework, 28, 42–3, 98, 103n35, 129; conceptual, 42, 137; movement building, 103n35
Freeman, Jo, 329
Fritsch, Kelly, 96, 98–9
Frobisher, Martin, 345
Frost, Corey, 20, 173
Frye, Northrop, 71
Fulton, Warren Dean, 57
Furlonge, Nicole Brittingham, 4, 19–20; collaborative ear, 20, 161; *Race Sounds* (book), 4, 156

Gable, Clark, 238
Galvin, Robert, 338n29
gay, 143, 263–4, 284n2, 329; liberation, 253, 263, 265–6, 271
gaze, 21, 118, 124, 233–5, 237–9, 241–2; male, 234, 239; settler, 234; veiled, 238, 241
gender, 94, 198, 204–5, 262, 273, 275, 290; binary, 94; identities, 273–4
genres, 11, 58, 110, 114, 146, 177, 180, 182, 206, 208, 214; of music, 263; oral-based, 5; poetic, 199
Gilbert, Gerry, 287, 292, 296
Ginsberg, Allen, 289, 297, 299, 305; *Howl*, 289, 297; "Wichita Vortex Sutra" (poem), 305
Girouard, Scott, 250, 271
Glazner, Gary, 208
Glennie, Evelyn, 158
Glück, Louise, 138
Gold, Artie, 327, 338n29
Goldsmith, Kenneth, 28, 30–1, 49n3
Goto, Ayumi, 344–5, 353
Grimaud, Daniel, 332
griots, 180, 181

Haley, Alex, 66, 68, 74; *Roots* (novel), 66
Halfe, Louise, 227
Hall, Stuart, 201
Hallett, Carla, 302
Halq'eméylem (language), 341–2
Hamraie, Aimi, 96, 98–9
Hannah-Moffat, Kelly, 106
Hannigan, Lee, 286, 291
Hastings, Dan, 331–3
hearing (sense), 158, 231
hegemony, 33, 141; political, 5
heteronormative, 274–5, 347
Higgins, Dick, 151
High Park Literary Festival, 75n7
Hindmarch, (Gladys) Maria, 294

INDEX

hip hop, 52–3, 55, 65, 142–3, 145, 181, 184, 208; culture, 55; roots, 205
histories: activist, 277; Canadian queer, 273; collective, 249, 275, 282; lesbian, 275, 278; literary, 289–90; women's, 280
Hogan's Alley, 124
Holman, Bob, 208
horror, 21, 234, 242; acousmatic, 235
Höstman, Anna, 105
Howe, Fanny, 113
Huelsenbeck, Richard, 151
humanities, 95, 132, 148, 161; digital, 186
Humanities Data Lab, 253, 271
Hume, Christine, 160
Huovinen, Inez, 300
Huse, Peter, 118

identity, 66, 69–72, 98, 100n1, 179–80, 182, 191, 196, 198–200, 204–10, 216, 218–19, 267, 269–70; Canadian, 71; cultural, 70, 72; expression of, 199, 206–7; racial, 198; vocal, 198
ideological, 139, 204; affinities, 202–3; climate, 334; preference, 335
ideology, 94, 204, 257; post-identity, 204
improvisation, 8, 19–20, 80, 129, 190, 328; musical, 160
inclusion, 20, 97, 173, 206, 333, 349
Indigeneity, 21, 216, 218, 222
Indigenous artists, 349, 351; communities, 9, 125; culture, 8; languages, 83, 341; music, 341; nations, 253; peoples, 7, 342–3; performance, 349, 351; rights, 330; song, 100–1n3; writers, 8, 216
Inspired Word Café, 10, 165, 168, 193
institutional, institutions, 9, 12, 149, 214, 223, 266, 271, 347, 351; cultural, 215, 261, 263, 266; economies, 143; regulation, 329

intentionality, 111, 325–6, 342
interactions, 6, 10, 12, 17, 64, 69, 94–5, 97, 128, 132, 157, 161; bodily, 123; historical, 343; problematic, 140; textual, 4
interdependence, 96, 103n31, 133
interdisciplinarity, 38, 122, 165, 214, 330
intergenerational, 22, 256, 275, 281; bridges, 276, 283; conversations, 255–6, 281; dialogue, 249, 268, 276, 281–4; trauma, 21, 223, 226
interpellation, 236, 341
interpretation, 24, 103n31, 113; strategies of, 243; of voice, 97
interrogation, 6, 60, 79, 81–2
intersection, intersectionality, 14, 64, 73, 89, 94, 103n35, 123, 126, 137, 157, 186
intersubjective, intersubjectivity, 342; activity, 18; experience, 344; sound practices, 23–4
interventions, 172; acoustic, 61n2, 65; radical, 277; therapeutic, 102n16
interviewees, 11, 29, 46
interviewers, 14, 29
interviews: in print, 11; process, 30; space, 31, 33–4; subjects, 265
Inuit, 345, 347–8, 350
isolation, 32, 136, 231, 250, 274, 324
iterability, 289, 294
iteration, 10–11, 256, 282
iterative process, 48
Itter, Carole, 38, 288, 321

Jackson, D.D., 151
Jameson, Fredric, 242
jazz, 65, 152, 158, 203, 304, 307
Joans, Ted, 208
Jones, El, 8, 9, 15, 20, 163, 196, 199–200, 202, 205, 207–8
Jones, Keith, 99
Jones, Reed, 179

INDEX

Joplin, Janis, 262, 264
Joseph, Miranda, 200
justice, 6, 176, 238; social, 164, 175

Kafer, Alison, 100n1, 102n11
Kahn, Douglas, 29–30, 44
Kamboreli, Smaro, 7, 335–6n1
Kanngieser, Anja, 99
Kant, Immanuel, 238
Kask, Janet, 333–4
Kearns, Lionel, 297, 305, 310
Kellough, Kaie, 8
Kelowna (BC), 10, 163, 165, 194, 308; community, 178
Kentaro Ide. *See* DJ Kentaro
Keteku, Ian, 184
Killjoy's Kastle (installation), 255–6, 281–2; structure, 255–6, 281–2
Kirkpatrick, Bill, 89–90
Kiyooka, Roy, 59, 287, 289, 291, 296, 300, 311
knowledge, 14, 92, 99, 100–1n3, 102n11, 127, 219, 237, 246, 263, 284, 345; creation, 336n2; exchange, 335–6n1
Koizumi, Maya, 301
Konyves, Tom, 327, 329, 332, 338n29
Krasinski, John, 21, 233, 235; *A Quiet Place* (film), 21, 233–5, 239–43
Krip-Hop, 90
Krip-Hop Nation, 99
Kubrick, Stanley, 158

LaBelle, Brandon, 6
labour, 14, 18, 32, 34–6, 68, 73, 78, 83–4, 90, 187, 190, 325; archival, 336n3; collaborative, 98; creative, 17; curatorial, 330; division of, 260, 335; emotional, 78; feminized, 32; gendered, 287; mutual, 94
Lacan, Jacques, 21, 233–4, 239, 242

Lacanian, 21, 233–5; argument, 234; gaze, 237; psychoanalysis, 237; subject, 234
Lang, Fritz, 240
language: coding, 186; poetic, 7, 70, 112; written, 11, 17
Lapp, Claudia, 327, 338n29
Latta, John, 307
law, 188, 267, 315
layering, 43, 66, 133, 334, 348; polyrhythmic, 45; of voices, 66
layers, 32, 68, 80, 159, 216–17, 223, 304, 348
learning, 44, 50, 92, 94, 98, 159, 178, 229, 256, 260, 289; oral, 189
Lee, Dennis, 70
Lemon, Ralph, 136–8, 312–13, 319
Lennix, Harry, 150
lesbian, 246, 254–5, 262, 266, 282; collectives, 274; liberation communities, 280. *See also Killjoy's Kastle*
Lesbian and Gay Liberation in Canada project, 253, 271
Lesbian Liberation Across Media (LLAM), 10, 22, 250, 268–9, 273–80, 283–4
lesbian liberation films, 22, 250, 254, 268, 273–5
lesbian organizations, 255, 261; Lesbian Organization of Toronto (LOOT), 261–5
Leveroos, Rob, 123
Lewis, Talila, 101n5
LGBTQ2+, 274, 278; activists, 276; communities, 268, 274–6, 281–4; debates, 274
L'Hirondelle, Cheryl, 344
liberation movements, 276; lesbian, 250, 257, 274–5, 281–2
libraries, university, 254, 295

INDEX

Lingis, Alphonso, 206
listening, 21, 33, 159, 243, 283; active, 172, 178, 237; acts of 15, 348; attentive, 14; close, 26, 30; critical, 43; intentional, 4; intersubjective, 20; normative, 100–1n3
listening practices, 15, 33, 99, 102n16, 156, 268–9, 287, 289; appropriative, 6; default, 6; ethical, 42, 161; self-reflexive, 18
literary: events, 23, 278, 286, 324–5, 329; exceptionalism, 17; resistance in Canada, 9; value, 8, 219, 326, 329, 333, 335
LLAM. *See* Lesbian Liberation Across Media
logic, 21, 42–3, 74, 213–14, 234–6, 241, 270, 343; extractive, 236; resistant, 74; settler-colonial, 344
LOOT. *See under* lesbian organizations
Loveless, Natalie, 214
Lukin Linklater, Tanya, 340, 345

MacKenzie, Bridget, 303
manipulation, 81, 86, 330; of language, 81
Margaret, Sebastian, 103n35
marginality, 143, 204, 327
marginalized people, 202, 204
Marlatt, Daphne, 23, 38, 287–90, 292–5, 300, 308, 312, 318, 321
Marxist analysis, 35
Mash, Cole, 10, 19–20, 27, 136, 138, 163, 165, 196
material conditions, 21, 96, 276–7; footprint, 33; meaning, 290; postbody, 69; product, 36
materiality, 10, 12, 17, 24, 83, 344; forensic, 24
Mathur, Ashok, 51, 59, 335–6n1

Maud, Ralph, 295
MC, 55
McAuley, John, 327, 338n29
McCall, Sophie, 349
McFadden, David, 299
McGowan, Todd, 237
McGregor, Hannah, 249, 271
McLeod, Dan, 310
McLeod, Dayna, 209
McLeod, Lateef, 90, 99
McMurray, Darcy, 123
McNeilly, Kevin, 57
McWhorter, John, 211n5
media, 17, 51–2, 87, 89, 91, 107, 112–14, 242, 250, 254, 259; analog, 258; archaeology, 242; ecology, 239; formats, 8, 289; globalized, 52; public, 315; social, 141, 180, 240, 272; tour, 85, 87
mediation, 19, 80, 196, 216, 246; digital, 5
medicine, narrative, 172
meditation, 7, 16, 19, 126, 184, 231
memory, 128, 189, 220, 261, 276, 280, 287, 308–9, 316, 337n21, 353; living, 344, 353; public, 278; writerly, 290
metaphors, 4, 79, 88n1, 100–1n3, 157, 199, 209
methods: citational composition, 246; collaborative, 18; for listening, 91–2; therapeutic, 77
mic, open, 6, 23, 141, 143, 172, 178, 194
Michigan Womyn's Festival, 262–4
Middleton, Emma, 250, 271
mimesis, 261, 263
Minden, Robert, 288, 302
Mingus, Mia, 92, 97–9, 103n35
mix, mixing, 55, 57–8, 65–6, 68, 72–4, 75n1
mobility, 12; issues, 35; restrictions, 283

· 373 ·

INDEX

modes, 7, 48, 58, 109, 112, 172, 182, 318, 324, 326, 335; autocratic, 109, 168; dominant, 17; patriarchal, 167; of poetry, 20; settler-colonial, 21
monsters, 235–6, 239–42
Montreal, 27, 58, 116, 209, 221, 253, 277, 286, 300, 306, 326–7
Moore, Leroy, 99, 103n35
Moores, Margaret, 246–7, 261, 263–4; *Labyris Rising* (film), 246–7, 250, 254, 261, 263–5, 274, 285n5
Moreton, Judy, 262
Morin, Peter, 241, 340, 344–6, 350, 353
Morris, Tracie, 15, 19–20, 38, 107, 136, 138–9, 141, 143–4, 146–7, 149, 151, 153, 160, 181, 229, 235
Morris, Wesley, 235
Moten, Fred, 138, 139–40, 153, 156, 159
mother, motherhood, 31, 42, 165, 167, 191, 309
Moure, Erín, 116, 164–5, 167, 173, 177, 183, 193, 286, 290–1, 311–12, 335–6n1
movies, 202, 209, 250, 254, 264, 298
Mullen, Harryette, 160
multiculturalism, 71–2
Multiculturalism Act, 71
multimodal, 4, 17, 41; practice, 62
multiplicity, 7, 9, 17, 22, 66, 109, 133, 198
Mulvey, Laura, 234
Muntean, Reese, 6, 18–19; *A Small Piece of Sky* (performance), 6, 19, 122–3, 126, 129–30, 134
Murakami, Sachiko, 216
Murch, Walter, 317
museums, 300, 342, 344–5; curators, 336n3; public, 324; studies, 325
music: improvisatory, 300; inclusionary, 349; instrumental, 51, 67, 250, 259, 261, 268, 271; synthetic, 64
Musqueam, 123, 342
myths, 95, 98, 152, 329

Nancy, Jean-Luc, 206
Nasca Lines, 114–15
nationalism, 17, 62, 74; literary, 70
National Slam, 175
nations, 70, 123, 343; coastal, 345
nation-states, 9, 71, 344
Navas, Eduardo, 268
Nemiroff, Diana, 326–7, 331, 334
neoliberalism, 143, 183, 237, 247
New York, 145, 149, 151, 208
Ngai, Sianne, 281
Nicolson, Marianne, 343
Ning, May, 250
Nisga'a: community, 231; culture, 229–30
Nock, Samantha, 225–8
noise, 19, 63–4, 73, 91, 108, 133, 296, 347; music paradigm, 17; pollution, 63, 118
normalcy, 91, 94, 100n1, 100–1n3, 102n16
norms, 90, 349, 335–6n1; cultural, 203
Norris, Ken, 327, 329–30
nostalgia, 55, 64, 250, 255, 280–1
notation, 4, 310, 314

objects, 93, 144, 146, 148, 224, 233–4, 240, 242, 336n3, 339, 344–5; cultural, 21, 243, 351; personal, 278, 283; physical, 52; remixed, 12; sonic, 5; textual, 224
objet petit a (Lacan), 242
Obrist, Ulrich, 336n3
OCR (optical character recognition), 31, 49n3
October Crisis, 326
O'Driscoll, Michael, 236
Olson, Charles, 294, 304, 308–10, 312, 314–15; *Causal Mythology* (lecture), 295, 312
Ondaatje, Michael, 317

openness, 14–15, 20, 23, 122, 325–7, 329–30, 332, 334
oral: accounts, 275; artifact, 198; culture, 13–14, 188–9, 199; history, 10, 13, 22, 38, 224, 247, 274–5, 283–4, 287, 312, 318–19; and literature, 9; traditional, 14; traditions, 14, 20, 180, 182
orality, 4, 11, 14, 170, 189, 199
organizations, 253, 257, 260, 349; community-art, 193; lesbian liberation, 258; non-profit, 119
Orlandersmith, Dael, 146

page poetry, poets, 71–2, 147, 183, 205
pandemic, 10, 165, 196, 216, 268, 274, 283, 339. *See also* COVID-19
pareidolia, 66–7, 70, 72
Park Hong, Cathy, 204
parody, 175, 207–10; self-, 209
Patchen, Kenneth, 307
pedagogy, 153, 155, 159, 189, 213, 305
PennSound, 49n3, 295, 306
Perdomo, Willie, 145
performance: art, 57, 145, 330; live, 66, 123, 215; literature, 199; poetry, 183, 200, 208; practices, 23, 122, 183, 344; studies, 13, 324; technologies, 17
performative utterance, 140
performativity, 55, 147, 160, 197, 205, 207; of spoken word, 20
perlocutionary, 139n1, 153–4n1
pheneticization, 15, 60, 67, 75n13
Philip, M. NourbeSe, 74
philosophy, 153, 156
photographs, 114, 222, 228, 275, 314, 337n21
photography, 115–16, 128, 197
physicality, 16, 43, 78, 80, 90, 289, 333
Pico, Tommy, 214
Piepzna-Samarasinha, Leah Lakshmi, 103n35

Pietri, Pedro, 208
Pink Type, 266–7
pitch, 4, 305; gender-nonconforming, 93
Pluth, Ed, 241
podcast, 10, 22, 51, 65, 89–90, 92, 235, 246–50, 269, 271–2; audio collage, 248, 269
Poe, Edgar Allan, 139–40, 155, 229
poems: breath, 310; bus, 307; experimental, 137; oral, 170, 316; visual, 13, 24; voiced, 305
poésie pure, 209
poetics, 3–4, 79, 82–4, 142, 144, 146, 289, 294, 302, 304–5; open source, 73–4; postmodern, 314
poetic voice, 147, 197–8; individual, 71
poetry: communities, 23, 200, 204; conceptual, 30, 211n13, 315; readings, 208, 287, 292, 297, 309, 330–1, 335; slams, 144, 173, 178, 202, 208–9
poets: beat, 142, 203, 208; young, 173, 291, 304
Poggioli, Renato, 202–3, 206
poiesis, 122–3, 133–4, 147
political correctness, 256, 282
politics: citation, 246, 250, 268; crip, 90, 100n1; racial, 20; radical, 330
Pollak, Nancy, 276–7
polyvocality, 19, 68, 274
positionality, 15, 43, 86, 94, 96–7, 348, 350; critical listening, 24, 42–3, 348
Potrebenko, Helen, 78
Pound, Ezra, 298, 316
power: dynamics, 128, 200, 280; imbalances, 7, 35, 329; structures, 81–2, 98, 280, 340
practice: aesthetic, 213, 345; art, 163–4, 166–7, 181, 191, 193–4; contemporary, 132, 233; creative, 11–12, 22, 215, 219; poetic, 165, 186,

224, 286, 288; political, 16–17, 164; resistant, 47, 213–14; social, 262, 277, 332. *See also* listening practices; performance: practices
practitioners, 5, 14, 64–5, 183, 325
Pratt, Mary Louise, 66
Press Gang (collective), 251, 256–8, 260, 265, 274, 276, 278–80, 282–3; members of, 274–5, 278, 282; Publishers, 274
prOphecy sun, 6, 18, 123; *A Small Piece of Sky* (performance), 6, 19, 122–3, 126, 129–30, 134
Prusic, Elvis, 298

queer, 23, 101n5, 103n35, 257, 265, 269, 275; communities, 14, 22, 246, 274, 276; histories, 274, 276
quiet, 63, 84, 113

racialization, 12, 21, 216
racism, 17, 23, 32, 71–2, 74, 94, 140, 150, 155, 229, 236
Radford, Deanna, 11, 16, 28, 29, 50, 136
Rankine, Claudia, 160
rap, 45, 65, 205
Rault, Jasmine, 247
rawlings, angela, 86
Raza, Asad, 336n3
reading: events, 23, 286; series, 306, 325–6, 328, 338n29
recognition, 34, 67, 71–2, 100, 101n5, 102n16, 203
Reconciliation Commission on residential schools, 8, 21, 237, 347, 351
recordings, 66, 86, 242, 287, 289, 308–9, 311, 331; amateur, 295–6; reel-to-reel, 8, 23, 242, 291, 299; video, 57, 196, 198, 246, 248
relationality, 6, 24, 170, 324
remediation, 10, 19, 246, 249, 290

repetition, 159–60, 215
representation, 11, 80, 89, 112, 197, 202, 228, 236, 262, 325; artistic, 18; non-binary, 273; non-hierarchical, 13; textual, 9
research, 35, 110, 116, 168, 215, 228, 287, 331, 335, 337n21
research-creation, 119, 214
residential schools, 227–9, 237; intergenerational survivors of, 229, 231
resistance, 4, 7, 9, 23, 168–9, 243; collective, 73; linguistic, 81; literary, 9; political, 5, 24, 81, 213
resonance, 7, 9, 12, 19, 118, 157, 159, 243, 301, 303
Resonant Practices (conference), 213
response: bodily, 35, 288; creative, 228; patterns, 129; visceral, 129; vocal, 157
reverberation, 39, 110, 112, 321
rhythms: collective, 129; daily, 128; human, 69; musical, 68
Riddle, Emily, 219
risk, 39–40, 64, 139, 156, 207, 229, 237, 247–8
Robinson, Dylan, 6, 15, 23–4, 33, 39, 42–3, 93, 100–1n3, 236, 241, 339–41, 353; *Hungry Listening* (book), 6, 15, 33, 42–3, 47, 100–1n3, 236, 339–40, 343, 348–50
Rodgers, Tara, 33
Rogoff, Irit, 325
Romania, Romanian, 105–7
Roque Ramírez, Horacio N., 275
Rose, Tricia, 45
Rosner, Mireille, 123, 130
Ross, Becki, 262–3, 271
round table, 22–3, 286–8, 290–1; discussion, 286; proceedings, 10
ruptures, 45, 62, 65, 71, 82
Ryan, Faith, 6, 15, 18

samples, sampling, 51, 65–8, 72–4, 75n7
Sanchez, Sonia, 152
Sankofa, 192
Sayers, Jentery, 318
Schafer, Murray, 6, 17, 63–6, 70, 73, 118, 339–40
schizophonia, 64–5, 69
schizophonophilia, 51, 61n2, 63, 65
Schmaltz, Eric, 17
scholarship, 6, 18, 35, 196, 214–15, 247, 289, 294
Schwartz, Michelle, 251–7, 271, 273–5, 282–3, 285n5
Schwitters, Kurt, 151–2, 157–8; *Ursonate* (performance), 55, 151–2, 157–8
scores, 22, 106, 129, 132–3, 176, 261, 349, 351
Scott, Erin, 20, 163, 196
Scott, Jordan, 18, 28, 30, 41, 47, 88n1, 90, 99, 102n16, 213, 220; *blert* (poetry volume), 4, 79–83, 88n1; *Lanterns at Guantánamo* (poetry volume), 81, 84–5, 115
scratching, 62, 66, 68, 75n7
Scream in High Park Literary Festival, 75n7
screenings, 253–4, 257, 274–5
self, 44, 70, 78, 168, 171, 178, 270; reflexivity, 10, 177, 237
sensibilities, 54, 144, 179
sensitivity, 29, 44, 47
settler-colonialism, 70, 94, 213, 347; forms, 7; structures, 21
settlers, 9, 42, 70, 93, 100–1n3, 218, 234, 340–1
sexism, sexist, 23, 32, 140, 205, 327, 333, 327
Shakespeare, William, 38, 140–1, 144–5, 149–50, 152, 158, 309; *Taming of the Shrew*, 140, 149

Shearer, Karis, 22, 227, 280, 286–7, 290, 295, 301, 321, 335–6n1
Sholette, Gregory, 143
Siegler, Karl, 312
Signal+Noise Media Art Festival, 66–7
signals, 19, 73, 89, 95
signifiers, 83, 236, 262; acousmatic, 242
Siklosi, Kate, 13, 24, 69, 353
silence, 3, 7, 24, 64, 70, 85, 241, 288, 303, 332, 346–7
Simmonds, Millicent, 236
Simon, Vida, 116
sincerity, 209–10
singers, singing, 105–6, 147, 185, 191, 206, 341, 349
Sir George Williams University Reading Series, 287, 290, 299
slam, 19–20, 143–5, 172–80, 202, 208; communities, 20, 178; poetry, 10, 20, 144–5, 180, 199–202, 205; scene, 142, 145, 151, 178, 205
solidarity, 15, 82, 206, 242, 247, 253, 269; in poetics, 82; work, 15, 269
Somé, Malidoma, 172; *Ritual* (book), 172
Somers-Willett, Susan, 180, 201; *Cultural Politics of Slam Poetry* (book), 85, 93, 180, 201
sonic, 8–9, 12–14, 17, 74, 160; aesthetics, 92; approaches, 8; compositions, 20, 68, 157, 261; elements, 19, 123, 223; practices, 5, 9, 16; works, 12, 22, 24
sound: acousmatic, 84; ambient, 22, 87; archives, 234, 236, 291; coded, 236; collective, 9; crip, 91; diegetic, 242; lesbian liberation print, 257, 259; non-diegetic, 258; non-sound, 346; practitioners, 10, 14
sound poetry, sound poets, 13, 33, 82, 147, 149, 151, 216–17

INDEX

sound recordings, 22–3, 57, 86, 312, 315–16
soundscapes, 6, 62–4, 66–7, 70, 73–4, 87, 268, 339
sound studies, 6, 18, 183
soundwalks, 118–19, 122–3, 127, 129, 132–3
space: acoustic, 6, 64, 67; dialogical, 22, 275, 282–3; personal, 273, 277–8; physical, 168, 276, 278; polysonic, 68; polyvocal, 71; social, 18, 66, 277, 284; sonic, 268, 334; virtual, 268, 278, 283–4
speakers: attached, 321; disabled, 18, 89–90, 102n11
speech: disability, 93; nonnormative, 18, 91–2, 95, 99; patterns, 18, 45, 91
SpokenWeb, 250, 253–4, 268, 271–2, 285n5, 286, 290; Podcast, 236, 249, 271–2; Symposium, 9, 77; team, 271. *See also* Camlot, Jason
spoken word: albums, 164–5; artist, 146, 164, 181–5; communities, 200, 203; performance, 164, 196, 207–9; poetry, 99, 180, 206; scenes, 204, 206–7
Stanley, George, 307
Starnes, Jason, 3, 9, 77, 83, 84
Stein, Gertrude, 158, 160, 316
Sternberg, Josef von, 238, 240; *The Devil Is a Woman* (film), 240; *The Scarlet Empress* (film), 238, 240
storytellers, storytelling, 146, 180–1
Straw, Will, 334
stutter, stuttering, 3–4, 18, 28, 77–83, 90–1, 96
subjectivity, 28, 39, 100–1n3, 133, 225, 233, 236, 341–2
Sufi, 166, 184–5
suicide, 233, 237, 239
Swanson, Raegan, 264, 271, 273, 274
syntax, 11, 80, 108, 310

Tagaq, Tanya, 8, 349–50
Tallman, Kenny, 307
Tallman, Warren, 286–7, 291–2, 294, 301, 309
tape recorder, 197, 291–2, 294, 296–7, 304, 306, 308, 310, 319–20
tape recordings, 242, 286, 294, 314, 317; magnetic, 286, 289, 291
tapes, 227, 287, 289–96, 298–9, 301, 303, 306–9, 312–15, 317
Tayler, Felicity, 10, 22, 250–1, 254, 268, 271, 273–5, 281–2, 285n5, 326–8, 334
teachers, teaching, 44, 137, 142–3, 153, 156–7, 214, 219, 305, 307
technologies: digital, 32, 55, 197; electroacoustic, 64–5, 73; recording, 9, 33, 287–8, 318; sound, 17, 23, 69, 73
TEMiC (Textual Editing and Modernism in Canada) (summer institute), 286
temporality, 10, 114, 132, 290; retroactive, 220
testimony, 224, 226–9, 237
Thakur, Gautam Basu, 239
theory, 12, 56, 202–3, 234, 237, 243, 339; critical race, 18; decolonial, 234; psychoanalytic, 239
Thesen, Sharon, 23, 289–90, 292–3, 295–6, 312, 315–16, 318–19
Thomas, Audrey, 295, 320
Thomas, Dylan, 297
Thomas, Leon, 152
Thompson, Marie, 63–4
timbre, 3–4, 43, 94, 96, 99, 100–1n3, 197
tin ear, 100–1n3, 101n5, 347
TISH (poetry community), 23, 294, 296–7, 320
Toronto, 105, 253, 257, 260, 265–6, 271, 277, 279, 281, 298, 308
Torres, Edwin, 152
TransCanadas (conference), 223

INDEX

transcriber, 26–30, 33–4, 36, 38–40, 42–3, 46, 48
transcription, 4, 10, 16–17, 22, 26, 28–31, 34–7, 40–3, 46–8, 49n3, 223, 312–13, 318, 320; process, 30–1, 38, 44–5, 224
translation, 19, 48, 108, 153
trauma, 85, 225–6, 233, 235, 237–8
Travassos, Almarinda, 246–7, 261, 264; *Labyris Rising* (film), 246–7, 250, 254, 261, 263–5, 274, 285n5
Truth and Reconciliation Commission, 8, 21, 237, 347, 351
turntables, 51, 53, 57–9, 65
turntablism, 17, 50, 54, 68–9, 73. *See also under* Compton, Wade
Tyler, Mike, 146
typesetting, 266–7
typewriter, 31, 319–21
Tzara, Tristan, 81–3, 151

UBC, 56–7, 286, 292, 294, 304, 306–7, 313–14, 342, 351; Okanagan, 22, 286, 290, 350
United States, 70, 176, 326
universities, 57, 193, 271, 339, 341
Urbaniak, 74
utterance, 147, 151, 160, 198, 209

Vancouver, 122–3, 175, 178, 185, 257–8, 260, 274, 276–7, 279–80, 306, 312
Vancouver Poetry Conference (1963), 280, 286
Véhicule Art Inc., 23, 325–7, 330–1, 334–5, 338n29
Véhicule Press, 23, 164, 326–34, 337n21; Poets, 329–30
violence, 21, 85, 159, 217, 228, 234, 332
Vision Festival (1996), 151
VIVO archives, 258, 271
vocabularies, 4–5, 108, 264; visual, 108

vocal, 5, 64, 95–6, 108, 160, 198, 288, 297, 302
Vocal Fries Podcast, 92
vocalization, 62, 64, 66, 90, 103n31
voices: appropriated Indigenous, 280; of disabled speakers, 89; and gaze, 21, 234; human, 7, 29–30, 45, 199; in poetry, 301, 315; resistant, 147, 160; uttered, 147, 160; women's, 319. *See also* poetic voice
Voyce, Stephen, 73–4

Wah, Fred, 23, 56, 287, 288, 290, 292
Walker, Bill, 313
Waters, Juliet, 210
Webb, Phyllis, 308, 321
Weheliye, Alexander, 69
Westerkamp, Hildegard, 118, 126
Wheeler, Lesley, 335–6n1
white: people, 52, 187, 216, 241; supremacy, 8, 72, 94, 98
whiteness, 174, 204–5, 207, 236, 256, 281, 348
Whitman, Walt, 208, 297
Willard, Tanya, 350
Williams, Raymond, 201
Williams, Saul, 185, 202
Williams, William Carlos, 298, 305, 316
Wilson, Jordan, 340, 342
witness, 21, 32, 39, 87, 130, 225, 287, 353; attentiveness of, 40; historical, 159
witnessing, 87, 225–8; act of, 225, 228
Women's Press Collective, 260, 279
Wong, Alice, 89–90, 92, 94–5, 99
Woodcock, George, 293, 295, 301
Woodley, Baylee, 255, 271
Working Women's Collective (film), 250, 257–9, 274, 278, 280, 282, 285n5
World Soundscape Project, 118
Wortham, Jenna, 235

INDEX

Yamashiro, Takeo, 300
Yergeau, Remi, 95
Younging, Greg, 349
YouTube, 51, 186
Yu, Timothy, 203–5

Zeiher, Cindy, 241
Žižek, Slavoj, 234, 241
Zolf, Rachel, 74; *Janey's Arcadia* (book), 74
Zukofsky, Louis, 306
Zupančič, Alenka, 240